THE MASTER MUSICIANS

DEBUSSY

SERIES EDITED BY R. LARRY TODD
FORMER SERIES EDITOR, THE LATE STANLEY SADIE

Contents

Appendices

Preface

N O COMPOSER OF CLASSICAL MUSIC IS MORE POPULAR TODAY THAN CLAUDE
Debussy. Probably the best indication is the thousands of recordings of his
music. There are more than 100 of the *Préludes* for piano, for example, and nearly
300 of one of his earliest works, the *Prelude to the Afternoon of a Faun* (with several
of the recordings more than a half century old). The popularity of his music has
helped define current performance practice. Debussy's piano pieces are part of
the canon—taught and studied at practically all levels of skill and proficiency. In
opera houses and concert halls around the world, his compositions have become
staples of the repertory.

What is unusual about Debussy's popularity is the breadth of its appeal. It is rare
to find a composer whose music attracts in substantial numbers those with little or
no background in classical music as well as those who have made it their life's work.
Like the music of Chopin—one of Debussy's favorite composers—his music has the
ability to entice listeners on many levels.

The basis of that appeal is the distinctive sound of his music. Although there have
been many imitators, more than a century after much of it was created, Debussy's
music remains fresh and original. The core of its attraction is not a specific attribute
(its tunefulness, for example), but the effect of many elements—the combination of
melody, harmony, and rhythm, as well as its instrumentation and timbre. At its heart
is an engaging simplicity that defies traditional analysis and lends mystery to what
ultimately is an extremely refined and highly personal approach to composition.

Debussy lived long enough to experience fame, and his response to it was mixed.
He welcomed it for the income it provided, although there was never enough for
him to live without debt. But he resented the intrusions into his private life that
accompanied it. And he disliked being well known and categorized—as an
"Impressionist," for example.

He was suspicious, too, of strict demarcations between "popular" and "classical"
music. Since he made a point of turning his back on much of the recent tradition
in Western classical music, he probably would have resented being viewed solely as
a "classical" composer in the sense that we use the term today. At the same time he
was wary of being "popular"—whether as a composer of "popular" music or as a
popular "classical" composer. To Debussy, popularity was usually the consequence of

pandering to public taste. He was proud of what he perceived of as his indebtedness to no one and, especially at the outset of his career, was convinced his music would be little appreciated by the masses.

A respectable portion of Debussy's fame today is based on the popularity of a dozen or so works, pieces like the *Prelude to the Afternoon of a Faun*, "*Rêverie*," and "Clair de lune." But they are early compositions and representative of only a small part of his work. Over a nearly forty-year period, Debussy composed several hundred pieces, in a multitude of genres and a variety of styles. He made a point of not repeating himself as a composer, and for listeners there are always surprises and discoveries to be made.

One of the purposes of this book is to present Debussy's music in all its variety. But another, equally fascinating, is to explore his personality, at times elusive, often contradictory, but centered in his devotion to music and in his ambition to create a name for himself as a composer unlike any other.

This work is the first study of Debussy's life and music in twenty years. During that time a great deal of new information has become available concerning both his life (especially the student years) and compositions. Notable publications include François Lesure's comprehensive biography of Debussy, first published in 1994. Complementing it is the first complete, annotated edition of Debussy's *Correspondance*. Debussy wrote thousands of letters. But prior to the publication of the correspondence in 2005, many had not appeared in print, and those that had, had often appeared in periodicals rare and difficult to access.

In a similar manner, Debussy's music is now accessible in a scholarly, complete edition, started in 1985. To date, sixteen volumes (of a proposed thirty-four) have appeared. Each supplies primary sources and subsequent revisions, and is more reliable and indicative of Debussy's final thoughts than the standard editions available (many of which rely on outdated texts, decades old). Thanks to a detailed *Catalogue* of Debussy's works, also prepared by François Lesure, new material has also been provided on the dating of the music.[1]

Debussy is divided into separate biographical and musical sections. But I encourage all readers, especially those uncomfortable with music terminology, to look at the chapters that focus on music (Chapters 9–14). The opening of each discusses in a broad manner Debussy's developing musical style. I have avoided using jargon, instead focusing on Debussy's changing approach to writing music.

---

1. An updated version of the catalog was published posthumously (Lesure died in 2001) in the republication of his Debussy biography in 2003. It serves as the basis of the online list prepared by the Centre du Documentation Claude Debussy (http://www.debussy.fr; available in both French and English translation).

There are two chapters in *Debussy* that focus neither on his life nor music. In his development as a composer, Debussy drew not just on musical models, but on all the arts, including poetry and painting. His interest in the arts led to a wide variety of labels being associated with his music and a great deal of confusion as to their validity. Debussy's fascination with the arts, its effect on his music, and the merit of classifying his music as Impressionist or Symbolist is the subject of Chapter 8. The final chapter of *Debussy* (Chapter 15) focuses on Debussy's career as a music critic. He was one of the finest of his time, and the reviews he wrote reveal a great deal not just about his musical taste but about what he felt the role and function of music should be.

Primary sources for this book are in French. Many of the English translations are my own, but I have tried whenever possible to direct attention to English-language editions and have used translations from them (Roger Nichols's selection of Debussy's letters, for example). In those instances, I have compared the translation with the original for accuracy and updated in the footnotes any changes that might have occurred in dating, using the *Correspondance* as the source.

Debussy is a continuation in the Master Musicians Series of the volume written by Edward Lockspeiser, first published in 1944, and revised and updated five times over the next thirty-eight years. It was a book that inspired generations of readers (myself included; I first read it nearly forty years ago). It is an honor to be part of the tradition established by him, and a pleasure to be able to contribute to it.

My thanks to Suzanne Ryan, Editor-in-Chief of Humanities and Executive Editor of Music at Oxford University Press, for her support and patience in preparing this book for publication. Professor R. Larry Todd, editor of the Master Musicians Series, provided timely criticism and insight. Jessen O'Brien, editorial assistant at Oxford, has been a pleasure to work with and an expert guide in preparing the book for the press.

Peter Veracka, director of the A. T. Wehrle Memorial Library of the Pontifical College Josephinum, has been especially kind and helpful, and provided a large number of the books and articles I needed for research. My thanks, too, to Alexandra Laederich, Curator at the Centre de Documentation Claude Debussy, for her assistance in providing the illustrations.

My wife, Allie, died shortly after I completed the first draft of *Debussy*. She was an exceptional musician, and a great help and support in writing this book. *Debussy* is dedicated to her memory.

Eric Frederick Jensen
Columbus, Ohio, 2013

Abbreviations for Frequently Cited Sources in Notes

C   Claude Debussy, *Correspondance (1872–1918)*, ed. François Lesure and Denis Herlin. Annotated by François Lesure, Denis Herlin, and Georges Liébert. Paris: Gallimard, 2005.

D   Marcel Dietschy, *A Portrait of Claude Debussy*. Oxford: Clarendon Press, 1994.

DL   Claude Debussy, *Debussy Letters*, ed. François Lesure and Roger Nichols. Cambridge, MA: Harvard University Press, 1987.

DM   Claude Debussy, *Debussy on Music*, ed. Richard Langham Smith. Ithaca, NY: Cornell University Press, 1988.

DR   Roger Nichols, ed. *Debussy Remembered*. Portland, OR: Amadeus Press, 1992.

Ecrits   Claude Debussy, *Monsieur Croche et autres écrits*, ed. François Lesure. Paris: Gallimard, 1987.

LK   Edward Lockspeiser, *Debussy: His Life and Mind*. 2 vols. London: Cassell, 1962, 1965.

LS   François Lesure, *Claude Debussy*. Paris: Klincksieck, 1994.

DEBUSSY

CHAPTER ONE

A Musician's Apprenticeship

Men of genius are incapable of study in their youth. They feel intuitively that
they must learn everything differently from the masses.

Tolstoy, *Notebooks* (January 1857)

EBUSSY RARELY SPOKE ABOUT HIS CHILDHOOD. HE ALWAYS MADE A POINT OF
guarding his privacy. But in this instance additional incentive was provided by
the stigma associated with the poverty and hardships of his youth. At times it had
been a struggle for him simply to survive.

In addition to the hard times, there had been profound differences between
himself and his family, distinctions that could only have become more unsettling as
he grew older. Approaching his fiftieth year, he dryly noted that one's soul is
"bequeathed to us by a crowd of perfectly unknown people"—a remark probably
intended to refer more to his immediate family than to his ancestors, about whom
he knew little.[1]

The de Bussys (as they were originally known) have been traced as far as the
seventeenth century. They were wine-growers and tradesmen of little or moderate
means and lived in Burgundy. Around 1800 a member of the family settled in
Paris. Claude-Alexandre (1812–1889), the composer's grandfather, was a carpenter.
Manuel-Achille (1836–1910), Debussy's father, tried his hand at several trades,
including those of merchant, salesman, and marine. He was unsuccessful at all and
did not find steady employment until his son was an adult.

1. Letter to André Caplet of 22 December 1911 in Claude Debussy, *Correspondance (1872–1918)*,
ed. François Lesure and Denis Herlin (Paris: Gallimard, 2005), p. 1473. Hereafter abbreviated *C*.

Even as a child Debussy was distinctive. But what was most striking about his family and ancestors was their normality. Business and trade was their sole occupation. With the exception of a paternal uncle who settled in England in the 1870s and possibly taught piano privately, there is no indication of any particular interest among the Debussys in the arts.[2]

Debussy's father never received training for any profession. When he was eighteen, he joined the marines serving part of the time in undetermined tropical isles. In November 1861 when his enlistment had ended, he married Victorine-Joséphine-Sophie Manoury (1836–1915), also of Burgundian heritage, and they lost little time in starting a family. The first of five children was born on 22 August 1862 and baptized Achille-Claude.[3] A sister, Adèle, followed less than a year later.

Debussy's childhood coincided with the final years of the reign of Napoleon III but reflected none of the glitter and pomp associated with it. These were difficult times for the Debussy family. At first they lived above a small china shop that they operated in Saint-Germain-en-Laye. But it was not successful and closed by the end of 1864. Over the next few years the Debussys moved frequently, Victorine working as a seamstress and Manuel as a traveling salesman. Not until 1868 did he find regular employment as bookkeeper with a printing firm—only to have it end two years later when war broke out with Prussia.

The Franco-Prussian War of 1870 culminated in the swift defeat of the French forces and the capitulation of Napoleon III. It created months of political instability. In Paris there was wide-spread refusal to accept the terms of surrender, and the city prepared for a siege. Political radicals—many of them militant socialists—took charge. The result was known as the Commune, and it resisted not just Prussian forces but the remnants of the defeated French army who eventually were assigned the duty of subduing what had become a bloody and protracted revolt.

During the Commune, Manuel Debussy enlisted in the National Guard, the force that now found itself defending Paris against the assault of the French army. He rose swiftly in the ranks, became a captain, and led an abortive attack at Issy, one of the forts south of the Seine. Whether he was a supporter of the Commune or merely one of thousands caught up in the events remains uncertain. But when the movement was crushed in May 1871, he was put on trial and—despite his wife's appeal—was sentenced to four years in prison. The term was commuted (after he had served one year) to four years' suspension of his civil and familial rights. Virtually nothing is known of the Debussy family during those years, but the times must

2. No connection has been found with N. de Bussy, a sixteenth-century composer of chansons.

3. During his youth, Debussy was known as Achille, and at the start of his career added some luster to his name by the use of "Claude-Achille" and "de Bussy." He did not begin consistently to refer to himself as "Claude" until he was thirty.

have been extraordinarily challenging for them. Financial support from relatives or friends would have been essential for their survival.

The Debussys' eldest child was spared at least some of the horrors of the war and the Commune. In 1870 he accompanied his mother to the south of France to visit his paternal aunt, Clémentine. She was a year older than Debussy's father and recently married to Alfred Roustan, an innkeeper in Cannes.

Clémentine was a colorful character. In the 1860s she had mingled with high society and for several years had been the mistress of a wealthy stockbroker, Achille Arosa. She and Arosa were Debussy's godparents, but it is uncertain how much contact they actually had with the Debussy family.[4] Perhaps Arosa gave his godson expensive gifts, such as the tricycle seen in a photograph of Debussy at the age of five. From time to time, he may have helped the family financially.

But beyond the wealth he possessed, Arosa was a man of culture with considerable interest in art. As he grew up, Debussy displayed similar tastes, and it has long been assumed they had been fostered by meeting Arosa. That now seems unlikely. Their relationship was not close. Even though he and Debussy stayed in touch after the affair with Clémentine ended, Arosa in time became critical of his godson's "distant manner" and maintained that he would amount to nothing.[5]

Clémentine's marriage to Alfred Roustan was an indication that her life had entered a more stable and respectable phase. For Debussy the visit was one he long remembered. In a letter written nearly forty years later he vividly recalled the countryside and the sea:

> I remember the railway which passed in front of the house and the sea in the distance.... And there was also the road to Antibes where there were so many roses that never in my life have I seen so many at one time.... With the recollection of a Norwegian carpenter who sang from morning to night—some Grieg, perhaps?—I bring my "Souvenirs" to a close. Rest assured that I will not turn them into an orchestral work ("The Carpenter's Apprentice"?).[6]

Debussy's comments provide a rare glimpse of his youth. But they reveal more about himself at age forty-five than about his childhood. Humor—such as the reference to the musical carpenter and the play on Dukas's *Sorcerer's Apprentice*—is

---

4. On Debussy's 1864 baptismal certificate, Clémentine's identity is concealed by the fanciful pseudonym, Octavie de la Ferronière. It is not known why the Debussys delayed their son's baptism for two years after his birth. His sister, Adèle, who was nearly a year older, was baptized before him.

5. Marcel Dietschy, *A Portrait of Claude Debussy* (Oxford: Clarendon Press, 1994), p. 9. Hereafter abbreviated *D*.

6. Letter to Jacques Durand of 24 March 1908 in *C*, p. 1076.

intended to divert attention from more intimate details. And the recollections themselves focus on the countryside and casual encounters. There is no mention of people whom he would have known well—such as his aunt—nor is there any reference to the circumstances surrounding the trip to Cannes.

Yet Clémentine—who is not mentioned in any of Debussy's published correspondence—was by all accounts caring and loving, and to a great extent actually raised two of the Debussy children. In comparison, Debussy's mother seems to fare poorly. She herself admitted that she had no great fondness for children—and that helps to explain Clémentine's enlarged role. Victorine was also the disciplinarian in the family, and according to one source (but not an eye-witness) she was "very severe...frequently slapping" the children.[7] One of Debussy's friends in the 1880s described her as "very excitable."[8] But she had another side. She was a good cook and "passionately devoted" to Claude.[9] He was her favorite, and it was Victorine Debussy—not the father—who took a more active role in his education and the early stages of his career.

Debussy's attitude toward his father was ambivalent. He once described him as an "old scoundrel."[10] Yet he seemed to view his father's conduct with tolerance and amusement—and the man himself with affection. Not long after his death Debussy described it as "a loss felt all the more deeply with each day that passes." But, he added, "we hardly ever had a thought in common."[11] The differences between them could scarcely have been greater. His father's taste in music, for example, was for light opera (not surprisingly, a favorite among his son's compositions was one of the earliest and most conventional, *L'Enfant prodigue*). Claude, on the other hand, seemed drawn to what was unconventional and distinctive, and in his adolescence he displayed a refinement in taste and interests that could only have been puzzling to many in his family. Yet there is no sign that these differences alienated him from his parents. Perhaps the strongest indication of the regard in which Debussy held them was the pleasure he experienced later in life in witnessing their enjoyment of his growing fame.[12]

7. Dolly Bardac in Roger Nichols, ed., *Debussy Remembered* (Portland, OR: Amadeus Press, 1992), p. 200. Hereafter abbreviated *DR*.

8. Paul Vidal, "Souvenirs d'Achille Debussy," *La Revue Musicale* 7 (May 1926), p. 13.

9. Ibid.

10. Edward Lockspeiser, *Debussy: His Life and Mind*. 2 vols. (London: Cassell, 1962, 1965), I, p. 9. Hereafter abbreviated *LK*.

11. Letter to André Caplet of 21 November 1910 in *C*, pp. 1331–1332.

12. During an eleven-year period, five children were born to Manuel and Victorine Debussy. Debussy's sister Adèle (1863–1952) eventually became a seamstress and never married. According to an article published in the *New York Times* in 1909, she had "no sympathy with his compositions" and "always refused to take any money from him" (David Grayson, "Claude Debussy Addresses the

Debussy's father wanted his son to become a sailor, an idea that seemed to appeal to the boy. But the visit to Cannes led to a change of plans. Clémentine arranged for Debussy to have piano lessons with a local musician, Jean Cerutti (actually a violinist by training). Years later Debussy described Cerutti to his first French biographer as an "elderly Italian professor."[13] But although he may have appeared old to the nine-year-old, Cerutti was only forty-two. From him, Debussy remembered learning the "first rudiments" of music, but he also noted that Cerutti found nothing special in him.[14]

Cerutti's evaluation did not discourage Debussy's parents. After the family returned to Paris, they mentioned the piano lessons to Charles de Sivry, a friend whom Manuel Debussy had probably met in prison after the Commune. De Sivry was a true *bohémien* and actively involved in Parisian artistic circles. He had close connections with the literary scene and was a good friend of the writers Paul Verlaine and Villiers de l'Isle-Adam. He was also an amateur musician, and his mother, Antoinette-Flor Mauté de Fleurville, taught piano. De Sivry suggested that Claude study with her.

Mme Mauté de Fleurville was forty-eight when she began teaching Debussy. She was fond of playing the grande dame, as the flowery name she created for herself indicates: Mauté was the name of her second husband, "de Fleurville" was a fanciful appendage. Her claim to fame was her assertion that she had been a student of Chopin. On the surface, Mme Mauté did not seem much better qualified than Cerutti, and in biographies of Debussy she has been routinely portrayed as a pretentious dilettante who fortunately did her gifted pupil little harm.

But her affectations obscured her accomplishments. She was a good pianist who actually may have studied with Chopin.[15] And she was a superb teacher. Three years before his death Debussy recalled her with extraordinary fondness, noting that she had taught him "the little I know about the piano." At the time he was preparing an edition of some of Chopin's piano pieces and wished that she were still alive so that he could draw upon her knowledge: "she knew so many things

---

English-Speaking World: Two Interviews, an Article, and *The Blessed Damozel*," *Cahiers Debussy* 16 [1992], p. 25). There were three other brothers: Eugène-Octave (1873–1877) died of meningitis. Emmanuel (1867–1937) became a farmhand. Alfred (1870–1937) in his youth had artistic interests similar to Debussy's. He was later employed as an inspector for a railroad, and, according to Debussy, his musical tastes favored the cabaret.

13. Louis Laloy, *Claude Debussy* (Paris: Les Bibliophiles Fantaisistes, 1909), p. 11. *D*, p. 12.

14. Laloy, p. 11.

15. Chopin had many students—not all have been identified. No evidence has surfaced that she was not his pupil (see Jean-Jacques Eigeldinger, *Chopin: Pianist and Teacher*, tr. Naomi Shohet, Krysia Osostowicz, and Roy Howat [Cambridge: Cambridge University Press, 1986], p. 129).

about Chopin."[16] On another occasion—again, late in life—he noted that he had been privileged to hear "only two fine pianists": Liszt, and "my old piano teacher, a small, stout woman who plunged me into Bach and who played his music as it is never played now—putting life into it."[17] Debussy liked to exaggerate to make a point. By placing Liszt and his "old piano teacher" on the same level there was no better way to emphasize how greatly she had inspired him. He later said that she had played a "considerable" role in his "musical formation, not only as pianist, but also as creator."[18] Debussy never gave comparable praise to any other of his teachers.

Mme Mauté—who charged nothing for her lessons with Debussy—provided impetus to his growth as a musician. Unfortunately, details of her instruction are not known, nor even how long Debussy studied with her. But at most it could only have been for about a year. She must have encouraged Debussy's parents to cultivate their son's gifts and probably suggested to them (who knew so little about music) that their son would be best served by attending the Paris Conservatoire. She was convinced that the standard approach of private piano study at home was insufficient both to challenge him and develop his skills.

The decision was made to prepare Debussy as quickly as possible for the Conservatoire. It might have been more prudent to go at a slower pace and gradually refine his technique. Not only had Debussy begun the study of music fairly late, but in applying to the Conservatoire he would be compared to students older and far more mature. There was always the risk that those who heard his performance for admission might fail to recognize his accomplishments or would prefer more established skills to developing the potential of a child. That autumn, Debussy and 156 other students applied for admittance to the piano program. He performed Weber's "Invitation to the Dance," a challenging piece, and on 22 October 1872—exactly two months after his tenth birthday—he learned that he was among the thirty-three who had been admitted.

At the Conservatoire

Founded during the French Revolution, the Paris Conservatoire was the oldest conservatory in Europe. The musical education offered to Debussy was substantial and in all ways conventional—representative not just of the nineteenth century, but of much of the twentieth century as well. Its goal was to produce skillful and

16. Letter to Jacques Durand of 27 January 1915 in *C*, p. 1871.

17. Conversation with Victor Segalen of 17 December 1908 in Annie Joly-Segalen and André Schaeffner, eds., *Segalen et Debussy* (Monaco: Editions du Rocher, 1961), p. 107.

18. Alfred Casella in *DR*, p. 97.

competent musicians thoroughly grounded in their craft. Musical genius of any kind had not been a concern of those drafting the curriculum.

In addition to study of their instrument, performers received training in music theory and harmony, and participated in ensembles (the study of music history was not yet a requirement). The goal was for all students to be immersed in studying and making music with few other distractions. Debussy's musical skills benefited from that approach. But in time he found the academic rigor at the Conservatoire intolerable. His true growth as a musician came not from what he was taught but from his opposition to it.

He spent nearly a dozen years at the school. Unlike his brothers and sister, it was the only formal education of any kind he ever received. His mother took responsibility for teaching him non-musical subjects at home. But although there is no reason to believe that she did not take her duties seriously, the depth and breadth of Debussy's schooling outside of the Conservatoire was limited. It was not an uncommon situation. Lack of a formal education was widespread in France at the time. A quarter of those intending to marry were unable even to write their names on their marriage certificates.[19]

The musical concentration at the Conservatoire developed Debussy's musicianship in much the same way that rigorous physical training produces an athlete. It made him aware of the extent of his musical abilities and, by comparison to classmates, encouraged his competitive spirit. But Debussy's interests went well beyond music. As he matured, he hungered for knowledge, especially about the arts. He accomplished a great deal by educating himself, but gaps remained, and occasional difficulty with grammar and syntax would sometimes prove an embarrassment.

Although it is unlikely that he grasped it at the time, Debussy's admission to the Conservatoire was an event of extraordinary significance to his parents. All their hopes became centered on him. He was by far the most gifted of their children, and the vision of him as a renowned pianist provided hope and solace for the difficulties in their own lives. There is no indication that Debussy was thrust into that position against his will or, as had been the case with Beethoven, driven to it. He seemed to enjoy the challenges of his study and, as they increasingly came his way, the successes. Perhaps he welcomed the stability provided by study at the Conservatoire. For their part, Debussy's parents willingly entrusted their son to the school, firm in the conviction that it was the ideal source to develop and ripen his musical gifts.

Debussy's formal study at the Conservatoire began on 25 October when he enrolled in the piano class of Antoine Marmontel. It seemed to be a good choice.

19. Not until 1882 did attendance at secondary school become compulsory. At the time it was estimated that more than half a million children were not enrolled. See Jacques Chastenet, *La République des Républicains. 1879–1893* (Paris: Hachette, 1954), p. 74.

Marmontel was one of the most prominent figures at the Conservatoire, having taught there since 1848. He was well regarded by his colleagues and had taught a number of exceptional musicians—Bizet, for example.

But there were disadvantages to studying with him of which the Debussys were unaware. He was a teacher, not a performer, and he lacked the technique to demonstrate difficult passages for students. In addition he had no reputation for producing outstanding pianists. His most famous students had been composers.

Part of the problem can be traced to Marmontel's appointment to the Conservatoire. The leading candidate for the position had been Charles-Valentin Alkan. Not as well known today as he should be, Alkan was one of the most exceptional pianists of his generation, as well as a gifted composer and teacher. But his candidacy fell victim to the politics of the Conservatoire. Since being hired, Marmontel had focused on piano pedagogy, and had written a book (*Les Pianistes célèbres*) containing biographical sketches of more than two dozen eminent pianists of the century.

All this should not detract from Marmontel's strengths: his musical sensitivity and ability to teach not merely how to play the piano (that is, technique), but also music. It was those traits that had so impressed pupils like Bizet. But if a student was intent on a career as a piano virtuoso—and that was the obvious goal of both Debussy and his parents—Marmontel's teaching was open to criticism. An interesting parallel is provided by the American composer Edward MacDowell who came to Marmontel in 1876 with goals similar to Debussy's. He was fifteen, highly talented, and eager to learn. But he found Marmontel too pedantic. MacDowell stayed with Marmontel for only about a year. After hearing a virtuoso performance by Anton Rubinstein, he concluded: "I'll never learn to play like that in the Paris Conservatoire."[20] During the years when Debussy studied with Marmontel, his studio was mediocre at best. The finest pianists were Debussy, Camille Bellaigue, and Gabriel Pierné. Bellaigue became a music critic, Pierné a conductor and composer.

Debussy's study with Marmontel began well enough. The piano class met three times a week, and Marmontel was impressed by what he saw. In his first detailed evaluation, he described Debussy's "marvelous progress" and predicted that he would "become a great artist" (29 January 1873). Six months later he noted Debussy's "true artistic temperament."[21] These initial reactions emphasize Marmontel's ability to see beyond the piano and to recognize Debussy's outstanding musicianship.

20. Alan H. Levy, *Edward MacDowell. An American Master* (Lanham, MD: Scarecrow Press, 1998), p. 12.

21. John R. Clevenger, "Debussy's Paris Conservatoire Training," in *Debussy and His World*, ed. Jane Fulcher (Princeton, NJ: Princeton University Press, 2001), pp. 324, 325.

He made rapid progress. Debussy was soon playing pieces requiring substantial technique, such as Ignaz Moscheles's *Allegri di bravura*, op. 51. In July at the annual jury, he was awarded a second certificate of merit (ranked seventh in a group of fifteen) for his performance of the first movement of Chopin's Second Piano Concerto. The following year he received a first certificate of merit (fourth of fourteen), once again for a work by Chopin (the Ballade No. 1, op. 23). Both are demanding pieces, and for a twelve-year-old to perform them—and win an award in the process—was impressive.

Even more astonishing was the rate at which Debussy learned. To be able to play the Chopin concerto after only three years of piano study was exceptional. Although it has become customary to deprecate his skills as a pianist, Debussy was extraordinarily gifted—in fact, a prodigy. Certificates were awarded at a public ceremony, and these must have been occasions of celebration for the Debussy family—especially when the critic for *L' Art musical* described him as "a budding virtuoso of the first order."[22]

There was a similar response to his first recitals. Marmontel arranged for Debussy to participate in two concerts (16 January and 18 March 1876) in the small town of Chauny. Debussy had a prominent role, performing fashionable fantasies on operatic tunes, accompanying Léontine Mendès (a gifted fellow-student) in arias by Fromenthal Halévy and Ambroise Thomas, accompanying a cellist in a Donizetti fantasy, and participating in the performance of a Haydn trio. Local criticism was rhapsodic. "This budding Mosart [*sic*] is a real devil," exclaimed one reviewer, "What verve! What spirit!" It seemed obvious, noted another, that he would become "a renowned artist."[23]

With less than four years of study at the Conservatoire, Debussy's future could not have appeared more promising. He made a striking impression—not just a result of his youth, but also because of his demeanor and the intensity of his performances. In appearance he resembled his father—small in stature, lively, somewhat swarthy. His prominent forehead attracted attention. It had several bony protuberances (most likely a result of benign bone tumors), and Debussy was self-conscious enough to attempt during his adolescence to conceal them by combing his hair over them.

Most memorable was his gaze. It was described by fellow students in a variety of ways: "ardent," "concentrated," "intense." To some he seemed "fierce," and "unsociable," a bit like a wild animal.[24] That marked his approach to the piano as well: at times he seemed to attack it.

---

22. François Lesure, *Claude Debussy* (Paris: Klincksieck, 1994), p. 28. Hereafter abbreviated *LS*.

23. Ibid., p. 30.

24. Ibid., p. 24.

But his refinement also set him apart. Classmates noticed that he preferred to buy a delicacy to eat rather than purchasing something more substantial for less. It was attributed to his "aristocratic tastes."[25] And he was fascinated by art. In one instance, he mutilated a friend's copy of the magazine *Le Monde illustré*, tearing illustrations from it to hang on his wall—reproductions of paintings by Ernest Meissonier, known for his vibrant and colorful scenes of the Napoleonic Wars.

Piano study was only one component of the program of study at the Conservatoire. In November 1872 Debussy enrolled in a sight-singing (solfège) class taught by Albert Lavignac. Lavignac later became famous as the editor of the monumental *Encyclopédie de la musique et Dictionnaire du Conservatoire*. But at the time of his contact with Debussy he was at the beginning of his career.

The solfège class became the foundation of Lavignac's reputation. He did not limit it to sight-singing and dictation but made it a general musicianship course that was one of the most important—and most challenging—in the curriculum. Facility was required for reading at sight in all the clefs (not just the treble and bass clefs taught today), as well as skill in transposition. Debussy excelled and, despite being the youngest, in his final year of study with Lavignac (1876) received a First Medal in solfège.

But that same year also brought the first indications of problems. In their evaluations, both Marmontel and Lavignac complained that Debussy needed to work harder. They were convinced that he was relying too much on natural ability and not putting enough effort into his studies. His jury appearance in 1876 seemed to justify their concern. Debussy performed the first movement of Beethoven's Piano Sonata, op. 111, was only ranked eighth out of eighteen, and won no prize at all. Marmontel described Debussy's work during the year as "a bit *muddled* and *scatterbrained*...he can do much better"—a judgment seconded by Lavignac.[26]

His jury performance the following year did not show much improvement. Although Marmontel seemed pleased with what he saw as renewed effort on Debussy's part, it only resulted in a shared second prize (ranked fifth in a group of twenty-one) for a performance of the first movement of Schumann's Second Piano Sonata, op. 22. Preparation for other classes provided no excuse. Study with Lavignac had ended, and, although he was enrolled in a required ensemble class, Debussy (like most other students) rarely bothered to attend. To some, Debussy's piano playing now seemed bizarre, capricious, and undisciplined. "He would literally throw himself at the keyboard and force all his effects," one student recalled. "He seemed to be enraged with the instrument, abusing it with impulsive gestures, and

25. Ibid., p. 28.

26. Evaluations of 2 February and 20 June 1876 in Clevenger, "Training," pp. 325, 326.

breathing noisily during the difficult passages."[27] Such idiosyncrasies could only have worked against him at the juries. But those who heard Debussy play the piano later in life—both in public and private—invariably remarked on his skill, artistry, and extraordinary sensitivity.

A change in teacher might have improved the situation. During the two previous juries not only had Debussy done poorly, there had been broad criticism of Marmontel's students in general. If nothing else, Debussy might have found a new teacher and a different approach refreshing. He had been studying with Marmontel for about a half dozen years. What had begun well had turned stale. Distancing himself from the disastrous events of the previous two years might have been helpful, but he made no change in instructor. During his final two years with Marmontel (1878 and 1879)—despite a generally positive evaluation—he won no additional awards and was ranked at about the middle with other competitors (ninth of seventeen; eighth of fourteen).

It was a dismal showing, and Debussy's performance in his academic classes offered no consolation. In November 1877 he enrolled as auditor in the harmony and accompanying course (officially changed solely to harmony in the following year) of Emile Durand.[28] He was in the class for three years, but he and Durand never established a rapport. Although Durand praised his musical aptitude, he characterized his work in a manner identical to Marmontel: "muddled" and "scatter-brained."[29]

Fortunately, during this bleak period in Debussy's life, Marmontel provided encouragement. Despite the failures, he arranged for Debussy to become pianist and musician factotum at the chateau of Chenonceaux in the summer of 1879. It was a wonderful opportunity for him. The contrast between it and his mundane existence (notably the crowded, three-room apartment he shared with his family) could not have been more striking.

The chateau—a magnificent residence that had once been home to Diane de Poitiers—was owned by Marguerite Pelouze, née Wilson. Daughter of a wealthy Scottish engineer (who had presented Chenonceaux to her as a wedding gift) she was charming and elegant (and the mistress of Jules Grévy, president of France). She had a great interest in the arts and a particular admiration for Flaubert, who was an occasional guest. In music, Wagner was her passion. Unfortunately, little is known of

27. Gabriel Pierné, "Souvenirs d'Achille Debussy," *La Revue Musicale* 7 (May 1926), p. 10.

28. Harmony students were expected to attend the music history class taught by Louis Bourgault-Ducoudray. But there were no exams for this course—and no indication that Debussy ever bothered to attend.

29. Evaluations of 19 January and 19 June 1878 in Clevenger, "Training," pp. 334, 335.

Debussy's experiences at Chenonceaux—not what music he played for Mme Pelouze, not even the precise nature of his duties.

The music of Wagner, it may be presumed, made some appearance. At the time, his stature in France was hotly debated. The performance of *Tannhäuser* at the Paris Opéra in 1861 had created a scandal, and it was not until 1893 that the Opéra performed another of his works. Although there were occasional performances in France of excerpts in a concert version, those who wanted to see staged versions of Wagner's most recent music generally needed to travel to Germany.

Many of Wagner's strongest supporters in France were writers or had distinct literary interests. The *Revue Wagnérienne* (1885–1888; Mme Pelouze was one of its founders) was created to gain wider appreciation for his music and included among its contributors some of the most notable writers of the day, including Stéphane Mallarmé, Catulle Mendès, and Villiers de l'Isle-Adam.

Among musicians, progressives often emulated Wagner. Conservatives (and this would have included many of Debussy's professors) castigated him. To play and study Wagner's music at Chenonceaux, even if only in piano reduction, would have been exciting to Debussy—particularly given his later fascination with some of it. But it would not have been his first contact with Wagner's compositions. One memorable evening after class at the Conservatoire he had been introduced to the overture to *Tannhäuser* by Lavignac—who was to become one of the best known of Wagner's supporters in France. They became so immersed in their study that they forgot the time, and on leaving found that the night watchman had locked them in.

Debussy never made any direct reference to his stay at Chenonceaux, but at least it provided distraction to the difficulties he was encountering at the Conservatoire. Because of academic regulations, it had become impossible for him to continue studying piano: students were dropped from a program of study if, after winning a prize, they captured no additional prize in two consecutive years or did not win one in three consecutive attempts.

On his return to Paris, Debussy continued in Durand's harmony class and enrolled in a new course devoted to accompanying. Taught by August Bazille, it covered more than accompanying and included extensive sight-reading, sight transposition, improvisational accompaniment to a melody, and piano reduction of orchestral scores.

Debussy excelled. He was awarded the First Prize in accompanying—astonishingly, the *only* First Prize he ever received at the Conservatoire.

Earlier in his study, the award might have had some significance. Now, it had little value. He had failed in piano. And his work in Durand's harmony class had not been much better: in the only two harmony competitions that he entered (1879 and 1880), he had done poorly. Debussy was now at a crossroads in his career, and the study in Bazille's class—no matter how successful—could only reinforce how much he needed to evaluate his future.

Without a First Prize in piano, a career as a concert pianist was unrealistic. Debussy's only notable success—in Bazille's class—would probably lead to little more than journeyman work as an accompanist, possibly for an opera house or choral group. According to his professors, Debussy's predicament had been brought about by his laziness and carelessness, and, given his musical gifts, by his unwillingness to study. But a closer look reveals that Debussy's failure was not a result of his laziness, but of his challenging the program of study.

He consistently questioned the value of what he was taught and rejected what appeared to be misguided and routine. He was also strongly independent and, compared to other students, self-assured and unusually mature—not in the ways of the world, but in assessing his artistic convictions.

Debussy's professors found him to be a difficult pupil. The question he asked most often was "Why?": Why were only certain modulations acceptable? Why were only particular chord sequences approved? Why did the sight-singing exercises contain so little rhythmic inventiveness?

Much of Debussy's questioning—long remembered by other students—focused on rules that existed for their own sake. He was convinced that many were being enforced only to enable students to compose like their teachers. In Bazille's class he was rebuked for his unconventional modulations (with understatement, Bazille described him as being a "*good harmonist* but a bit fanciful").[30] In Durand's harmony class his homework presented solutions that were "ingenious, elegant, charming, but in no way academic."[31] Although Debussy often seemed playful in these confrontations—enjoying the role of devil's advocate—in the process he was developing characteristics of his own musical style.

Seen in that light, Lavignac's assertion that Debussy was "scatter-brained in theory, even though he understands it very well" makes some sense.[32] He was careless because he was bored. And sometimes what was perceived as carelessness was intended defiantly. In general his professors did not take it personally. Lavignac seemed particularly understanding. At times even Durand (described by one student as "a good professor, but intractable") at least found Debussy's unorthodoxy to be clever.[33] In his final evaluation he described Debussy as a "talented student who has made great progress this year."[34] But what "progress" Debussy had made had

30. Evaluation of 21 June 1880 in ibid., p. 336.
31. According to fellow-student, Paul Vidal, *LS*, p. 37.
32. Evaluation of 9 June 1876 in Clevenger, "Training," p. 333.
33. Vidal, "Souvenirs," p. 12.
34. Evaluation of 18 June 1880 in Clevenger, "Training," p. 335.

been against the grain and was the result of a calculated adherence to the rules. "The best thing one could wish for French music," Debussy wrote in 1902, "would be to see the study of harmony abolished as it is practiced in the conservatories."[35]

Marmontel was also familiar with Debussy's probing. It generally took the form of improvisations, often preceding a lesson, and Marmontel admired their independence and resourcefulness.[36] Although Debussy never revealed his reaction to him as a teacher—and thought more highly of Mme Mauté—Marmontel had been a great help. During these difficult years at the Conservatoire, he consistently responded in an encouraging manner, convinced of Debussy's musical gifts, even if they were not directed toward the piano. While he turned out to be the wrong type of teacher to guide Debussy's career as a piano virtuoso, he was an ideal one to foster his musicianship.

Yet another instance of Marmontel's support occurred in the summer of 1880, when he arranged for Debussy to serve for several months as pianist for Nadezhda von Meck and her family. This was the first of three occasions that Debussy would spend with the von Mecks—an invaluable experience that, like his association with Marguerite Pelouze, brought him into contact with people and ideas out of the ordinary.

Nadezhda von Meck was a wealthy and eccentric Russian widow whose passion was the music of Chaikovsky. For more than a dozen years she provided him with a stipend to enable him to compose. But it was a gesture, generous as it was, that Mme von Meck could easily afford. She lived extravagantly and owned residences in and near Moscow, as well as in Ukraine. During the summer and autumn, much of her time was spent traveling with family and servants to fashionable locations throughout Europe.

Debussy's duties for the von Mecks varied: playing in a piano trio; accompanying her daughter, Julia (a singer, twenty-seven); teaching piano to her daughter, Sonia (thirteen) and theory to her son, Alexander (sixteen). Perhaps the most trying part were the piano duets with Mme von Meck. These almost always consisted of pieces by Chaikovsky, far from a favorite with Debussy. Mme von Meck adored his music: "When I play [the Fourth Symphony], a fever penetrates every fiber of my being," she wrote to Chaikovsky after a session with Debussy. "For an entire day I am unable to recover from its effects."[37]

---

35. "The Orientation of Music" in Claude Debussy, *Debussy on Music,* ed. Richard Langham Smith (Ithaca, NY: Cornell University Press, 1988), p. 84. Hereafter abbreviated *DM.*

36. Years later, as Debussy began his career as a composer, Marmontel jokingly referred to him as "my second-prize winner of 1877." *LS,* p. 66.

37. Ibid., p. 45.

In 1880 Debussy's stay with the von Meck family began in July in Switzerland, moved to France (the Midi, Paris, and Nice), and concluded in Italy. He quickly grew in their affections. His musical abilities—particularly his facility in sight-reading—were much appreciated. The von Mecks also enjoyed his quick wit and lively sense of humor, especially his skill at mocking the musical styles of popular composers such as Charles Gounod and Ambroise Thomas. It was an exhilarating and exciting time for him. To surrender this opulent and stimulating environment for the dreary routine of life in Paris was difficult. When he left in November, Mme von Meck was astonished to see him cry.

It was he who wrote asking to return. In July 1881 he traveled to Russia to meet them, and then accompanied the family to Vienna and Italy, not returning to Paris until early in December. In September of the following year he returned again and followed a similar itinerary: Moscow (September) and Vienna (November), arriving in Paris at the end of the month. Those three residences with the von Mecks were a wonderful opportunity. Unfortunately, none of his letters from the time have survived, so many of the details of his stay—as well as Debussy's reaction to them—are lacking. But the trips served the purpose of the traditional "Grand Tour" and exposed him to portions of Europe and a way of life he would never have been able to experience on his own. It came at an ideal time, too—precisely when he was giving thought to his future and had need of a more expansive frame of mind.

Debussy became attached both to the von Mecks and to their affluent way of life. But his musical experience was also enriched, often in unexpected ways. He long remembered hearing some gypsies perform in Moscow. And the daily musical activities required him to maintain his skills as a pianist. By necessity, he became familiar with much of Chaikovsky's music and even prepared for publication a four-hand piano transcription of portions of *Swan Lake*.

He was anxious to gain the approval of the von Mecks. In the beginning, unsure of himself and eager to create an impression, Debussy added three years to his age and claimed that he had won the First Prize in piano. Not content with being a mere performer, he went on to talk of his accomplishments as a composer and his study in the composition class of Jules Massenet, at the time the most popular composer in France. His goal, he told them, was winning the Prix de Rome, the Conservatoire's prestigious award for the best student composer.

There was at least some measure of truth in what he was telling them. Debussy was writing music: his first compositions were created around 1880 and include a piano trio (written for the von Meck ensemble), several songs, his only symphony (for piano, four-hands, from which an allegro survives), and a piano piece (*Danse bohémienne*). They are far from accomplished pieces, but they do reveal talent. Most seem to have been conceived with the von Mecks in mind, both as a means of displaying his skill and as a token of his esteem.

Debussy presented the score of the symphony as a gift to Mme von Meck. In her gracious response, she thanked him for his "charming symphony," an apt reaction to many of these early works.[38] They are attractive, elegant, lyrical, and generally a cut above the typical salon piece whose intention is merely to please—so much so that it seems likely that Debussy had earlier composed other pieces which have not survived. What is surprising is the amount of originality. Even if only present in a subtle manner, from the start Debussy seemed determined to set himself apart.

These compositions were Debussy's response to the crisis of 1880. They also help to explain his failure as a virtuoso and his incessant questioning of musical grammar. By 1877 he found himself attracted more to music than to playing the piano, more interested in creating music than in performing it. And his probing in the classes of Lavignac, Durand, and Bazille helped lay the foundation both for his study as a composer and for his musical style.

When he described himself to the von Mecks as a student of Massenet, in his own mind Debussy was probably stretching the truth only a little. It seems likely that he had decided to enroll in Massenet's class in the autumn. He was not unknown to Massenet (who had been on the juries which had heard him perform the Chopin Ballade in 1875 and Beethoven the following year). For anyone who wanted to study composition, Massenet's fame as a composer and popularity as a teacher made him the obvious choice.

But in December 1880—about a month after his return to France—Debussy enrolled not with Massenet but in the composition class of a comparative unknown: Ernest Guiraud. It is not clear what happened. Although he later showed little sympathy for Massenet's music, at this stage in his career the prestige of Massenet's name would probably have been sufficient attraction in itself. Perhaps, because of his late return, Debussy found Massenet's class closed. Or Guiraud may have been recommended by Marmontel, who thought highly of him. There also remains the possibility that Debussy was actually denied admission to Massenet's class—the result of an academic career memorable for its failures.

But while the reason Debussy found himself in Guiraud's class may never be known, it turned out to be a stroke of good luck. Guiraud was skilled, knowledgeable, and open-minded. The three and a half years that Debussy was to spend as his student had its share of trials and tribulations. But it led to mutual respect, substantial growth in Debussy's musicianship, and the first recognition of his skills as a composer.

38. Letter of 20 February 1881 in *C*, p. 12.

CHAPTER TWO

The Prix de Rome

To be popular, one must be a mediocrity.
Oscar Wilde, *The Picture of*
Dorian Gray (1890)

WHEN DEBUSSY ENROLLED IN THE COMPOSITION CLASS TAUGHT BY GUIRAUD, he knew little about him, and—since this was the first composition course Guiraud had taught—absolutely nothing about the class. But Guiraud knew something of Debussy. He had been on the juries that had heard him perform Chopin in 1875 and Schumann two years later. It is also likely that he had discussed Debussy with former professors, especially Marmontel. Guiraud had been a student of Marmontel and winner of the First Prize for piano in 1858.

Debussy may have realized that he was fortunate to be studying composition at all. He came with far fewer accomplishments than others in the program, as comparison with recent winners of the Prix de Rome reveals. Prior to winning the Prix in 1882 Gabriel Pierné had won First Prizes in piano, organ, and counterpoint and fugue. Paul Vidal, his successor in 1883, had won a pair of First Prizes: in harmony, and in counterpoint and fugue. Those were the two areas in which composers were expected to excel. But Debussy's study had been conspicuous by its failure.

From a strictly practical point of view, it would have been far better to be in the composition class of Jules Massenet. The function of a composition professor was not just to teach. It was to assist students in finding employment and commissions—and in those areas the prestige of Massenet was unequaled. Appointed professor of composition in 1878 after the success of his opera *Le Roi de Lahore*, his classes usually contained about a dozen students and numerous auditors. He seemed to have the

Midas touch: former winner of the Prix de Rome, good friend of the current director of the Conservatoire (Ambroise Thomas), recently elected to the Institut de France—and he was only thirty-eight.

Debussy's greatest fear may have been his concern that any composition teacher would try to mold students in his image. But there would have been no danger of that occurring with Massenet. He was, in the words of a former student, "an educator of the first rank....By no means shallow or reactionary, and never academic. He was able to understand natures that were very different from his own."[1]

Guiraud was five years older than Massenet and had won the Prix de Rome in 1859. But none of the handful of operas and ballets he had composed since then had met with particular success. In 1876 he became a member of the faculty at the Conservatoire teaching harmony—a result not so much of his accomplishments but of his friendships. Today he is mostly remembered because of his association with Georges Bizet. After Bizet's early death, Guiraud helped to popularize his work by composing recitatives for *Carmen* and preparing the second of the *L'Arlésienne Suites*. But in both instances, his efforts seem heavy-handed compared to Bizet's.

In addition to study with Guiraud, that autumn Debussy was hired as accompanist in the private voice studio of Victorine Moreau-Sainti. It was the type of work frequently done by composition students at the Conservatoire. Debussy supplemented it by teaching piano privately.

Moreau-Sainti came from a distinguished family of singers. Her class (which met twice weekly from November to June) attracted a large number of students, especially well-to-do amateurs. Debussy took no pleasure in his association with the group. He never cared for amateurism of any kind, especially when, as in this case, snobbism played a role.

One student eventually caught his attention: Marie Vasnier. She was charming, attractive, and artistic, with an exceptional soprano voice. At the time of their meeting, Mme Vasnier was thirty-two and had two children, aged nine and eleven. Her husband Henri (who was eleven years older) was a buildings registrar and an amateur archaeologist. The Vasniers lived well and mixed in stylish circles. Debussy soon became a frequent guest at their house, so much so that it seemed like a second home to him. The Vasnier's daughter, Marguerite, recalled that "between his father, pretentious and not very intelligent, and the petty and narrow-minded ways of his mother, [Debussy] was not happy at home"—a biased view of his family life tailor-made by Debussy to gain sympathy.[2] He must have been flattered by the attention shown him. Mme Vasnier (whose name he persisted in spelling "Vanié")

1. Robert Orledge, *Charles Koechlin (1867–1950). His Life and Works* (Chur, Switzerland: Harwood Academic, 1989), p. 5.

2. Marguerite Vasnier, "Debussy à dix-huit ans," *La Revue Musicale* 7 (May, 1926), p. 17.

encouraged him to compose, and a room was even set aside for him to work in. Her husband took an interest in Debussy's studies. And the children enjoyed his unpredictable sense of humor—such as when he pretended his walking stick was a guitar and serenaded them, or when he invited some passing street musicians into the house and improvised with them.

Much was done to make him feel at home. He gave piano lessons for a while to their daughter, who was amused by his ineptness. "An appalling teacher [with] not an ounce of patience" was her verdict. Although he could be "moody" and "unsociable" to guests invited to their home (it seems that he wanted the Vasniers all to himself), he was "utterly charming with those he liked."[3] Charm is not a trait noted by Debussy's classmates; however, in addition to his improved social skills, it seemed to have blossomed during his stay with the von Mecks.

"You felt," recalled Marguerite Vasnier, "that here was a personality."[4] He seemed exotic: a Florentine from the Middle Ages, a Venetian nobleman of the Renaissance— that was how two friends from school described him. His manner of speaking was also distinctive: restrained ("as happens so often with people who are not satisfied with clichés and think for themselves"). In his conversations it seemed as if he were "trying his hardest to find a word supple enough to get across the nuance of an impression or a point of view."[5]

At the Conservatoire Debussy was hoping for a clean break with his piano study—and of the disappointment associated with it. But his first year as a composer did not go well. Guiraud's evaluation was adequate ("Intelligent. Good student"), but he did not think highly of the class as a whole—which had only three other students in it.[6] The academic year did not end on a positive note. Debussy's jury composition was criticized severely. "Shilly-shallying," one judge concluded. "Too much modulation, a poor path."[7]

Guiraud became known for being relaxed with students, perhaps even a bit slack. That may help to explain why Debussy decided to investigate the organ class of César Franck. Franck, a gentle and fatherly figure revered by his students, had been teaching organ at the Conservatoire since 1872. The administration paid little attention to his accomplishments as a composer, and despite a growing reputation (Franck had recently completed *Les Béatitudes* and the Piano Quintet), he was never asked to teach a class in composition. As compensation, Franck expanded the

3. Marguerite Vasnier in *DR*, pp. 20, 19.

4. Ibid., p. 17.

5. Raymond Bonheur in ibid., p. 10.

6. John R. Clevenger, "Debussy's Paris Conservatoire Training," in *Debussy and His World*, ed. Jane Fulcher (Princeton, NJ: Princeton University Press, 2001), p. 339.

7. Théodore Dubois in *LS*, p. 53.

content of his organ classes. Improvisation (and, as a corollary, composition) played an important role, and it was not unusual for young composers to attend. Debussy was curious about Franck. Although not enthusiastic about most of his compositions (which, like much nineteenth-century music, he found burdened with sentiment), Debussy was fond of several, especially *Les Béatitudes*. Perhaps he thought that Franck's teaching would provide some stimulus to his work with Guiraud. But while Debussy ended up enjoying aspects of the class, overall it was a disappointment. He was amused by Franck's encouragement of students to modulate, only to cut them off if he felt they became inventive ("Not too much…not too much").[8] But he retained respect for Franck, at least in part for what he felt was his absence of worldliness (what he later described as Franck's "soul of a child").[9]

That summer Debussy returned to the von Mecks for the second time, visiting both Russia and Rome. Writing songs was his primary interest, and he composed more than a dozen in 1881. They are lyrical, often with great sensitivity to the text. It has become commonplace to compare them to those of Massenet whose songs—primarily written for the salon—were extremely popular. But the comparison does Debussy an injustice. Although intended for the salon, Debussy's are surprisingly refined and original.

Many of these songs—as well as the nearly two dozen more he was to write over the next three years—were intended for Mme Vasnier. She must have been an extraordinary musician. The music he tailored for her voice is challenging and requires unusual agility and sensitivity. After returning from his stay with the von Mecks in December, Debussy spent more time with the Vasniers than ever, in the process neglecting his study at the Conservatoire. Guiraud, who was not pleased by his late return, was concerned. In a report of 11 January 1882 he continued to note Debussy's intelligence but felt that he "needed to be reined in."[10] His evaluation of Debussy at the conclusion of the academic year was not particularly encouraging: "Some progress. Poorly balanced temperament, but intelligent. Will succeed, I believe."[11] But, despite his concerns, that May he gave Debussy permission to enter the competition for the Prix de Rome.

The Prix de Rome had been established in 1803 (the same year Berlioz was born), its sponsor being the venerable Institut de France. Of the five academies that comprised the Institut, it was the Académie des Beaux-Arts (that is, the Fine Arts: visual arts and music) which was responsible for administering the Prix. In addition to composition, prizes were offered in sculpture, engraving, painting, and architecture.

8. Paul Vidal, "Souvenirs d'Achille Debussy," *La Revue Musicale* 7 (May, 1926), p. 14.

9. Review of 13 April 1903 in *DM*, p. 173.

10. Clevenger, "Training," p. 339.

11. 26 June 1882 in ibid., p. 340.

The objective of the Prix de Rome was admirable: to provide a period of financial independence for young artists at the start of their career, creating an opportunity for them to study and develop their skills. A modest stipend was supplied for four years. Usually winners spent the first three years in Rome as the guest of the Académie, but there was flexibility in the length of stay.

For composers, there were two stages in the competition. The preliminary round lasted six days and was primarily academic. Entrants were housed at the Conservatoire and were required to write a four-voice fugue (on a given theme) and a short choral work, all without the use of a piano. Generally about a half dozen students were permitted to pass from that trial to the more challenging final stage: the setting of a cantata (the text was supplied) for soloists, chorus, and orchestra. That round lasted twenty-five days during which the competitors were given access to a piano but kept secluded. Conversations were monitored, as well as visitors, who were only allowed at seven in the evening. About a week and a half after the cantatas had been completed, they were performed in a version accompanied by piano, four-hands, before the members of the music section of the Académie des Beaux-Arts—and a preliminary vote was taken. A performance before the entire Académie followed. Journalists were present, and a final vote was held to determine the winner. It was a prestigious affair and one in which politics had its share.

To be successful as a composer in France, many thought it was essential to win the Prix. More important than the stipend was the fame associated with it. Employment and commissions followed. During Debussy's involvement with the Prix, the pupils of Massenet dominated the competition.

In this, his first attempt, Debussy did not get beyond the preliminary round. But even entering the competition seemed premature. Known more for his iconoclasm than his accomplishments, Debussy had only recently begun to study composition. And he was the student of a teacher to whom few favors were owed.

During the year Debussy's reputation as an enfant terrible had continued to grow. In March 1882 he had attended the premiere of Edouard Lalo's ballet, *Namouna*. It met with a mixed reception: boos from conservative season-ticket holders, cheers from young supporters—including Debussy. Years later, he reported that he had been booted out of the performance because of his "noisy but forgivable enthusiasm."[12] All of the composition students paid a price for his rowdiness: the Conservatoire box was closed to them for several months.

Since his shift from performer to composer, Debussy had become more self-assured and increasingly more self-centered. From his earnings as accompanist he regularly purchased books and small objets d'art, despite the fact that money was

12. Review of 19 January 1903 in *DM*, p. 94.

still in short supply at home. And he ordered a set of visiting cards engraved with the name "A. de Bussy," an aristocratic touch intended to complement his association with the Vasniers and a reflection of what he perceived as his growing stature as a composer. On 12 May 1882 several of his works (including a *Nocturne et scherzo* for cello and piano) received their premiere at the salon of the piano-maker, Flaxland, sponsor of a series of recitals for amateurs. Debussy figured prominently in the program as pianist, but what made the concert particularly meaningful for Debussy was the participation in it of Mme Vasnier. She sang two of the songs he had written for her ("Les Roses" and "Fête galante") with himself as accompanist.

While Debussy that summer and autumn was enjoying the society of the von Mecks for a final time, Guiraud traveled to Germany to hear the music dramas of Wagner. The theater which Wagner had opened in Bayreuth in 1876 solely to perform his own compositions provided musicians from around the world with the opportunity to attend superlative performances of his work. Debussy was to make the pilgrimage to Bayreuth later. In 1882 Guiraud was among a sizable but select French contingent and he enjoyed what he heard, particularly *Parsifal*. He was in good humor as the 1882–1883 academic year started. But Debussy once again prolonged his stay with the von Mecks, and that, coupled with lax class attendance, was enough to set Guiraud on edge.

"A bizarre, but intelligent temperament," he wrote of Debussy in January 1883. "Writes music poorly. Nonetheless has made progress."[13] The remarks emphasize Guiraud's exasperation, and they were seconded by other composers at the Conservatoire who described Debussy's work as "disorderly" and "strange."[14]

Although Guiraud's frustration is understandable, his assertion that Debussy wrote music "poorly" comes as a surprise. What did he mean by it? One possibility may be found in his use of the verb "écrire" ("to write") instead of "composer"—since, despite his fine musical hand, Debussy was generally careless in the use of accidentals and other indications for performance.[15] But rather than taking Guiraud's comment literally—that Debussy did not put music down on paper well—it seems more likely that he felt Debussy's apparent ignorance of academic methodology led him to write music that was peculiar and violated textbook rules. In fact, by 1883 Debussy had been creating compositions—some of the songs for Mme Vasnier, for example—that were in many ways more interesting than the work of his teacher. But Guiraud knew nothing of them since Debussy chose to keep them to himself.

13. Report of 9 January 1883 in Clevenger, "Training," p. 340.

14. Comments of Thomas and Delibes concerning the *Première Suite d'orchestre* (1 February 1884) in ibid., p. 341.

15. See Roger Nichols, *The Life of Debussy* (Cambridge: Cambridge University Press, 1998), p. 17.

At the time of Guiraud's perplexing evaluation, Debussy was in the process of arranging his songs for Mme Vasnier into an album to give her as a present. The best of the set had been composed fairly recently and were settings of the poetry of Paul Verlaine. Verlaine was an unusual choice for a student composer. He was not well known, and Debussy's enthusiasm for his poetry was a mark of discernment. It elicited a new type of music from him, freed from convention, with greater use of dissonance and with more declamatory vocal lines. These songs hardly seem the work of a student. In works like "Mandoline" Debussy anticipates the more pungent style of songs of twentieth-century composers such as Francis Poulenc (the *Chansons gaillardes*, for example, completed in 1926).

At some point over the next few months Debussy showed Guiraud some of the music he had been writing outside of class, in particular a large-scale project from Théodore de Banville's drama, *Diane au bois*. It was a decisive move. Had Guiraud been small-minded, the quality and originality of Debussy's work might have aroused some envy. Instead he became a supporter, an advisor, and, in time, a good friend. It was an uncommon relationship and attracted attention. Paul Vidal, a student of Massenet, felt that Guiraud pampered Debussy and treated him "like a spoilt child."[16]

Guiraud's change in attitude is evident in Debussy's second attempt at the Prix that May. He told Debussy that if he wanted to win, he needed to be more conventional. This time Debussy was among the five who passed the preliminary round. The next stage—the setting in seclusion of the cantata text—was an ordeal, but Debussy managed to keep his sense of humor. The Vasniers were among his visitors, and their daughter, Marguerite, seeing bars in the windows of his room wondered why they were there. "No doubt because they think we're wild beasts," he replied.[17]

Assigned cantata texts tended to be stiff and archaic. That year's selection, "Le Gladiateur" by Emile Moreau, was somewhat better than average. Debussy did what he could to find inspiration. He must also have felt pressured, for he was not a quick worker. But he did a more than respectable job, producing moments of surprising intensity in what has been described as a "miniature Wagnerian music drama."[18]

On 22 June all the versions of "Le Gladiateur" were performed. As it turned out, Debussy's setting was not considered for the first prize but managed to get the second prize (after being tied for it). That was an unexpected success, especially in light of the typically strong showing by Massenet's pupils. Winning the second prize usually meant winning the first prize the following year, so there were expectations for Debussy.

16. *DR*, p. 24.

17. Ibid., p. 20.

18. John R. Clevenger, "Achille at the Conservatoire, 1872–1884," *Cahiers Debussy* 19 (1995), p. 34.

Music critics present at the performance of the cantatas reacted favorably to his work. The judges' response was also encouraging, and mention was made of Debussy's "bountiful musical nature," as well as "some striking dramatic effects." But their praise contained a warning. His music was, they felt, "ardent to the point of intemperance"—a hint that if he hoped to win the first prize he had better create a blander product.[19]

Paul Vidal was awarded the first prize in 1883. Now that he was to leave for Rome, Vidal gave up his position as accompanist for an amateur choral society, La Concordia, and recommended Debussy as his successor. It was not a particularly accomplished group.[20] By Debussy's standards, its repertoire was narrow: a favorite with the group were the choral works of Charles Gounod who was honorary president of the society. But this was to turn to Debussy's advantage. Much of Gounod's fame had been created by the success of two operas: *Faust* (1859) and *Mireille* (1864). Although more recent works by him had not been as popular, his reputation remained formidable. Gounod and Debussy knew one another, and their association with La Concordia drew them into more frequent contact. In time Gounod became a powerful supporter.

Despite his reservations, Debussy benefited from his association with La Concordia. There were performances of significant works new to him: in January 1884, for example, excerpts were performed from Liszt's *Legend of St. Elizabeth* as well as Bach's Cantata No. 106, one of his finest. But Debussy's relationship with the society was strained. He could not be relied upon to attend rehearsals and often gave flimsy excuses for absences.

Still, his association with La Concordia entailed some recognition of his musical accomplishments. Coupled with an improved relationship with Guiraud, the recent second place in the Prix, and the inspiration provided by his friendship with the Vasniers—Debussy's spirits could only have been lifted. His self-assurance soared. On one occasion he served as a substitute teacher in a composition seminar. "My dear orphans," he announced from the doorway, "in the absence of your parents, I shall provide nourishment for you!" Instruction followed: "a rustling of misshapen arpeggios, a gurgling of trills on three notes simultaneously, in both hands, and chains of harmonic progressions which could not be analyzed according to the sacrosanct textbook."[21]

Contributing to Debussy's self-confidence were the strides he had been making as a composer. The nearly dozen songs he composed in 1883 and 1884 maintain

---

19. *LS*, p. 61.

20. Gabriel Fauré described the chorus as "very mediocre, with a heavy, dull sound." Jean-Michel Nectoux, "Debussy et Fauré," *Cahiers Debussy* 3 (1979), p. 14.

21. According to Maurice Emmanuel who was a member of the class (*DR*, p. 21).

high standards. Most are settings of the poetry of Paul Bourget (whom Debussy knew slightly and admired). But also among them is the first indication of his interest in the esoteric poetry of Stéphane Mallarmé ("Apparition"). This out-pouring of song was a direct result of Debussy's association with Mme Vasnier. She was, he confessed, "the only muse who has ever inspired in me anything resembling musical sentiment (to speak only of that)."[22] She had opened her home to him, and offered praise, support, and encouragement. But by 1884 she had become more than an inspiration: she and Debussy had become lovers.

The songs themselves give some indication of it. Many are love poems, increasingly intimate in detail and desire: "This pillow during nights of madness/Saw our brows united in sleep"; "The ardent intoxication of life/Weakens the delighted lover"; "For love is stronger/Than the gods and death." Debussy became hesitant to compete in the forthcoming Prix de Rome, afraid that if he won, he would be separated from her.

Discretion was not foremost in his mind, and the affair did not long remain private. Family and friends were horrified. To Debussy's mother, Marie Vasnier was immoral, preying on her son's youth and inexperience. For Paul Vidal, it was "a sin-ister tale of adultery...his succubus is battening on to all his little weaknesses. She's pretty and much pursued by admirers.... I thought for a moment, last year, that art had recovered its hold over him.... But his present behavior fills me with remorse....His moral sense is undeveloped, he's nothing but a sensualist."[23]

Their affair lasted for several years. Debussy's letters are the primary source of information about it but contain few direct references. What is most striking is the intensity of his passion. For at least a time, it became an obsession. But Vidal's reac-tion was excessive. Yes, there was a sensual side to Debussy—an aspect of his character that over the years seemed to alienate several of his friends. But "Art" had not lost its attraction. The large number of songs he produced are evidence of it. And, despite reservations, Debussy continued to keep the Prix de Rome in mind. That May he competed once again. The selected cantata text—"L'Enfant prodigue" by Edouard Guinand—was a version of the biblical parable of the return of the prodigal son. Debussy successfully completed the preliminary round and entered into seclusion for the composition of the cantata. On 27 and 28 June the completed works were performed. Debussy profited from outstanding singers supplied by Guiraud to enhance the performance. Gounod too gave his support and, unlike the previous year when there had been debate over giving him any prize at all, he was awarded the first prize. "Very marked poetic sensibility, warm and brilliant coloring, dramatic and lively music" was the response of the judges.[24]

22. From Debussy's dedication to her of "Tragédie."

23. Letter of Paul Vidal to Henriette Fuchs of 12 July 1884 in *DR*, pp. 24, 25.

24. *LS*, p. 69.

For this, his third and final attempt at the Prix, Debussy had made a point of following Guiraud's advice. Some of the music he wrote for it is deliberately popular in style, resembling Massenet, for example, or Delibes. Debussy wrote what he knew would have broad appeal. But at the same time *L'Enfant prodigue* is an accomplished and skillful work, so much so that it is difficult to see how the judges could have avoided giving him the prize.

News of his victory spread widely. "I'm not surprised," wrote Nadezhda von Meck when she learned of it. "He's extremely gifted."[25] At home his success was met with enthusiasm—and a sense of relief.

But Debussy reacted quite differently. He learned of his triumph while gazing at some boats on the Seine, waiting outside the building where his cantata had just been performed:

> All at once someone tapped me on the shoulder and breathlessly said, "You have won the prize." Now I don't know if you are going to believe this, but my heart sank. I had a sudden vision of boredom, and of all the worries that inevitably go together with any form of official recognition. I felt I was no longer free.[26]

Rome

Debussy was expected to arrive in Rome no later than January 1885. The primary attraction the Prix held for him was its stipend: about 4,000 francs annually for four years. In 1884 the city of Paris was sponsoring a music competition that offered awards of 10,000 and 6,000 francs for a new composition, and it occurred to Debussy that if he won that competition, the financial freedom it provided would enable him to decline the Prix de Rome and remain in Paris with Marie Vasnier. It was the type of impulsive act that was characteristic of him for much of his life.

For the Paris competition Debussy needed to submit a work for soloists, chorus, and orchestra—similar to what he had just done with *L'Enfant prodigue*, but of greater length—on a theme neither theatrical nor religious. The deadline for entries was 29 September. He had one work on hand that could have served as the basis for a competition entry, a setting of Leconte de Lisle's *Hélène*. But he was a deliberate worker, and, despite his hopes, in the end had nothing ready.[27]

---

25. Ibid., p. 59.

26. Review of 10 June 1903 in *DM*, p. 211.

27. The winning entry was Vincent d'Indy's *Chant de la cloche*. Because he was a private student of Franck and not of composition professors at the Conservatoire, d'Indy's success came as a shock—a point that Debussy savored.

There now seemed little choice but to prepare for Rome. But his infatuation persisted. In the autumn he approached a recent acquaintance, Count
Giuseppe Primoli (a descendant of Napoleon Bonaparte's brother, Lucien),
requesting a loan to repay some debts and to buy "some flowers for *her who
loves them so much!*"[28]

Primoli was well known in both France and Rome, where his salon (which
included Henry James among its visitors) was one of the most exclusive. He had a
great interest in the arts, was a strong supporter of the Prix, and made a point of
being helpful to its winners. Debussy was to turn to him more than once for
assistance after he moved to Rome. But in this first instance Primoli did not respond
quickly enough, and Debussy wrote again, now claiming that he needed money for
a fine binding for his songs—a special album intended for Marie Vasnier.

Debussy delayed his departure for as long as possible, not leaving until 27 January
1885. That day he wrote from Marseille to Henri Vasnier, Marie's husband, the first
in a series of letters to him. They make interesting reading. "I will never forget,
Monsieur," he wrote not long after his arrival in Rome, "all that you have done for
me, and the place you made for me inside your family. I will do all that I can to
prove to you that I am not ungrateful."[29]

In their correspondence Debussy shared thoughts, ideas, and concerns. Vasnier
responded with fatherly advice. Debussy had two ulterior motives: to maintain
contact with Marie, no matter how tenuous, and to complain bitterly of his lonely
and miserable existence in Rome.

Of the four years associated with the Prix, it was expected for winners to spend
at least the first two in Rome. Their residence was an elegant villa, the Villa Medici,
built in 1540 and renovated by the French early in the nineteenth century. The site
had been selected both for its beauty and for what was hoped was its ability to
foster in students a love for the arts. By all accounts (except Debussy's) the villa was
exceptionally attractive, particularly the extensive gardens. Debussy found it all a
bore. "You speak of the tranquility the Villa has to offer," he wrote to Vasnier that
September, "God knows, I could do with a bit less of it."[30]

Years later, Debussy's recollections of life at the Villa had not mellowed. The type
of communal life it represented would never have been congenial to him. But
nearly everything associated with the Villa became an irritation. He remembered
his room as one which the students had nicknamed "The Etruscan Tomb." According
to Debussy, its green walls "seemed to recede as you moved toward them." The meals,

28. Letter of [November? 1884] in *C*, p. 19.

29. Letter of early February 1885 in ibid., p. 23.

30. Letter of 16 September 1885 in Claude Debussy, *Debussy Letters*, ed. François Lesure and Roger
Nichols (Cambridge: Harvard University Press, 1987), p. 11. Hereafter abbreviated *DL*.

he claimed, were unforgettable, particularly the "roba dolce," a mixture that tasted like gasoline and soured cream. All in all, it was "a diet that ruined one's stomach for life!"[31]

Debussy said that he spent little time with other students and described the supposed "artistic milieu and jovial camaraderie" as "much overrated."[32] His aloofness is confirmed by another Prix winner, Gabriel Pierné: "There was no real intimacy between [Debussy] and the other students. He was very solitary, and fled our company. He went out a great deal, roamed through antique shops, and made a clean sweep of tiny Japanese *objets* which delighted him. He was scarcely seen except at mealtime."[33] Unlike other composers in residence, he did not attend any of the musical salons in the city.

But Paul Vidal—still in Rome as a result of his win in 1883—remembered Debussy's life as being quite different: "Even though he complained from time to time of the lack of camaraderie in the Villa, he used to appear at the soirées given by the director...playing piano duets and singing his songs, which everyone adored....He and I spent most of our time together, playing piano duet arrangements of Bach's organ works, which he was passionate about. We also studied the two-piano arrangement of Beethoven's Ninth Symphony, Chabrier's *Valses romantiques*, etc."[34]

Vidal was also aware of Debussy's complaints and realized that he was "terribly bored. His only dream is of returning to Paris."[35] He knew firsthand why Debussy was upset, for Vidal agreed with some of Debussy's objections. "Rome is intolerable," Vidal had recently written. "Life in the Villa is odious; there's no stimulus to compose anything."[36]

The truth concerning Debussy's life at Rome lies somewhere between Pierné's and Vidal's accounts. He could keep to himself—just as he had at times at the Conservatoire. But he never led the life of a hermit and would have chosen the company of Vidal to that of Pierné (with whom he was not close). He preferred associating with adults—such as Count Primoli—to mixing with students, in part because he did not want to be seen as a student. But life in Rome was not as desolate as he wanted others to believe. That autumn he was more truthful (although the root of his unhappiness—separation from Marie Vasnier—could not be revealed):

31. Reviews of 10 June 1903 and May 1903 in *DM*, pp. 212, 198.

32. Letter of early February 1885 to Vasnier in *C*, p. 23.

33. Gabriel Pierné, "Souvenirs d'Achille Debussy," *La Revue Musicale* 7 (May, 1926), p. 11.

34. *DR*, p. 8.

35. Letter of 16 February 1885 in "Debussy de 1883 à 1885 d'après la correspondance de Paul Vidal à Henriette Fuchs," *Revue de Musicologie* 48 (1962), p. 100.

36. Letter to Henriette Fuchs of 12 July 1884 in *DR*, p. 25.

"I'm not well and I'm not ill. I'm simply suffering from a malaise which can't be described, but which is a result of being where I don't belong."[37]

The purpose of his persistent complaints was to somehow justify leaving Rome. "I may return to Paris sooner than you think," he warned Vasnier shortly after his arrival.[38] Although Vasnier did everything he could to put him in a better frame of mind—pointing out the beauties of Rome and the advantages of his situation—for months Debussy continued to threaten to give it all up and return.

During his stay in Rome Debussy confided in Claudius Popelin (an artist living in Paris), and in his son Gustave (a recent Prix winner). To them, he spoke of his predicament, as well as the depth of his infatuation and despair. "My desires and conceptions exist only *through her*," he wrote. "This love is insane, I know, but the madness prevents me from thinking."[39] It was the "madness" which tempted him to resign the Prix, and it also was at the heart of his dissatisfaction and determination to return to France.

Winners of the Prix were not allowed to leave Italy without permission. In 1885 Debussy left twice. His first departure (perhaps without approval) occurred in late April. He returned on 5 May, after having seen the Vasniers. His second visit to France—in this instance he presented a trumped-up excuse for the director—was in early July and lasted about two months. During this absence he visited the Vasniers in Dieppe, where they were vacationing (during a later visit to Dieppe, the painter, Jacques-Emile Blanche, claimed that he had seen Debussy scaling a rope ladder, Marie waiting at the window).

The visits did nothing to temper either his ardor or dissatisfaction with life in Rome. There was some relief that September in a working vacation at the seaside residence of Count Primoli in Fiumicino. Primoli was away and Debussy had the house all to himself. As always, the sea was a refreshing experience. To Vasnier, he described Fiumicino as "a charming spot where the Romans come to bathe in the sea. There is a little harbor with little boats—most entertaining and picturesque."[40] In addition to the vacation, Debussy had an unexpected musical pleasure: a performance of masses by Palestrina and Orlando di Lasso in a small church in Rome. It was a time of renewed interest in Renaissance music, and Debussy became an enthusiastic admirer. "The effects which are produced simply from a profound knowledge of counterpoint are truly astonishing," he wrote to Vasnier. "There is a twisting in the melodic lines that brings to mind the effect of the illuminations in very old missals—and that also underlines the sentiment of the words."[41]

37. Letter to Vasnier from the end of November 1885 in *DL*, p. 15.

38. Letter of early February 1885 in *C*, p. 23.

39. Letter to Claudius Popelin on 24 June [1885] in ibid., p. 31.

40. Letter of 29 January [1886] in ibid., p. 49.

41. Letter from the end of November 1885 in ibid., pp. 44–45.

Palestrina was not new to Debussy. The Kyrie of the *Pope Marcellus Mass* had been performed in April 1884 by La Concordia. But there were a number of elements which combined to make the Roman experience more memorable: a better performance, the setting (a church about which Debussy raved), and the general paucity of worthwhile music for him to hear. The striking comparison he made to Renaissance visual art was characteristic of him. Debussy tended to think of the arts in broad terms and often discovered fascinating correspondences. And there was yet another attraction for Debussy in the music of Palestrina and Lasso: their distance from the musical canon taught at the Conservatoire, which relied almost exclusively on eighteenth- and nineteenth-century models.

The Renaissance music Debussy heard also provided a welcome departure from the usual. Contemporary musical life in Italy held no attraction for him, particularly Italian opera which Debussy dismissed as bloated and bombastic. But there were some additional musical opportunities at the Villa. The director of the Académie for most of Debussy's stay was Ernest Hébert, a painter. He was a passionate music lover and became fond of Debussy. Debussy dined regularly with the Héberts, performed frequently for them (including several of his Bourget songs), and even served as occasional accompanist for the director, an amateur violinist.

It was through Hébert that Debussy met Franz Liszt. Liszt was seventy-four and spent part of each year in Rome. He enjoyed occasional contact with the Prix winners at the Académie. On 8 January he was the dinner guest of the Héberts, and in his honor Debussy and Vidal played a two-piano arrangement of his *Faust Symphony*—during which Liszt fell asleep. The next day Debussy and Vidal accompanied the Héberts on a follow-up visit to Liszt, where it is likely they played Chabrier's *Valses romantiques*, a lively work whose novelty would have made it more difficult for him to doze off.

Liszt had yet to play for them, and despite his age his virtuosity remained impressive. The opportunity came on 13 January when he once again visited the Héberts with Debussy present. For the past decade or so Liszt had been creating a series of astonishing works, bold in their use of dissonance and audacious in their expansion of tonality. They remained little known and mostly unpublished (some who knew them even suspected that Liszt had become senile). Unfortunately, the present occasion was entirely social, and foremost in Liszt's mind were the tastes of his hosts. He played not his new compositions, but several nearly a half century old: "Au bord d'une source" (from the *Années de Pèlerinage*; Book I) and his transcription of Schubert's "Ave Maria." Debussy long remembered the effects Liszt created with his use of the pedals, but had he played a more recent work—*Nuages gris* or *En rêve*, for example—Debussy would have been spellbound, both by their originality and by their break with the tradition associated with the teaching at the Conservatoire.

By 1886 Debussy's passion for Marie Vasnier was waning, or at least in abeyance. That February the Héberts were visited by friends, the Hochons (he was a professor of medicine). Mme Hochon was exceptionally pretty, and interested in music. Debussy was seen kissing her at the Villa, an incident that was recorded with surprise by Mme Hébert in her diary—since for months the Héberts had known of Debussy's affair with Marie Vasnier.[42] During July and August, Debussy was on vacation in France. No references appear to the Vasniers, and about this time his correspondence with Henri Vasnier lessens considerably.

With the attraction of Marie Vasnier dwindling, Debussy was spending more of his time on music, as well as doing a great deal of reading. He wrote on several occasions to a book dealer in Paris, Emile Baron, asking for recent works—including Symbolist and Decadent writers (such as Joris-Karl Huysmans, Jean Moréas, and Charles Morice), a translation of Shelley, the *Revue indépendante* (a leading artistic journal), and Rosicrucian literature (the occult was much in vogue at the time). The reading confirms Debussy's eagerness to educate himself. But it also reveals a strong interest in current literary trends in Paris and helps to explain why Rome became little more than a prison to him. Debussy's reading may have been stimulating, but he accomplished little as a composer during 1885 and 1886. He was required each year to complete a work of substance (referred to as an envoi) and to submit it to the Académie for evaluation. Beyond those works, he only composed about a half dozen songs. Eight months after his arrival in Rome, Debussy concluded that his life there was "*a wasted experience [that] has merely set me back.*"[43] In many ways, he was right.

The Prix de Rome had been created with a focus on the visual arts. It was the intention for young painters and architects who won the prize to experience the grandeur that was Rome (especially its antiquities and Renaissance masters) and use them as a foundation and source of inspiration. But for a composer—particularly one concerned with modernity like Debussy—living in Rome contributed far less. For him, there had only been one notable musical experience: the moving encounter with the music of Palestrina and Lasso. But that could just as easily have occurred in Paris where there was a similar resurgence of interest. Contemporary Italian music had little to offer him. Precisely at a time in his career when he wanted to keep abreast of developments in the arts, Debussy found himself isolated from them. While in Rome, he missed the final Impressionist exhibit (including Seurat's *La Grande Jatte*), and could only have learned belatedly of the publication of Jules Laforgue's *Complaintes* and Jean Moréas's *Symbolist Manifesto*.

42. According to Debussy's friend, Pierre Louÿs, it was Mme Hochon who "ravished" Debussy. See *LS*, p. 420.

43. Letter to Vasnier of 16 September [1885] in *DL*, p. 12.

It might have been assumed that for someone with as strong an interest in the arts as Debussy the exposure to Italian painting and architecture would have had a profound effect. It did not. He noted with interest some work of Signorelli and Raphael. But in general his mood was hardly receptive, feeling, as he did, like a captive. Unlike other winners of the Prix, there was no novelty in his situation. He had already spent a fair amount of time in Rome with the von Mecks. All of this only served to emphasize how different Debussy was from the usual winner of the Prix. He had never fit the mold of a "student composer." But to his professors in Paris— those who evaluated what was supposed to be his yearly progress—he was not only a student, but one on probation.

Their attitude was made clear in their criticism of the yearly envoi he sent to them. The first was a symphonic ode *Zuleima* (an adaption of Heine's *Almanzor*), based on a poem by Georges Boyer. Debussy began the project with enthusiasm; like all the envoi, it had been selected by him. But he soon tired of it, complaining of its Verdian and Meyerbeer-like qualities. What provided Debussy's attraction to Heine's tale is hard to fathom. It is an old-fashioned love story set among the Moors in Spain, with all the trappings of grand opera. The committee that examined the score concluded that Debussy seemed "tormented by the desire to produce the bizarre, the incomprehensible, the unperformable"—a clear indication in their eyes that he had returned to his old ways.[44] Unfortunately, *Zuleima* has been lost (perhaps destroyed by Debussy), so there is no way of knowing why the committee found so offensive what he had felt was so bland. But it is interesting to note that the envois of Vidal and Pierné— both of whom were to have far smoother careers than Debussy—were praised.

Debussy's second envoi, *Printemps* (Spring; for wordless chorus, piano, and orchestra), was written in haste in 1887. He did not complete the orchestration. For the committee, he supplied the piano score and a tale that the full score had been destroyed in a fire at the bindery. The inspiration for it was a painting by a fellow student at the Villa, Marcel Baschet—a work which in turn had been inspired by Botticelli's *Primavera*. Botticelli's painting was widely admired in France at the time, and Debussy was not alone in responding to it. In 1886 Ernest Chausson—who was to become a good friend of Debussy—considered composing a tone poem based on it.

Debussy explained his intentions for the work in a letter to Emile Baron, making clear to him that there was no detailed program associated with it because of his dislike of them. "I wanted to express the slow and languid genesis of beings and things in nature," Debussy wrote, "then their flowering—concluding with a dazzling delight at being reborn to a new life."[45] Debussy later returned to *Printemps* and

44. John R. Clevenger, "Debussy's Rome Cantatas," in *Debussy and His World*, ed. Jane Fulcher (Princeton, NJ: Princeton University Press, 2001), p. 71.

45. Letter of 9 February 1887 in *C*, p. 59.

began to orchestrate it in September 1908. But he soon lost interest. It is known today in a revision—charming and tuneful—made by Henri Büsser in 1913 with Debussy's approval and assistance.

It is hard to believe that this is the same work that led to one of the most famous criticisms in the history of music. When they received *Printemps* the committee was outraged and detected at its core a "vague impressionism which is one of the most dangerous enemies of truth in works of art."[46] What was meant is not at all clear. The occasionally nebulous tonality and structure of *Printemps* might have been perceived as "impressionistic," but much of it, like *L'Enfant prodigue*, is (for Debussy) quite tame.

The concept of "impressionism" in music—as we think of it today—did not exist in 1887. What was probably intended was an attack upon new and unusual elements in Debussy's musical style, not that they sounded in some way "impressionistic." Impressionism in painting had been present in France for about a decade and was still controversial. That it was new, different, and unconventional aroused strong opposition and led to its being perceived by some as a threat to tradition. In that sense, as being representative of new developments in the arts, Debussy's music was impressionistic—and unacceptable.

Printemps was Debussy's final envoi from Rome. He left early in March 1887. Most winners spent three years there, but he had spent two, all that was required. Not long after his return to Paris, he wrote to Hébert thanking him for his kindness. The last months spent in Rome, he confessed, now seemed like a "dreamlife, immersed in my work, all my efforts devoted toward an elevated ideal of art without concerning myself with the opinions of anyone."[47] Financial security, freedom from daily concerns, the opportunity to be original and even experimental in one's work—those had been possible while living at the Villa. In Paris, forced to confront the realities of life as a composer, Debussy finally realized that, with all its disadvantages, there had been some benefit to his life in Rome.

46. *LS*, p. 96.
47. Letter of 17 March 1887 in *C*, p. 61.

CHAPTER THREE

Establishing a Reputation

The world is myself. It owes me its existence. I have created it with my senses.
It is my slave, and no one else has power over it.

Rémy de Gourmont, *Sixtine. Roman de la vie cérébrale* (1890)

AFTER ENDURING A TWO-YEAR EXILE IN ROME, DEBUSSY COULD ONLY HAVE been exhilarated by his return to Paris. It was an unusually exciting time to live there, especially for anyone with an interest in the arts. There was a constant stream of new books, new music, and new paintings—all in a variety of styles that provoked broad debate. Each set its own standard: Dynamism, Syntheticism, Integralism, Neo-Romanticism, Primitivism—to name only a few. But among the literally dozens of "isms" that flourished in the decades prior to the First World War—an indication both of the vitality of the arts and of their disarray—three drew conspicuous attention: Impressionism, Symbolism, and Naturalism.[1]

Impressionism, despite its popularity today, was unquestionably the most controversial. It was criticized for what was seen as its peculiar, visual distortions of the world and for its rejection of tradition. Everyday life served as its basis (often with a modernist slant), but the deeply personal technique used to represent it—short brushstrokes emphasizing dazzling color and light—was revolutionary.

In contrast, Symbolist art turned its back on the real world and focused instead on a spiritual and visionary one founded in idealism. Content drew heavily on myth and dream. But unlike Impressionist painting, the technique of Symbolist art

---

1. A fuller discussion of Impressionism and Symbolism is found in Chapter 8. For additional reading, see Belinda Thomson, *Impressionism: Origins, Practice, Reception* (London: Thames and Hudson, 2000), and Kenneth Cornell, *The Symbolist Movement* (New Haven, CT: Yale University Press, 1951).

could not have been more traditional in basis, using a meticulously academic style to represent increasingly bizarre and mysterious images.

There was no literary counterpart to Impressionism, but Symbolist poets, novelists, dramatists, and critics formed the avant-garde of the 1880s. Their work—a favorite of Debussy—was attacked for its obscurity, eroticism, and extreme individuality. It was frequently described as decadent, but among the Symbolist movement itself "Decadence" was perceived as a separate trend, its defining trait being an absence of idealism.

Symbolist literature often presented itself as an antidote to Naturalism, a popular movement associated with the novelist Emile Zola and his followers. Naturalists—and the academic school of painting which was in many ways their counterpart—extolled realism, and their work was fastidious in its attempt to re-create the everyday world, including aspects of it that would have been regarded as prosaic (or even offensive to the moral standards of the day). They adopted a measured approach focusing on detail, and, in the visual arts, prized accuracy and objectivity.

Compared to the developments occurring in literature and the visual arts, the musical world seemed rather dull. As always, opera remained the major musical genre in France. But there was no sign of the changes that were occurring in the other arts, except perhaps for the occasional exotic locale that bore superficial resemblance to the Oriental and Middle Eastern settings favored by many Symbolists. Massenet's operas set the standard, and they were logical continuations of the grand opéra formulated by Meyerbeer in the 1830s and the opéra-lyrique of Gounod.

What revolutionary tendencies existed in French music of the day were found not in opera but in the activities of the Société Nationale de Musique. Founded in February 1871, its goal was to foster French music, especially instrumental compositions. Symphonies, concertos, sonatas, chamber ensembles—all were part of a genre that had been perceived as predominantly German, and in that sense the formation of the Société Nationale was a response to the defeat suffered at German hands in 1870. But there was a practical reason for the move as well. Performing instrumental music required fewer resources and expense than opera or oratorio.

A large number of composers benefited from the sponsorship of the Société. But as good as much of this music was—including not a few masterpieces—to some it resembled a mutual admiration society. To those with more radical tastes like Debussy, the works were too traditional. New ideas and new techniques had changed French painting and literature. French music seemed poised for similar change.

Debussy's first concern on returning to Paris in 1887 should have been the practical one of laying the foundations for his career as a composer. He needed to maintain connections with the Conservatoire as well as to develop friendships with those in positions of influence in the musical world. It would be helpful, for example, to establish relations with Edouard Colonne and Charles Lamoureux, conductors of the two major concert series in Paris. Equally important was becoming active in the Société Nationale. But fame—and financial success—ultimately involved creating a successful opera. As a recent winner of the Prix de Rome, the path for Debussy had been made easier. His success assured recognition, and it was traditional for the directors of opera houses in Paris to be receptive to Prix winners.

For most composers, the primary purpose of winning the Prix was to facilitate entry into the highly competitive musical life in France. But as his letter to Hébert revealed, almost immediately upon his return Debussy became disenchanted. Winning the Prix was supposed to open doors. But that would be the case only if the music he composed were in an easily understandable style. In other words, to become popular Debussy needed to continue the deception he had begun with *L'Enfant prodigue*. During the next half dozen years he was often at war with himself, unsure of what to do, and frustrated by his inability to make a name and earn a living.

For a young composer, the Société Nationale provided an essential outlet. But Debussy delayed becoming a member until January 1888. There had recently been a change in administration, one that should have worked to his advantage. In November 1886 Camille Saint-Saëns, a founder and prominent member, had resigned. He was critical of Debussy's music, and during his long life did all he could to hamper his career. With Saint-Saëns's departure, leadership more receptive to Debussy had come into power. The new president was César Franck, but he was merely the figurehead. Actual management of the organization was in the hands of the two secretaries, Vincent d'Indy and Ernest Chausson. Both were former students of Franck, and their standing in French musical circles was growing. Debussy soon became friendly with them, if only on a superficial basis.

Of the two, d'Indy was the more powerful. He was nine years older than Debussy, aristocratic, devoutly Catholic, and (despite his hero worship for Napoleon Bonaparte) a monarchist. These were all traits that endeared him to a conservative establishment for which Debussy had little sympathy. But there was common ground. Like Debussy, d'Indy's artistic interests went beyond music. He was well read, interested in current trends, and a skillful watercolorist.

Both d'Indy and Debussy had received a standard musical training, although in d'Indy's case his—befitting his social standing—had been conducted privately (and included study with both Marmontel and Lavignac). In 1872 he became a private student of César Franck whom he greatly admired. He later did much to promote Franck's music and became his first biographer.

Study with Franck solidified d'Indy's musical taste. He venerated a great deal of the eighteenth- and nineteenth-century tradition that Debussy chose to ignore. But after Franck was snubbed by the Conservatoire, d'Indy became wary of the musical establishment and more receptive to composers who were not part of it. Like Debussy, he was critical of popular composers like Massenet. And he revered Wagner. In d'Indy's case, it was an admiration that began cautiously. And what he particularly admired—the use of music to express sentiment and ideas—was not what attracted Debussy.

During the 1880s d'Indy's compositions were drawing attention. *Wallenstein,* op. 12 (a collection of three overtures inspired by Schiller and completed in 1881), reflected his study with Franck. They are fairly conventional pieces, resembling at times Liszt's tone poems, but imaginatively orchestrated. Five years later, d'Indy completed the *Symphonie sur un chant montagnard français,* op. 25, one of his most popular works. It is a piano concerto of sorts, possessing great charm, and displaying its Franckian tendencies both by its structure and concern with thematic unity. By the mid-1880s, d'Indy was widely regarded as the most promising young composer in France. But he was generous in his support of others, and was in a position to be helpful to Debussy.

Debussy's membership in the Société was a sensible first step in self-promotion, but any attempt to launch his career was hampered by life at home, much of which was in disarray. He still lived with his parents, and their financial situation had worsened. There was pressure on Claude (who was now twenty-five) to establish his livelihood in a hurry. Debussy continued teaching piano, but never with pleasure. Starting in 1889, he earned additional income by arranging for publication piano transcriptions of orchestral compositions by Saint-Saëns. That, too, was unpleasant, both because of the routine involved and because of his dislike of Saint-Saëns's music.

Prix winners frequently began their careers by doing some teaching at the Conservatoire or taking minor posts at the Opéra. That also had no appeal to Debussy. But he did maintain cordial relations with Guiraud and even visited Marmontel on occasion. The relationship with Guiraud was of real value—not because it served to advance Debussy's career, but because it provided an opportunity for him to speak his mind. Even if Guiraud sometimes regarded Debussy as eccentric, he was at least willing to listen.

Instead of ingratiating himself with the musical establishment, Debussy preferred to avoid it. In September 1888 he was asked to supply an overture for a concert sponsored by the Institut de France intended to honor recent Prix de Rome winners. His eminently polite and sarcastic refusal—Debussy claimed he felt incapable of providing a work "worthy of the Institute"—could only have irritated precisely those musicians he should have been trying to charm.[2] He also made no attempt to enter the salons of the upper class—such as those of the Polignacs and Greffulhes—which, for composers like Gabriel Fauré, became important sources of patronage.

2. *LS,* p. 97.

From a purely practical point of view, it should have been important to Debussy to cultivate the acquaintance of those who could advance his career. Instead, he seemed eager to satisfy his curiosity and to become friends with those from whom he could learn—in the process encountering new ideas and stimulus for his work.

In general during these years Debussy tended to avoid musicians, preferring instead the company of writers and artists. He was intensely curious about the arts and eager to learn more. The artistic and literary circles in which he moved were informal, the number of participants fluctuating, the primary basis being a fondness for debate and a habitual curiosity about the arts. Meetings were held in favorite cafés and bistros, and Debussy soon became a habitué of several. At a tavern, Chez Pousset, he probably came into contact with two of the best-known writers of the time: Villiers de l'Isle-Adam and Catulle Mendès. Both were devoted Wagnerians who earlier had been associated with the Parnassians—a literary group popular in the 1860s and 1870s. At Pousset's, Debussy would also have met Jules de Brayer, an organist and ardent advocate of the music of Musorgsky, in addition to Gabriel Mourey, a translator of Poe, one of Debussy's favorite writers. He could also have renewed acquaintance with Charles de Sivry, who was a regular visitor to Pousset's.

At Thommen's, Debussy met the poet and amateur musician Maurice Rollinat, author of the popular *Les Névroses* (*Neuroses*), and the writers Louis le Cardonnel and Charles Cros. Also a frequent visitor was the artist Adolphe Willette, a friend of Vincent d'Indy and one of the first to treat the poster as an art form. Debussy would have been attracted to his work, much of which recalls the commedia dell'arte and the world of Verlaine's "Fêtes galantes." Willette provided an illustration for Debussy's early setting of Verlaine's "Mandoline" (1890).

Similar surroundings were found at Weber's, a tavern Debussy visited regularly in the 1890s, and Reynold's, a favorite haunt of Toulouse-Lautrec. More elevated in the artistic hierarchy was the Café Vachette where Debussy also spent time. A regular guest there was the poet Jean Moréas whose *Symbolist Manifesto* of 1886 helped define the movement. Debussy knew Moréas and, according to the reminiscences of friends, was a participant in the aesthetic debates that raged at the time.

During these years Debussy developed unusually close friendships with two young men roughly his own age: Raymond Bonheur and Robert Godet. Bonheur was a musician and a good friend of Chausson. He shared with Debussy a curiosity and interest in all the arts. Godet's abilities were many: novelist, journalist, linguist, reclusive amateur composer (and Wagnerian). He was widely traveled, and also friendly with Chausson. Those who knew him well described him as a humanist in the true sense of the word.

Perhaps the most significant relationship for Debussy at this stage of his career was with the bookseller and publisher, Edmond Bailly. Bailly had studied briefly at the Conservatoire, but then had turned to literature and established a bookstore and press: the Librairie de l'art indépendant. It became a meeting place for many prominent and promising writers and artists, including Villiers, Henri de Régnier, Pierre Louÿs, André Gide, Odilon Redon, and Félicien Rops. The premises were used for occasional art exhibitions. Musicians, too, were welcome, and a piano was kept in the back.

Bailly's interests were eclectic. His knowledge of Swedenborg and the occult was extensive. And he was so fascinated by theosophy (a mystical religion that attracted Alexander Scriabin and the painter, Jean Delville) that he became editor of a popular, theosophical journal, *Le Lotus bleu*. Everything out of the ordinary seemed to attract him. In music his tastes even included oriental music—a topic about which Debussy was ignorant, but curious.

Debussy soon became a regular visitor to Bailly's shop. While he admired Bailly's "truly artistic ideas," he seemed most impressed by "his determination [that] sometimes puts mine in the shade."[3] Bailly became a supporter, and two of Debussy's earliest works, the *Cinq Poèmes de Baudelaire* and *La Damoiselle élue* were published by him, the latter in a luxurious limited edition.

The number of composers in whom Debussy showed interest was few. In the late 1880s he became friendly with Paul Dukas, several years younger, and a student of Guiraud at the Conservatoire. But although Debussy stayed in touch with Dukas over the years and admired some of his music, they never became close.

That was not the case with Erik Satie. "We never had to explain things to each other," Satie recalled. "Half a sentence was enough, because we understood each other and, it seemed, had always done so."[4] Satie and Debussy probably first became acquainted in 1887, but it was not until five years later that they began to spend time with one another—discussing music, playing billiards, and also visiting *Le Chat noir*, one of the most popular artistic cabarets in Paris.[5] The meetings—usually at least once a week—continued for more than twenty-five years. What ultimately drew them together was the recognition that they were different from everyone else: two kindred spirits bound by their unconventionality. When Debussy gave Satie a copy of his Baudelaire songs, it was inscribed with humor and affection: "For Erik Satie, genial musician of the Middle Ages, who has strayed into this century to the joy of his good friend, Cl. A. Debussy."[6]

3. Letter to André Poniatowski of February 1893 in *DL*, p. 42.

4. *DR*, p. 104.

5. The *Chat noir* regularly produced plays, often with music. Debussy enjoyed the entertainment there, but was not, as has often been maintained, the house piano player. Nor, as it had been earlier thought, had he been frequenting the café since the early 1880s.

6. *LS*, p. 128.

The summer of 1889 marked the centenary of the French Revolution, and it was celebrated by a grandiose exposition intended to put France's prosperity on display. French artistic and industrial accomplishments were the focus with the Eiffel Tower, at the time the world's tallest structure, created to exemplify it. The Exposition was extensive—covering the Champ-de-Mars, the Trocadéro Gardens, and part of the Esplanade of the Invalides—and drew huge crowds, in part because the novelty of electricity attracted visitors at night. One of the most popular portions of the Exhibition was devoted to France's growing success as an imperialist power.

In the past decade France had substantially increased its holdings and protectorates in Africa and Asia. There were exhibits devoted to these recent acquisitions, as well as to those of other European nations. The intent was to present exotic cultures, with scenes from daily life, along with examples of clothing, art, music, and cuisine. Those displays were among the most popular at the Exhibition. To many, they offered confirmation that life in much of the world was curious, barbaric, primitive—and vastly inferior to Western civilization.[7]

Debussy responded differently. Two exhibits in particular drew his attention: a drama with music by a theatrical troupe from Saigon, and concerts by a Javanese gamelan (percussive, tuned instruments on which performers play modal music that is exceedingly complex rhythmically). Ernest Chausson and the painter Henri Lerolle were among the 875,000 visitors to hear the gamelan, and drew comparisons between the gamelan dancers and the exoticism of Symbolist art, describing them as "figures from the paintings of Gustave Moreau come to life."[8] But Debussy was captivated by the originality of what he saw and heard, and admired it all the more because of its remoteness from Western tradition. These were, Debussy felt, pure musicians with nature itself as their tutor. His romanticized perception (actually, mastery of the gamelan requires long study and meticulous rehearsal similar to that for an orchestra) provided him with inspiration, and, as when he had seen gypsies performing in Moscow, led to a far broader grasp of music's potential than that held by most of his contemporaries.

Associated with the Exposition were two concerts of Russian orchestral music, including works by Borodin, Rimsky-Korsakov, and Musorgsky. Much of it was a novelty, for at the time in France knowledge of Russian music was mostly limited to that of Chaikovsky. The non-traditional elements in these concerts would have piqued Debussy's interest. Because his music was soon to show some similarity—

---

7. For more information, see Annegret Fauser, *Musical Encounters at the 1889 Paris World's Fair* (Rochester: University of Rochester Press, 2005).

8. Letter to Ernest Chausson of [June 1889] in Ernest Chausson, *Ecrits inédits*, ed. Jean Gallois and Isabelle Bretaudeau (Paris: Editions du Rocher, 1999), p. 214.

especially in the use of modality and timbre—the resemblances have sparked debate concerning both the amount of Russian music Debussy actually knew, and when he became familiar with it.

It had been assumed that he encountered a good deal of Russian music when living with the von Mecks. But that was not the case. Chaikovsky dominated their interest. Robert Godet recalled that Debussy showed him some songs by Borodin and Balakirev that he had acquired while in Russia. But as for Musorgsky, whose music was to have the most profound effect on him, Debussy stated firmly that when he was in Russia "his name was never mentioned."[9] Within a few years Debussy would acquire more in-depth knowledge of Russian music, especially of Musorgsky's *Boris Godunov*. But at the time of the Exposition, much of the music would have been new and fascinating to him.

Additional influence on Debussy's development as a composer was provided by trips to Bayreuth in the summers of 1888 and 1889 to hear Wagner's music dramas. His visits coincided with those of a large French contingent undertaken for a variety of reasons: to pay homage, to satisfy curiosity, or simply to be seen. Bayreuth was a brilliant social as well as a musical event, and it was costly. Fortunately for Debussy, Etienne Dupin, a wealthy financier with strong interests in the arts (and to whom Debussy dedicated his Baudelaire songs), came to his assistance.

Debussy saw three of Wagner's works: *Parsifal* and *Die Meistersinger* in 1888, and *Tristan* in 1889. It was an unforgettable experience for him. Hearing *Parsifal*, he was "moved to tears."[10] But he was also able to maintain some objectivity. Other French composers who traveled to Bayreuth—including d'Indy, Chabrier, Magnard, and Chausson—were overwhelmed. Wagner's accomplishments appeared so stupendous that they felt intimidated.

Debussy was more dispassionate. He discovered strengths and weaknesses in Wagner's music. Although he was aware of its innovations, Debussy's musical convictions were so strong (and in time his individuality so pronounced) that he was able to dissect and analyze Wagner's musical style to his advantage.

The opportunities to hear Wagner, the gamelan from Java, music by Musorgsky and Borodin—all within about a year—had a profound effect on Debussy as a musician. But focusing on his artistic development makes it easy to lose sight of his personality. What was he like during these years? What captured his interest? How did he perceive himself? Some intriguing answers can be found in the responses he made in 1889 to a questionnaire, a popular form of amusement at parties at the time:

9. Letter to Pierre Lalo of 23 June 1908 in *DL*, p. 192.

10. Louis Laloy, *Claude Debussy* (Paris: Les Bibliophiles Fantaisistes, 1909), p. 23. Debussy's reaction was not unique: Hugo Wolf and Chabrier also wept during *Parsifal*; Guillaume Lekeu reported that he fainted on first hearing the prelude to *Tristan*.

Your favorite virtue?	Pride
Your favorite qualities in men?	Will
Your favorite qualities in women?	Charm
Your idea of happiness?	To love
Your idea of misery?	To be too hot
If not yourself, who would you be?	A sailor
Your favorite prose authors?	Flaubert and Edgard-Poè
Your favorite poets?	Baudelaire
Your favorite painters and composers?	Botticelli, Gustave Moreau, Palestrina, Bach, Wagner
Your favorite heroes in fiction?	Hamlet
Your favorite heroines in fiction?	Rosalind
Your favorite food and drink?	Russian food, coffee
Your pet aversion?	Dilettantes, women who are too pretty
Which character in history do you most dislike?	Herod
For what fault do you have the most toleration?	Errors in harmony
Your favorite motto?	Always upward [Toujours plus haut][11]

There are many favorites of the Symbolists among his answers: Poe (the spelling always seemed to present challenges to the French), Baudelaire, Botticelli, and Moreau—all in their way Symbolist icons. These were unusual tastes, as were his musical preferences (although the growing cult of Wagner placed him dangerously close to fashionable trends). Shakespeare also makes an appearance, and Debussy's fondness for him was no passing fancy. Rosalind is a character in *As You Like It*, one of his favorite plays. For many years he considered it for an opera. The tolerance for "errors in harmony" speaks volumes for those who knew him at the Conservatoire. But the manner in which he avoided answering the question about who he would be, if not himself, is curious. A specific person would be the expected response, possibly someone rich or famous. Instead he chose not an individual, but a rather common profession (but one that reflected his own love for the sea). His preference for "Pride" and "Will" bring to mind his admiration of Edmond Bailly's "determination." As for his favorite motto—"Toujours plus haut"—it was one to which he would remain constant all his life.

During the years following his return from Rome Debussy needed regularly to draw on his store of will and determination, for establishing a reputation came

11. The questions are in English in the original. Debussy's responses were first published in December 1903. The entire questionnaire is reproduced in *D*, pp. 56–57.

slowly. Few of his compositions appeared in print. In 1888 a set of songs, the *Ariettes*, was published though not with a distinguished firm. Over the next few years they were followed by a half dozen pieces for solo piano, a mixed bag including the *Deux Arabesques* (printed by a noted publisher, Durand), as well as several bland salon works such as the *Tarentelle styrienne* and *Valse romantique*. The primary purpose of publication is to stimulate performances, but there were few of those. Two of the *Ariettes* were performed on 2 February 1889 in a concert at the Société Nationale. A lone reviewer praised them, but Debussy must have taken pleasure in the reference to his "searching out what is new, and fleeing from banality."[12]

The most notable opportunity to present his music to the public occurred in April 1890. Debussy's final envoi for the Prix de Rome—a three-movement Fantaisie for piano and orchestra—was scheduled for performance by the Société as part of a concert conducted by Vincent d'Indy. This was the first occasion for both the public and his peers to hear a work by Debussy of some length. But at the last moment, he abruptly withdrew it. After rehearsal, d'Indy had decided to perform only the first movement (apparently because of the length of the concert). Debussy quietly removed his copies of the score from the stands of the musicians and wrote to d'Indy explaining that he would prefer to have "a passable performance of all three movements than a fine performance of the first."[13]

Most composers would have been annoyed by d'Indy's proposed cuts. Some might even have considered withdrawing their work from performance. But few would have walked away from an opportunity to have their music heard in such an important setting. In the end Debussy's impulsive act created no animosity with d'Indy. Perhaps he felt that, since all the movements of the *Fantaisie* were united thematically, there was sense to Debussy's action. And in many ways it was just as well that there was no performance. The *Fantaisie* does not show Debussy to advantage. He always remained dissatisfied with it, and it was neither published nor performed in his lifetime.

Debussy placed much greater faith in the other major composition that occupied his attention at the time: *La Damoiselle élue*. This was the third of his envois, and much of 1887 and 1888 was spent on it. In both structure and content it is precisely the type of cantata he would have preferred to have composed for the Prix de Rome competition. Its text is taken from Dante Gabriel Rossetti's poem, "The Blessed Damozel." Rossetti, and the Pre-Raphaelite School he represented, were very popular in France in the 1880s, particularly among the Symbolists. More than any other of Debussy's compositions of the time, *La Damoiselle élue* had the potential to appeal to a broad base of the public. But Debussy did little to promote it, and nearly five years passed before it was heard.

12. *LS*, p. 102.

13. Letter to d'Indy of 20 April 1890 in *DL*, p. 30.

In addition to his work on larger-scale compositions such as the *Damoiselle*, he continued to be attracted to song. The *Ariettes*—his first song album (later issued as the *Ariettes oubliées*)—was started in 1885, and completed two years later. It contains settings of six poems by Verlaine. Like the earlier Verlaine songs, they are distinctive and accomplished. Unfortunately, their partial performance in 1889 attracted little attention. On completing the *Ariettes* Debussy began a set of songs devoted to poetry of Charles Baudelaire—another poet whose work enjoyed favor with the Symbolists. But he was unable to find a publisher for them, and the *Cinq Poèmes de Baudelaire* were published by subscription in February 1890 in an edition limited to 150 copies (once again, the financial assistance of Etienne Dupin played a vital role).

The Baudelaire songs are very different in style from the *Ariettes*. They are chromatic, extremely difficult to perform, and challenging enough to assure limited recognition. That was Debussy's intention. Their limited edition made clear that they were intended not for the masses, but for the select few Debussy hoped would find value in his music. Yet he surely had no idea that it would be fifteen years before they were actually performed in public, and then only in part.

The esoteric appeal of the Baudelaire songs reappeared in a set of four songs begun in 1892. For the *Proses lyriques* Debussy wrote not only the music, but the words as well. Although his use of chromaticism is not as pronounced as in the Baudelaire settings, the mannered text and music seemed once again to confirm Debussy's determination to attract the attention of a chosen few.

Debussy also wrote during these years a variety of works for piano. Several—especially the *Deux Arabesques* and *Petite Suite*—are today among his most popular. Much in them appears improvisatory, and probably grew from improvisations at the piano. But this effect was one he deliberately cultivated, similar to the manner in which an Impressionist painting often conveys the feeling of a sketch.

In Debussy's piano compositions, melodies often trace graceful, flowing lines, similar to an arabesque—a noticeable visual trait of art nouveau (an arts and crafts movement allied to Symbolism). There is languor and studied simplicity, as well as avoidance of any semblance of the grandiose. In appearance they are salon pieces, but, unlike several other piano pieces from these years (such as the *Tarentelle* and the *Valse*), Debussy transcends the genre. His pianistic style has been copied so frequently that its originality is easily overlooked. But these early piano compositions confirm both his affinity for the instrument and distinctive approach to it.

Like the songs, Debussy's piano compositions at first attracted little attention. Writing opera remained the usual means in France to achieve popularity, but it was a path Debussy so far had avoided. There were two major, state-funded opera houses in Paris: the Opéra and Opéra-Comique. Traditionally, they had been quite different, with the repertoire at the Opéra-Comique being lighter in subject and with spoken dialogue in place of recitative. But by 1900 these distinctions had blurred, the only real difference being the more conservative taste of the Opéra. To have a work accepted for performance at either house was difficult, and all the harder for Debussy who seemed less concerned with courting public favor than with bringing into prominence his originality.

Although the idea of composing an opera never seemed far from his mind, the decision to write one was thrust upon him. In 1890 he began to set to music *Rodrigue et Chimène* by Catulle Mendès, a prolific novelist, poet, dramatist, and critic. An old friend of both Villiers and Mallarmé, Mendès had begun his career as a poet associated with the Parnassians in the 1860s. His writings covered a broad assortment of topics, but a sizable portion of his reputation was based on his use of taboo sexual themes—incest, for example, in *Zo'har* (1886) and lesbianism in *Méphistophéla* (1890), a copy of which he gave to Debussy.

Mendès also had a strong interest in music. He was a devoted Wagnerian (he published a study of Wagner in 1886) and had been among the first to champion his work in France. Although strictly an amateur, Mendès was unusually knowledgeable about music and musical life, at least in part because of his common-law marriage with the composer, Augusta Holmès. Prior to working with Debussy, Mendès's most notable musical collaboration had been with Chabrier, for whom he wrote *Gwendoline* (1885). But Chabrier was only one of many composers with whom he worked. Among the list are d'Indy, Massenet, Camille Erlanger, Reynaldo Hahn, and Debussy's future disciple, André Caplet.

Mendès had heard Debussy's Baudelaire songs in a private performance at Chausson's. Impressed by them, he decided to help find a publisher for the recently completed *Fantaisie* (eventually purchased by Choudens, through his efforts). That assistance has led to speculation that Debussy felt forced into collaborating with Mendès. But he probably viewed Mendès's progressive reputation with an open mind and may even have hoped that his distinctive literary tastes could work to their mutual advantage.

For a composer of Debussy's youth and inexperience, the association with Mendès lent plausibility to the project.[14] *Rodrigue et Chimène* was based on the tale of El Cid, and used as its primary source Corneille's *Le Cid* (1636) and Guilhem de Castro's *Las Mocedades del Cid* (1621). But although the idea of the project may have looked promising, Debussy probably did not know that the libretto given to him was an old one, first written in 1878 and already rejected by other composers.

Whatever hopes Debussy may have had could only have vanished after reading Mendès's text. Thoroughly conventional in style and content, in many ways it actually resembled *Zuleima*, the envoi of which Debussy had been so critical. But even

---

14. During this period Mendès was also working with Gabriel Pierné on a pantomime, *Le Collier de Saphirs* (1891), and a ballet, *Les Joyeuses Commères de Paris* (1892).

if it had been better written, the chances that the opera would be successful—or even performed—were slim. In 1885 Massenet had completed his own El Cid opera, *Le Cid*. It was performed regularly through 1891, and by 1919 had been given 152 times at the Opéra—not an overwhelming success, but reason enough to avoid duplication.

Debussy's work on *Rodrigue* continued intermittently for nearly three years. He never completed it. "My life is hardship and misery thanks to this opera," he wrote to Robert Godet, "Everything about it is wrong for me.... I long to see you and play you the two acts I've finished, because I'm afraid I may have won victories over my true self."[15] Most of three acts were completed (Mendès spoke of the opera as containing four, but nothing of the fourth act has survived). It was a chore for Debussy, but, despite his pessimism, in the end he produced some surprisingly effective music for portions of it.

Although it may have seemed paramount at the time, Debussy's work on *Rodrigue* was of far less consequence to his career than his meeting with Mendès's good friend, Stéphane Mallarmé—a meeting that in many ways seemed inevitable. They were introduced to one another by the writer Ferdinand Hérold in the autumn of 1890. Mallarmé was forty-eight, and, famous both for his poetry and translations of Poe, was regarded by many as the greatest writer in France. Like Debussy, he had broad tastes in the arts, particularly in the visual arts where his interests ranged from Japanese painting and woodcuts to, among the moderns, both the Impressionists and Symbolists. Several painters were good friends, especially Whistler (Mallarmé translated his "Ten O'Clock Lecture") and Manet (with whom he collaborated on a limited edition of Poe's "The Raven").

To many, Mallarmé's poetry remained an enigma. Deliberately obscure and ambiguous, it was impossible to grasp in a traditional manner—so much so that it opened him to ridicule, making acceptance of his work difficult. Mallarmé actually made his living as a teacher of high school English. But as prosaic as life in a lycée could be, he managed to remain immersed in his art, convinced of the sacred basis of poetry. In his final years he was at work on what he simply called "Le Livre," a work he described as an "Orphic explanation of the Earth."[16]

Mallarmé's home was regularly opened to guests on Tuesday evenings. At first only old friends such as Mendès or Villiers regularly attended. But by the mid-1880s—the result of growing mention of him in books like Verlaine's *Poètes maudits* (Cursed Poets) and Huysmans' *Against Nature*—attendance at the salon started to pick up. It began to attract a large number of young writers: Francis Viélé-Griffin, André Gide, Paul Valéry, Charles Morice, René Ghil, Félix Fénéon, Gustave Kahn,

15. Letter of [30] January 1892 in *DL*, p. 34.

16. Gordon Millan, *The Life of Stéphane Mallarmé* (New York: Farrar, Straus and Giroux, 1994), p. 232.

Camille Mauclair, Georges Rodenbach, Henri de Régnier, Pierre Louÿs—virtually every writer of note of the coming generation. Although most of the guests were poets and novelists, artists and composers were also welcome. Topics of discussion were far-ranging. The atmosphere was relaxed, with humor and a continuous flow of conversation usually gently guided by Mallarmé.

It was not easy to gain entry: Mallarmé made a point of meeting privately with those he was considering inviting. But Debussy passed scrutiny. How frequently he attended the salon is not known. It never became, as it did for many, a weekly ritual. But Debussy was a regular guest and became friendly with Mallarmé, admiring both the man and his work.

Mallarmé could only have been intrigued by Debussy. He was fascinated by music, and composers were a rarity in his salon. Music for Mallarmé existed in multiple dimensions. He was obsessed, for example, with the sound and musicality of his own writings, both poetry and prose. But he was also actively involved in contemporary music life—interested in Wagner and, since 1885, a regular visitor to the Lamoureux concert series.

Mallarmé knew some of Debussy's music, notably the Baudelaire songs, which impressed him as they had Mendès. It was his esteem for Debussy that led to a proposed collaboration. In 1862 Mallarmé had begun work on a poem intended for the stage: *Le Faune, intermède héroïque*. As was so often the case with his poetry, it was reworked for many years finally appearing in a limited edition in 1876 as *L'Après-midi d'un faune*. A second edition appeared a decade later. Debussy knew the work, and even gave a copy of it to Paul Dukas in May 1887.

In November 1890 Mallarmé took steps to have the poem staged at the Théâtre d'Art, a theater that specialized in the avant-garde. Three months later an announcement appeared in the press noting that the performance would include music by Debussy. Here was a project that could provide Debussy both with a sense of personal accomplishment and the potential to bring him before an artistic elite whose opinion he valued. But for reasons unknown, plans for performance of the poem were dropped. It must have been a disappointment, but Debussy was not put off. He continued to think both about the poem and music suitable for it.

Since the possibility of a staged collaboration with Mallarmé seemed remote, Debussy continued to work on *Rodrigue et Chimène*. His personal life at the time remains a bit of a mystery. Early in 1891 in a letter to Robert Godet, he made passing reference to a love affair that ended "miserably and cheaply.... I loved her so much."[17] To whom he was referring remains unknown. But there were romantic interests. In the late 1880s he had been attracted to Catherine Stevens, daughter of the painter Alfred Stevens. Known for her beauty (and familiar enough with music

17. Letter of [2 February 1891] in *DL*, p. 32.

to try her hand at composing), Debussy had made a point of sending a copy of his Baudelaire songs to her. He was also an admirer of the sculptor, Camille Claudel. Although their relationship is unclear, one of her works, *La Valse*, was displayed in his workroom throughout his life.

Debussy's most enduring relationship during these years was with Gabrielle (Gaby) Dupont (1866–1945). They met in the spring of 1890. She was twenty-four and a striking beauty with green, "catlike eyes."[18] Gaby, who had little interest in the arts, had a good sense of humor as well as a strongly practical side. In the summer of 1892 (after finally moving out of his parents' apartment) she and Debussy began living together. It was the beginning of an affair that lasted for nearly eight years.

Debussy's professional prospects at the time continued to be gloomy. He felt, as he confessed to Godet, like "an exile with no future except to plod on dismally from day to day."[19] By the autumn of 1892 he was describing his existence as little more than a "black hole." The situation was complicated by his parents who, anxious for him to earn a living (his Prix stipend ended in the spring of 1889), inaugurated what Debussy called a "needling campaign."[20]

It had been more than five years since his return from Rome, and Debussy had little to show for it. His former companions at the Villa seemed much better off. Paul Vidal, for example, had become assistant chorus director at the Opéra (1889–1892), and then director of singing and a conductor there (1892–1906). His operetta, *Eros*, was produced in 1892. A ballet, *La Maladetta*, was performed at the Opéra the following year. Vidal had not strayed from the path expected for a Prix winner. Debussy had made a point of doing so, and found it rough going.

Had he taken a more active role in the Société Nationale, his situation might have been more secure. A good pianist was always needed there, but he rarely volunteered, and in the nine years after Debussy became a member, he performed in only five concerts.[21] Performances of his own music at the Société were infrequent: the *Ariettes* previously mentioned, and then nothing until *La Damoiselle élue* in April 1893. It was galling for him to witness the success of those he was convinced were far less gifted than himself—such as that of a recent Prix winner Gustave Charpentier, the future composer of *Louise*. Charpentier's *La Vie du poète* had been performed to acclaim in May 1892. Debussy could not have been stronger in his criticism; he

---

18. René Peter in *DR*, p. 33.

19. Letter of [30] January 1892 in *DL*, p. 34.

20. Letters to André Poniatowski of 5 October 1892 and February 1893 in ibid., pp. 39, 40.

21. In February 1889 he accompanied two of his *Ariettes*. Nearly five years passed before he returned: in January 1894 in a four-hands performance of Rimsky-Korsakov's *Capriccio espagnole*, followed in the next month as accompanist to two of the *Proses lyriques*. In February 1896 and January 1897 he was the pianist in performances of Guillaume Lekeu's Piano Quartet.

described the piece as crude and sensational, and complained that it represented ideals totally opposed to his own.

But there were some encouraging developments. The publication of the Baudelaire songs was followed in late spring 1892 by *La Damoiselle élue*, issued by Bailly in a handsome edition with a frontispiece by Maurice Denis. Although known mostly for publishing young writers like Régnier and Louÿs, Bailly's press was a prestigious one, and Debussy's latest compositions were attracting a small but devoted following.

A more tangible form of support appeared later that summer when Prince André Poniatowski, a friend of Bailly, took an interest in Debussy. It led to an offer which seemed too good to be true: a concert solely devoted to Debussy's music to be performed in the United States. Poniatowski had a strong interest in the arts and was married to an American. He was eager to promote relations between the two countries, and was even hopeful that he could persuade Andrew Carnegie to support Debussy for a time.

Debussy responded with enthusiasm. "I gladly accept your proposal—because, no matter how you look at it, to be *successful* in Paris actually means relying on all that is mediocre, sordid, petty, and shameful.... Whatever may happen, I shall always be grateful to you for having—in the midst of a utilitarian world—the imagination to keep me in mind."[22] In the end, nothing came of Poniatowski's project, but he continued to take an interest in Debussy and, as he later put it, felt "morally obliged" to provide him with financial assistance for several years.[23]

Poniatowski's financial aid probably started in 1893. The performance on 8 April of that year of *La Damoiselle élue* at the Société Nationale provided real justification for it. Although attacked by some critics (there were complaints of excessive chromaticism), it was well received by connoisseurs and colleagues, and received an encouraging review in *Le Figaro*. Among those warm in their praise were the artist Odilon Redon (who gave Debussy one of his lithographs as a token of his appreciation) and Vincent d'Indy.

But while an artistic success, the performance of *La Damoiselle élue* did not ease any of Debussy's financial concerns. The following month he grudgingly served as a pianist for three lectures on Wagner (associated with the French premiere of *Die Walküre*) presented by Mendès. The lectures were simplistic, and extraordinarily popular. In the past, being involved in such a project would only have added to Debussy's gloom and frustration. But something had recently happened that provided hope and encouragement. On 17 May—in the midst of his chores for Mendès—he attended a performance of Maurice Maeterlinck's drama, *Pelléas et Mélisande*.

22. Letters to Poniatowski of 9 September and 5 October 1892 in *C*, pp. 109, 111.
23. *LS*, p. 133.

Maeterlinck had a strong following in Paris, and Debussy knew a great deal of his work. He admired his poems, *Serres chaudes* (Hot-House), and had been so taken with the drama, *La Princesse Maleine*, that he had tried to get approval to set it to music (as it turned out, Maeterlinck had already promised it to d'Indy). It was the illusory qualities of Maeterlinck's dramas that provided the basis of much of their attraction. "They are real," explained the Symbolist critic Rémy de Gourmont, "by dint of their unreality."[24] Perhaps as early as 1892 Debussy had purchased a copy of *Pelléas et Mélisande*.

As had been the case with Mallarmé's *Faune*, the Paris premiere of *Pelléas* was intended for the Théâtre d'Art. Two of Maeterlinck's earlier dramas, *The Intruder* and *The Blind*, had been given there to acclaim. *Pelléas* was scheduled for performance on 11 March 1893, but financial complications delayed and then threatened to cancel any performance at all. It took a heroic effort to arrange a single matinee at the Bouffes-Parisiens.

For Debussy, it was an extraordinary experience. *Pelléas et Mélisande* is, by any standard, remarkable : dream-like, evocative, and ethereal. Here, Debussy felt, was an ideal basis for opera—not stilted and orthodox like *Rodrigue et Chimène*, but a drama that complemented his own conception of what opera should be.

He asked his friend Henri de Régnier to serve as intermediary and to approach Maeterlinck for permission to set *Pelléas* to music. No objections were raised, and when he received word of Maeterlinck's consent early in August, Debussy eagerly began to set the text to music. From the start, *Pelléas* was intended to be different from other operas. No librettist was consulted to turn the play into an opera. Nor did Debussy attempt an adaptation himself. He set to music Maeterlinck's drama as published with surprisingly few cuts.

Debussy's discovery of *Pelléas* provided a sense of direction to his work, similar to his earlier discovery of the poetry of Verlaine. He found in it drama new in content, new in style—so different from the typical productions of the day, that it seemed to demand music free from convention and constraint. Although it would be nearly a decade before *Pelléas* was performed, more than any other of his compositions it would establish his reputation and bring him fame so unexpected that in many ways it was as much a burden as a blessing.

24. Rémy de Gourmont, *The Book of Masks*, tr. Jack Lewis (Boston: John W. Luce, 1921), p. 23.

CHAPTER FOUR

Years of Struggle

The average man hates the artist from a deep instinctive dread of all that is
strange, uncanny, alien to his nature.

Arthur Machen, *The Hill of Dreams* (1907)

HE THIRTEEN YEARS FROM 1887—WHEN DEBUSSY RETURNED FROM ROME—
until his marriage in 1900 have been portrayed as Debussy's Bohemian
years. He associated almost exclusively with artists, writers, and musicians. Even
the expected mistress was part of the scene. It resembled a real-life dramatiza-
tion of the romanticized fiction popularized in books like Murger's *Scènes de la
Vie Bohème* and Du Maurier's *Trilby*—a concept that lives on in the image of
the "starving artist" existing on the fringe of respectable society.

But Debussy's Bohemian life had only superficial similarity to one found in the
pages of a book. His need for money seemed continually to hound him. And tied
to it was his limited success in establishing a reputation. Progress in that area
remained slow because he seemed lackadaisical, at times even apathetic. *La Damoiselle
élue* provides the best instance. After he completed it, more than four years passed
before it was performed. Other composers—Magnard, for example—arranged special concerts devoted to their own music. That possibility never seemed to occur to
Debussy, although he had friends who could have helped with the costs.

The time of his discovery of *Pelléas* coincided with a broadening of friendships for
Debussy. Probably the most important for the establishment of his reputation was the
relationship that developed with Ernest Chausson. Although they had known one
another for several years (a result of Chausson's work as secretary for the Société
Nationale), their association had only been casual. Over the next year they became good
friends. Chausson, who was seven years older than Debussy, became an elder advisor.

Chausson's interest in Debussy was very much in character. He recognized Debussy's gifts, soon became aware of the difficulties he was having, and was eager to help. But he must also have recognized that he and Debussy had much in common. Both were critical of a great deal of contemporary French music. And both shared a deep interest not just in music, but in all the arts. Chausson admired contemporary French painting and had broad tastes—from Corot to Gauguin. Odilon Redon (who, in addition to being an artist, was a fine pianist and violinist) was a good friend with whom Chausson performed chamber music. Literature, too, was an attraction. Prior to taking up music, Chausson had given serious consideration to becoming a writer, and had even begun a novel.

In artistic matters, Chausson could be unusually open-minded. Although active in the Société Nationale, he was aware of its weaknesses. Its concerts, he wrote to Debussy, sometimes resembled "doctoral exams" where composers seemed more interested in showing off their skills than in writing good music.[1] At the time of their friendship Chausson's stature as a composer was substantial and growing. Among his most recent works were the *Poème de l'amour et de la mer,* op. 19 (1893), the Symphony, op. 20 (1890), and the *Concert,* op. 21 (1891).

But despite having points in common, there were substantial differences, too. The most obvious one was their social standing. Chausson had been raised in the upper middle class amid wealth and comfort. His completion of law study in 1876 had been unnecessary: there was never any need for him to earn a living. Unlike Debussy, he could indulge his artistic tastes to the full, and he collected paintings by Degas and Renoir, as well as manuscripts of writers whom he admired such as Villiers.

There were also differences in the musical training they had received. Chausson had begun by studying composition at the Conservatoire with Massenet—but, like d'Indy, he decided to become a private student of César Franck. That led to the adoption of Franckian musical ideals, concepts that Debussy regarded with suspicion.

With the exception of the final years of his life, Chausson seemed tentative as a composer. In Debussy he encountered a composer who, although much younger, was both more original and self-assured. This artistic maturity could be intimidating to Chausson and created a major source of friction between the men. But ultimately the greatest difference between them was one of aesthetics. "One day or another," Chausson wrote in 1884, "I have no doubt that I can write a piece of music of interest to some unconventional minds—but between that and a true work of art there is a world of difference."[2] For Debussy, by its very nature "a true work of art" would be unconventional—and often its appeal was esoteric.

---

1. Letter of 12 November 1893 in *C,* p. 174.

2. Letter to Paul Poujaud of [1884] in Ernest Chausson, *Ecrits inédits,* ed. Jean Gallois and Isabelle Bretaudeau (Paris: Editions du Rocher, 1999), p. 172.

Chausson owned a fine home in Paris, but, as a fashionable member of society, he spent summers outside the city. In the summer of 1893 he rented a house in Luzancy, along the Marne. Debussy was invited there twice, staying first from 30 May until 3 June and again in mid-June. In addition to Chausson's family (and its four young children), also present at various times were Henri Lerolle (a painter, and Chausson's brother-in-law), and Raymond Bonheur. Bonheur and Debussy were already good friends; Lerolle became one. This was the first extended opportunity for Debussy and Chausson to know one another better, and photographs taken during the visit have vividly captured the atmosphere—from boating excursions (showing the men wearing vest and tie, a reminder of how formal the days before the First World War could be) to Debussy at the piano.

One of their most interesting activities involved the music of Musorgsky. Chausson had a copy of *Boris Godunov*, and he and Debussy went through the score in detail. Four years earlier, Debussy's friend Robert Godet had borrowed a copy of *Boris* from Jules de Brayer, an admirer of Musorgsky, and lent it to Debussy. But he had only glanced at it, mostly because of his unfamiliarity with the Russian language. Now he was fascinated by the music. Its use of modality would not have been a novelty to him, since he had encountered similar instances in music of Glinka while with the von Mecks. But Musorgsky's original harmony—free of academic restraint—would have intrigued Debussy, as would the dramaturgy, so different from both Wagner and French opera. These were both concepts that later influenced his work on *Pelléas*. And they were reinforced by additional study of Musorgsky's music, especially the songs.

During his stay with Chausson, Debussy was completing the *Proses lyriques* and working on a string quartet. Chausson was busy as well. That summer he began setting to music Maeterlinck's poetic cycle, *Serres chaudes*. But his major concern was the opera, *Le Roi Arthus*, for which he had written his own libretto based on the Arthurian legends. He had started work on it in 1886 but did not finish it for nearly a decade.

Debussy's letters to Chausson reveal a great deal about their relationship. From the start, he was deeply appreciative of Chausson's interest in him and openly expressed his gratitude, admitting that he was "profoundly happy" to be his friend—"because in you artistic qualities are completed by human ones."[3] Their friendship, Debussy felt, would become "the best and most profound" of his life.[4] Chausson responded warmly. "The affection you have shown me gives me great pleasure, and I am deeply moved by it," he wrote. "You know that you can count on my

3. Letter of 26 August 1893 in *DL*, p. 48.
4. Letter of [3 October 1893] in ibid., p. 59.

friendship—completely."⁵ Chausson's support went beyond words. He lent Debussy money and was anxious to see him "relieved of material worries."⁶

But although he felt indebted to him, Debussy was frank in explaining their different musical approaches, asking pardon if in commenting on Chausson's scores he had "sometimes spoken a bit brusquely."⁷ When Chausson brought *Arthus* to him, he bluntly pointed out what he felt to be its strong and weak points.

Chausson took the criticism in stride and became in Debussy's words "a bit like a big brother." He felt Debussy needed someone to provide guidance to his life. "As for your sermons," Debussy dryly commented, "I'll always value them."⁸ Chausson was a champion of middle-class values and was eager for his young friend to settle down, have a job, and marry. He suggested that he take on more pupils or find a music position of some sort. In the autumn of 1893 he tried to secure an assistant conducting post for him at the casino in Royan, precisely the type of position that Debussy had made a point of avoiding. Two years earlier it had been held by Albéric Magnard who had had a miserable time, describing the work as "absurd and anti-artistic."⁹ But, although Chausson realized that Debussy deserved better, he remained convinced that such a position was better than nothing at all, and an essential first step toward more stable employment.

While at Luzancy, Debussy and Chausson spoke of Maeterlinck and of Debussy's work on *Pelléas*. Debussy began by setting one of the most dramatic scenes, the death of Pelléas (Act IV, scene iv), but in early September he confessed to Chausson that the result was too Wagnerian, and started over. He also continued to work on the String Quartet. Debussy had extraordinary difficulty with the finale, which he reworked three times. On its completion that November he sold the quartet to Durand, but the 250 francs he received was token payment for his efforts.

That same month Debussy traveled to Belgium, the first trip of any length he had made since returning from Rome. There were two people he wanted to meet. In Brussels he was introduced to Eugène Ysaÿe, a virtuoso violinist who had done much to promote the careers of d'Indy, Chausson, and Lekeu. He was active both as a conductor and soloist (in addition to founding a string quartet). It was Debussy's hope to interest him in his own quartet. Chausson had paved the way by writing to Ysaÿe, and he was receptive. Debussy played a great deal of his music for him and was pleased by his enthusiastic response.

5. Letter of [4 June 1893] in *C*, p. 134.

6. Letter of [28 August 1893] in ibid., p. 152.

7. Letter of 26 August 1893 in ibid., p. 151.

8. Ibid.

9. Letter to Emile Cordonnier from the end of September [1891] in Albéric Magnard, *Correspondance. (1888–1914)*, ed. Claire Vlach (Paris: Publications de la Société Française de Musicologie, 1997), p. 59.

From Brussels, Debussy traveled to Ghent where he met Maurice Maeterlinck. Although Debussy had already received permission to set *Pelléas*, he wanted to discuss details—and probably was also simply curious about an author whose work he admired. Their meeting went well. But if he had hoped to establish a close friendship, he was disappointed. Maeterlinck professed total ignorance of music, but gave Debussy full authority to proceed, even suggesting sections of the play he might want to cut.

Debussy was accompanied on the trip by a new friend, Pierre Louÿs—a writer whom he had probably first met in the autumn of 1892 at Mallarmé's. Over the next eight years, Louÿs was to become extremely close to Debussy.

It was an unusual and in many ways an unlikely friendship. Louÿs—whose real name was Louis (he changed the spelling to add an exotic touch, the final "s" not being pronounced)—was eight years younger than Debussy. He possessed broad culture and refinement, in addition to what his friend the writer Paul Valéry described as "a seductiveness and an elegance which I have never come across in anyone else."[10]

Louÿs was well connected in the literary world. In 1893 he had just begun his association with the *Mercure de France*, one of the leading Symbolist journals. His best-known work, the novel *Aphrodite*, followed two years later. The collection of poetry, *Chansons de Bilitis* (1894), and several novellas such as *La Femme et le pantin* (*The Devil Is a Woman*; 1898) sold well and made him much better known than Debussy during the time of their friendship.

Although he mixed in circles associated with Symbolism, Louÿs's writings had little in common with it. In his work, sensuality was a major characteristic; *Aphrodite* was a defense of hedonism. The plot (set in antiquity) focused on the sexual encounters of a prostitute and included frequent graphic, sexual descriptions as well as scenes of cruelty and depravity (including a crucifixion described in gory detail). At times the novel borders on the pornographic—and that helps to explain the many French and English editions (usually privately printed) copiously illustrated.

Pornography was one of Louÿs's hobbies. He collected it and wrote thousands of pages of it: poems, novels, tales, dramas, and parodies. None of it was published during his lifetime—it was so explicit that no legitimate publisher would have touched it—but it was shared with friends, and it is reasonable to assume that at some point Debussy was shown works like Louÿs's *Le Livre obscène*, *Scènes de la vie érotique*, or *Trois Filles de leur mère*. In sexual matters, Louÿs's life reflected his writings. He was fond of grisettes and prostitutes, many of whom found their way into his "Chronological and Descriptive Catalogue of All the

---

10. "At the Grave of Pierre Louÿs," in Paul Valéry, *Masters and Friends*, tr. Martin Turnell (Princeton, NJ: Princeton University Press, 1968), p. 285.

Women with Whom I Have Slept," a project started in February 1892 and embellished with photographs.

Eroticism is an essential trait in nearly all of Louÿs's work, so much so that "the majority saw nothing in his splendid books but apologies for the flesh and its pleasures."[11] But, concluded Valéry, animating it all was Louÿs's "cult" for beauty as an ideal.[12] His writings also provide insight into aspects of human nature rarely depicted by contemporary authors—what Joris-Karl Huysmans, in writing about the erotic art of Félicien Rops (with whom, incidentally, Louÿs has much in common) described as a "dark descent into the depths of the soul."[13] Louÿs was adamantly opposed to what he believed was the rampant sexual hypocrisy of his day. His writings, he felt, were one way to expose and attack them.

Debussy enjoyed spending time with Louÿs. The unconventionality of his tastes fascinated Debussy: the distinctive, oriental decor of his apartment, the presence of Zohra bent Brahim (Louÿs's Algerian mistress), the fascination with all of the arts, and the casual, unpretentious atmosphere—usually smoke-filled, for both Debussy and Louÿs were heavy smokers. But to Louÿs's surprise, even though he described Debussy as "handsome, virile, and very passionate," he showed no interest at all in participating in any of Louÿs's sexual escapades.[14]

Debussy admired Louÿs's urbanity and broad culture (he knew English and German), even at times emulating it. But it is a mistake to perceive their relationship as one dominated by Louÿs—as many studies of Debussy have done, several even stating that Louÿs molded Debussy's literary taste. Debussy's preferences were already well formed by the time of their meeting.[15] In fact, it was their shared artistic interests—Mallarmé and Bach, for example—that reinforced their friendship. As for Louÿs's fanatical Wagnerism, Debussy was gracious enough to overlook it, though he did try to temper it.

Not much time passed before the trip taken with Louÿs in the autumn of 1893 brought tangible benefits to Debussy's career. On 29 December 1893 his String Quartet was performed at the Société Nationale by Ysaÿe's quartet. Debussy's piece paid some homage to the style of César Franck, an approach that many members of the Société welcomed. Although public reaction in general was tepid, there was one particularly encouraging sign: praise for the quartet in the journal *Art moderne*.

11. Ibid., p. 287.

12. Ibid., p. 288.

13. Joris-Karl Huysmans, *Certains* (Paris: Plon, 1908), p. 77.

14. According to Louÿs, in contrast to his own promiscuity, Debussy limited his sexual relations to five women during his life, all of them blonde. *LS*, p. 420.

15. This misconception of their relationship can be traced to the chatty, unreliable, and often spiteful recollections of the painter, Jacques-Emile Blanche.

It was the work of the influential Belgian critic, Octave Maus. Maus was associated with Les Vingt (later known as La Libre Esthétique), a modernist art group that encouraged a variety of styles from Impressionist to Symbolist. Their exhibits provided an important venue for new music as well, and Debussy would soon benefit from their support.

Chausson also continued to be of help. He arranged for Debussy to present a series of "Wagnerian Seances" at the home of his mother-in-law. Debussy was to perform at the piano for two hours on Saturday afternoons, playing transcriptions of *Parsifal, Tristan, Die Meistersinger,* and portions of *Siegfried.* He received an extraordinary amount of money for the job. But it was an exhausting chore. Chausson also attempted to launch Debussy into the upper echelons of Parisian society. He provided entrée to the salon of Mme de Saint-Marceaux who had a strong interest in music, especially that of Fauré. Debussy played much of his music for her, including the *Damoiselle,* the *Proses lyriques,* and some excerpts from *Pelléas.* Mme de Saint-Marceaux liked what she heard and took a genuine interest in him, but Debussy found little in the salon that appealed to him.

Occasional performances at the Société Nationale remained the primary outlet for Debussy's music. Two of the *Proses lyriques* were performed on 17 February 1894 with Debussy as accompanist. Thérèse Roger, a member of Chausson's circle, was the singer. Critical reaction to the *Proses* was not kind. These were far more challenging than the Quartet, and at least one critic found them to be astonishingly bizarre.

Roger (1866–1906) had also sung in the performance of the *Damoiselle* and—although there is no indication that Debussy was captivated by her performances—a great deal must have gone on behind the scenes. To the surprise of everyone, that spring Debussy announced that he and Mlle Roger were engaged to be married. A date was set for mid-April. The impulsiveness of Debussy's act seemed in character, but the idea of marriage did not—and some suspected the hand of Mme de Saint-Marceaux who was known for her match-making skills. Chausson described himself as being "literally stupefied."[16] So was Louÿs. He was opposed to it, and characterized Mlle Roger as a "drawing-room singer." "I am convinced," he wrote to his brother, "that it would be a bad marriage, and I am distressed about it for my friend's sake."[17]

Other than their musical backgrounds, Thérèse Roger and Debussy seemed to have little in common. She was not a beauty, like Gaby. And despite her skill in performing songs by Chausson and Fauré, she was not known as a particularly gifted singer. But Chausson and Henri Lerolle, eager to put the situation in the best light possible, seemed pleased. Debussy confessed to Lerolle that it was all very

16. *LS,* p. 149.
17. *D,* p. 88.

much like a fairy tale, and that for some time he had felt a "profound tenderness" toward her which he had not dared to express.[18]

At the time of his engagement Debussy was still living with Gaby Dupont, who remained oblivious of what was happening.[19] He now needed to find a way to end their relationship amicably and at the same time to keep it all a secret from Mlle Roger and her family. Unfortunately for Debussy, the Rogers received an anonymous note telling them of his duplicity. Although the contents of the letter are not known, it seems that matters other than his affair with Gaby were mentioned— debts, for example, perhaps even his previous relationship with Marie Vasnier.

The Rogers were outraged. Friends did not rush to his defense, and Debussy soon found himself ostracized. Chausson wrote he was "despondent" about the "sordid affair" and decided that it would be inappropriate for Debussy to continue his Wagner seances.[20] What seemed to make the matter worse was Debussy's refusal to admit the truth. "I can see," explained Chausson, "how he might have told lies, watered down the truth or put a different slant on things, even though that's a stupid and pointless way of behaving, but to lie directly to her face, with indignant protests, about something so serious, that I cannot comprehend."[21] The engagement was broken off in mid-March.

Debussy tried to present a defense and even visited Mme de Saint-Marceaux in an attempt to right the situation. Through it all, his most vigorous supporter was Louÿs. On 22 March he wrote to Mme de Saint-Marceaux to try to exonerate Debussy. Concerning the relationship with Gaby, Louÿs noted that Debussy had intended breaking with her but was still searching for a gentle and appropriate way to do so when news of his engagement was revealed. "As for the rumors you have heard of his earlier life," Louÿs wrote, "I can assure you that they are monstrous slanders." He concluded with sensible advice on the merit of anonymous letters— "usually written by a liar and in any case by a coward."[22]

Because of the scandal, many of Debussy's friends broke with him. The most severe loss was Chausson. A coolness developed between them, not merely because of what was perceived as cavalier treatment of Thérèse Roger but also because of Debussy's financial irresponsibilities. But the entire affair seemed to cause Debussy little pain. Perhaps—as his enemies had claimed—her dowry had been the major attraction. As for the salons into which he had been introduced and which were now closed to him, he had long felt they were a waste of his time.

18. Letter to Henri Lerolle of [c. 24 February 1894] in C, p. 197.

19. Although he mentioned in passing to Lerolle that Gaby had left in February, that does not seem to have been the case.

20. Letter of Chausson to Lerolle of 19 March 1894 in DR, p. 45.

21. Letter of Chausson to Lerolle of 6 April 1894 in ibid.

22. Letter of 22 March 1894 in ibid., p. 46.

What puts the incident in perspective is Debussy's conduct not long before the engagement. At that time, he seemed charmed with Yvonne Lerolle, daughter of Henri Lerolle. He gave her an exquisite Japanese fan, embellished with a few measures from *Pelléas* and inscribed: "In memory of her little sister, Mélisande." He also dedicated to her a set of piano pieces, *Images*—not the well-known collection of later years, but an earlier group, first published in 1978. It seems possible that during these months Debussy was looking for a way out of his relationship with Gaby. His engagement to Thérèse Roger had been hasty—probably conceived as a way of following the "respectable" path endorsed by Chausson and others in his circle.

Debussy's professional life seemed to suffer little from the scandal. Gradually, his works were becoming better known. Prior to the incident, a concert devoted solely to his music had been presented on 1 March 1894 in Brussels sponsored by Maus. It was an extensive program, including the String Quartet, two of the *Proses lyriques*, and the *Damoiselle*. Debussy was present and was pleased both by the quality of the performances and by the audience's reaction. Originally intended for inclusion was his music for Mallarmé's *Faune*, but it was not finished in time. He had been working on it for months, not—as had been originally discussed—to accompany a presentation of the poem but as an independent composition inspired by it. After his break with Chausson, Debussy continued work on it and spent an increasing amount of time on *Pelléas*, devoting the summer primarily to Act III.

Late in August Debussy began a new project, a collection of three pieces for violin and orchestra that probably eventually became the *Nocturnes*. It was to be an experiment in timbre, with the first using strings, the second winds (flutes, four horns, three trumpets) and two harps, with all the forces united in the finale. Debussy intended it for Ysaÿe, but he showed surprisingly little interest. In 1897 Debussy began to convert it to a more standard orchestral piece, but it was not completed for another three years.

The premiere of the *Prélude à l'après-midi d'un faune* finally occurred on 22 December 1894 at the Société Nationale. The performance was especially important in Debussy's mind because of its association with Mallarmé, and he took particular interest in it, even attending rehearsals. Performances of his works had never been wildly successful, and Debussy had relied on the scattered appreciation of connoisseurs. In this instance—even though the performance was not polished—audience response was so enthusiastic that, contrary to policy, the *Faune* was encored.

But although the audience may have been charmed, critics were not. The *Faune* avoids many of the musical traditions that critics relied on as a basis for evaluation. Its structure is nebulous, its tunefulness unconventional, its harmony audacious, even its genre is uncertain: is it a short tone poem? an overture? Long familiar with hostile reaction to his work, Debussy placed far greater weight on the opinions of colleagues, and on that of Mallarmé himself who was enthralled by it. Additional performances on 13 and 20 October 1895 as part of the Colonne concert series were better in quality. Several critics—generally those with little musical training— were delighted by it. But music critics in general continued to be hostile, one concluding that it was "empty and pretentious."[23]

All of Debussy's work thus far had been brought out by a variety of publishers. He would gain greater prestige and stability if he were connected with a single publisher—one who would not only guarantee to print his music but could also provide either a stipend or advances on his work. After completing the *Faune*, Debussy had the good fortune to become associated with Georges Hartmann, an established publisher with a distinguished roster including Massenet. He bought the *Faune* from Debussy at the bargain price of 200 francs. But it was the beginning of a beneficial relationship. Hartmann helped to promote Debussy, whom he recognized as a rising star. Probably starting in mid-1895, he gave Debussy a monthly stipend of 500 francs.

It was money the composer very much needed. Debussy earned little from his compositions, and not much more was available from other sources. He took occasional musical odd jobs, continued to teach piano privately, and directed a small choral group formed in 1894 by his friends the Fontaine family who were helpful supporters. One member remembered his "angelic patience" with the group, not a trait much in evidence in his work as a piano teacher where he ignored matters like fingering and poked fun at repertoire that bored him.[24] He even returned to his Wagnerian duties in 1896 with weekly performances at the salon of Mme Godard-Decrais. They must have been memorable—as he accompanied himself at the piano, singing in a voice invariably described as rough and somewhat nasal.

With many of his friends vanished because of the Roger scandal, the two major sources of stability in his life were his association with Louÿs and Gaby. Despite his engagement to Thérèse Roger, Gaby stayed with him, contributing to their income by work as a milliner. And through it all, Louÿs maintained a good relationship with her. He genuinely cared for her, and treated Gaby with kindness and respect.

Despite the success of the *Faune*, this was a time when Debussy had real need of support. On occasion he tried to brush off his problems with cynical observations on the age: a time in which "Art," he claimed, was no longer "something lofty and disinterested, but just a way of making money within the reach of those who are wedded to the respectable professions."[25] But remarks like these were only attempts to minimize his depression, the "black melancholy" he had once mentioned to

23. *LS*, p. 164.

24. Mme Gérard de Romilly, "Debussy professeur, par une de ses élèves (1898–1908)," *Cahiers Debussy* 2 (1978), p. 3.

25. Letter to Jules Huret of 19 January 1898 in *DL*, p. 93.

Chausson.[26] He expressed himself openly to Louÿs, whose frequent travel abroad gave Debussy little choice but to unburden himself in letters. In 1898 while in Egypt, Louÿs received an especially bleak letter. "I feel alone and helpless," Debussy wrote. "Nothing has changed in the black sky which is the basis of my life, and I scarcely know where I am going if not towards suicide—a foolish ending to something that perhaps deserved better. I am tired of struggling against idiotic and contemptible impossibilities."[27] Louÿs replied: "YOU ARE A GREAT MAN. I have never said that to anyone before. Whatever your problems may be, that thought must be foremost in your mind."[28] And he advised Debussy to continue to immerse himself in his work, and to do all that he could to assure a performance of *Pelléas*.

During these years *Pelléas* remained Debussy's primary concern. It was his most substantial work, and he realized that his future would in all probability be determined by it. As he finished portions, he played them for friends to gauge their response. Prior to their break Chausson had heard some of the early sections, but, because of his work on *Le Roi Arthus*, refused to hear more—convinced that the originality of Debussy's work would affect his own.

Henri Lerolle, who had remained close despite the Thérèse Roger incident, heard a great deal more of *Pelléas* and was enthusiastic. In December 1894 he invited Debussy to play what he had completed thus far for several acquaintances. The setting was more competitive than convivial, for Vincent d'Indy was scheduled to play portions of his new opera, *Fervaal*. It was d'Indy's major composition during these years and was intended to rejuvenate French opera. On arriving, Debussy claimed that he had left his own score at home, but after hearing *Fervaal* his coyness vanished, and his score miraculously appeared. Its originality "really astonished" many of them, not least d'Indy.[29] As a result of private performances such as these, word of *Pelléas* spread, creating not only interest but extraordinary curiosity about it as well.

Debussy finished *Pelléas* (in piano score) in 1895. Soon after, several opportunities to perform it appeared. In August or September Paul Larochelle, the new director of the Théâtre Libre (an avant-garde theater), expressed interest in it, as did the Théâtre de l'Oeuvre in 1896—but nothing came of either proposal. That same year Eugène Ysaÿe attempted to convince Debussy to allow him to perform excerpts from *Pelléas* in Brussels. But Debussy rejected the offer, in part because he was offended by the aggressive and self-serving manner in which Ysaÿe proposed the project. But he replied with tact, writing that a partial performance would destroy the dramatic unity intended. He also felt that there was always danger that the work

26. Letter of [2 July 1893] in ibid., p. 47.
27. Letter of 21 April 1898 in *C*, p. 398.
28. Letter of 5 May [1898] in ibid., p. 400.
29. Reaction of Paul Poujaud in *D*, p. 85.

would be perceived as being presented incomplete simply because no opera house was willing to stage it in its entirety.

In 1898 Debussy was asked to supply incidental music for a performance in England of *Pelléas* as a drama. Once again, he declined, and, without his approval—which should have been necessary since he had the musical rights for the play—music was provided by Gabriel Fauré. Debussy was furious. But he told Georges Hartmann that he was not worried. There was, he wrote, considerable difference between his music and that of Fauré, "the musical servant of a group of snobs and imbeciles."[30] He was right about the differences in their music, but might have been more concerned that whatever popularity Fauré's production might have—and it *had* been a success—would detract from the novelty of his own setting.

All of this interest in *Pelléas* should have been heartening to Debussy and should have encouraged him to push for its premiere. But he left the matter in the hands of Hartmann who was not aggressive. He recognized Debussy's ability—and its potential to earn money—but even though he was familiar with *Pelléas*, he seemed unaware of its significance. So, as had been the case with *La Damoiselle élue*, a work that could have opened doors for Debussy and made life much easier for him remained unperformed.

Although *Pelléas* was Debussy's major concern in the 1890s, there were quite a few abortive projects stemming from his friendship with Louÿs. The first, dating from September 1894, was a drama, *Oedipe à Colonne*, for which Debussy was to supply incidental music. The play was intended to be jointly written by Louÿs and Ferdinand Hérold, but it never went beyond the planning stage. A second project followed seven months later. At first referred to as *Le Roi des Aulnes*, it was a fairy tale conceived as an opera. It became *Cendrelune* (Cinderella), and two scenarios (both in two acts) have survived. Although it continued to be mentioned as late as May 1898, Debussy and Louÿs were unable to agree on its content, and no music was composed. Of greater interest to Debussy was a setting based on a series of poems ("Willowwood") translated by Louÿs from Rossetti's *The House of Life*. *La Saulaie* occupied Debussy in 1896 and 1897, and portions (intended for baritone and orchestra) were completed. But despite assertions in 1900 that he was working on it, little was actually finished.

Louÿs seemed far more eager than Debussy that they collaborate. In November 1895 he approached him with the scenario for a ballet, *Daphnis et Chloë*. It was a hasty and fairly nebulous plan, and, although Debussy wrote to Louÿs in May 1896 that he was working on it, his claim appears doubtful. An equally vague project concerned Louÿs's novel, *Aphrodite*. Debussy had written to Louÿs not long after its publication offering praise ("unique...prodigiously supple"), but the generalities he

---

30. Letter of 9 August 1898 in *DL*, p. 100.

used indicate that he was choosing his words with care.[31] Although he received unofficial permission from Louÿs to adapt *Aphrodite* as an opera, he never did so.[32] Related to an *Aphrodite* opera was Louÿs's suggestion in 1897 for an *Aphrodite* ballet or pantomime. Debussy did not oblige. Speed always seemed important to Louÿs in these proposed collaborations. He failed to grasp Debussy's meticulous pace, and from the start that seemed to doom their work together. But it also seems clear that none of the proposals caught fire with Debussy.

The comparatively few compositions completed by him in the period from 1895 to 1900 (that is, after *Pelléas* was finished) are indicative of the difficult times he was having. Work continued on the *Nocturnes*, but with slow progress. Mostly it was a question of projects or ideas for projects, all for various reasons abandoned. Only one composition actually resulted from his friendship with Louÿs. In the spring of 1897 he set to music "La Flûte de Pan," the first of what would become three songs from Louÿs's *Chansons de Bilitis*—a popular collection of prose poems originally presented by Louÿs as translations from ancient Greek. Debussy added to it "La Chevelure" (The Tresses), and in the following year, "Le Tombeau des naïdes" (The Tomb of the Naiads), the entire set being published in 1899 as *Trois Chansons de Bilitis*.

In addition to these songs, Debussy worked on setting several of his own poems, similar to what he had done with the *Proses lyriques*. They were given the title *Nuits blanches*, and two (from a projected set of five) were written. But Debussy never completed the set, and left them unpublished.

Perhaps the most obvious indication of how difficult a time Debussy was having writing music is his involvement with Erik Satie's piano pieces, *Trois Gymnopédies*. In 1896 Debussy orchestrated the first and the third of them for performance at the Société Nationale. It was a generous gesture for a good friend, and a gracious attempt to make Satie's work better known. But this was the *only* time that Debussy ever orchestrated the music of someone else—and had his own muse not deserted him, he might not have found time for it. Orchestration was never routine for Debussy, but a crucial aspect of composition. His arrangements of the *Gymnopédies* are inventive, extraordinarily sensitive, and extremely beautiful—all reasons that Debussy's settings remain today among the most popular of Satie's music.

Debussy's hopes remained focused on *Pelléas*, and, until it was accepted for performance, he seemed incapable of applying himself for any length of time on any other project. This uncertainty was a major source for his depression, and it affected his life with Gaby, a relationship that at least in Debussy's eyes was becoming

31. Letter of 10 April 1896 in *C*, p. 310.

32. Several composers showed interest in *Aphrodite*, including Puccini. It was set by Camille Erlanger in 1906.

increasingly meaningless. In late 1895 or early in 1896, he proposed marriage to Catherine Stevens. She turned him down, suggesting that he ask again after *Pelléas* was performed. Then in February 1897 Gaby discovered a letter that gave proof of his involvement with another woman. Debussy described the incident for Louÿs in a curiously detached manner:

> Gaby, she of the piercing eye, found a letter in my pocket which left no doubt as to the advanced state of a love affair, and containing enough picturesque material to inflame even the most stolid heart. Whereupon…Scenes…Tears… A real revolver and *Le Petit Journal* there to record it all.… It would have been nice to have you here, my dear Pierre, to help me recognize myself in all this third-rate literature.[33]

Debussy's remarks are all that is known of the incident, and, while it has been assumed that Gaby attempted to kill herself with the pistol, it would have been equally acceptable in the canons of "third-rate literature" for her to have taken a shot at Debussy. Nothing has been found in *Le Petit Journal* or any other newspaper. Given the bantering tone often assumed by Debussy and Louÿs in their correspondence, Debussy may have been more imaginative than factual in his account. Whatever may have occurred, no one was seriously injured by it. A month later, in a postscript to a letter, Debussy forwarded to Louÿs at Gaby's request "her nicest smile."[34] But their reconciliation, if it can be described as one, appeared casual and haphazard.

A breakup seemed only a matter of time, and it was Gaby who made the first move, leaving him in December 1898 to become the mistress of Count de Balbiani, a South American banker. But despite the coldness of their final months, Debussy did not forget their years together. In June 1902, after the long-awaited premiere of *Pelléas*, he presented a score of it to her, inscribed: "To Gaby, princess of the mysterious kingdom of Allemonde. Her old devoted friend, Claude Debussy."[35]

Debussy did not remain alone for long. Earlier that summer, he had met Marie-Rosalie Texier (known as Lilly or Lilo, 1873–1932), a friend of Gaby. She was about ten years younger than Debussy and had been living in Paris for three years working as a model for fashion houses. Their first meeting did not impress him favorably. But in the spring of 1899 Debussy began to see her regularly. The series of letters which he wrote to her over the following months become extraordinarily intimate. When, after about a month, Lilly attempted to break off their relationship, Debussy intensified his courtship. What may have added to his passion was the announcement by Louÿs of his engagement to the daughter of the poet, José Maria de Hérédia.

33. Letter of 9 February 1897 in *DL*, p. 88.
34. Letter of 9 March 1897 in ibid., p. 92.
35. *D*, p. 71.

The wedding on 24 June was a major social event, for which at Louÿs's request Debussy wrote a march (now lost). The marriage of his closest friend heightened Debussy's sense of isolation.

In writing to Lilly, he made a point of describing not merely his love for her, but what he could provide, mentioning how *Pelléas* would improve his stature. He assured her that it would be performed that year. That was only a hope, but there was at least some substance to it. In May 1898 Debussy had played *Pelléas* for Albert Carré, manager of the Opéra-Comique, and André Messager, the music director. Both had told him that they would stage the work, but no date had been set—for, in addition to the formalities of a contract, Debussy had yet to orchestrate it.

The marriage of Debussy and Lilly occurred on 19 October in a quiet civil ceremony which included Satie and Louÿs among the witnesses. That day Debussy quickly gave a piano lesson in order to have enough money to dine out with his bride. Marriage seemed to agree with him, and his mood became brighter than it had been in months. "Mademoiselle Lilly Texier," he reported to Robert Godet, "has exchanged her inharmonious name for that of Lilly Debussy, much more euphonious as I'm sure everybody will agree."[36] But it is odd that just five months earlier, when he had learned of Louÿs's engagement, he had offered his congratulations, but seemed to rule out anything similar for himself. "My old liaison with Music," he wrote, "prevents me from marrying."[37]

36. Letter of 5 January 1900 in *DL*, p. 109. This is an instance of Debussy imitating Louÿs. Writing to Debussy, he announced his wedding in a similar manner: "Mademoiselle Louise de Hérédia has exchanged her name for that of Louise Louÿs, more symmetrical and balanced."
37. Letter of 16 May 1899 in *C*, p. 479.

CHAPTER FIVE

Divagations, 1900–1904

If you think of someone you have loved deeply, it will not be their words or gestures that you will recall, but the silence you have shared. The *quality* of those silent moments alone revealed the *quality* of your love, and your souls.

Maurice Maeterlinck, *On Silence* (1896)

DEBUSSY'S ENGAGEMENT TO THERÈSE ROGER IN 1894 HAD LARGELY BEEN THE result of trying to meet the expectations of a new circle of friends. But his marriage to Lilly Texier was his own doing. To some extent it appears that he wanted companionship, especially after the recent breakup with Gaby. But Debussy also seemed anxious for more stability in his life.

The home which he soon established with Lilly was cosy. Their small apartment was meticulously clean and tidy....From the windows you could see a little greenery, and the peace and quiet were only troubled at certain times by the happy cries of children in a school courtyard.

There was an atmosphere of intimacy and calm in the two small rooms joined by a bay. One was Debussy's studio where, on the desk, manuscripts, inkwells and pencils were laid out in perfect order. There was also a divan, several Oriental carpets and, on the walls, pictures by Henri Lerolle, Jacques-Emile Blanche, Thaulow, and drawings representing Lilo Debussy, then at the height of her beauty. She had delicate features surrounded by fair hair; she appeared to be the very incarnation of Mélisande. In the other room there was an upright piano, books and scores.

If Lilo was not a musician (which her husband was glad of), she was an accomplished mistress of the household, always on the lookout for treats and cooking exquisite little meals for him which he appreciated greatly and consumed with relish.[1]

1. Madame Gérard de Romilly in *DR*, p. 58.

Adding to the ambiance were two cats. Debussy had a longstanding relationship with cats. The pair he had with Lilly were granted unusual favors, including being permitted to lounge "solemnly on the desk and, if they so wished, to sow disorder among the pencils."[2] As had been the case with Gaby, Lilly managed much of the household and kept it going on a small amount of money.

But even with his newfound domesticity, Debussy had little peace of mind. He described himself as being in a "moribund, depressed state," in part because of concern over *Pelléas et Mélisande*.[3] Albert Carré appeared willing to perform it during the 1901 season, but no firm date had been set. Not having a performance date was unsettling, and adding to Debussy's apprehensions was the recent triumph of Charpentier's *Louise* at the Opéra-Comique, so very different from *Pelléas*. "It fills to perfection," he told Louÿs, "the need for vulgar beauty and imbecile art proclaimed by the many."[4] Hartmann urged Debussy to complete the score for *Pelléas*. There will be no real commitment, he wrote, until Carré has "*the score in hand*."[5]

Debussy continued to do what he could to provide additional income, including occasional salon performances of Wagner. The *Nocturnes*, finally finished to his satisfaction, appeared in print in February 1900, and both Debussy and Hartmann were hopeful that this substantial orchestral composition would do much to increase his reputation. The two best venues for it were the Colonne and Lamoureux concert series. But Colonne would not schedule it, and when it was shown to Camille Chevillard, the new conductor of the Lamoureux series, he was far from enthusiastic. He agreed to schedule it, but only the first two movements because the third movement required a female chorus. It was a fitting commentary on Debussy's beleaguered state that the sole performance of any of his music during these months was of a salon piece: the *Tarentelle styrienne*, performed at a Société Nationale concert on 10 March.

Just when it seemed that matters could not be bleaker, on 23 April 1900 Georges Hartmann died. Hartmann and Debussy had not been close—they were far too different in temperament—but the stipend that Hartmann supplied Debussy remained his primary means of support. "I am truly sorry for his death," Debussy wrote. "He played his part with good grace and a smile, fairly rare among philanthropists of art."[6] In his dealings with Debussy, Hartmann had been a businessman with a touch of generosity. But the executor of his estate lacked even the semblance of a

2. Ibid.
3. Letter to Robert Godet of 5 January 1900 in *DL*, p. 109.
4. Letter of 6 February 1900 in ibid., p. 110.
5. Letter to Debussy of 4 January 1900 in *C*, p. 531.
6. Letter to Louÿs of 25 April 1900 in ibid., p. 557.

philanthropist and was soon demanding that Debussy pay back advances that he had received for his work.

Lilly was profoundly discouraged. Debussy did his best to lift her spirits, telling her that they needed to "struggle a bit more. And for that I am counting on you—my joy, my delight, my happiness, and also my greatest and most beautiful hope."[7] Then in the midst of their worries, they discovered that she was pregnant. Because of their precarious finances, there was a mutual decision for an abortion, and Lilly spent about a week in mid-August at a clinic. Her health, which had never been robust, became yet another cause for concern when an examination revealed that she might have an early stage tuberculosis. Debussy tried to remain positive. "So I conjure up smiles," he confessed to Louÿs, "which feel like tears."[8]

There was some encouraging news that summer. On 24 August *La Damoiselle élue* was presented as part of the official French contingent of concerts at the Universal Exposition held in Paris. Its selection was an indication of Debussy's growing fame. And the performance itself he described as "unforgettable."[9] The primary role was sung by Blanche Marot. "It was not possible for anyone to have interpreted *La Damoiselle élue* with greater sensitivity and sincere feeling," Debussy told her. "At times you were able to withdraw so completely from the world around you that the effect was unearthly."[10] She had also performed the *Chansons de Bilitis* on 17 March at the Société Nationale, and in time would become closely associated with Debussy's music.

The *Damoiselle* met with a favorable reception by the public—and the usual mixed one from critics. But one unusually supportive voice stood out: Pierre Lalo, son of the composer, praised Debussy's "melodic invention" as well as the originality and refinement of his harmonic approach.[11] Lalo was to become one of Debussy's most ardent supporters, and Debussy took the unusual step of writing to thank him for his review.

Criticism in general seemed to be gradually turning Debussy's way. Some of this was a result of the changing of the guard, as younger critics like Lalo and Gaston Carraud stepped forward. But it was also becoming more common for composers to serve as critics, even in major newspapers. That was particularly helpful for the premiere of the *Nocturnes*, the first two of which ("Nuages" and "Fêtes") were given

7. Letter of 25 April 1900 in ibid., p. 556.

8. Letter to Louÿs of 14 May 1900 in *DL*, p. 113. According to the editors of Debussy's *Correspondance*, Lilly had suffered a miscarriage (p. 566).

9. Letter to Blanche Marot of 24 August 1900 in *C*, p. 565.

10. Ibid.

11. *LS*, p. 198.

at the Lamoureux series on 9 December. Among those who wrote reviews of the *Nocturnes* were Pierre de Bréville, Alfred Bruneau, and Paul Dukas—all of whom were composers of some stature—and they tended to be more receptive and understanding of Debussy's style. Overall, his music was beginning to receive a more balanced and insightful appraisal.

Debussy could only have been heartened by reaction to the *Nocturnes*, and he began 1901 in a better frame of mind. After what had been a period of comparative stagnation, he started work on a new composition, a collection of three piano pieces which would become *Pour le piano*. The surprising simplicity of the title was revealing: its ambiguity set it apart from the programmatic titles for most piano music. After their completion in April, *Lindaraja* (for two pianos, four-hands) followed. His industry was a good sign. And his homelife with Lilly also seemed to be going well. In January he gave her the score of the *Nocturnes* with the inscription: "This manuscript belongs to my little Lilly-Lilo, all rights reserved. It is also a token of my deep and passionate joy in being her husband."[12]

Still, performances of Debussy's works remained irregular. One of the most unusual occurred on 7 February on the premises of the newspaper, *Le Journal*. It was the result of a suggestion made to Debussy by Louÿs the previous October. For the performance a series of a dozen tableaux vivants (with implied nudity) was presented to the recitation of poems from the *Chansons de Bilitis*. Debussy provided music arranged for two harps, two flutes, and a celesta (only the parts for the flutes and harp have survived). The music was not intended to accompany the reading of the poetry, but as a backdrop for the tableaux themselves. The entire concept was a bit dated by 1901—it had been particularly popular in Symbolist theater, where tableaux were often presented as an auxiliary to the evening's main entertainment—so it is not surprising that no additional performances followed.

The need for more money provided the impetus two months later for Debussy's entry into the world of music criticism. Even though it had become an increasingly common way for composers to supplement their income, Debussy's credentials set him apart. Not only was he a rising star, he also wrote well and with originality. But becoming a music critic was not something he looked forward to. Writing did not come easily to him, and the time spent attending concerts and preparing reviews he would have preferred to spend composing.

Debussy served as music critic for *La Revue blanche*, one of the leading artistic journals of the time, for about eight months (from April to December 1901). It was an association of benefit both to himself and the paper. Debussy was engaging,

12. *D*, p. 125.

witty, iconoclastic, and often startling in his unconventionality. He showed little concern in offending anyone, and that in itself helped contribute to his popularity. Much of what he wrote was imaginative and inventive, especially when Debussy brought into play his fictional creation, Monsieur Croche. Croche, an outspoken and opinionated anti-dilettante, made infrequent but unforgettable appearances in the reviews, always adding spice with his blunt and controversial observations.

That May—not long after beginning work as a music critic—Debussy finally received written assurance from Carré that *Pelléas* would be performed the following year. While it was certainly welcome news, it was also a reminder that he needed to begin orchestrating it. Maeterlinck soon learned of the forthcoming production, and on 30 May he met with Debussy to discuss it in general terms. He was interested in giving the role of Mélisande to his longtime mistress, Georgette Leblanc, a singer and actress. But Debussy put off making a decision, noting that it was not his alone to make. Privately, he was extremely critical of Leblanc: "Not only does she sing out of tune," he told a friend, "she speaks out of tune."[13]

That August Debussy took the first of what would become a series of regular summer vacations visiting Lilly's parents in Bichain in Burgundy. He stayed for about a month, and enjoyed it. The countryside provided a welcome escape from life in the city. As he explained to Raoul Bardac, a young man who had recently started taking lessons in composition with him, in Burgundy it seemed as if he were "at the opposite end of the earth from Paris."[14]

On his return, he continued to work on the orchestration of *Pelléas*, all of which was probably completed by September. But time was also devoted to the full premiere—that is, all three movements—of the *Nocturnes* on 27 October at the Lamoureux concerts. Debussy felt that the conductor, Chevillard, was insensitive and incapable of doing the score justice, suspicions that seemed to be confirmed during rehearsal:

Debussy: "I would like it to be more nebulous."
Chevillard: "Quicker?"
Debussy: "No, more nebulous."
Chevillard: "Slower?"
Debussy: "More nebulous."
Chevillard: "I don't know what you mean. Gentlemen, let us begin again!"[15]

The performance was not as well-received as had been the premiere of the first two movements; the final movement ("Sirènes") was a bit rough, and there were

13. Madame de Romilly in *DR*, p. 56.
14. Letter of 31 August 1901 in *DL*, p. 120.
15. *LS*, p. 208.

complaints from critics about excessive chromaticism. But Lalo was fairly generous in his praise, noting the "exquisite melodic contours" of the finale.[16]

Lalo was also supportive of *Pour le piano* which received its premiere at the Société Nationale on 11 January 1902. The pianist was Ricardo Viñes, a friend of Maurice Ravel and a great enthusiast for Debussy's music. Viñes was thirteen years younger than Debussy and passionate about literature (Poe and Baudelaire were two of his favorites). His first meeting with Debussy the previous November—to go over *Pour le piano* prior to its performance—was one Viñes had looked forward to for a long time. Although they never became close (privately Debussy criticized his playing as "too dry"), Viñes was entrusted with the first performances of several of Debussy's most important piano compositions.[17] In his journal, Viñes described the success of *Pour le piano* as "phenomenal."[18] Audience response was enthusiastic, but critics tended to focus on the superficial charm of the pieces.

Two days after the performance of *Pour le piano*, rehearsals began for *Pelléas et Mélisande*. For the next three months Debussy was to devote much of his time to preparing for the premiere. He began by coaching the singers and was pleased by the one chosen for Mélisande—not Georgette Leblanc as Maeterlinck had expected, but Mary Garden, a member of the Opéra-Comique ensemble for several years. "Your ears would have to be plugged to resist the charm of her voice," he wrote of her. "For my part, I can not imagine a more smoothly insinuating timbre. It is as if it were tyrannical in its effect, for it is impossible to forget."[19]

Pelléas et Mélisande required extraordinary sensitivity from the singers, who had to abandon the type of vocal and dramatic display characteristic of the operatic repertoire. Much has been made of the ability of those who created the roles, especially Mary Garden, with the implication that she had been sought out and nurtured for her part. But nothing could be farther from the truth. She had recently won praise in the title role of Charpentier's *Louise*. In the year following *Pelléas*, she was to be equally successful in *La Reine Fiammette* by Xavier Leroux—a tale of love and intrigue set in the Italian Renaissance—to a text by Catulle Mendès and in a musical style resembling Massenet's. She excelled in standard repertoire. That she

---

16. Ibid., p. 209.

17. Conversation of 17 December 1908 in Annie Joly-Segalen, and André Schaeffner, eds., *Segalen et Debussy* (Monaco: Editions du Rocher, 1961), p. 107.

18. Nina Gubisch, "Le Journal inédit de Ricardo Viñes," *Revue Internationale de Musique Française* 1 (1980), p. 224.

19. Letter of 8 July 1902 to André Messager in *C*, p. 674. Mary Garden's memoirs (an "as-told-to" variety written with Louis Biancolli and published in 1951) contain some colorful Debussy anecdotes and are unreliable. In addition to her fondness for the picturesque, starting in 1945 she began to suffer from senile dementia.

was able to enter so successfully into the world of *Pelléas et Mélisande* was a tribute to her skill and sensitivity. For Debussy, it was simply a stroke of good luck that she was available.

Although the selection of Mary Garden turned out to be ideal, it made a bitter enemy of Maeterlinck. He regarded it as a personal affront that Georgette Leblanc had been passed over and refused to let it go unchallenged. On 7 February he brought the matter before the Société d'auteurs dramatiques, claiming that his rights as author had been violated. At no time, he claimed, had Debussy been given free rein to stage the opera as he saw fit. But in a letter to him of 1895 Maeterlinck had done just that.

In mid-February both Debussy and Maeterlinck met with the Société to present their case. But, as it became clear that Debussy had conducted himself in a manner entirely within his rights, Maeterlinck decided to drop the Société, and go to court. To Debussy, his behavior was "little short of pathological."[20] But worse was yet to come. On 13 April—about two weeks before the premiere—Maeterlinck wrote an open letter to *Le Figaro*. He claimed that the performance of *Pelléas et Mélisande* did not acknowledge his "most legitimate rights"—and he hoped that its failure would be "prompt and resounding."[21]

After waiting for years to bring *Pelléas* to the stage, Debussy now found himself in the odd position of being publicly attacked by its author. At the same time he needed to avoid being distracted by Maeterlinck's malice and focus his attention on rehearsals. For, despite its uncommon musical style, the amount of rehearsal devoted to *Pelléas et Mélisande* was no more than usual for a new work. Debussy took full advantage of it and became involved with many details of production, such as the stage lighting. Fortunately, he was dealing with a conductor sympathetic to the score and eager for its success. André Messager's skill and dedication soon earned Debussy's esteem. "You knew how to bring the music of *Pelléas* to life with a tender delicacy I dare not hope to find elsewhere," he wrote him not long after the premiere.[22] The greatest challenge for Debussy during the weeks prior to the first performance was, slow worker that he was, the hurried creation of additional music to allow more time for changes of scene.

With Maeterlinck's open opposition and the absence of influential friends to support the production, Debussy remained apprehensive and concerned about "possible manifestations on the part of Leblanc-Maeterlinck."[23] The public dress

---

20. Letter of 27 January 1902 to René Peter in *DL*, p. 123.

21. *D*, pp. 114, 115.

22. Letter of 9 May 1902 to Messager in *DL*, p. 126.

23. Letter of [28 April 1902] to Gabriel Mourey in *C*, p. 651.

rehearsal on 28 April was tense, and starting in the second act there were complaints about the preciosity of the setting and Garden's foreign pronunciation (she was Scottish). But the premiere two days later was better received. Response from critics and the public was generally favorable. Present were a number of young supporters, such as Emile Vuillermoz, who were outspoken in their praise. But even more conservative musicians, like Massenet and Fauré, acknowledged some of the work's qualities.

Pelléas was so different from the usual fare that Debussy's concerns were understandable. For, despite the eagerness expressed in avant-garde musical circles for change in French opera, few could have expected a response as radical as Debussy's. Vincent d'Indy, whose *Fervaal* was regarded by many as providing new direction for French opera, was disconcerted by its success—but fair-handed in his reaction to it. "M. Debussy is something like a Monteverdi to us," he drily noted.[24]

There were more than a dozen performances of *Pelléas*. "Each evening," wrote *Le Figaro*, "it wins a new victory with the public, and it is applauded by the most famous composers. It has been a long time since a dramatic work has been so passionately discussed as *Pelléas*. . . . Such a production will remain a date in the history of dramatic music."[25] Its success provided Debussy with the recognition to broaden his reputation. Henri Büsser, who directed the chorus and made his debut as a conductor with the final performances of *Pelléas*, recalled visiting Debussy shortly after the premiere: "His young wife wanders in and out, arranging the flowers I've brought them in a vase. This little room we're in, with oil paintings, watercolors and drawings on the walls, radiates happiness. The delightful Lilly is its source. She's happy that *Pelléas* is being produced. 'It's my work too,' she says, 'because I gave Claude encouragement when he was despairing of ever seeing his work reach the stage!'"[26]

For Debussy, it was exhilarating, but exhausting as well. "I'm suffering fatigue to the point of neurasthenia," he confessed to Godet. "I can only think that the labor and nervous strain of these last months have finally got the better of me."[27] As a break, he visited London from 12 to 20 July, a short trip undertaken at the invitation of Messager who was director at Covent Garden from 1901 to 1905. Debussy enjoyed it. Mary Garden was also there and made her Covent Garden debut as Manon that same month. Particularly memorable was a performance of *Hamlet* Debussy attended at the Lyric Theater. Mary Garden went with him and was

---

24. 26 March 1904 in the *Revue bleue* quoted in *D*, p. 120. The allusion is to Monteverdi's role as the founder of opera.

25. Issues of 21 May and 22 June 1902 quoted in ibid., p. 121.

26. *DR*, p. 80.

27. Letter of 13 June 1902 in *DL*, p. 128.

astonished at the depth of his reaction: "He seemed like a child in a trance. So profoundly was he affected that it was some time before he could speak. I have never known anyone to lose himself so completely in the spectacle of great art."[28]

Debussy made the trip without Lilly, and his letters to her provide glimpses into their relationship. The courtship had been passionate. Marriage had become routine. Much of his attraction seemed to have been based on what he saw as her child-like simplicity. That helps to explain the increasingly infantile manner he adopted in writing to her—a pose so unlike him, that whatever novelty it may have possessed could only have become tiresome. "I loved your lack of courage very much," he wrote while in England. "You see, it is very nice to be the strong little wife, but there are times when the strong little wife must have her weaknesses. That adds an extra charm to her graciousness.... Would you believe that it is impossible to get a good cup of tea? That makes me think of my rue Cardinet and the dear little wife, who, among other gifts, possesses that of making tea. Ah! in England there are no such wives as that; here they are wives for horseguards with their complexions of raw ham and their movements like those of a young animal."[29]

When Debussy returned from England, Lilly was ill, and her doctor recommended a change of air. They went to Bichain, not returning to Paris until 15 September. But despite the nearly two months of free time, Debussy accomplished little. There was some revision of *La Damoiselle élue* in preparation for a new edition—yet another indication of his growing fame (the Baudelaire songs had also been republished). And as a means of settling with Hartmann's executor (who sold the rights of many of Debussy's pieces in July 1902 to another publisher), new editions appeared of early piano works like the *Ballade*, *Mazurka*, and *Valse*. The success of *Pelléas* made them far more valuable.

The remaining months of 1902 were concerned not with composition but with preparations for the return to the stage of *Pelléas* on 30 October. Debussy continued to take an active role in the production. A primary concern was the need for a new Pelléas (Jean Périer, who had done well as its creator, was not on the roster at the time). And the producers also decided to have a woman rather than a child assume the role of Yniold, a change that worked out well. There was even some thought to having Pelléas portrayed by a woman—as had actually been the case in the stage performance Debussy had seen in 1893—but after consideration the idea was abandoned. In addition to *Pelléas*, that November the *Faune* was performed by Chevillard. And in the following month, the *Damoiselle* was performed at the Colonne Concert Series with Mary Garden. Both works provided an outlet for what had become clamorous support for his music by a growing number of admirers.

28. *DR*, p. 73.
29. Letter of 16 July 1902 in *D*, pp. 122–123.

Official recognition of Debussy's stature came early in the new year and was a complete surprise. He was named a chevalier of the Legion of Honor. Debussy owed the honor to the efforts of a recent friend, the music theorist and historian Louis Laloy. Laloy's academic background was enough to make Debussy wary, but they got along well. Their friendship had as its basis an insightful review of *Pelléas* that Laloy had written. He had wide-ranging interests. Like Debussy, he was fascinated by the Far East and later became a specialist in Chinese music.

Another new friend was the writer, Paul-Jean Toulet. Toulet was five years younger than Debussy and a dedicated non-conformist (his daily routine was to go to bed at seven in the morning, and breakfast in the mid-afternoon). Like Satie, he had a great sense of the absurd. For years he sent droll postcards and letters to himself, a selection of which were published posthumously as *Lettres à soi-même* (1927).

Toulet worked as a journalist and at the time he met Debussy had published little: one novel and a translation of Arthur Machen's *The Great God Pan*, neither of which had attracted notice. He was soon to publish *Mon Amie Nane*—a novella about a woman of easy virtue—followed by the works that are the basis of his growing reputation today: the novel *La Jeune Fille verte* and the collection of poems *Les Contrerimes*. Despite being an accomplished stylist—rich, polished, and fanciful—Toulet was little known during his life, and Debussy's admiration for him is yet another indication of his discriminating taste.[30]

The project that drew Toulet and Debussy together was a proposed adaptation of Shakespeare's *As You Like It*, a favorite of Debussy. Initial stages of the collaboration were interrupted by Toulet's visit to Southeast Asia in 1902–1903 (the fascination with the Orient was an additional interest he shared with Debussy). But even though it was announced in the press in 1903 as forthcoming—and in one instance as finished—this was another of Debussy's projects that never made much progress.

Debussy's fame led to a brief return to music criticism. For about four months beginning in January 1903 he wrote reviews for *Gil Blas* and was treated more as a celebrity. His writing continued to probe contemporary musical life, such as d'Indy's new opera, *L'Etranger*, and a rare performance of Wagner's *Ring* in London. But there was a subtle change in his stance. Debussy now seemed more nationalistic. He became impassioned in his defense of French music of the past—especially that of Rameau—and argued that for more than a century French taste had been corrupted by foreign influences.

---

30. Both of Debussy's new friends were habitual users of opium. It may come as a surprise to those who view Debussy's music as a series of dreamy reveries that he strongly disapproved of their habit. It led to a rare lecture, and a warning to Toulet about the "sinister drug…an imagination as finely balanced as yours is just the sort to suffer from it most." Letter of 28 August 1903 in *DL*, p. 138.

As his fame grew so did performances of his music, not just in Paris but throughout France. In addition to orchestral compositions like the *Faune* and *Nocturnes*, the piano pieces, songs, and string quartet were regularly performed. Sometimes it seemed more like a sporting event than a concert, with youthful fans chanting: "De-bus-sy!" On 21 April 1903 the Schola Cantorum—a music school co-founded and directed by d'Indy and, although devoutly academic, a welcome alternative to the Conservatoire—presented a program devoted solely to Debussy's music. That same year *La Damoiselle élue* was performed by La Concordia, the choral group for which Debussy had been accompanist prior to winning the Prix de Rome.

In May Lilly left once again to visit her parents in Bichain. But Debussy did not follow until later. With all the trials of *Pelléas et Mélisande* now behind him, he was ready once again to focus on composition—a major reason he decided to stop writing for *Gil Blas*. First if not in prominence then in need of being completed was a commission two-years old to write a rhapsody for saxophone; the money received for it had long been spent. The project itself was a challenge. "The saxophone is a reedy animal with whose habits I'm largely unfamiliar," he wrote to Louÿs. "Is it suited to the romantic sweetness of the clarinets or the rather vulgar irony of the sarrusophone (or the contra-bassoon)? In the end I've got it murmuring melancholy phrases against rolls on the side drum."[31]

More significant was a series of twelve *Images*. In July Debussy had signed a contract with Durand for two sets of six pieces, one for solo piano, and another (five were eventually completed) for either two pianos or orchestra. For the solo piano pieces, Debussy had already chosen titles. What would eventually become the orchestral *Images* had also been given titles at this early stage, but "Ibéria," "Gigue triste," and "Rondes" would change to "Gigues tristes," Ibéria," and "Valse" in May 1905 before assuming their final titles.

Debussy went to Bichain in mid-July and did not return to Paris until 1 October. He and Lilly rented a house that had formerly been an inn. "Here we are far from the empty noise of the big cities," he wrote.[32] Debussy enjoyed the countryside, took frequent walks, and even considered buying land there.

The peace and quiet provided stimulus for work beyond the *Images*. Debussy completed *Estampes* (Prints), a collection of three pieces for solo piano ("Pagodes" [Pagodas], "La Soirée dans Grenade" [Evening in Grenada], "Jardins sous la pluie" [Gardens in the Rain]). And he started work on an orchestral composition—not the *Images*—but an equally ambitious concept which at this stage he described as

---

31. Letter of [early August 1903] in ibid., p. 136.
32. Letter of [14 July 1903] to Fromont in *D*, p. 128.

"three symphonic sketches entitled: 1. 'mer belle aux îles Sanguinaires'; 2. 'jeu de vagues'; 3. 'le vent fait danser la mer'; the whole to be called *La Mer*."[33] Debussy eventually decided on a different set of titles: "De l'aube à midi sur la mer" (From Dawn to Noon on the Sea), "Jeux de vagues" (Play of Waves), and "Dialogue du vent et de la mer" (Dialogue of Wind and Sea). He made substantial progress, and the entire composition was written in a year and a half—a rushed pace for Debussy. It was all an indication of how eager he was to return to composition after the months of distraction with *Pelléas*.

He did not write much music for the remainder of the year, the most notable work being *D'un cahier d'esquisses* (From a Book of Sketches), an intriguing, short piece commissioned by a magazine and which passed with little notice. But there truly was little time available for writing music. *Pelléas* returned to the Opéra-Comique at the end of October (with Debussy's usual involvement), and there were two new contracts. For Durand, Debussy agreed to write an opera based on Poe's tale, "The Devil in the Belfry." It was a curious choice—a little-known work, not in Poe's typical macabre style. Debussy intended to complete the work by May 1905, at which point he hoped it would be taken up by the Opéra-Comique.

The second contract (a provisional one) engaged Debussy to complete Chabrier's opera, *Briséis*; Chabrier had been working on this for many years, but as his health declined, he had been unable to complete it. Only one act was in a finished state. For the remainder (on a text by Catulle Mendès and Ephraïm Mikhaël) there were sketches. D'Indy, a good friend of Chabrier, had originally consented to complete the score but had discovered that there simply was not enough to work with. Although Debussy was fond of Chabrier's music, the idea that he would continue the project seemed odd. *Briséis* may very well be Chabrier's dramatic masterpiece— but Debussy's musical style is far removed from it. Perhaps, like d'Indy, Debussy eventually came to the conclusion that Chabrier's sketches were too meager. For whatever reason, nothing came of the project.

In 1903 the number of performances of Debussy's music continued to grow. That November the *Faune* was given in both the Colonne and Lamoureux series. The German premiere occurred the same month with Ferruccio Busoni conducting the Berlin Philharmonic—the most notable indication that interest in Debussy was moving beyond the borders of France. The following year saw performances of *Estampes* (at the Société Nationale on 9 January and soon elsewhere), the *Damoiselle*, the *Faune*, and the *Nocturnes*. As an additional mark of acceptance Debussy was appointed to the jury that determined the winner of the composition prize sponsored by the city of Paris, the same competition he had considered entering in 1884.

---

33. Letter of 12 September 1903 to Messager in *DL*, p. 141.

The income that was provided by his growing fame was welcome, but the popularity was not. Celebrity was a mixed blessing for Debussy and in many ways unexpected. He wanted to retain some of his anonymity and all of his privacy—and did not, for example, like being recognized in public. The irony of the situation could not have escaped him. For years he had ridiculed composers like Massenet and Charpentier when they were in fashion. Now *he* was in fashion, and, for one who had always distrusted the approval of the masses, it must have been a bit unsettling.

As Debussyism and Debussyists came into existence, he did what he could to distance himself from them. The most disturbing indication of his popularity was a series of articles entitled "Pelléastres" that appeared in January 1904 (published as a book six years later). They were the work of Jean Lorrain, born Paul Alexandre Martin Duval. Lorrain, who was seven years older than Debussy, was a popular writer and critic. There were two sides to his literary skills. His novels—such as *Monsieur de Bougrelon* (1897), and *Le Vice errant* (1902)—exemplified the decadent style. But he was better known as a newspaper critic whose sharp and caustic comments often bordered on defamation.

Lorrain's criticism was intended to be provocative. "What gives meaning to my existence," he boasted, "is the knowledge that I am odious to so many people. It's a delicious pleasure."[34] His diatribes had led to duels, including one with Marcel Proust in 1897. But notoriety sold papers, and Lorrain was the highest paid journalist of his day. Although still widely read, by 1904 his popularity was on the wane. In *Pelléastres* he attacked those who admired Debussy, and by implication Debussy himself. The articles described in detail the "snobs and poseurs" infatuated not just with Debussy's opera but with his music in general.[35]

Over the years Debussy had encountered a good deal of adverse criticism. His usual response was to ignore it. But he took personal offense at what Lorrain had written and asked Louÿs how best to respond. He was advised to do nothing—and to hold any response, should it be needed, for important music critics. It was good advice, but there was cause for Debussy's anger. Lorrain's Debussyists were thrill-seekers, eager for sensation in any form—jaded, pretentious, superficial, and, in some instances, depraved. Debussy ("the leader of a new religion") was represented as seeming to share their ideals.[36] It was a mockery for him to be associated with such a crowd and understandable that he felt a response was needed. But in the end

---

34. Thibaut D'Anthonay, *Jean Lorrain* (Paris: Plon, 1991), p. 55.
35. Jean Lorrain, *Pelléastres* (Paris: Albert Mericant, [1910]), p. 25.
36. Ibid.

he followed Louÿs's advice. He was being baited, and a reply would have only drawn more attention to what Lorrain had written.

During the first half of 1904 Debussy worked neither on *La Mer* nor the Poe opera, but on several short works. The *Trois Chansons de France* was the first set of songs he had written in five years. The poets selected (Charles d'Orléans and Tristan L'Hermite) dated from the fifteenth and seventeenth centuries, respectively, and were an indication of regard for France's heritage similar to that expressed by Debussy in his criticism for *Gil Blas*. He also spent time on incidental music for a proposed performance of *King Lear*, although little was actually completed.

There was a more successful outcome for two dances intended for jury performance at the Brussels Conservatory. Written for the chromatic harp with orchestral accompaniment, the *Deux Danses* are among Debussy's most engaging works and were completed in a short period of time. But their charm and serenity are a reminder of how dangerous it is to interpret a composer's life by his music. At the time he was writing the *Danses*, Debussy's personal life was in turmoil.

The source of the tumult was the dedicatee of the *Trois Chansons de France*: Emma Bardac. She was the same age as Debussy, married to a banker, and "pretty with auburn hair and topaz-colored eyes." She possessed, according to her daughter, "an incomparable charm, to which nobody could remain insensible."[37] There were similarities to Marie Vasnier. Both were sophisticated, wealthy, and part of an elegant society which appreciated the arts. And like Marie Vasnier, Emma Bardac was also a singer. She had inspired Fauré's collection of songs, *La Bonne Chanson*, and for a time had been his mistress.

Debussy had known Emma casually for several years. She was an admirer of his music, and it was probably as a result of her interest that her son, Raoul, had taken some private lessons with Debussy. How their relationship became more intimate is not clear. In the fall of 1903 Debussy made a point of giving her a dedicatory copy of *Estampes*. They began to meet frequently during the first months of 1904.

As late as July everything still had an appearance of normality in the Debussy household. Louis Laloy visited the Debussys for lunch: "I was their only guest, and both laughing made me admire their faience plates that they had caused to crackle in the frying pan in order to imitate the real stoneware."[38] On 15 July Lilly left for Bichain. Debussy told her he would follow in about a month as he had the previous year. But she could only have sensed something was wrong. "You mustn't think I got any pleasure out of putting you so deliberately on the train," Debussy wrote to her. "It was hard for me! Only, for reasons I'll explain to you later, it had to be

37. Dolly Bardac in *DR*, p. 200.

38. *D*, p. 133.

done.... Also, I've got to find something new, otherwise my reputation will suffer; for some time I've been worried because I'm revolving in the same old circle of ideas.... Life has its dangerous turning-points and in my case they're complicated by the fact that I'm both an artist (what a business!) and your husband. Try to understand me and not be resentful."[39]

A few days later he wrote again to his "little Lilly-Lilo," explaining that an artist was a "deplorable husband," but that "a perfect husband often produced a pitiful artist.... It's a vicious circle. You'll say that in that case, one shouldn't marry? How can I reply to such a question, sincerely believing as I have, that I'd be able to make you happy entrusting yourself to me!"[40]

Debussy seemed to be preparing Lilly for a separation, implying that the problem was not with her, but with him—a composer whose "old liaison with Music" made marriage impossible. But despite reservations he may have had about marriage in general, at the root of the situation were specific problems that had developed between himself and Lilly. Debussy had married her attracted by her youth, beauty, charm, and girlishness. It was her vulnerability—that she would be his "dear little wife"—which had appealed to him. As with Gaby, it had never been intended that she would be a "soul mate," one with whom he would share his music.

The same traits that had served as the basis of his attraction became the root of his discontent. He questioned her fragility and lack of support during difficult times, occasions when he had had to "conjure up smiles" to keep things going. He later told her that he had "often tried to put on a bold front against adversity, but a word from you would shatter all."[41] And her natural fondness for domesticity— their neat, little apartment and the routine of their married life—now seemed to be precisely what he did not want. During their divorce proceedings, Debussy accused her of maintaining a "daily tyranny over my thoughts," proof of which he claimed in the reduced number of compositions he had produced during their marriage.[42]

It seems that, more than anything else, Debussy felt stifled and oppressed by their relationship. But he had no idea how to improve it or resolve his predicament. He had never told Lilly how difficult living with her had become. And she knew nothing of his relationship with Emma Bardac.

"Everything about me is instinctive, unreasoned," Debussy once confided to a friend. "I'm not at all master of myself. And then there are times I can do nothing— when I'm before a wall, asking myself if I'm going to jump over it or not."[43] In this

---

39. Letter of 16 July 1904 in *DL*, pp. 147, 148.
40. Letter of 19 July 1904 in *C*, p. 853.
41. Letter of 11 August 1904 in ibid., p. 195.
42. *LS*, p. 189.
43. Conversation of 8 October 1907 in *Segalen et Debussy*, p. 71.

instance, Debussy took the leap. On 30 July he fled with Emma Bardac to Jersey. They soon settled in Pourville, not far from Dieppe.

It was not until mid-August that Debussy wrote to Lilly. He began with a lie— "This letter comes to you from Dieppe where I am staying for a few days prior to leaving for London with J. E. Blanche"—and then he asked her forgiveness for what would follow. He admitted that he should have spoken to her before leaving, but that he had never found the right moment and "perhaps, lacked the courage." "I have the greatest possible affection for you," he wrote, "and that only makes more difficult what I must frankly say to you today. After these days spent far from you— where for the first time I was able to think dispassionately about our life—I am convinced that I have never made you as happy as I should have. . . . I also remember those moments of irritation when you asked me to *give you your freedom.* . . . It is clear that this letter will cause you pain; it has been painful for me to write it. . . . My final request is to ask you to preserve the memory of what we had without mixing into it the narrow and ridiculous opinions of people who have never known love or devotion."[44]

There is no mention in the letter of Emma Bardac, although it was foolish of Debussy to think that she would remain unknown. Instead, he tried to give the impression that his flight had been selfless and generous. Since he had never been able to make Lilly happy, he would set her free. But no matter how unhappy Lilly may have been, the main reason Debussy left her was because *he* was unhappy. With Emma Bardac he seemed to find the happiness that was missing. He may have felt that in writing a letter to Lilly which skirted the issues and avoided the truth he was taking the first step to resolve their problems. All it did was make matters worse.

Debussy's initial reaction to the separation was one of relief. By escaping to Pourville with Emma, he had distanced himself from a problem which, he seemed to think, would soon take care of itself. He wrote to Jacques Durand, telling him not to let anyone know where he was. And he returned to composing in a countryside he described as "delightful; even better I am at peace here, and completely free to work—which hasn't happened to me in a long time."[45]

44. Letter of 11 August 1904 in *C*, pp. 861, 862.
45. Letter of [between 31 July and 4 August 1907] in ibid., p. 859.

CHAPTER SIX

Notoriety and Respectability, 1904–1910

> This life is a hospital where every patient is possessed with the desire to change his bed. This one would prefer to suffer before the stove, and that other thinks that he would recover by the window. It always seems to me that I will be better where I am not, and that question of removal is one that I discuss incessantly with my soul.
>
> Baudelaire, "Anywhere Out of the World"
(1868; translation by Stuart Merrill [1890])

DEBUSSY SEEMED CONVINCED THAT HIS SEPARATION FROM LILLY WOULD BE A simple matter of obtaining a divorce. He never considered how friends and associates might react to his affair with Emma Bardac, nor did he anticipate Lilly's response. In mid-September 1904 he interrupted his stay in Pourville to meet Lilly in Paris. He no longer knew, he told her, "what to do or what to think....More than ever I need tranquility—to the point of wishing I were dead, since, whatever I do, someone will certainly be harmed by it."[1] On 20 September he returned to Paris with Emma, apparently at least for a time living by himself. Negotiations with Lilly became protracted and charged with emotion. She made it clear that she did not want the divorce and pleaded with Debussy to return. On four occasions she threatened to kill herself.

It could not, then, have come as a surprise when on 13 October she attempted suicide. She was rushed to a hospital after having shot herself in the stomach—a severe wound from which recovery was slow. Details of the incident—including Debussy's initial reaction to it—are not known. But many of his friends responded

---

1. Letter to Lilly of 14 September 1904 in *C*, p. 864.

sympathetically to Lilly, some even offering to help pay her medical expenses. Through it all she continued to hope that it would somehow work out, as late as March 1905 proposing a reconciliation to Debussy.

For months, Debussy's marital problems had remained a private affair, though with repercussions in musical circles. Then on 4 November the press assured a wide audience for his troubles:

> The young wife of a distinguished musician—regarded as the leader of the new school and whose recent work, performed at a national theater, was much applauded and discussed—attempted suicide a few days ago. This young woman—whose dark beauty was well known in artistic circles—abandoned herself to despair on learning of the infidelity of her husband. Oppressed by her great sorrow, she tried to starve herself to death, refusing all nourishment. Then she decided to hasten her end by means of a revolver. Wounded by two bullets, she was taken to a clinic in the Rue Bizet. Her condition today is somewhat reassuring. But a divorce is pending. Her husband did not reconsider his original stance, and the hoped-for reconciliation did not take place. The musician in question will marry the young wife (already divorced) of a financier and devotee of the arts equally well-known in Paris.[2]

There was little accuracy in the lurid report: Lilly was not brunette; there was a single gunshot wound; she was not taken to a clinic in the rue Bizet, but one in the rue Blomet, and Emma Bardac was neither young nor "already divorced" (her divorce did not become effective until May 1905). Lilly's hunger strike seemed real enough, but Debussy privately dismissed it as an act. Everything about the article was intended to be sensational. In early January *Le Figaro* erroneously reported that Lilly had tried once again to take her life.

The press coverage turned Debussy's divorce into full-fledged scandal. There was enough to make it juicy gossip, with aspects touching both the artistic world and high society. Debussy always came off poorly—the prominent composer coldly abandoning his young and beautiful wife, ignoring her pleas and suffering, driving her to suicide, and taking solace in the arms of a wealthy socialite. He could only have been horrified at seeing his life become a public spectacle. But there was little he could do about it. There was enough truth in the account for it to stand unchallenged. And Debussy found the whole situation so distasteful that the last thing he wanted was to become further enmeshed in it.

"The nightmare"—as Debussy called it—seemed to come to an end in July 1905: a court-sanctioned resolution that required him to pay monthly alimony of 400 francs.[3] But the disastrous consequences lingered and continued to affect both

2. From *Le Temps*. The *New York Herald* had a similar report. *LS*, p. 265.

3. Letter to Jacques Durand of [8] August 1905 in *DL*, p. 154.

his personal and professional life for years. It created a decisive break with the past—a break which, at least in part, he clearly wanted. But it blackened him in the eyes of many people.

To some, Debussy's liaison with Emma Bardac and abandonment of Lilly provided confirmation of his character: "a dreamer, a sensualist, a voluptuary."[4] "People have said," wrote Paul Dukas, "that he was heartless, an egoist, a trifler with the feelings of others, and Heaven knows what else!"[5]

In his correspondence, Debussy gave two reasons for leaving Lilly: their incompatibility, and his conviction that his creativity was stifled while living with her. But few were aware of his view of the situation. And there were always those who seemed unwilling to accept any explanation, who were convinced that Debussy was a "trifler" and that Lilly was his innocent victim. Adding to it all was the wealth of Emma Bardac's family. One of her uncles was enormously rich. Debussy's relationship with her was seen as merely a ploy to marry money. But when the uncle died in February 1907, most of his wealth was left to charity.[6]

Debussy was aware of all the charges and insinuations—and was hurt by them, particularly when their source was those whom he had believed were his friends. The most steadfast in their support were Louis Laloy and Jacques Durand, but there were many defections. Debussy became unusually sensitive, seeing snubs where none were intended—as when on one occasion he wrote to a friend who in public had failed to greet him, asking if it had been intentional. To Laloy he unburdened himself: "I have seen desertions taking place around me…! Enough to be disgusted forever with anything associated with the human race.…I will not recount what has taken place: it is shabby, tragic and sometimes bears an ironic resemblance to cheap novels.… In the end, it has caused me a great deal of pain. Was there some forgotten debt to life I had to pay? I do not know."[7]

Although Debussy was aware of the depth of the animosity toward him, he was surprised by it and seemed unaware that there might be some justification for it. While it would have been senseless for him to remain in a marriage he felt was preventing him from writing music, he had acted egotistically and precipitately—which was completely in character—and had given little thought to what might be the consequences. His reaction to the incident was also completely in character: "It seems I'm not permitted to have a divorce, like anyone else," he told Durand.[8]

4. Jacques-Emile Blanche in *DR*, p. 109.

5. Ibid., p. 98.

6. Emma was not, as had been assumed, disinherited because of disapproval of her association with Debussy. See *LS*, p. 281.

7. Letter of 14 April 1905 in *C*, p. 900–901.

8. Letter of [31? October 1904] in ibid., pp. 872.

A decade earlier his divorce and affair might have passed without comment. But now that he had become a celebrity, it was certain to attract attention.

Since by society's standards the circumstances were unfavorable to Debussy, it was not easy to defend him. Among his oldest friends, Satie continued his visits. But not Louÿs. He came out strongly in support of Lilly. Writing to his brother about the incident, he began by referring to "poor Mme Debussy" who had been "abandoned by her husband," and expressed his willingness to have her stay at his home during her convalescence.[9] Over the years he and Debussy had drifted apart. They saw one another with less frequency, and there was no longer the rapport they had once had. In the summer of 1903, Debussy had removed a dedication to Louÿs from the second of the *Estampes*. During this time Louÿs was entering a stage in his life which would lead to tragedy—dependency on cocaine and alcohol, followed by physical ills and increasing poverty.

The loss of friends made Debussy bitter and heightened his willingness to distance himself from others. He had never been easy to approach or to know. But after his divorce he became even more remote. This side of him—described variously as a "show of paradox and often sarcastic and unkind irony" and "ill-restrained wrath and irony"—became well known and gave him the reputation of being cantankerous.[10] According to Emile Vuillermoz, "Debussy lived in a kind of haughty misanthropy, behind a rampart of irony, protecting himself fiercely from bores and fools. A triple, barbed ring of defensive paradoxes, biting persiflage and acute mockery kept intruders at a distance."[11]

But the misanthropy was not merely intended to ward off "intruders." It was a barrier, and a test for those whom he might eventually consider for friendship. It had the unfortunate effect of preventing him from knowing some people whom he might have liked: when the young, Hungarian composer, Zoltan Kodály, wanted to meet Debussy in 1909, acquaintances assured him it was a waste of time because he was so unapproachable. But there were at least a few who saw Debussy's behavior for what it was, "an almost incredible shyness which he disguised under a show of paradox and often sarcastic and unkind irony."[12]

The notoriety now associated with Debussy did not hamper his professional reputation. But it was to his advantage that during these years the concert scene in Paris was expanding. New series were being formed, including one sponsored by Jacques Durand. And discontent with what was perceived as the insularity of the

9. *LS*, p. 265. It was, incidentally, an odd stance for Louÿs to adopt. For years he had been having an affair with his wife's sister (married to Henri de Régnier).

10. Reminiscences of Alfredo Casella and Georges Jean-Aubry in *DR*, pp. 97, 121.

11. Ibid., p. 95.

12. Alfredo Casella in ibid., p. 97.

Société Nationale led in 1910 to the creation of the Société Musicale Indépendente (SMI). Gabriel Fauré served as president with the participation of a number of young composers, including Ravel, Vuillermoz, Florent Schmitt, and André Caplet.

Performances of Debussy's piano pieces and songs continued unabated. And the String Quartet—which had become especially popular—was heard regularly. In February 1905 there were premieres of two new piano pieces (*Masques* and *L'Isle joyeuse*), as well as a major orchestral work eight months later: *La Mer*. In April *Pelléas et Mélisande* reappeared at the Opéra-Comique in what was now a regular occurrence. Even the bastions of the Conservatoire were stormed with a performance of the *Faune* in December. As an indication of his prominence, in July Debussy signed an exclusive contract with Jacques Durand, an association similar to the one he had had with Hartmann. Debussy received 25,000 francs for the orchestral score of *Pelléas*, and advances and loans regularly. He and Durand also became good friends, and their correspondence provides many details of Debussy's life during these years.

The amount Durand paid for *Pelléas* was a smart investment. It continued to become increasingly better known, and there were gradually performances outside of France: Brussels and Frankfurt in 1907, and Cologne, Munich, Prague, Berlin, Milan, and New York in 1908. Rome and London staged *Pelléas* in the following year. Reaction was mixed—lukewarm at best in Germany, and hostile in Italy. But the performances in Brussels and London were enthusiastically received. In both latter instances Debussy went to supervise some of the rehearsals, and, in what was to become his usual reaction, was critical of what he found. In Brussels he condemned the singers and orchestra "whose Flemishness is about as flexible as a 100 kg. weight...the woodwind thick and noisy, the brass, on the other hand, stuffed with cotton wool....Added to which they have a disconcerting gift for mangling the simplest rhythm....In short, a constant and utterly exhausting struggle to arrive at something tolerable."[13] In London he complained that he had "to take on the role of electrician, stage-hand—God knows how it will end!...They want to do in a week what would require a month's work....I've done all that I can and my artistic conscience will be clear."[14]

As his fame grew, Debussy found he was even welcomed by musical officialdom. In a surprising move in February 1909 he accepted a position on the Conseil Supérieur at the Conservatoire, his reputation as an iconoclast being secure enough for the appointment to be noted with astonishment by *Le Figaro*. But the Conservatoire, now under the direction of Fauré, was making an attempt at modernization—so the overture to Debussy made sense. He found the

---

13. Letter to Louis Laloy of 23 January 1907 in *DL*, pp. 176–177.
14. Letter to Durand of 18 May 1909 in *C*, p. 1179.

Conservatoire to be "the same gloomy, dirty place" of his youth "where the dust of unhealthy traditions still sticks to the fingers."[15] But he did discover some compensation in the juries he attended, with some fine woodwind players, and, in Guiomar Novaes, a young pianist of distinction. His association also led to the composition of several pieces for the juries.

The increasing number of performances of his work fed the growth of Debussyism. The critic Camille Mauclair was unusual in noting that Debussy was actually "an isolated figure…the exact opposite of the leader of a school of composition."[16] Most critics were eager to associate him with the work of a large number of younger composers, from Florent Schmitt to Déodat de Séverac. It seemed to make no difference to them that their musical styles differed widely.

No composer suffered more from this than Maurice Ravel. In time, both he and Debussy were generally perceived as the embodiment of Impressionism in music, much as Haydn and Mozart have been paired with eighteenth-century Classicism. The label has done a great deal to blind many to the substantial differences in their music.

Debussy and Ravel knew one another and had mixed reactions to each other's work. Ravel was fifteen years younger and had long admired Debussy's music. He prepared at Debussy's direction a piano reduction of the third movement of the *Nocturnes*. And his enthusiasm for *Pelléas* led him to attend all fourteen performances of its first run. Debussy was aware of Ravel's accomplishments. Several of Ravel's most characteristic works date from early in their association: *Jeux d'eau* was composed in 1901, and the String Quartet followed two years later.

The first indication of friction between them occurred in April 1907 when Pierre Lalo published a letter which Ravel had written to him in the previous year. In it Ravel took offense at supposed innovations in Debussy's manner of writing for the piano—noting that they had first appeared in *Jeux d'eau*. Lalo was by this time no supporter of Debussy, and his publication of the letter was obviously intended to stir up trouble. Debussy was annoyed by the remarks, and in private became increasingly critical of Ravel's music: he described the *Histoires naturelles* as "artificial and chimerical," while conceding that "Le Cygne" was "very pretty music."[17]

But what really seemed to anger Debussy was Ravel's assertion that Debussy had actually *stolen* from him, placing in "La Soirée dans Grenade" (one of the piano *Estampes*) a device for the pedal first used in Ravel's "Habanera." The accusation in no way hampered Ravel's continued admiration for much of Debussy's music. But Debussy became increasingly disparaging. Ravel, he concluded, was "extraordinarily

15. Letter to Caplet of 25 November 1909 in *DL*, p. 216.

16. Camille Mauclair, *La Religion de la musique* (Paris: Fischbacher, 1924), p. 268. Written in 1908.

17. Letter to Jacques Durand of 25 February 1907 in *DL*, 177.

gifted, but what annoys me is the attitude he adopts of being a 'conjuror,' or rather a Fakir casting spells and making flowers burst out of chairs."[18] When he heard Ravel perform his *Valses nobles et sentimentales*, Debussy concluded that "a good deal more can be done with that music!"[19]

In keeping with the growing international scope of his fame, the first biography of Debussy was published in 1908 in London by Louise Liebich. The first French biography (written by Laloy) appeared a year later. Both books were brief and included little biographical information. Each was intended more as an appreciation of Debussy's musical style than an in-depth study of his work.

Laloy's book was followed in 1910 by a pamphlet, *The Case of Debussy*. It contained an article, "M. Claude Debussy et le snobisme contemporain" by Raphaël Cor (published the previous year in the *Revue du temps présent*), and the results of a questionnaire about Debussy sent to 100 notables (of whom twenty-nine responded). The booklet was largely unflattering, and the article was highly critical, condemning both Debussy's music and its influence on musical taste. Should anyone at the time have felt smug about Debussy's stature, the pamphlet was confirmation that there remained a contingent adamantly opposed to him. Perplexed by his newest works (especially *La Mer*), some critics who had praised Debussy's earlier work— Pierre Lalo, for example—now became hostile. Convinced that Debussy was leading an entire generation down the wrong path, they were eager to present other French composers as alternatives.

The music of d'Indy was frequently put forth as an antidote. D'Indy held a prominent position in French musical life, both as teacher and composer. His compositions—such as the Second Symphony, op. 57 (1903)—had a strong following and drew on precisely the type of tradition Debussy shunned. But it was simplistic to regard d'Indy and Debussy as being on opposite sides of the fence. D'Indy was not necessarily the traditionalist and conservative that some portrayed him as being. In works such as the *Jour d'été à la montagne,* op. 61 (1905), there are, beyond the "impressionistic" program of the music itself, occasional harmonies as provocative as any by Debussy, and an inventive and subtle handling of the orchestra.

The situation was further complicated by d'Indy's admiration for some of Debussy's music. In frequent demand as a guest conductor, d'Indy made a point of performing Debussy's works, including the *Faune* in Russia and the *Nocturnes* in both Italy and the United States. He also came out in support of *Pelléas*. But starting in 1905 criticism of d'Indy's music from ardent Debussyists such as Vuillermoz set the stage for warfare between the two camps.

18. Letter to Louis Laloy of 8 March 1907 in ibid., p. 178.
19. Reminiscences of Casella in *DR*, p. 97.

Privately, both Debussy and d'Indy could be critical of one another. Debussy felt that the Schola Cantorum (which d'Indy directed) was rigidly dogmatic, and several times he commented on "the mediocrities who run it."[20] But neither d'Indy nor Debussy gave public support to their partisans. The differences between both their compositions and their musical aesthetic were obvious. But in his occasional forays into music criticism Debussy made a point of being fair-handed in his evaluation of d'Indy and unusually generous in his praise. Each respected the another despite reservations about the music. "I love and admire you because of your art," d'Indy once wrote to Debussy—and while the warmth of feeling was never shared by Debussy, he supported d'Indy's artistic integrity.[21]

In addition to d'Indy, at about this time Paul Dukas was put forth as a rival to Debussy. Dukas did not compose a great deal, and his previous works—such as the Symphony (1896) and *The Sorcerer's Apprentice* (1897)—presented few of the modernistic traits of Debussy's music. But the moderate success of his opera *Ariane et Barbe-bleue* (1907) increased his standing. Both it and the piano Variations (1903) were presented by critics as preferable to the "debaucheries" and "exquisite seductions of the Debussyists."[22] He and Debussy had long been friends, but their relationship had taken a turn for the worse following Debussy's divorce. By the time of *Ariane*, they had become amicable once again, but in private Debussy was critical of Dukas's opera and irritated by the attempt to present it as superior to his own work. Fortunately, as had been the case with d'Indy, neither Dukas nor Debussy permitted himself to be drawn into a public debate.

Debussy's detachment from musical politics was characteristic. He showed little interest in politics in general. The major political events of his day—the rise of Boulangerism in France in the late 1880s, the extraordinary scandals associated with the attempt to build the Panama Canal in the 1890s, the confrontation with Germany in Morocco in 1905—all passed without comment. As for the Dreyfus case, indications are that he was pro-Dreyfus. In January 1899 he signed a manifesto (published in *Le Temps*) calling for moderation in the affair. And the *Revue blanche*, for which he had been music critic, was avowedly a Dreyfus supporter. What is clear is that he did not share the opinion of adamant anti-Dreyfusards like d'Indy and Louÿs.

Attacks on Debussy's music and the promotion of d'Indy and Dukas did nothing to stem the tide of Debussyism. But despite Debussy's aversion to the entire concept (and loathing of the supposed existence of a "Debussy School"), the advantage to it lay in the opportunity it presented for him to come into more frequent contact

20. Nina Gubisch, "Le Journal inédit de Ricardo Viñes," *Revue Internationale de Musique Française* 1 (1980), p. 193.

21. Léon Vallas, *Vincent d'Indy. La Maturité, La Vieillesse (1886–1931)* (Paris: Albin Michel, 1950), p. 321.

22. Jean Huré in the *Monde musical* of 15 March 1907 quoted in *LS*, p. 301.

with young composers. Once the preliminaries were over, Debussy could be kindly and helpful. To both Edgard Varèse and Manuel de Falla, Debussy offered advice, encouragement, and even recommendations to publishers. He was, wrote Varèse, "a man of great kindness, intelligence, fastidiousness, and wide culture....He was in his middle forties when I first knew him, I in my early twenties, but he treated me simply as a colleague without the least condescension."[23]

One young composer with whom Debussy became particularly close was André Caplet. In many ways Caplet—both a conductor and a Prix de Rome winner in 1901—became his amanuensis. They first met in October 1907, and Debussy soon developed a high regard for him. Caplet shared with Debussy an interest in literature, especially Poe. And he became helpful in a number of ways. As a conductor, he was able to promote Debussy's music. But he also did not turn away from more routine tasks, such as in the summer of 1909 helping correct the proofs for *Rondes de printemps*, one of the orchestral *Images*.

Debussy also became friendly during these years with the young writer, Victor Segalen. Segalen had long been an admirer of Debussy's music when, in 1906, he took the decisive step of knocking on his door. His purpose was to approach Debussy about collaborating on an opera, Siddartha, based on the life of Buddha. The idea appealed to Debussy, and rather than turning his back on the offer of an unknown author, he considered the concept. It eventually led to work on an opera based not on Buddha, but on the legend of Orpheus. Debussy went through Segalen's text in detail in 1908, but despite his fascination with it, he never wrote any music for it.

As Debussy's fame increased it led to increased demand for his music and countless imitations. Vuillermoz warned that if Debussy did not "decisively retake" leadership of contemporary music, he would discover that "the entire young, parasitic generation which has grown around his work [would produce] music *à la Debussy*...better than himself!"[24] Vuillermoz was also irritated by old works of Debussy which were now presented in new garb—such as Debussy's orchestration of "Jet d'eau" from the *Cinq Poèmes de Baudelaire*. It is obvious that Debussy was doing all he could to use as many of his earlier compositions as possible. In 1907 he worked on *L'Enfant prodigue* for a new edition. That same year saw the first performance of Henri Büsser's orchestration of the *Petite Suite*.

Part of the problem was that during the four years following his break with Lilly, Debussy actually composed little. It comes as no surprise that he found it hard to write music during the stressful time of the divorce. "I feel nostalgia," he confessed

23. Louise Varèse, *Varèse. A Looking-Glass Diary* (New York: Norton, 1972), p. 45.
24. Review of 3 March 1907 in *LS*, p. 289.

to Messager, "for the Claude Debussy who worked so enthusiastically on *Pelléas*— between ourselves, I've not found him since."[25] But during those first months Debussy still managed to complete a fair amount of music for *La Mer*. The comparatively dry period followed. In 1905 he finished the first three *Images* for piano. In the summer of 1906 he worked on *Ibéria* from the orchestral *Images*, but, as he admitted to Durand, he continued "to wallow in the midst of Nothingness."[26] The following year was more fruitful with the completion of the remaining *Images* for piano, and some work on the *Rondes* for the orchestral *Images*. But in 1908 the small set of piano pieces, *Children's Corner*, was the most sizable work he composed. In addition there was his usual involvement with projects, all of which were abortive, including the projected opera with Segalen on Orpheus and one with Gabriel Mourey on the Tristan legend.

With the continued success of *Pelléas*, Debussy's interest in operatic projects never faltered. Despite his involvement with Segalen and Mourey, in the summer of 1908 he began work on another opera, an adaptation of Poe's tale, "The Fall of the House of Usher"—a project that would occupy him off and on for the rest of his life. He even signed a contract with the Metropolitan Opera House in New York, granting them first performance rights (as part of a double bill with *The Devil in the Belfry*). But despite his assurance to Durand that he was "working like a factory," there was not a great deal of music to show for it.[27] These were obviously not the times of plenty that he had hoped would result from his separation from Lilly.

In December 1908 the short scores for both *Ibéria* and *Rondes de printemps* were finally completed. That for *Gigues* followed the next month—and with it the arduous task of creating the orchestral *Images* neared completion. In December 1909 he began work on a rhapsody for clarinet as part of the jury evaluation at the Conservatoire. And that same month saw the beginning of work on the first book of *Préludes* (a set of twelve) for piano, the set being rapidly completed in January 1910. A collection of songs, the *Trois Ballades de François Villon*, followed four months later.

But even with the promotion of student compositions like *L'Enfant prodigue*, Debussy was unable to keep pace with his living expenses. Since his separation from Lilly, he had been living well above his means. He and Emma (including for their first six years together, her daughter Dolly) settled in an aristocratic neighborhood near the Bois de Boulogne. It was a good home for entertaining: elegant and fashionable. Regular visitors included Laloy and Caplet. Satie came frequently for lunch, Toulet for dinner on Thursday. There was a room set aside for Debussy's

25. Letter of 19 September 1904 in *DL*, p. 149.
26. Letter of 18 April 1906 in *C*, p. 951.
27. Letter of 17 July 1907 in *DL*, p. 180.

work located on the ground floor "with spacious bay windows which flooded it with light."[28]

> His study, the "sacred room of the house," was typical of its master. It was not a large or cluttered room, such as one is accustomed to associate with a busy composer. Everything in it was carefully selected and refined. In spite of the fact that he was a man of wide reading, the books in his study did not number more than a hundred or so, and these were only authors that Debussy had chosen as his particular favorites—Rossetti, Maeterlinck, François Villon in an old edition, Mallarmé. There was a small upright piano, in one corner between the light high windows, a desk on which there were several small carved wooden animals, a bowl of beautiful goldfish. The colors of the room were subdued, the furnishings practical. Only a few precious prints and watercolors adorned the walls.[29]

His work table was always in order, with pens ready for use. Prominently in place was a wooden statue of a toad Debussy had named Arkel (after the character in *Pelléas*), and which was regarded as a good-luck charm. There was also a profusion of cut flowers, even during the winter.

The study looked out on what Debussy liked most about his new home: the garden. He had designed it and did some work in it. It was a constant source of inspiration. "On fine days, he walked along a garden path and noted down his musical ideas in a little red leather notebook which never left his pocket."[30] "I can look into my garden," he once told a newspaper interviewer, "and find there everything that I want."[31]

With the exception of 1908 and 1909 (when there was not enough money), Debussy and Emma took vacation trips each summer. These were in many ways essential for him. He needed the change of scene—just as he had welcomed the summer trips to Burgundy while married to Lilly. In 1909 he noted that staying in Paris for the summer necessitated adapting to the noise of "the suburban railway" near his home. His quip—"one doesn't need to hear the song of the nightingale—the song of the trains is much more in tune with modern artistic preoccupations"—shows what he missed.[32] In July 1905 he and Emma visited Eastbourne, and briefly London. Eastbourne (which he described as a "charming, peaceful spot") he enjoyed, but London he found to be "rather dreary."[33] Most of August 1906 they

28. E. Robert Schmitz in *DR*, p. 194.

29. Ibid., p. 168.

30. Dolly Bardac in ibid., p. 199.

31. Interview of 16 May 1909 in David Grayson, "Claude Debussy Addresses the English-Speaking World: Two Interviews, an Article, and *The Blessed Damozel*," *Cahiers Debussy* 16 (1992), p. 24.

32. Letter to Jean-Aubry of 9 September 1909 in *DL*, p. 214.

33. Letters to Durand of 26 July 1905 and to Laloy of 13 September 1905 in ibid., pp. 153, 160.

spent near Dieppe, and August 1907 in Pourville. As always, Debussy loved being near the sea, but he hated the hotel they stayed in and described Pourville as "apart from the sea…an odious place where the people are slightly more ridiculous than elsewhere. My strongest desire is to escape as soon as possible."[34] It was impossible for him to write any music.

Debussy's vacations were intended to provide both a relaxing change of scene and inspiration. Those in 1906 and 1907 failed to provide the stimulus he had hoped for. But at least life at home seemed more agreeable. There were indications of his attachment to Emma, who, unlike Lilly, became associated with several of his works. His term of endearment for her was "chère petite mienne" (my own little dear), often abbreviated "p.m." It found its way into the completed draft of *La Mer* (5 March 1905): "for my own little dear whose eyes laugh in the shadows."[35] For *Fêtes galantes* he asked Durand to include a "slightly mysterious" dedication: "In gratitude for the month of June 1904, followed by the letters, A.l.p.M."[36] The letters were an abbreviation for "à la petite mienne," the date a reference to their declaration of love.

Debussy also gave Emma little piano pieces as gifts on her birthday and Christmas (including one with a humorous commentary on its seventh and ninth chords). But what provided the strongest of bonds to their relationship was the birth on 30 October 1905 of a daughter, Claude-Emma. She was soon nicknamed Chouchou (Darling), and Debussy's attachment to her and enchantment with her could not have been greater. Fatherhood added a new dimension to his life. "Let me wish you happiness on the birth of your little daughter," Debussy wrote to Varèse. "You will see how much more beautiful this is than a symphony and that the caress of a child of one's own is better than glory."[37]

But despite his joy at being a father, Debussy's reservations concerning marriage persisted. "Calm does not inhabit my soul," he wrote to Laloy in the autumn of 1907. "Is it the fault of the feverish landscape in this part of Paris…? Is it because I am definitely not made for domestic life?"[38] There is no more substantial proof of this ambivalence than his reluctance to marry again. Debussy and Emma had been living together for nearly three and a half years before they were married on 20 January 1908. More than six years later Debussy reiterated his conviction that— despite the love he had for his family—"an artist needs to be as free as possible

34. Letter to Victor Segalen of 26 August 1907 in ibid., p. 183.

35. *D*, p. 137.

36. Letter of [between 31 July and 4 August 1904] in *C*, p. 859.

37. Letter of [23 October 1910] in Varèse, *Diary*, p. 91.

38. Letter of 15 October 1907 in *C*, p. 1036.

in life."[39] He feared domestication. And judging from a formal portrait of himself and Emma taken in 1912 in which Debussy appears as an uneasy embodiment of bourgeois contentment, there was justification for his concern.

Adding to Debussy's apprehension was the cost of maintaining "domestic life." He was earning far more money now than he had in the past—both because of more performances and because of his association with Durand. At a time when 90 percent of the population in France earned less than 2,500 francs per year, he received 25,000 francs for the orchestral score of *Pelléas* alone.

In 1906 in Paris a member of the middle class earned from 4,000 to 5,000 francs per year. A doctor earned 14,000.[40] But Debussy discovered that it was necessary to earn far more to maintain the type of household—including servants—associated with his new lifestyle. His annual rent was 8,000 francs. Servants cost an additional 2,000. With food, clothing, and miscellaneous expenses, he would probably have needed at least 20,000 francs yearly.[41] Despite substantial advances from Durand, he was consistently short.

From 1907 to 1914, Debussy received on average about 16,000 francs per year from Durand. His average deficit during these years exceeded 28,000 francs—and at his death he owed Durand more than 66,000 francs.[42] Some additional income was provided by Emma who had inherited a 5,000-franc annuity from her uncle, Daniel Osiris. But maintaining a sufficient income became a losing battle to Debussy. "Whatever ingenious plans I invent," he wrote to Durand, "I always end up 3,000 francs short, and even by selling my soul to the devil I don't know where I shall find them."[43] In 1912 Debussy asked Laloy if he knew anyone willing to lend him 20,000 francs as quickly as possible. He was even willing to pay 5,000 or 6,000 francs interest on the loan.

It has generally been assumed that Debussy's predicament was his own fault—that it was "his craving for luxury and his extravagance" that led to the need for more money.[44] But although Debussy was the first to admit that he managed money poorly, the life that he was leading with Emma was one that she had always had and expected to continue. Debussy obviously enjoyed aspects of this new lifestyle. But

39. François Lesure, "Une Interview romaine de Debussy (février 1914)," *Cahiers Debussy* 11 (1987), p. 7.

40. Jacques Chastenet, *Histoire de la Troisième République. Jours inquiets et jours sanglantes. 1906–1918* (Paris: Hachette, 1955), pp. 157–158.

41. Christophe Charle, "Debussy in Fin-de-Siècle Paris," in *Debussy and His World*, ed. Jane Fulcher (Princeton, NJ: Princeton University Press, 2001), p. 287.

42. Ibid., pp. 288, 289.

43. Letter of 19 July 1911 in *DL*, p. 244.

44. Léon Vallas, *Claude Debussy. His Life and Works* (Oxford: Oxford, 1933), p. 242.

the costs of maintaining it became a frightful burden for him, and, more than once, he considered moving elsewhere to save money.

The need for more money was the primary reason Debussy decided to start conducting his own music. Earlier in his career he had shown little interest in it, turning down the chance to conduct *La Damoiselle élue* for Colonne in December 1902, and an offer in August 1906 from the London Philharmonic. But conducting paid well, and on 12 January 1908 Debussy made his debut with *La Mer*. It was because of the challenges it presented that he received the offer. Colonne had been scheduled, but rehearsals had gone poorly and Debussy was cautiously approached. Chevillard had also had problems with the score for the premiere in 1905, resulting in a performance barely satisfactory. "The man should have been a wild beast tamer," Debussy concluded. "There is clearly so little of the artist in him."[45]

La Mer is filled with challenge for a conductor, and Debussy was nervous about accepting the offer. But despite his "furiously beating heart," rehearsals went well. "It's the first time I've tried my hand at orchestral conducting," he commented, "and certainly I bring to the task a candid inexperience which ought to disarm those curious beasts called 'orchestral musicians.'"[46] Audience response was enthusiastic—not because of his conducting skills but because of the opportunity it presented to pay homage to the composer. Debussy was called back on stage nearly a dozen times to clamorous applause. But the incident did not lead to a swelled head. "It is entertaining to search for orchestral color by means of a little baton," he concluded, "but it resembles an exhibition—and the success awaiting you isn't all that different from an illusionist, or an acrobat who has completed a dangerous leap."[47]

The following month Debussy conducted *La Mer* and the *Faune* in London for a high fee. In February 1909 there was a return engagement, this time for the *Faune* and the *Nocturnes*. Thus far fortune had favored him. In London the orchestra had even rehearsed the pieces prior to his arrival. But during the performance of "Fêtes" he made a mistake during a tempo change, and tried to get the orchestra to stop. It did not—and the performance continued without a hitch.

Debussy never wanted to conduct and never enjoyed it. "I am ill before, during and after!" he admitted.[48] Nerves were obviously a factor, but there was no sign of them on stage. He appeared calm and collected—if anything, too much so. It soon became evident to musicians that his conducting skills were limited and that he was content—like many composers before and since—to go through the paces, though at times it must have felt like walking through a minefield.

45. Letter to Durand of 10 October 1905 in *C*, p. 925.

46. Letter to Segalen of 15 January 1908 in *DL*, p. 186.

47. Letter to Paul-Jean Toulet of 22 January 1908 in *C*, p. 1061.

48. Reminiscences of Casella in *DR*, p. 96.

What bothered Debussy more than the conducting itself was the time it consumed. Conducting and writing music criticism were both activities that took him away from what he wanted to do: write music. But in the end, it made little difference how successful his compositions were. Composing simply did not bring in enough money to maintain the fashionable lifestyle he had adopted. He had assumed that with success his life would become both more productive and more manageable. Instead the need for additional income was as much of a burden as it had ever been. At times he longed for the old days: "for the Claude Debussy who worked so enthusiastically on *Pelléas*"—a time when life seemed less complicated, and when achieving a measure of recognition seemed to be the solution to all of his problems.

CHAPTER SEVEN

The Final Years, 1910–1918

The higher civilization rises, the more vile man becomes.
General Karl von Einem, Commander, German
Third Army, April 1915

DEBUSSY TURNED FIFTY IN 1912—THE SAME YEAR IN WHICH THE ONE hundredth performance of *Pelléas* was celebrated. A decade had passed since its premiere, and during those years his fame had continued to grow. But he now seemed more driven than ever, not because of ambition unsatisfied, but because of growing debt. As it mounted, he desperately asked for 6,000 francs from Durand. "It hasn't been a question of 'advances' between us for a long time!" he admitted. "But I no longer know what to do."[1]

It was the lack of money that led to his eagerness to take on more substantial—and better paying—projects. In September 1910 Debussy was asked to compose music for an unusual ballet. *Khamma* had a fanciful Egyptian scenario and was being commissioned by Maud Allan, a dancer who (like Loïe Fuller and Isadora Duncan) was known for her provocative performances. The commission, Debussy confessed, had been accepted for "reasons of domestic economy."[2] He would soon discover that this was one project it would have been better to avoid.

Maud Allan (1873–1956), a Canadian who had settled in San Francisco, was gifted musically, but not until in her early twenties did she decide to try music as a profession. In 1895 she traveled to Berlin to study, and six years later entered the master piano class of Ferruccio Busoni. Busoni was one of the finest pianists of the

1. Letter of 3 September 1913 in *C*, p. 1662.
2. Letter to Godet of 6 February 1911 in *DL*, p. 235.

day, but his students varied widely in their ability. Entry to the master classes (for which there was no charge) often seemed capricious.

Allan never drew on her music study to make a career as a pianist. Instead, despite having no formal training in dance, she began to experiment with the possibilities of applying natural and spontaneous movements to popular pieces like Mendelssohn's "Spring Song." Busoni and others were impressed and offered encouragement. It led to Allan's dancing debut in Vienna in 1903, followed by successful appearances a year later in Paris and London.

Her signature piece became *The Vision of Salomé* (with music by Marcel Rémy)—a subject whose mixture of morbidity and sexuality contemporary audiences seemed to find irresistible. There were expressions of concern over supposed nudity and indecency in the production, but extraordinary praise as well. It was, concluded one London critic, "a reincarnation of the most graceful and rhythmic forms of classic Greece . . . music turned into moving sculpture."[3]

Allan remained in London for nearly a year and a half—the time of her greatest triumphs. But she soon realized that to maintain a measure of novelty she needed to expand her repertoire. Commissioning a new piece from Debussy seemed a certain means of attracting publicity. And he could only have been dazzled by the amount he was offered: 20,000 francs, with an advance of 10,000.

Many of the problems that grew out of the project resulted from the ambiguity of the contract. Despite his exclusive association with Durand, the firm was not consulted (Debussy may have hoped to avoid paying any commission). But had Durand's staff been involved, the contract would have been far more precise: omitted from it were essential matters, such as the length of the score and the size of the orchestra.

Disagreements between Debussy and Allan soon developed, and Durand was finally contacted in desperation in April 1912 to rewrite the contract. He provided an accurate and detailed transcription of the original, but Allan wanted more. She demanded that the score not be published until she performed it. And she felt that the music (at that stage completed in piano score) was too short. There were other concerns. Why, she wondered, had the work not been dedicated to her?

The matter of dedication was the easiest for Debussy to solve (he dedicated it to no one). But her proposed alteration of the score created an impasse. When Debussy refused to comply, Allan responded with a mixture of wheedling and threats: "I am sure both you and Mons. Durand would be the last persons to wish me to feel unhappy with the result of our labors. Of course, if you will not lengthen and revise it in parts I shall be compelled to have this done by another. . . . This, however, would

3. In the *Observer* (March 1908) quoted in Felix Cherniavsky, *The Salomé Dancer. The Life and Times of Maud Allan* (Toronto: McClelland and Stewart, 1991), p. 164.

not be in keeping with either your or my artistic ideas, therefore, I see only one way out and that is for you to realize the position I am in and how very much it means to me and *be kind* and do as I ask you."⁴ Allan was nothing if not persistent, and the project was to drag on for years with continued attempts at resolution.

In addition to *Khamma,* the autumn of 1910 saw the birth of another major project, one more flattering to Debussy, but equally hair-raising in its effect. In late November Debussy received an effusive letter from the Italian writer, Gabriele d'Annunzio, asking whether Debussy "loved" his poetry and announcing that he wanted to work with him on a "long-meditated Mystery."⁵ The letter was the initial step in a calculated campaign. D'Annunzio spared no effort to captivate Debussy, as well as his family and friends. In the end Debussy became involved in a hybrid project that seemed destined at best for limited success.

Although little remembered today, d'Annunzio was one of the major literary figures of the time. He was very highly regarded in France where, for over a decade, translations of his work had appeared soon after their publication in Italy. In novels like *Il piacere* (*The Child of Pleasure*, 1889), and *Il fuoco* (*The Flame of Life*, 1900; serialized that May in the *Revue de Paris*), d'Annunzio became known for his decadent tone and scandalous content—with murder, madness, and eroticism as recurring themes. His dramas—written for the greatest actresses of the day such as Sarah Bernhardt and Eleonora Duse (d'Annunzio's mistress for eight years)—had been less successful. But while that did not bode well for his work with Debussy, his well-publicized love affairs and extravagant tastes assured d'Annunzio of the type of celebrity that attracted audiences.

D'Annunzio arrived in Paris in March 1910 to flee his creditors. He soon became the darling of fashionable society—including the Rothchilds and Countess Greffulhe—and for months was a frequent item in newspapers. Although the two men had friends in common like Gabriel Mourey and Count Primoli, d'Annunzio's social circles were not Debussy's, and there was no contact between them. Debussy's knowledge of and reaction to d'Annunzio is not known. But it would have been impossible for him not to take notice of his arrival in France.

By 1910 much of d'Annunzio's writing seemed out of fashion, heavily indebted to Symbolist and Decadent themes that had been popular decades earlier. But Debussy had never been associated with a writer so widely known, and when d'Annunzio approached him he probably felt that d'Annunzio's celebrity in itself was an indication of the probable success of their collaboration. "The thought of working with you," he quickly responded, "gives me a kind of fever in advance."⁶

4. Letter of 26 June 1912 in *C*, p. 1524. In English.
5. Letter of 25 November 1910 in ibid., p. 1335.
6. Letter of 30 November 1910 in ibid., p. 1339.

Debussy's enthusiasm would have been dampened had he known that a number of other composers had been considered for the project before him, including Schmitt, Roger-Ducasse, and Henry Février.

D'Annunzio favored flamboyance—in their correspondence Debussy soon became "O Claude roi" and "Claude de France." But Debussy took it in stride, admitting annoyance with the relationship only "now and then."[7] Through it all he maintained a positive attitude. After text and music were completed, a more relaxed and genuine relationship emerged between the two.

Debussy soon discovered that d'Annunzio's "long-meditated Mystery" was a free adaptation of episodes from the life of St. Sebastian. Rather than a drama, ballet, or an opera, the work was an unpredictable mixture of them all, intended to show-case the dancer Ida Rubinstein (who would portray the saint). Debussy offered no criticism of the premise, and both the bizarrely androgynous casting and its religious association seemed to intrigue him: "the cult of Adonis is connected with that of Jesus, which is very beautiful."[8]

The horrific martyrdom of St. Sebastian (bound to a tree, his body was riddled with arrows) was, like Salomé, a theme dear to Symbolism. It had become an obses-sion for d'Annunzio. He traced the source of his fascination to one of his mistresses who, after a session of lovemaking, observed that d'Annunzio's body was "speckled with violent kisses" in a manner resembling the saint's fatal wounds.[9]

D'Annunzio's goal for his *Martyrdom* was to produce a spectacle focusing on the clash between pagans and Christians in the first century. He conducted research in the Bibliothèque Nationale, and, despite having limited knowledge of the language, decided to write in French in order to circumvent any rights of his Italian publisher. He also benefited from the help of friends, including the poet and socialite, Robert de Montesquiou. Montesquiou—who had served as the primary model for the eccentric hero of Huysmans's *Against Nature*—was also a good friend of Ida Rubinstein, and he was eager to assist in the project.

For d'Annunzio, the participation of Ida Rubinstein was essential. She, too, was a flamboyant personality. Born in Russia to wealth and privilege, her exotic and singular beauty had attracted extraordinary attention in Paris, this despite her hav-ing only minor roles in the Ballets Russes productions of *Cléopâtre* (June 1909) and *Schéhérazade* (June 1910). Like Maud Allan, she had had no formal training in dance and relied on her skills as an actress and mime. D'Annunzio was convinced that she would create the ideal St. Sebastian.

7. Claude Debussy, *Lettres de Claude Debussy à sa femme, Emma*, ed. Pasteur Vallery-Radot (Paris: Flammarion, 1957), p. 48.

8. Letter to Godet of 6 February 1911 in *C*, p. 1384.

9. John Woodhouse, *Gabriele D'Annunzio. Defiant Archangel* (Oxford: Clarendon Press, 1998), p. 56.

Debussy was well paid for his part in the project. The contract, signed on 9 December, assured him 20,000 francs (with an immediate advance of 8,000), as well as a percentage from performances. He was optimistic, but admitted to Caplet that he "perhaps still had time to indulge in a folly, even to . . . make a mistake."[10]

It was just as well that Debussy had few illusions about the project. He had yet to see a word of d'Annunzio's text. And the premiere was scheduled for May. "They say some composers can write regularly, so much music a day," Debussy once said in an interview. "I admit I cannot comprehend it."[11] Yet that was precisely what he would have to do to complete *Le Martyre de Saint Sébastien* in time.

The text began to arrive bit by bit in mid-January. Debussy, adopting the style of d'Annunzio, praised the "ever-burgeoning splendor" of the work.[12] The text, he claimed, was "so lofty and other-worldly, the music is very difficult to find."[13] But the rushed pace became too much. Panic set in, and Debussy eventually called in Caplet to help with the orchestration. Without his assistance, it would have been an impossible task: rehearsals actually started in April—even before all the orchestration was finished.

The production was expected to be spectacular and attracted a good deal of attention. Less than a week before the premiere, what was perceived as the sacrilegious nature of d'Annunzio's Mystery led to it being denounced by the Archbishop of Paris. For d'Annunzio—who believed that all publicity was good publicity—it provided an opportunity to heighten the controversy and increase ticket sales. Rather than offering a detailed defense, he and Debussy countered by describing their work as "profoundly religious."[14]

The premiere on 22 May perplexed both public and critics. A mixture of drama and ballet more than four hours in length seemed to test the patience of everyone. There was praise for the exotic scenery created by Léon Bakst, but broad criticism of Ida Rubinstein's strong Russian accent. Many found the text pretentious; some found it vulgar. And devotees of Debussy's music complained that there was less than an hour of it scattered throughout the work. Eagerly anticipated, the *Martyre* was regarded as a disappointment, and it had only ten performances.

D'Annunzio appeared satisfied nonetheless. For years, he continued to mention to Debussy the possibility of another collaboration. That nothing came of it was just

10. Letter of 14 February 1911 in *C*, p. 1392.

11. *New York Times* interview of 26 June 1910 in David Grayson, "Claude Debussy Addresses the English-Speaking World: Two Interviews, an Article, and *The Blessed Damozel*," *Cahiers Debussy* 16 (1992), p. 26.

12. Letter to d'Annunzio of 29 January 1911 in *DL*, p. 233.

13. Letter to d'Annunzio of [20 February 1911] in *C*, p. 1396.

14. *LS*, p. 340.

as well. Two other d'Annunzian extravaganzas were similarly unsuccessful: *La Parisina* (1913) with music by Mascagni, and *La Pisanelle ou la mort parfumée* (1913) with music by Ildebrando Pizzetti (and Ida Rubinstein in the title role).

Complementing his involvement with *Khamma* and the *Martyre*, Debussy continued to work as a guest conductor in major European cities. In late November 1910 he appeared on the podium in Vienna, scheduled to conduct a lengthy program, including the *Petite Suite*, the *Faune*, the *Nocturnes*, *La Mer*, and *Ibéria*. But he was hampered by both lack of rehearsal time and the awkwardness of having his instructions to the orchestra transmitted by an interpreter. It was a challenge, and Debussy joked with Emma that "with these 'brutes,' it's like being an animal trainer in a cage of wild beasts. He can't take his eyes off them or he's 'done for.'"[15] Perhaps he gained in the process some sympathy for Chevillard, whom he had criticized in nearly identical words five years earlier. In the end, it was necessary to cut both *La Mer* and the *Nocturnes*, but Debussy was enthused by what he described as a "stunning" performance of *Ibéria* ("I've never heard it like that before").[16] Vienna was followed by three days in Budapest (from 3 to 6 December). There he was not called upon to conduct but to perform as pianist—including *Estampes* and *Children's Corner*—and serve as accompanist for the *Proses lyriques*.

In the following year, the major conducting trip was in June to Turin where, as part of a series of concerts associated with an international exposition, Debussy conducted the *Faune* and *Ibéria* in addition to short works by Chabrier, Dukas, and Roger-Ducasse. Accompanied by Emma and Chouchou, it was intended to be more in the nature of a diversion. But it turned out to be a disaster. All of his short-comings as a conductor were revealed. Fortunately, the young conductor Vittorio Gui assumed direction of rehearsals, and when Debussy conducted the performance, all went well. Gui's assessment of Debussy as a conductor was damning: "His beat was uncertain, his head was always buried in the scores (and it was his own music!), he lacked control over others and over himself, and even turned over the pages of the score with the hand that held the baton!...He conducted as best as he could, woodenly, mechanically, without fire and without really leading his forces; no calamities, but no poetic feeling."[17] Debussy would hardly have endorsed Gui's evaluation of his skills as a conductor, but he would have admitted that conducting was never more than a job, and, as he once put it, was intended "to win the approval of an audience made up for the most part of idiots."[18]

---

15. Letter to Emma of 2 December 1910 in *C*, p. 1342.
16. Letter to Emma of 3 December 1910 in *DL*, p. 229.
17. *DR*, pp. 226, 229.
18. Letter to Emma of 2 December 1910 in *DL*, p. 228.

Debussy's experience in Turin had been exhausting, and on his return his physician advised rest. August was spent in Houlgate, not far from Pourville. But as always, while he found the sea and nature restful, Debussy was annoyed by the crowds and their noise. "I'm doing precisely nothing," he wrote to Caplet, "not out of idleness but because it's impossible to think amid this caravanserai."[19]

That October Debussy gave serious consideration to traveling to the United States where he was becoming better known. There was already the contract with the Met for the Poe operas. Now he received an invitation to conduct *Pelléas* at the Boston Opera House, where Caplet was conductor and where in 1909 *Pelléas* had already been given. The new performance was to be a model one, and Debussy was excited by it.

Some attraction for the trip seemed to be provided by the opportunity to spend time away from Emma. Married life continued to be a trial for Debussy. Unlike Lilly, Emma was a talented musician, and in marrying her perhaps he had hoped to share more of his artistic interests. But the real problem was Debussy's worldview—overwhelmingly self-centered, and, as he himself admitted, often at war not merely with convention, but with reality. "Those around me persist in not understanding that I have never been able to live in a real world of people and things," he told Durand. "And that is why I have this irrefutable need to escape and become involved in adventures which seem inexplicable because they involve a man no one recognizes. And perhaps that is what is best in me! Besides, an artist by definition is a man accustomed to dreams and who lives among phantoms. . . . How could it be expected that this same person would be able to follow in his daily life the strict observance of traditions—laws and other barriers erected by a hypocritical and cowardly world."[20]

This stance deeply affected his relationships and his work as a composer. It was, he felt, essential to "suppress what devours the best of our thought in order to reach a point where we only love ourselves with a fierce scrupulousness. But it is the opposite which happens: first a family—which clutters and obstructs the way, either with too much kindness or by providing blind serenity. Then come the Mistresses or the Mistress (with whom one hardly reckons), too happy to lose oneself in oblivion."[21]

The situation was not helped by Emma's reaction to Debussy's proposed trip to Boston. She strongly opposed it. "You know what a horror I have of contradiction?" he wrote to Caplet. "And I imagined the natural thing would have been to support me as lovingly as possible! The thought of describing to you the continual arguments

19. Letter of 15 August 1911 in ibid., p. 246.
20. Letter of 8 July 1910 in *C*, p. 1299.
21. Letter to Caplet of 22 December 1911 in ibid., p. 1473.

and battles was so painful, I've put off writing to you as long as possible!...Frankly, I'm extremely depressed."[22] At one point Debussy felt he was at "a dangerous turning point," and a separation was considered.[23] He and Emma discussed it, and she went so far as to contact an attorney.

To Debussy, married life could be a numbing experience. Near the end of their stay at Houlgate, he wrote to Durand: "The truth is that we have to admit we don't know why we came. Is it really that we've lost the ability to enjoy things together? I don't know. But apart from the air we're breathing, which human industry hasn't been able to do anything about, everything else is less than mediocre."[24] The latter half of 1911 was a low point in Debussy's marriage. In later years, although friction continued, the bond between him and Emma seemed much stronger.

His love for their daughter, Chouchou, added another dimension to marriage. "Chouchou's smile helps me through some of the darker moments," he confessed to Godet.[25] To those who saw them together, the depth of his love for her was obvious: "she was the center around which his affections revolved and everything else in his life was subordinated to this dominating emotion."[26]

He took extraordinary interest in her development, watched as she learned to play the piano, and was amused by her childish attempts at writing music. There was a striking physical resemblance between the two. And their temperaments were alike as well: strong-willed, independent, sensitive, and gifted. All of Debussy's friends were charmed by her. The extent of his own attachment can be seen not just in the music she inspired—*Children's Corner*, for example—but in his willingness to immerse himself in her world, such as in the following series of postcards he sent to her while visiting Vienna in 1910:

1. Once there was a papa who lived in exile…
2. and every day he missed his little Chouchou.
3. The inhabitants of the city saw him walking past and murmured 'Why does that gentleman look so sad in our gay and beautiful city?'
5. So Chouchou's father went into a shop run by an old, very ugly man and his even uglier daughter; he politely removed his hat and using deaf-mute gestures asked for the most beautiful postcards they had, so that he could write to his darling little

22. Letter of [17 November 1911] in *DL*, p. 247.
23. Letter to Caplet of 23 March 1910 in *C*, p. 1259.
24. Letter of 26 August 1911 in *DL*, p. 246.
25. Letter of 18 December 1911 in ibid., p. 250.
26. Maggie Teyte in *DR*, p. 150.

daughter.... The ugly old man was very moved by this and as for his daughter, she died on the spot!

6. The said papa went back to his hotel, wrote this story which would make a goldfish weep, and put all his love into the signature below, which is his greatest claim to fame.

LepapadeChouchou[27]

The difficulties with Emma and cancellation of the trip to Boston were only part of the reason for Debussy's depression. First, there had been the less than positive public and critical response to the *Martyre*. And then, after all the effort it had involved, Debussy had been able to compose little. Work on the Poe operas was stagnant. "Everything is as dull as a hole in the ground," he wrote.[28]

It was not until the first half of 1912 that he became more involved with music with a return to *Khamma*. Although he knew that the complications with Maud Allan lowered expectations for a performance soon, he remained hopeful of becoming involved in a project that could be both financially and artistically rewarding.

The most likely source for work of that type seemed to be the Ballets Russes directed by Serge Diaghilev. Since their first productions in Paris in 1909, they had been phenomenally popular, much of it a result of Diaghilev's sharp business and artistic sense. He excelled in providing novelty.

Diaghilev had first made a name for himself as founder and editor of the journal *Mir Iskusstva* (The World of Art, 1898–1904). Its success was due in part to his comprehensive knowledge of contemporary art, literature, dance, and music. In 1908 he had staged Musorgsky's *Boris Godunov* in Paris. It became the hit of the season and led in the following year to performances of excerpts from Glinka's operas, as well as ballets to music by Borodin and Rimsky-Korsakov.

There was much about Diaghilev's productions that enthralled French audiences, but one of the major attractions was their exoticism. Much of the music was new and novel, and the subject matter was colorful and distinctive. Originality was heightened by the astonishingly gifted group Diaghilev had assembled. His dancers were superb, especially Vaslav Nijinsky. Michel Fokine, an admirer of Isadora Duncan, was the primary choreographer. Fokine's ballets were distinctive, innovative, and frequently inspired by Russian folklore. The ballets themselves were complemented by extraordinarily bold and colorful scenery (exemplified by the work of Bakst).

27. The text has been written on six postcards (the fourth is missing) which depict "Austrian soldiers in a variety of humorous situations." *DL*, p. 229.

28. Letter to Caplet of 22 December 1911 in ibid., p. 252.

Debussy had been the first French composer of note approached by Diaghilev to write for the Ballets Russes. He had been asked to prepare a score for the 1910 season on a scenario set in eighteenth-century Venice (*Masques et bergamasques*). Although Debussy, unlike most of Paris, had been far from enthusiastic about the performances of the Ballets Russes, this topic—with possible echoes of Verlaine and the commedia dell'arte—was of interest to him. He wrote the scenario himself (in the process angering Laloy who thought that he was going to collaborate on it), but did not write any music—probably because of his preoccupation with the Maud Allan and d'Annunzio projects.

The phenomenal success of the Ballets Russes continued with Stravinsky's *Firebird* (1910) and *Petroushka* (1911). For the 1912 season Diaghilev decided to produce a ballet using the *Prelude to the Afternoon of a Faun*. Instead of Fokine, Nijinsky was assigned to be the choreographer, his debut in this role. Using the images on Greek vases as an inspiration, Nijinsky created gestures deliberately stiff and angular. In striking contrast to Debussy's fluid and graceful score, "dancers moved in grooves across the stage, feet parallel, hips and faces toward the wings and upper bodies twisted toward the audience."[29] Debussy was horrified. He felt the dancers resembled "puppets" or "cardboard figures."[30] Adding to his disgust was the conclusion of the ballet where Nijinsky (as the faun) appeared to simulate orgasm.

But despite his dissatisfaction with the production, what reservations Debussy may have had about the Ballet Russes were overcome by financial need. On 18 June 1912 he signed a contract to compose music for a new ballet, *Jeux*. Its ambiguous scenario (by Nijinksy) was based on the search for a lost tennis ball. Debussy was to receive 10,000 francs for it, providing the piano score by the end of August, and the orchestral score by the end of March 1913. By Debussy's standards, it was going to be quick work—but at least at a slower pace than that for the *Martyre*. Debussy responded to the challenge, and completed *Jeux* within the guidelines.

Plans for the usual vacation by the sea were abandoned in 1912 and 1913. There simply was not enough money. In November 1912 Debussy even took up a short stint as music critic (at 500 francs per article) for *S.I.M* (*Société Internationale de Musique*), a journal more scholarly in tone and edited by Vuillermoz. He acquired additional income by conducting, including on 26 January 1913 the premiere of all of the orchestral *Images* (in the Colonne series), and *Ibéria* on 15 and 22 October (part of the short-lived Nouveaux Concerts aux Champs-Elysées).

29. Stephanie Jordan, "Debussy, the Dance, and the *Faune*," in James R. Briscoe, ed., *Debussy in Performance* (New Haven, CT: Yale University Press, 1999), p. 126.

30. François Lesure, "Une Interview romaine de Debussy (février 1914)," *Cahiers Debussy* 11 (1987), p. 5.

Despite his dislike of conducting, Debussy knew that he could substantially supplement his income by conducting more extensively outside of France. That led in 1913 to his acceptance of an offer from Serge Koussevitzky to visit Russia.[31] Koussevitzky had begun his career as a virtuoso double bassist and had traveled widely, appearing in 1908 as soloist with the Colonne orchestra. But his ambition lay in conducting and promoting new music, directions he was able to pursue thanks to the wealth of his wife's family. In 1909 he founded a publishing firm, the Editions Russes de Musique, and became a strong advocate for the music of Scriabin. That spring he appeared as guest conductor of the Colonne orchestra and in the autumn inaugurated a series of concerts in Moscow and St. Petersburg with his own orchestra. He hired the services of well-known performers—such as violinist, Fritz Kreisler— and made a point of including the works of contemporary composers in his programs. In 1910 he toured on the Volga, an ambitious attempt to bring music to many who had never before had the opportunity to hear an orchestra.

Although Debussy had mixed feelings about traveling to Russia, Koussevitzky did all he could to make it a success. He was a gracious host, and Debussy spent the first half of December in Russia as his houseguest. There were visits to both Moscow and St. Petersburg where he conducted staples such as *La Mer*, the first two of the *Nocturnes*, and the *Faune*. There was also time to meet with Diaghilev to discuss progress with *Jeux*.

The trip went well. Debussy was not unknown in Russia (among other works, the first two *Nocturnes* had been performed in Moscow in 1910), but there had been a mixed reaction to his music, with more old-fashioned musicians, such as Rimsky-Korsakov, expressing disfavor. During the visit, there was some criticism of his conducting: "In his performance there is not even a shade of temperament. Evidently he is pleased if he has not missed a bar or waved his baton an extra quarter."[32] But Debussy had nothing but praise for Koussevitzky's orchestra and could only have been moved by the testimonial of a group of Russian musicians presented to the "illustrious master" shortly before his departure.[33]

Debussy was missed at home, and that led to a testy exchange with Emma on a sensitive topic. "I have returned from rehearsal," Debussy wrote to her from Moscow, "and in great haste want to tell you that I love you, that you are my perfect *petite mienne*, and that nonetheless I feel wretched. Do you realize that you wrote: 'I don't

---

31. Prior to accepting Koussevitzky's offer, Debussy had agreed to perform with another Russian concert series, the Concerts Siloti. Alexander Siloti had performed Debussy's music and been a supporter. But Koussevitzky's payment was higher, and that was the determining factor for Debussy.

32. Vicot Walter in the *Russian Musical Gazette* in Moses Smith, *Koussevitzky* (New York: Allen, Towne, and Heath, 1947), p. 70.

33. *LS*, p. 373.

know how I will not bear a grudge against your music'? Don't you think that's enough to be a bit unsettling? First of all, between yourself and music—if there were to be any jealousy, it would be on music's side. And if I continue to make music and to love it, it is because I owe to it—this music which you treat so poorly—meeting you and loving you. Rest assured that if I were to stop composing, it would probably be you who would no longer love me, for neither the rather limited charm of my conversation nor my physical advantages would be sufficient to keep you."[34] Emma's remark had brought into the open once again what Debussy perceived as the unending conflict between his art and his role as husband, and by this time it probably seemed to him that there would never be a satisfactory resolution to the problem.

The trip to Russia was followed in February 1914 by visits to Rome (18–24 February) and the Netherlands (26 February–2 March). Neither was undertaken with any enthusiasm. In Rome he conducted *La Mer*, *Rondes de Printemps*, the *Faune*, and the *Marche écossaise*. In Amsterdam he conducted the first two *Nocturnes*, the *Faune*, and the *Marche*. Both visits went reasonably well, although response was more favorable in Amsterdam. For one young American sight-seeing in Rome, the opportunity to see Debussy was too good to be missed. But she left disappointed: "I had made a fine mental picture of him based on his erratic music; imagine my surprise when a stocky French-shopkeeper-looking person appeared and waved the baton absolutely without magnetism. . . . The large audience was divided in its opinion, some applauding, others hissing. One man finally expressed himself by yelling, '*Alla porta!*' (Show him the door!)."[35]

Italy and the Netherlands were followed by two more trips, Debussy's final journeys beyond the borders of France. On 28 April he made a quick visit to Brussels, where, as part of a private concert of his works, as pianist he performed the *Estampes*, two *Images*, and three *Préludes*. On 17 July he appeared as conductor at Queen's Hall in London, directing a program of smaller pieces that included the *Faune*. As he reflected on what had become the routine of his life, he could only have been disturbed by the absence of music as an ideal, and the prominent role it had assumed for him as a business.

Debussy wrote comparatively little music during the years 1912–1914. The first year—which included the completion of *Jeux*—was the most productive. *Gigues* was finished that October. Work was also continued on *Khamma*. By that autumn the piano score was ready to be engraved. But after beginning the orchestration, Debussy lost interest in it. It was completed by Charles Koechlin under Debussy's supervision early in the new year.

34. Letter of 8 December 1913 in C, p. 1717. It is curious that in Segalen's text of the Orpheus opera intended for Debussy, Eurydice expresses similar jealousy of Orpheus's music.

35. Pauline Stiles, *New Footprints in Old Places* (San Francisco: Paul Elder, 1917), p. 114.

The major composition for 1913 was the second book of twelve *Préludes* for piano, completed in January. Debussy himself performed the first three to an enthusiastic audience at the Salle Erard on 5 March, followed by a partial performance one month later by Viñes at the Société Nationale. During the summer there was a return to song. The *Trois Poèmes de Mallarmé* were completed in July. But Debussy's pleasure in the project was diminished when he learned that Ravel was also working on a Mallarmé set, even using (but in a chamber setting, as distinct from Debussy's version for voice and piano) two of the same poems.

Debussy also began work in 1913 on *La Boîte à joujoux* (The Box of Toys), a ballet for children conceived by the painter André Hellé. Debussy's love for Chouchou provided the inspiration. The piano version was finished in all essentials in October, but as usual the orchestration was a laborious process. Debussy worked on it intermittently until November 1917. It was eventually finished by André Caplet after Debussy's death. The remaining composition for the year was *Syrinx* (a short piece for solo flute)—the only piece that resulted from a proposed collaboration between Gabriel Mourey and Debussy for incidental music to his drama, *Psyché*, a project dating back to 1909. In 1914 only one work of substance was composed: the *Epigraphes antiques*, a collection of pieces for piano, four-hands, completed in July. They used as a basis the incidental music Debussy had written in 1901 for Louÿs's *Chansons de Bilitis*.

He was discouraged by this lack of productivity. "I have to confess that for a long time I have been sinking," he wrote to Godet. "I feel myself declining frightfully! Ah! the 'magician' which you once admired in me—where is he?"[36] His discouragement was heightened by the fate of the two most substantial compositions created during these years: *Khamma* and *Jeux*.

Difficulties with *Khamma* had never been resolved. Because of her dissatisfaction with the length of the score, in January 1913 Durand gave back to Maud Allan the 10,000 francs she had paid Debussy. She was even permitted to commission another composer to set her scenario to music.

But she still had hopes of using Debussy's score. Her concern with its shortness now shifted to its orchestration, and she asked Debussy to arrange it for a smaller ensemble, the type, she said, she would be more likely to encounter on tour. Debussy responded in his most courteous manner giving her permission to have it redone as she saw fit—at the same time making a point of taking no responsibility for the result. Maud Allan never staged *Khamma*, and its first performance had to wait until 1924.

Debussy held far greater hopes for *Jeux*. The long-awaited premiere occurred on 15 May 1913, but two factors were working against it. Nijinsky's choreography was even more stylized than what he had created for the *Faune,* the basis for it being the

36. Letter of 14 July 1914 in *C*, p. 1836.

rhythmic concepts of Jacques Dalcroze. Time was expressed by movement of the arms, and note duration by movement of the feet and body. The virtuosic display traditionally associated with nineteenth-century ballet was essentially eliminated. In many ways Nijinsky's choreography was innovative and anticipated later twentieth-century styles. But neither Debussy nor the audience cared for it.

The second factor contributing to *Jeux*'s being overlooked was the production two weeks later of Stravinsky's *Rite of Spring* (also choreographed by Nijinsky). So much attention was focused on what was seen as its scandalous nature, that *Jeux* was soon forgotten. The circumstances could not have been more unfortunate. One of Debussy's most interesting and distinctive works passed unappreciated. But that did not prevent him from having a warm—although somewhat diffident—admiration for Stravinsky's music.

Debussy was familiar with all of Stravinsky's major works of the time, including *Firebird* and *Petroushka*, and established a cordial friendship with him. To Stravinsky, Debussy spoke of the "sonorous magic" of *Petroushka* and the haunting "beautiful nightmare" of the *Rite*.[37] "My dear Stravinsky," he wrote, "you are a great artist!"[38] Chouchou also entered into the spirit of Stravinsky's music. She composed what Debussy described as a "fantasy on *Petroushka* to make tigers roar." "Although I have threatened her with all kinds of torture," he told Stravinsky, "she continues to assert that 'you'd find it very beautiful.'"[39]

In private Debussy was far more critical of Stravinsky, describing him as a "spoilt child" and a "young savage" who as he grew older would become "intolerable."[40] He expressed concern that he was "leaning dangerously towards Schoenberg," the type of music which—although his knowledge of it was limited—Debussy regarded as empty, pretentious, and stupefyingly Germanic.[41]

Although it had been some time since he had had a major success, the reception of *Jeux* did not diminish Debussy's reputation. A "Debussy Gala" organized by Vuillermoz about a month after the premiere of *Jeux* put a variety of his works on display, including several of the new *Préludes* and older compositions like the *Proses lyriques*—all a confirmation that his supporters remained ardent. But Debussy continued to worry, confiding to Durand that were it not for "my little Chouchou, I would blow out my brains, despite the baseness and absurdity of the act.... To struggle alone is nothing! But to struggle with a family is abominable!"[42]

---

37. Letters of 13 April 1912 and [7 November 1912] in *DL*, pp. 256, 265.

38. Letter of 24 October 1915 in ibid., p. 308.

39. Letter of [7 November 1912] in *C*, p. 1554.

40. Letter to Godet of 4 January 1916 in *DL*, p. 312.

41. Letter to Godet of 14 October 1915 in ibid., p. 306.

42. Letters of 30 August and 15 July 1913 in *C*, pp. 1659, 1641.

He seemed convinced that his situation could not become more unbearable. But like everyone else he failed to anticipate the effects of a world war. During the late summer of 1914 as political tensions rose after the assassination of Archduke Ferdinand in Sarajevo, to many the likelihood of war at first seemed a blessing. In France it was regarded as the ideal opportunity to reoccupy Alsace and Lorraine and to take revenge on Germany for the defeat of 1870. It was intended to be a short war—the armies would return victorious in time for Christmas. On 1 August France mobilized its troops.

Debussy had never been patriotic and had long been openly critical of the dangers of its excess. "I'm quite devoid of sang-froid," he wrote Durand, "and even more so of the military mentality, never having had occasion to handle a gun."[43] He seemed astounded at the depth of passion aroused by the outbreak of war, noting that even Paul Dukas "declares he's as ready to get his head blown off as the next man."[44] But Debussy soon found himself caught up in the fray, not least because Emma's son and son-in-law were in the army. When German forces, violating Belgian neutrality, came close to capturing Paris, Debussy along with many others fled the capital for safety. On 4 September he and his family received a safe-conduct pass for Angers, where they remained for about a month. As the severity of the war increased—and with it daily reports in the press of "Hun atrocities"—Debussy's attitudes hardened. He regarded the German forces with increased loathing and hatred.

After the battle of the Marne in the autumn of 1914, Paris seemed no longer in danger, but the conflict entered a new stage, that of trench warfare. Technological developments added new brutalities: poison gas, the tank, aerial combat, and bombings. Debussy was spared these horrors. But life in Paris was especially hard, with increasing shortages of food and fuel, and a steady increase in their cost.[45] Musical life was cut back as well.

Fortunately, additional work was found for Debussy with Durand. Not only did the war stir up resentment toward German music, it also made a substantial amount of music from German publishers unavailable. Durand attempted to fill the gap, and Debussy worked on editions of selected works of Chopin and Bach. He also entered the field of composer as propagandist. He contributed a short piano piece, *Berceuse héroïque*, to a collection honoring the King of Belgium—a widely sympathetic figure because of the invasion and occupation of his country by the Germans.

The *Berceuse* was followed by several other pieces similar in intent. In 1915 Debussy wrote both the words and music for a song, "Noël des enfants qui n'ont

43. Letter of 8 August 1914 in *DL*, p. 291.

44. Letter to Durand of 18 August 1914 in ibid., p. 292.

45. Debussy's last musical autograph—an improvisatory piano piece thirty-one measures in length—was presented as a form of payment to his coal-dealer, probably in February or March 1917.

plus de maison," in which his sentiments became more straightforward ("They burnt our school; they burnt our teacher, too"). And in the following year he began a cantata about Joan of Arc, *Ode à la France*, set in Rheims (whose cathedral, destroyed by German shelling, had become a symbol both of French fortitude and German barbarity).

During the first years of the war Debussy's spirits alternated between outrage and despair. He was pained and angered by Germany's invasion of France, and his sense of confusion and helplessness was only increased by the heavily censored accounts of the war he read each day in the press. It was impossible for him to write music. When he was offered the use for the summer of a small villa ("Mon Coin") near Pourville, he jumped at the chance. It became more than a welcome change of scene. Everything about "Mon Coin" seemed to lift his spirits. He was particularly enchanted by the garden, which at the summit presented a wonderful vista of the sea.

Debussy's letters reflected his new frame of mind. Rarely had he seemed so happy. At "Mon Coin"—isolated from the continual reminders of war, and installed in a home in which he wished he could live forever—Debussy's creativity returned in such profusion that even he seemed at times astonished by it.

During the summer of 1915 he composed a large body of his most imaginative and most innovative work, including *En blanc et noir* (for two pianos), the piano Etudes (a set of twelve), the sonata for cello, and the sonata for flute, viola, and harp. The sonatas were the first in an ambitious set of six, intended to include sonatas for violin; oboe, French horn, and harpsichord; trumpet, clarinet, bassoon, and piano; and for the last sonata, a return of all of them with the addition of string bass. These are not sonatas in the nineteenth-century sense but instead draw their inspiration from eighteenth-century French models—the type of music Debussy had been praising for years in his music criticism.

It was as if he were living a new life. "I am relearning music," he wrote. "There is an emotional effect one gets from placing the right chord in place which is impossible in the other arts. Pardon me. I am acting as if I have discovered music, but, in all modesty, that's a bit how I feel."[46] The idea of returning to the routine of life in Paris was inconceivable. "If I had a great deal of money," he told Durand, "I would immediately buy 'Mon Coin'—in gratitude for having once again found the ability to think and to work. When I think of the emptiness of last year, I get shivers up my spine, and fear returning to Paris and the factory of nothingness which my study had become!"[47]

But despite the serene setting in which they were produced, Debussy was convinced that these new compositions came into existence "not so much for myself,

46. Letter to D. E. Inghelbrecht of 30 September 1915 in *C*, p. 1937.
47. Letter to Durand of 1 September 1915 in ibid., p. 1926.

[but] to offer proof, small as it may be, that 30 million Boches can not destroy French thought.... I think of the youth of France, senselessly mowed down by those merchants of 'Kultur'.... What I am writing will be a secret homage to them."[48] At a time of horror and wanton destruction, it was his intention to replace "a little of the beauty" that was being lost.[49]

Debussy worked feverishly at "Mon Coin," waiting until the last possible moment before returning to Paris in mid-October. His spirits survived the change of scene well. But his physical condition had for some time been troublesome. It is not known precisely what the problem was, but that November he decided to see a physician. The diagnosis, coming as it did after the gloriously revitalizing experiences of the previous months, was a shock: cancer. Debussy was made aware of its serious nature but not told that his illness (cancer of the rectum) could be fatal.

Cancer had probably been present for years, but not enough is known of Debussy's medical history to determine when distinctive symptoms of the cancer— substantial bleeding, digestive complications including severe cramps, and gradual weight loss—first appeared. It is unlikely that the digestive complaints noted by Debussy in his correspondence in 1907 and 1909 (always assumed by his biographers to have been the first signs) were an indication of cancer—for it would have had to have spread at an astonishingly slow rate for Debussy to have continued a normal life until 1915.[50] But by that November the cancer had probably entered a calamitous stage; possibly a partial obstruction had occurred.

Debussy's physicians decided to perform a colostomy, an unusual and perilous procedure for the time. A primitive type of bag—probably of animal skin— would have been attached, and with no antibiotics, the danger of infection was high. The operation was scheduled for 7 December, and the night before—well aware that he might not survive it—Debussy wrote a note to Emma, telling her of his love, and asking her to love him "in the person of our little Chouchou . . . you are the only two for whose sake I do not want to leave this earth altogether."[51] The operation went well. But it was the beginning of months of pain and suffering.

Debussy was greatly weakened, and recovery was slow. For four months (and intermittently thereafter) he took morphine to ease the pain. It was essential to him, but its dulling side effects took their toll. "There is something broken in this curious

---

48. Letter to Durand of 5 August 1915 in ibid., p. 1915.

49. Letter of 14 October 1915 in *DL*, p. 305.

50. My thanks to Dr. Thomas Anderson (Columbus, Ohio), a cancer specialist who has provided me with details on the nature and historical treatment of cancer.

51. Letter of 6 December 1915 in *DL*, p. 310.

mechanism which was my brain," he told Godet.[52] Its continued use also contributed to the insomnia that plagued him.

In mid-January 1916 he received additional treatment: the use of radium to shrink and destroy his tumor. It was an advanced concept; only after the Second World War did it become more widely used. Fortunately for Debussy, as a result of the Curies' work, Paris was a center for the study of radium. For his treatment, pellets would have been inserted for monitored periods of time. The amount that he would have been given could only have been guessed at, since there were so few previous cases to use as a basis.

All in all, painful as it was, Debussy received treatment truly extraordinary for the time. Both the operation and the radium must have successfully localized the tumor, or he would never have been able to survive for as long as he did. But despite the best efforts of his physicians, the tumor remained active. That would explain the gradual change in his appearance, and the shock many experienced on seeing him "very emaciated, his complexion sallow and ashen."[53] Photographs taken in 1917 reveal an astonishing amount of weight loss, his clothes hanging limply on him. "I don't take this tattered body for walks anymore," he told Godet, "in case I frighten little children and tram conductors."[54]

Through it all Debussy remained stoic, and at first hopeful of a return to health. "I watch the hours go past, each the same as the other and still worth living when they're not too painful," he wrote in the midst of his radium treatment.[55] He inquired about the proofs of the *Etudes*, and that summer Emma reported that he was occasionally at work. But by June he was losing patience, wondering if his illness was "incurable," in which case, he told Durand, it would have been better had he known from the start.[56]

Like many, he began to view the war in a different light; 1916 had seen the horrors of Verdun and the Somme. Mutinies broke out in the French forces in May and June 1917 (although their extent was concealed from the public). The years of carnage had made a straightforward patriotic stance simplistic. "When will hate be exhausted?" Debussy wrote. "Or is it hate that's the issue in all this? When will the practice cease of entrusting the destiny of nations to people who see humanity as a way of furthering their careers?"[57] In the midst of it all, there were still financial worries (one wonders how he managed to pay for his treatment), including a court

52. Letter of 3 December 1916 in *C*, p. 2052.
53. According to one who saw him in 1917 in *D*, p. 183.
54. Letter of 11 December 1916 in *DL*, p. 320.
55. Letter to Godet of 4 February 1916 in ibid., p. 314.
56. Letter of 8 June 1916 in *C*, p. 2000.
57. Letter to Godet of 4 February 1916 in *DL*, p. 314.

order for payment to Lilly of 30,000 francs alimony. It had been nearly six years since Debussy had paid any (although she had received payments directly from his publisher).

He wrote to Durand noting his continued interest in the Poe operas, but although little work was done on them, music was not abandoned. The third of his sonata series—that for violin—was completed in the early months of 1917. And there were still thoughts of projects seemingly forgotten, such as the collaboration with Toulet on *As You Like It*. In November 1917 he sketched about a dozen pages for the *Ode à la France*. But nothing followed. "I feel only horrible fatigue and this distaste for activity, a result of my last illness.... Where are the beautiful months of 1915?"[58]

There was some attempt at normality. The premieres of his most recent compositions kept him before the public's eye—the Cello Sonata was performed in London in March 1916, and at the end of the year there was a performance of four of the Etudes and the Sonata for Flute, Viola, and Harp. "It's by a Debussy I no longer know," he told Godet.[59]

On occasion Debussy would attend a concert, and as late as December 1916 even performed *En blanc et noir* with Roger-Ducasse as part of a benefit to raise money for clothing for prisoners of war. Vacations remained important for the family. Part of the autumn of 1916 was spent in Moulleau near Arcachon, and the following summer in Saint-Jean-de-Luz. The trips provided some distraction. But he could not wait to escape from the hotel in Moulleau ("the very walls are hostile").[60]

Visits of friends helped to pass the time. Satie came by regularly and did what he could to provide some cheer. But his visits ended in the summer of 1917, the result of disagreement over his recent work. Each was too stubborn to give in to the other, until months later Satie, learning how ill Debussy had become, wrote to reestablish their friendship.

During the closing months of 1917 Debussy's condition worsened noticeably. He became so weak that Emma began to answer his correspondence for him. Hope for a recovery of any kind was abandoned.

The final days of his life occurred in the midst of a massive German offensive, begun on 21 March 1918 in a final, desperate attempt to capture Paris. Jacques Durand visited Debussy two days later. He tried to raise his spirits by talking of improvement—but Debussy affirmed that he knew the end was near ("only a matter of hours").[61] And he described the terror of the preceding night when,

58. Letters to Durand of 22 July 1917 and [12] September 1917 in *C*, pp. 2131, 2148.

59. Letter of 11 December 1916 in *DL*, p. 320.

60. Letter to Durand of 12 October 1916 in ibid., p. 318.

61. *LS*, p. 406.

during a bombardment, he had not had the strength to get out of bed to seek shelter in the cellar—only to have his wife and daughter refuse to leave his side.

After Durand's visit, Debussy's condition steadily continued to deteriorate. On 24 March he was substantially weaker and spoke with great difficulty. He died in his sleep during the evening of the following day and was buried four days later. There were few obituaries, and those that appeared were surprisingly perfunctory. It was Chouchou—twelve years old at the time—who, in a letter to her stepbrother Raoul, best expressed the sense of loss:

> Mama was called to Papa because the nurse found him to be 'very bad'!—Two doctors were sent for at once, and they both said he should be given an injection so that he would not suffer. Then I understood. Roger-Ducasse who was there said to me, "Come, Chouchou, kiss your Papa." Then all at once I thought that it was over. When I went back into the room, Papa was asleep and breathing regularly, but in very short breaths. He continued to sleep like that until 10 o'clock at night and then gently, like an angel, he fell asleep forever. What happened after, I can't describe. A torrent of tears wanted to flow from my eyes but I immediately held them back because of Mama. All night, alone in Mama's big bed, I was unable to sleep for a minute. I felt feverish and my dry eyes gazed at the walls and I couldn't believe the truth!
>
> The next day far too many people came to see Mama, so that by the end of the day she could hold out no longer—it was a release for her and for me. Thursday arrived, Thursday when he would be taken from us for ever! . . . I summoned up all my courage. I don't know where it came from. I didn't shed a tear: tears held back are worth as much as tears shed, and now it is night forever. Papa is dead. Those three words, I don't understand them or rather I understand them too well. . . . Think now and then of your poor little sister who would like so much to hold you and to tell you how much she loves you. Do you understand everything I feel and which I can not put into words?[62]

---

62. Letter of 8 April 1918 in *C*, pp. 2195–2196. Chouchou died from diphtheria sixteen months later.

CHAPTER EIGHT

Debussy and the Arts

The morbidness of the modern French mind is well known and universally admitted, even by the French themselves; the open atheism, heartlessness, flippancy, and flagrant immorality of the whole modern French school of thought is unquestioned. If a crime of more than usual cold-blooded atrocity is committed, it generally dates from Paris or near it;—if a book or a picture is produced that is confessedly obscene, the author or artist is, in nine cases out of ten, discovered to be a Frenchman. The shop-windows and bookstalls of Paris are of themselves sufficient witnesses of the national taste in art and literature,—a national taste for vice and indecent vulgarity which cannot be too sincerely and compassionately deplored.

Marie Corelli, Wormwood (1890)

M ORE OFTEN THAN NOT, COMPOSERS ARE CONTENT TO WRITE MUSIC, AND their interest in the other arts is minimal. There have been exceptions, and at first glance Debussy might seem to be one of them. But, by the standards of his day, it would have been odd if he had focused solely on music. Debussy lived at a time when composers in France appeared constrained by music, when they prided themselves not just on their knowledge of the arts, but on their accomplishments in them. Chausson, for example, was an art collector and unpublished novelist. Magnard and Lekeu were poets. D'Indy was a skillful water-colorist.

Composers' interests in the arts found a counterpart in artists' and writers' fascination with music. Some, like Whistler, gave their paintings titles based on musical compositions.[1]

---

1. One, the *Symphony in White #2*, inspired a poem by Swinburne, in the process combining image, word, and, by implication, music.

Poets, like Mallarmé, focused on the musicality of their verse. René Ghil went a step further and associated color and timbre with his poetry. In his *Traité du verbe* (1886, with a preface by Mallarmé) he assigned colors and specific instruments to vowels, for example: I (blue; violin); O (red; brass instruments)—all of which was meant to be seen and heard by the reader as a complement to the poems. There were attempts, too, to emphasize the kinship among the arts. The group of Belgian writers and artists, "La Libre Esthétique," promoted joint exhibitions and concerts (including one by Debussy in 1894).

But despite this widespread fascination with the arts, three factors set Debussy apart: the breadth of his interests, the discernment in his taste, and the manner in which the arts served as a source of inspiration—even at times as a model—for some of his music.

We know from his correspondence and from the recollections of his fellow students at the Conservatoire that Debussy's interest in the visual arts and literature began early in life. It was an interest that he pursued on his own, and it intensified in his late teens, largely as compensation for the formal education he had never received. He read voraciously, the well known (Balzac, Dickens) and the lesser known (Jean Richepin, Jules Laforgue). By the time he left for Rome he knew the literary scene in Paris well and complained about his isolation from it.

It was an extraordinarily robust time for literature. One contemporary text listed fifty-five distinct literary groups, running the stylistic gamut from free verse to "poésie scientifique" (René Ghil) and "poésie esotérique" (Edmond Schuré and Villiers de L'Isle-Adam).[2] Debussy was familiar with many of those groups, and enjoyed—especially in his youth—keeping up with literary trends. His interest led to association with writers such as Henri de Régnier (at the time, one of the most admired writers in Europe) and a close friendship with Pierre Louÿs. These relationships also bolstered his self-confidence and encouraged him to write and set his own poetry to music, as in the *Proses lyriques* and *Nuits blanches*.

In later years Debussy's literary discernment led him to select as friends and collaborators several of the most talented writers of a younger generation. Victor Segalen and Paul-Jean Toulet were little known at the time, but just as he had been among the first to detect special qualities in Verlaine's verse, he was among the first to appreciate their equally distinctive style.

Debussy never established a friendship with a visual artist comparable to the ones he had with writers. But we know that he was fascinated by the visual arts. "He was always sorry," wrote a piano pupil, "he hadn't taken up painting instead of music."[3]

---

2. Florian-Parmentier [Serge Gastein], *Histoire contemporaine des letters francaises de 1885 à 1914* (Paris: Eugene Figuière, [1914]).

3. Madame Gérard de Romilly in *DR*, p. 54.

To EdgardVarèse he confided: "I love images almost as much as music."[4] His tastes were broad and included among nineteenth-century artists Turner, Goya, the Pre-Raphaelites, Moreau,Whistler, Redon, Degas, Monet, and Hokusai.

Some of Debussy's interest in art can be seen in his concern about the appearance of his compositions in print—from the deluxe editions of the *Damozel* to ink color and word placement in those published by Durand. A more curious link to the visual arts is the monogram based on his initials that Debussy created for himself, with the "C" encircling the "D." It is a device often associated with artists, and that connection may have added appeal to Debussy.

There is not a great deal of evidence to make the case, but Debussy also had talent as an artist.The cover he drew for *Children's Corner*, for example, (including a fanciful interpretation of Golliwogg, one of the characters in it) is fanciful and charming.

From friends ("The most powerful influence on Debussy was that of writers, not of composers") to the press ("He is theVerlaine of music"), Debussy's interest in and indebtedness to matters artistic and non-musical became common knowledge.[5] When critics created a school of Impressionism in music, Debussy became its most senior member, so much so that over the decades the connection of Debussy with Impressionism has become all but unassailable. What was meant by use of the term? What were the advantages in applying it to his music?

Impressionism

"Impressionist" was first associated with Debussy's compositions in 1887 while he was a student at Rome. It was intended negatively by his teachers and referred not specifically to the movement (which was solely in the visual arts at the time), but to what was perceived as the non-traditional basis (and poor quality) of his music.

The initial Impressionist exhibition had occurred thirteen years earlier in Paris. From the start it was perceived as revolutionary. Among the artists first represented were many who would be closely associated with the movement, including Claude Monet, Camille Pissarro, Pierre-August Renoir, Alfred Sisley, and Berthe Morisot. The next Impressionist exhibition was held in 1876; the final one, the eighth, in 1886 (not all were marketed as being Impressionist, but that was how they were generally perceived). The very existence of the exhibitions gave them a revolutionary air—since they were created as a means of challenging the conservative taste represented in the annual official exhibits (known as Salons, and first established in 1667).There was strong public interest in the salons with typically several hundred

---

4. Letter of [12 February 1911] in *C*, p. 1389.

5. Paul Dukas in *DR*, p. 98; quoted in Stefan Jarocinski, *Debussy: Impressionisme et symbolisme* (Paris: Editions du Seuil, 1970), p. 139.

thousand visitors for each—and corresponding interest in the exhibits presented in contrast (or opposition) to them.

Debussy was only twelve when the Impressionists first made a name for themselves. The artists associated with the movement were not of his generation but of his father's. During the 1890s, when Debussy was beginning his career, many of the Impressionist artists were ending theirs. At the same time there was growing acceptance of their work, and appreciation of their style. Linking it to music was but a small step.

Contemporary attempts to define Impressionism tended to be polemical, but the Irish novelist (and occasional art critic) George Moore provided one in 1893 that, brief as it is, serves as a good point of departure. Moore had studied painting in France and knew many of the artists associated with the movement. "Impressionism," he concluded, "is a word which has lent itself to every kind of misinterpretation, for in its exact sense all true painting is penetrated with impressionism, but, to use the word in its most modern sense—that is to say, to signify the rapid noting of illusive appearance—Monet is the only painter to whom it may be reasonably applied."[6]

Although limiting Impressionism to Monet is deliberately provocative, Moore, in very few words, has captured much of the essence of Impressionism. The crux of his definition—the "rapid noting of illusive appearance"—was accomplished in painting with a focus on color and light (and less on line and detail). Bold, forceful brushstrokes were often used to produce a luminosity that resulted in blurred imagery.

Subject matter was equally distinctive. There was a concern with modernity. But there was an interest as well in subjective interpretation of natural scenes, and in painting out-of-doors. The goal was to work quickly and simply—to capture the substance of a scene, an approach that led to criticism that what was produced was not a finished product but hastily assembled sketches.

Critics were quick to pick up on a connection between Debussy's compositions and painters associated, if only vaguely, with Impressionism. The *Nocturnes*, for example, were linked to Whistler. But the initial basis for the connection—as in so many of Debussy's compositions—was that the artist and composer had used the same title. It was the similarity between the titles of some of Debussy's music and titles for Impressionist paintings that supplied what many were convinced were the strongest, initial linkage between them.

Descriptive titles found in both music and the visual arts seemed to invite interpretation. Debussy's first biographer singled out "Reflets dans l'eau" (Reflections in the Water, one of the piano *Images*), labeled it an "impressionist sketch," and, inventing a poetic program, described the piece as a "delicate reproduction in harmonic

6. George Moore, *Modern Painting* (New York: Charles Scribner's Sons, 1893), p. 84.

sound of shimmering waters and of the shifting, dazzling reflections seen in their depths. The rippling flow and trickle of a running stream is heard, the cool, translucent effect and gurgle of disturbed water is given, and throughout the piece the constant mobility of the trembling, wavering shadows is maintained."[7] Attaching programs to instrumental compositions without any had a long history in the nineteenth century. There is nothing new either in the approach or concept of the program created for "Reflets," except that it has been tailored to bring to mind what might be a verbal description of an Impressionist painting.

More often than not, Debussy's contemporaries labeled his music Impressionistic without explanation, the assumption being that listeners knew only too well why it was. "One can not imagine a symphony more delicately Impressionistic [than the *Nocturnes*]," wrote one critic.[8] But complicating any attempt to identify specific "Impressionistic" musical qualities in Debussy's music was the freewheeling use of identical terminology in both art and music criticism, a result of the kinship felt to exist among the arts (as when George Moore remarked on the "harmony of color, [and] the melody of composition" in a painting by Whistler).[9]

Debussy's friend and biographer Louis Laloy cautiously applied the term "Impressionist" to Debussy's music in the broadest possible sense. It was, he wrote, "purely auditory, just as Impressionist painting is completely visual"—a rather open-ended conclusion.[10] More commonly, Impressionist qualities were perceived as general components of Debussy's sound. Louise Liebich presented two: sound as color (timbre?), and harmony as color and light. Debussy, she explained, "employs sounds as colors and blends them in varied juxtaposition, forming them into delicately tinted sonorous aggregations; or he invests certain chords with an existence either sufficient unto itself or renders it capable of germination and developing a series of shaded, many-hued chord sequences [*sic*]. Fluid, flexible, vivid, these beautiful harmonies, seemingly woven of refracted rays of light, merge into infinite melody of a free, flowing rhythm....His own art and that of painting are in some instances almost identical in method, for his employment of chords and their combinations resembles the manipulation of colors by a Le Sidaner, a Whistler, or a Manet."[11] To Liebich, then, one of the primary similarities is the relationship between Debussy's harmonic approach ("chords and their combinations") and a painter's palette. But what precisely was meant? *How* did Debussy "employ" his chords?

7. Mrs. Franz Liebich, *Claude-Achille Debussy* (London: John Lane, 1908), p. 62.

8. Quoted in François Lesure, "Debussy, le Symbolisme, et les arts plastiques," *Cahiers Debussy* 8 (1984), p. 3.

9. Moore, p. 11.

10. Louis Laloy, *Claude Debussy* (Paris: Les Bibliophiles Fantaisistes, 1909), p. 51.

11. Liebich, pp. 27–28, 10.

And what direct connection was there between their use and a painter's "manipulation of colors"?

Contemporary definitions of musical impressionism are not much help. Reliance was on broad, innocuous generalizations. The one by Edward Dent in A. Eaglefield-Hull's *A Dictionary of Modern Music and Musicians* (1924), is one of the most comprehensive: "Impressionism: music intended to convey some suggestion of a landscape, or of a picture in which color is more important than outline, the melodic line in such cases being ill-defined and fragmentary, while subsidiary figures of accompaniment are much developed, often in rapid movement, the object of which is to produce a general effect of timbre rather than a clearly intelligible succession of notes. Similar effects are also obtained by slow harmonies based on chords which an older generation would have regarded as discords, but which the present day regards as agreeable consonances."[12] As with Liebich, color (timbre) is a key element with "slow harmonies" (in lieu of Liebich's "employment of chords") an important component.

Dent's definition, complemented by general comments made by Debussy's contemporaries, helps bring us closer to understanding why the similarity between Debussy and Impressionism was believed to be strong. There are musical correspondences to Moore's "rapid noting of illusive appearance," and specific musical devices to help explain the core of Dent's definition: the "general effect of timbre rather than a clearly intelligible succession of notes."

The Impressionist concern with color would have a counterpart in Debussy's nonfunctional harmony (where each chord can be heard as a separate entity, and not part of a conventional progression). In that sense, the blurred imagery of a painting by Monet, would be similar to the "blurred" harmonic effect in Debussy's music, the result of his slow harmonic rhythm, and the use of ninth and eleventh chords which, as Dent pointed out, "an older generation would have regarded as discords." Color, too, is a characteristic of Debussy's innovative instrumentation, one that focuses on the unique sound quality of each instrument, both by itself and as an ensemble instrument (mixing and blending with other instruments whether in a chamber or orchestral setting).

The Impressionists' lack of focus on line (a departure from tradition) could be seen as similar to Debussy's lack of interest in traditional musical structure. Their concern with sketches (as opposed to the meticulously finished work of an academician) brings to mind Debussy's interest in improvisation, specifically his attempts to create an illusion of improvisation in some of his compositions. Some critics, incidentally, referred to Monet's paintings as "improvisations."[13]

12. A. Eaglefield-Hull, ed., *A Dictionary of Modern Music and Musicians* (London: J. M. Dent, 1924).
13. Joris-Karl Huysmans, *L'Art moderne* (Paris: Plon, [1883]), p. 292.

But alongside these similarities, there are notable differences. In contrast to the illusive outline of many Impressionist works, Debussy's music can be extraordinarily precise and detailed. It had to be so to create the effect he wanted, and that is true even when he was trying to create the effect of improvisation. At the same time, there is no musical counterpart to the often bold, dynamic brush strokes found in some Impressionist art. On the contrary, Debussy's music is often astonishingly restrained and delicate (as, admittedly, can be the effect of Impressionist painting).

Although there are stylistic similarities between the music of Debussy and Impressionist art, it should come as no surprise that he did not like the comparison. He felt that it cast doubt on his originality. But he admitted a connection of sorts. Concerning the *Images* he wrote: "I tried to make 'something else' of them and to create—in some manner—*realities*—what imbeciles call 'impressionism,' a term as poorly used as possible, especially by art critics."[14] By "realities" Debussy seemed to be referring to the approach he also followed in *La Mer*, where he based his music not on an intermediary—like a painting of the sea—but on reality: the sea itself. That helps to explain a response he once made to a compliment by Emile Vuillermoz. "You do me a great honor," Debussy wrote, "by calling me a student of Claude Monet."[15] To Debussy, both he and Monet were constant students of nature, using it as a source of inspiration and basis for their art. And in that sense—and that alone—Debussy acknowledged an affinity with Impressionism.

Symbolism

From the start there were critics who refused to associate Debussy's music solely with Impressionism. "Debussyism," wrote Louis Laloy, "corresponds to symbolism in poetry and impressionism in painting."[16] Louise Liebich agreed: "By inclination and temperament Debussy is in close sympathy with the school of painters called impressionists and with the class of poets styled symbolists."[17] Because of profound aesthetic differences between the two movements, connecting Debussy's music with both Impressionism and Symbolism only seems to confuse the matter.

Symbolism took shape later than Impressionism (in tangible form, in September 1886 with the Symbolist Manifesto written by the poet Jean Moréas). Moréas, whose connection with Symbolism was short-lived, emphasized its idealism, its fondness for dreams, and its preference for feeling over intellect.

14. Letter to Jacques Durand of [end March–early April] in *C*, pp. 1080–1081. He is referring to the orchestral *Images*.

15. Letter of 25 January 1916 in *DL*, p. 313.

16. Laloy, p. 50.

17. Liebich, p. 24.

"What is the meaning of *Symbolism*?" asked Rémy de Gourmont, its most discerning critic. "Practically nothing, if we adhere to the narrow etymological sense. If we pass beyond, it may mean individualism in literature, liberty in art, abandonment of taught formulas, tendencies towards the new and strange, or even towards the bizarre."[18] Gourmont's list of characteristics hints at its connection with an allied movement: Decadence (identified by another contemporary critic, Arthur Symons, as differing from Symbolism by its "spiritual and moral perversity").[19] Yet another trait of Symbolism—and one that contributed to its mystery—was perhaps best expressed by Mallarmé. "Paint not the thing itself," he wrote, "but the effect which it produces."[20]

Symbolism, unlike Impressionism, was associated with both the visual arts and literature. In painting it exhibited a variety of styles, from the academic (Gustave Moreau) to the near abstract (Thorn Prikker). Subject matter focused on myth and dream. But even works that appeared straightforward, such as Puvis de Chavannes's "Young Girls by the Sea" (1879; a depiction of three young women in hieratic poses along the seashore) could, in Symbolist eyes, take on an entirely different meaning. Rather than three individual women, it was, in the interpretation of the poet and critic Gustave Kahn, "the same woman in three different physical attitudes...the same woman at three different times, in three different acts of her life: young at the moment of expectation, at the moment of the call, at the moment at which her throbbing drives bend back on themselves—when she comes to weep the eternal battle of the sexes."[21]

Gustave Moreau—selected by Debussy in 1889 as one of his favorite artists—was the most venerable of the Symbolist painters. One of his earliest paintings, "Oedipus and the Sphinx," had won a medal at the salon of 1864. His artistic credo was reflected in much of his work: "I believe neither in what I touch nor in what I see. I believe only in what I do not see and only in what I feel."[22]

Literary Symbolism embodied similar ideals and characteristics. During the 1880s and 1890s it had become the dominant movement in France for poetry, the novel, and criticism. Among its most famous writers were two closely associated

---

18. Rémy de Gourmont, *The Book of Masks*, tr. Jack Lewis (Boston: John W. Luce, 1921), p. 10. Gourmont's essay was first published in 1890.

19. From an essay by Symons written in 1893. Quoted in Roger Lhombreaud, *Arthur Symons* (London: Unicorn Press, 1963), p. 226.

20. Quoted in Gordon Millan, *The Life of Stéphane Mallarmé* (New York: Farrar, Straus and Giroux, 1994), p. 118. Mallarmé uses "paint" not literally but in a general sense, as "depict" or "represent."

21. Quoted in *Puvis de Chavannes. 1824–1898*, ed. Louise d'Argencourt et al. (Ottawa: National Gallery of Canada, 1977), p. 154.

22. Pierre-Louis Mathieu, *Gustave Moreau*. (Boston: New York Graphic Society, 1976), p. 173.

with Debussy's work: Stéphane Mallarmé and Maurice Maeterlinck. There was an astonishing variety of content within the movement, including a great deal that, to use Gourmont's words, exhibited "the new and strange": Georges Rodenbach's *Bruges-la-Morte* (1892), Edouard Rod's *La Course à la mort* (1885), and Rachilde's *La Marquise de Sade* (1887). Their cultivation of the bizarre was a factor in their popularity. There was also a concern with music in Symbolist literature, not just with the musicality of verse but in connecting poetry with music, as in Stuart Merrill's *Les Gammes* (Scales; 1887) and Gustave Kahn's *Palais nomades* (1887; it contained musical titles interspersed with prose poems).

In both Symbolist literature and the visual arts there was interest in états d'âme—soul-states, that indefinable complex of feelings and emotions that symbolized the ever-changing human spirit. Words were used to represent and elucidate soul-states in novels, poetry, and dramas. Artists represented them by color and line.

The connection between Symbolism and Debussy's music seems to make sense, not least because of his musical settings of two Symbolist masterpieces: *The Afternoon of a Faun*, and *Pelléas et Mélisande*. Beyond that there is Debussy's professed admiration for Moreau and Mallarmé (the latter, he wrote in 1913, had had "a considerable influence on the very quiet musician I was at the time").[23] But although contemporary critics took note of Symbolists traits in Debussy's music, they limited themselves to the broadest of generalities in attempting to describe them: "[Debussy's music] approximates to the art of the symbolists by its appeal to the imagination, by its power of suggesting the most subtle soul-states, and by its gift of evoking the magic atmosphere of legend and dream."[24]

Actually some prominent aspects of Impressionism can also be associated with Symbolism. There are, first of all, the titles. What may appear as generically Impressionist ones—"By the Seashore," for example—in different hands become decidedly Symbolist (see Puvis de Chavannes's painting mentioned earlier, or Emile Verhaeren's poem, "Au bord de l'eau"). Yet another point: the reference to "suggestion" in Dent's definition of musical Impressionism brings to mind Mallarmé's "Paint not the thing itself, but the effect which it produces."

What complicates any attempt at definition is that several of the musical characteristics associated in Debussy's compositions with Impressionism, can just as easily be associated with Symbolism. For example, the "blurred" tonal effect (slow harmonic rhythm, nonfunctional harmony) can create an effect comparable to dream-like, Symbolist reverie. Debussy's avoidance of traditional music structure and harmony can be seen as an instance of Gourmont's "abandonment of taught formulas."

23. Letter to Dr. Edmond Bonniot of 7 August 1913 in *C*, p. 1650.

24. Liebich, p. 29.

The music of Debussy the Symbolist sounds very much like that of Debussy the Impressionist. But by the 1970s increasingly he was linked to Symbolism instead.[25]

In the end, Debussy's interest in (and indebtedness to) the arts only confused the issue. In an attempt to understand music that is, on the one hand, fresh and direct in its appeal, and, on the other hand, elusive and difficult to classify, critics established links between it and well-known artistic styles of the day. Those links provided insight into some of Debussy's compositions. But as a description for all of his work—or a majority of it, or even for the most significant works—it was inadequate.

In addition to knowing about Debussy's interest in the arts, we know that he thought of music in broad terms and at times used the other arts to enhance his perspective. Privately he compared his piano pieces, *En Blanc et noir*, to works of art by Velázquez and Goya. When his friend Henri de Régnier remarked to him that words, used too frequently, lose their effect, he thought of how the same happened in music. As for painting, he felt that music in one respect had an advantage: "it can centralize variations of color and light of a similar aspect—a point rarely observed, though quite simple."[26] Such comments illustrate Debussy's sensitivity, as well as his willingness to compare and adapt the arts to musical ends.

But Debussy's interest in the arts did more than offer inspiration for his compositions. In the 1880s his settings of Paul Verlaine's poetry provided a new direction for his music. In a similar manner his songs based on the poems of Pierre Louÿs and Charles d'Orléans became extraordinary musical reflections on the texts.[27] These are instances of his sensitivity to poetry and of his ability to use its style to create a musical idiom intimately allied to it.

The same is true of his only completed opera, *Pelléas et Mélisande* (1893–1902). Here Debussy's sensitivity to Maeterlinck's prosody produced music of marvelous nuance, his goal being both to complement the text and enhance the drama. The concept of enhancement was also in his mind when writing the *Prelude to the Afternoon of a Faun* (1894). Here the intent was to interpret the sound and sense of Mallarmé's poem in an entirely subjective manner. And once again the result was music as free from convention as was Mallarmé's poetry—and so faithful in its way to Mallarmé's intentions as to astonish the poet.

Of the instances just mentioned, the settings of Verlaine, Maeterlinck's drama, and Mallarmé's poem have a strong connection to Symbolism. But a number of

25. See Jarocinski, *Debussy. Impressionisme et symbolisme.*

26. Letter to Raoul Bardac of 24-25 February 1906 in *C*, p. 942.

27. But not his settings of Charles Baudelaire, which were used more as an instance to adapt Wagnerian concepts.

Debussy's works have a similar kinship with Impressionism. Many of the *Images* for piano, for example, evoke an Impressionist gallery, as do the movements comprising the *Nocturnes* and *Estampes* (see Chapters 11 and 13).

But while there are compositions by Debussy whose connection to Symbolism and Impressionism helps to provide greater understanding of them, a substantial number stand apart. How can *Jeux* be categorized? Or the sonatas of his final years? In his later compositions Debussy increasingly moved away from influences in literature or the visual arts to write more absolute music. His concern was with sonority, with extending the types of sound usually associated with musical instruments, with malleability of structure, and with using select musical compositions from the past as a point of departure.

The purpose of associating a composer with a particular style—such as Classical, or Romantic, or Impressionist—is to provide insight into his or her work. Though it stands on its own merits, music does not exist on its own. It reflects the person who composed it and the cultural tastes of the time. That was particularly true of Debussy, who was enthralled by the arts. The breadth of his interests—from contemporary art and literature to eighteenth-century French chamber music—was extraordinary, and since those interests often found expression in his music, it complicates any attempt at a label. To classify him as an Impressionist, or Symbolist, or as a bit of both is simplistic. His music displays such variety that categorization only limits our understanding and appreciation of it.

CHAPTER NINE

Student Compositions

There is no excellent or supreme beauty without some strangeness in the proportion.

Frances Bacon, *Novum Organum* (1620)

Instrumental Works

Chamber: Piano Trio

Piano: *Danse bohémienne*; *Le Triomphe de Bacchus*; *Printemps*;
Première Suite d'orchestre (also for orchestra)

Vocal Works

Songs: "Nuit d'étoiles" (Banville); "Mandoline" (Verlaine); "Romance" (Bourget);
"Pantomime" (Verlaine); "Fleur des blés" (Girod); "Rondel chinois"(?); "Clair de lune"
(Verlaine); "En sourdine" (Verlaine); "Fantoches" (Verlaine); "Apparition" ((Mallarmé)

Cantatas and Works for the Stage:

Diane au bois; *Le Gladiateur*; *L'Enfant prodigue*
Hélène

MOST OF DEBUSSY'S STUDENT COMPOSITIONS WERE NOT PUBLISHED DURING HIS lifetime. Later in his career, when there was a market for any work by him, he was probably tempted to recycle some of these early pieces. But he must also have realized that had he authorized their publication, it would have seemed as if he were trying to profit from purely apprentice exercises. Still, it is surprising that it took so long for them to appear in print—and that nearly a century after his death, so many still remain in manuscript. One would have thought that for a composer of Debussy's stature, curiosity alone would have justified publication.

The reluctance to publish them is the result of hasty evaluation. Léon Vallas, for decades the most prominent of Debussy's biographers, examined in manuscript several of Debussy's student works and was critical of them. When some of the early songs appeared in print in the 1920s, Vallas concluded that they were clumsy, amateurish, and best left unpublished. Although his criticism was based on only a small portion of Debussy's youthful work (and, in some instances, only a brief examination of them), his opinion became widely adopted and led to the standard perception of Debussy as a late bloomer—one whose skills as a composer became apparent only years after he had left the Conservatoire.

Few bothered to take a closer look at Debussy's student works, yet anyone approaching them with an open mind could only have been struck by their accomplishments. There was much of interest—and not merely because they provided glimpses into his youthful tastes and development. Although awkward in spots, they show a great deal of craftsmanship, all the more noteworthy given the complex musical language of the late nineteenth century.

Ultimately what makes these early works so remarkable is their beauty. Craftsmanship can be taught, and Debussy worked diligently to acquire it. But from the start, the musical substance of his work—his inspiration—reveals him to be a superb musician of enormous potential.

Among Debussy's first compositions is his only piano trio, written in 1880 for the ensemble at Nadezhda von Meck's of which he was a part. Chamber music in general enjoyed increased popularity in France after the Franco-Prussian War, primarily because of the efforts of the Société Nationale. An area of particular interest was instrumental music—which (with the exception of solo piano compositions) had been neglected in France during the first half of the century. For Debussy's piano trio, there would have been no shortage of models from the regular concert series at the Société, including chamber compositions with piano by Alexis de Castillon, Vincent d'Indy, Edouard Lalo, and Camille Saint-Saëns.

Debussy's Piano Trio (not published until 1986) has a great deal of charm. As would be expected, it has four movements, but in this instance the second movement is an elegant scherzo (in which he makes clever use of pizzicato strings). The Trio is lyrical and overwhelmingly tuneful. Chamber music of this type would usually contain one or more movements in sonata form, but even at this early stage Debussy's disdain for set structures is apparent. Only one movement—the finale (twenty measures of which have been reconstructed from the cello part)—bears a remote resemblance to sonata form. Rather, Debussy's concern is with thematic contrast (there are four distinct theme groups in the first movement alone). The sheer profusion of melody serves as the basis of the trio's major flaw: its lack of cohesiveness. The effect is often that of a potpourri, with a series of striking melodies somewhat indiscriminately linked.

Still, the Trio is a respectable effort, especially since prior to it Debussy had composed very little. He presented a manuscript copy of the trio (with the dedication, "many notes accompanied by many regards") to his former harmony teacher, Emile Durand—a gesture which has been interpreted as indicating that, despite differences, their relationship was cordial.[1] But Debussy's presentation could just as easily have been intended as a declaration of independence, and proof, in spite of Durand's evaluation of him in class, of his accomplishments. No matter what the motivation may have been, Durand would not have been pleased by its structural laxness.

A few months before the trio, Debussy composed a *Danse bohémienne* for solo piano (not published until 1932). It was known to Mme von Meck who attempted to interest Chaikovsky in it, but his response was not encouraging. He dismissed it as a "pretty thing, but rather short, with themes which lead nowhere and an unsettled structure which lacks unity"—a frank evaluation.[2] The *Danse* is salon music, the type of piece which might have been included by a composer in an album of miscellanies. It is quite repetitive (dances tend to be) and not as accomplished or challenging as the Trio.

It is surprising that during these years Debussy did not draw on his training as a pianist to compose more substantial works for piano. Perhaps he was afraid of being perceived more as a pianist than as a composer. But instrumental music itself seemed to hold little attraction for him. Although he did compose several works for piano, four-hands—including a Symphony in three movements (December 1880 and January 1881), written for the von Mecks (the first movement, an allegro, sounds a bit Brahmsian), and an "Andante" and "Diane Overture" (1881; dedicated to Guiraud)—Debussy showed much greater interest in song.[3] From 1879 to 1885 he composed about forty songs on a variety of texts, and they constitute his major accomplishment as a composer during these years.

Most people familiar with nineteenth-century art song associate it with the German Lied and the songs of Schubert, Schumann, and Brahms. The French counterpart—the "mélodie"—has a much smaller following, in part because on first hearing the mélodie often seems less tuneful than the Lied. The mélodie was humble in origin, developing from the "romance," a genre popular in France from the Napoleonic era through the 1840s. Romances were generally slight pieces, intended for performance at home by amateurs. They tended to be lyrical, quite simple, and with rudimentary piano accompaniment.

---

1. *LS*, p. 48.

2. Ibid., p. 46.

3. In June 1882 he also composed two salon pieces: an "Intermezzo" for cello and piano (part of a projected suite for cello and orchestra), and a "Nocturne et Scherzo" (for cello with piano accompaniment). Both were arranged for violin as well. Another "Intermezzo" (intended for orchestra and surviving for piano, four-hands) was inspired by Heine's "Lyric Intermezzo."

The mélodie, although still directed toward the salon, displayed greater refinement. It began to make its appearance as enthusiasm for the romance waned. Berlioz, Meyerbeer, and Liszt composed quite a few, as did later composers such as Gounod, Delibes, and Saint-Saëns. But by the time Debussy turned to it, the mélodie was still more a popular than an artistic genre. Massenet was the most fashionable composer of mélodies. He wrote more than 250, issuing them individually and in albums. The poetry he set was frequently sentimental, written by popular poets of the day who often also wrote opera librettos. Massenet's mélodies were known for their lyricism (a reflection of his success in opera) with moderately difficult piano accompaniments. But his finest settings—such as the group of five comprising *Poème d'Octobre* published in 1878—rise above the usual level of the salon and, like the posters of Toulouse-Lautrec and Mucha, are strikingly evocative of *la Belle Epoque*.

Massenet's mélodies were representative of the most popular type. Those of his contemporary, Henri Duparc, tended to be more challenging and were directed toward connoisseurs. A student of Franck, Duparc was plagued by self-doubt and published little. His greatest accomplishment is seventeen songs, composed from 1868 to 1884 (although most did not appear in print until the 1890s). His choice of poets—including Jean Lahor, Leconte de Lisle, Théophile Gautier, and Charles Baudelaire—was far removed from the fashionable writers selected by Massenet. And Duparc's music was equally distinctive: adventurous, often daring harmonically, and intimately linked to the text. Duparc's mélodies are more characteristic of the type of mélodie Debussy was to create.

Debussy's first songs (composed in late 1879) were set to texts of the popular Romantic poet, Alfred de Musset.[4] It was a conventional choice, but Debussy was soon to find Romanticism—in both literature and music—sentimental and melodramatic. More characteristic was his next choice of poet: Théodore de Banville. Banville's poetry may not have been particularly innovative for the 1880s (he had been associated twenty years earlier with the Parnassians, who produced, in reaction to Romanticism, a more "classical" style). But his work remained distinctive enough to have a select following, an indication both of the breadth of Debussy's reading and the growing refinement of his taste.

Debussy's setting of Banville's "Nuit d'étoiles" (Starry Night) was composed early in 1880 and published two years later—the first of his works to appear in print. It represents well his earliest songs. The use of arpeggios in the piano to create a strumming effect imitative of the lyre referred to in the poem is a nice touch. But it is burdened by convention, with four-bar lyricism à la Massenet and a piano part

4. Two are known: "Madrid" (which remains unpublished) and "Ballade à la lune" (which is known only by a reference to it by Debussy's friend, Paul Vidal).

subservient to the vocal line. It can be gracious and tuneful, but the same may be said of many other mélodies of the day.

In 1881 Debussy composed about a dozen songs, using additional poems of Banville as well as poetry by Leconte de Lisle (who also had ties to the Parnassians). In general Debussy's very first songs can give the impression of melody thrust upon the text, but these new songs are far more skillfully handled. The music shows unusual sensitivity to the poetry and an increased role for the piano—all accomplished without sacrificing lyricism. His mastery of the Massenet-like mélodie of the day is demonstrated in little gems, such as his setting of André Girod's "Fleur des blés" (Wheat Flower). Several of the poems set in 1881 are love poems, not surprising given their association with Marie Vasnier—twenty-seven of Debussy's early songs were written with her in mind. But also present is wit and irony seen, for example, in the exoticism of "Rondel chinois," a fanciful parody of the current fad for exoticism found in operas such as Massenet's *Roi de Lahore* and Delibes's *Lakmé*.

What becomes increasingly apparent in these settings is Debussy's astonishing poetic sensibility. His reading and interpretation of poetry were intense—a passionate combination of intellect and imagination—and his music reflected it. In that sense, the finest of Debussy's songs exist both as a piece of music and as an interpretation of the text.

Poetry was a powerful source of inspiration to him, so much so that Debussy's music could be transformed by it. Such was the case in 1882 with his settings of Paul Verlaine. Although frequently associated with the Symbolists, Verlaine's poetry stands apart. He was about twenty years older than most of the writers connected to the movement. The scandal that surrounded him—his alcoholism and tumultuous affair with Arthur Rimbaud—attracted as much attention as his writing. Although Debussy is not believed to have known Verlaine, there was a personal connection. In the early 1870s during Verlaine's infatuation with Rimbaud, he was married to Mme Mauté's daughter and lived for a time with the family. Debussy was already studying at the Conservatoire so he probably had no direct contact with Verlaine, but it would be unlikely if he had not heard about him.

In his poetry Verlaine made a point of distancing himself from French literary tradition. For centuries, the standard line of verse in France had been the alexandrine: twelve syllables with a caesura (or cadence) at the halfway point. Verlaine played with the alexandrine in a variety of ways—altering the placement of the caesura, using an odd number of metrical feet, and introducing internal rhyme. As a result, he abandoned the traditional rhetorical style of much nineteenth-century French poetry. His rhyme schemes and meter became unpredictable; the use of assonance and alliteration became prominent.

To set Verlaine's poetry to music, a new and more flexible compositional approach was essential. Symmetrical phrasing, operatic lyricism, and luxuriant harmony in the style of Massenet would be incongruous. The music Debussy created for Verlaine's poems was unlike any he had written, with a free-flowing and declamatory vocal line, and considerable freedom in the use of dissonance (inevitably as a commentary on the text).

In choosing Verlaine, Debussy was well ahead of his time. Verlaine did not emerge from obscurity until the publication of *Jadis et Naguère* in 1884 (Gabriel Fauré's well-known settings of Verlaine's "La bonne Chanson," for example, were not completed until a decade after Debussy's). Debussy set four poems of Verlaine to music in 1882: "Clair de lune" (Moonlight), "En sourdine" (Muted), "Fantoches" (Puppets), and "Mandoline." They were written for Marie Vasnier, and because they were tailored to her strengths, make exceptional demands on the voice, especially in the upper register ("En sourdine" is a notable instance).

Debussy revised the first three of the Verlaine poems, publishing them in 1903 as the first set of *Fêtes galantes*. These later settings (that for "Fantoches" greatly resembles the 1882 version; the others are new) remain much better known than Debussy's student efforts. But the earlier versions have much to commend them.

The *enfant terrible* of the Conservatoire soon makes an appearance. In "Mandoline" (supposedly in C major, but with modal implications), the opening arpeggios consist of two open fifths placed on top of one another—emphasizing the ninth (A), but concocted to imitate the open strings of the mandolin. The reiterated Gs could not make the entry of the voice (outlining a D minor triad) more startling (Example 9-1a).

9-1a "Mandoline"

The role of the piano is pivotal—creating in its way duets for piano and voice. But even today what is most striking is Debussy's audacity: "Mandoline" seems to have no ending. Following a decisive statement of the tonic (C major), there is silence, then G—a playful ambiguity identical to the opening measures of the song (Example 9-1b).

9-1b "Mandoline" (1890 version; in the earlier setting the voice is an octave higher)

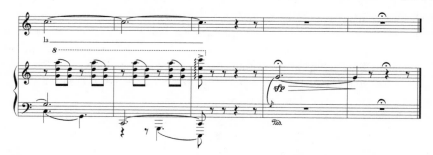

Because it has been routine for so long to belittle his student compositions, it is easy to overlook their innovations. Debussy's contemporaries did not. "Mandoline" was first published in 1890, and the composer Charles Koechlin was astonished by what he found in it. "There were several chords at the start," he recalled, "which revealed to me all sorts of modulatory possibilities."[5]

Debussy composed about a dozen songs in 1883 and 1884. Half use the poetry of Paul Bourget, a poet and novelist who was coming increasingly in vogue. These settings were among those Debussy performed to acclaim at the Villa during his stay in Rome, and their popularity is not surprising. They are lyrical in a more conventional manner than the Verlaine songs, but Debussy's more orthodox approach implies no abandonment of his poetic sensibility. For "Romance," a series of repetitive pianissimo seventh chords creates a marvelously static effect, intended as a musical counterpart to the silence referred to in the poem (Example 9-2).

9-2 "Romance"

5. Robert Orledge, *Charles Koechlin (1867–1950). His Life and Works* (Chur, Switzerland: Harwood Academic, 1989), p. 5.

One additional Verlaine poem was set in 1883: "Pantomime." Verlaine drew out the best in Debussy, and in this instance he seemed particularly attracted to Verlaine's irony—a characteristic of the poetry, incidentally, of another of Debussy's favorite writers, Jules Laforgue. "Pantomime" is a spirited work and an early indication of Debussy's fondness for the commedia dell'arte (similar themes in the poetry of Banville also attracted him). At times, its brash tunefulness brings to mind the music hall. The opening sets the stage for its mocking tone. Statements of the tonic are playfully avoided, as in Example 9-3 where the piano at first emphasizes the leading tone (D sharp; mm. 2–3, 5–6), but then descends by half step to F natural, making all the more startling the appearance of E major in the tenth measure:

9-3 "Pantomime"

As Debussy prepared for what was to be his final attempt for the Prix de Rome, fewer songs were composed. The most interesting is his setting of Mallarmé's "Apparition," a poem that had only recently appeared in print (November 1883) in the journal *Lutèce*. Mallarmé's hermetic poetry was to have a profound effect on Debussy, but this first encounter is a bit of a disappointment. Much of Mallarmé's work is visionary and dazzling. Ambiguity is an important element—with the sounds of words and their meaning often of equal significance, and with meaning itself condensed and obscured.

Unlike the Verlaine songs, Debussy's setting of Mallarmé does not go far enough in its unconventionality. There is too much that recalls his settings of Bourget's love poems, resulting in music that seems fragmented and at times at odds with the text. There is also a concern with the grand gesture, creating precisely the type of theatrical statement that Debussy made a point of avoiding in his later settings of Mallarmé. But perhaps it is unfair to expect so much so early in his career—for there is a great deal in the music that complements the poem, such as the wonderfully nebulous effects of the opening ninth chords in the piano's upper register (with the indication that they be performed "rêveusement": "in a dream-like manner").

Although songs were the major focus during these years, several projects indicated Debussy's interest in the stage. It was typical of Debussy throughout his career to contemplate writing for the theater; few projects, however, went beyond the planning stage. While in Rome he considered an adaptation of Flaubert's *Salammbô*, but nothing came of it. The most substantial project during these years was an adaptation of Banville's drama, *Diane au bois* (based on Ovid). Debussy was fascinated by its possibilities and worked on it intermittently from 1883 to 1886. His "Diane Overture" of 1881 (for piano, four-hands) may have been intended to be part of it. But only two additional segments were completed: parts of scenes iii and iv from Act II, a total of twenty-nine pages for soprano and tenor with piano accompaniment. Debussy probably was drawn to the dream-like elements of Banville's play (similar in that sense to his later interest in Maeterlinck's *Pelléas et Mélisande*). For a while he considered using *Diane* instead of *Zuleima* as his first envoi from Rome.[6]

Prior to *Diane au bois*, Debussy had shown interest in two other Banville works. In 1882 he set portions of Banville's play, *Hymnis*. And that same year, inspired by Banville's poem, "Le Triomphe de Bacchus à son retour des Indes," Debussy composed *Le Triomphe de Bacchus* for piano, four-hands ("Divertissement," "Andante," "Scherzo," "Marche et bacchanale"). It was followed (1883–84?) by a more ambitious suite, the *Première Suite d'orchestre* consisting of four movements ("Fête," "Ballet," "Rêve," and "Cortège et bacchanale").[7] In addition to the pieces associated with Banville, Debussy's work with Leconte de Lisle's *Hélène* was considered as an entry piece for the city of Paris competition in 1884. It was a "lyric scene" for soprano, chorus, and orchestra first started in 1881, but he completed only fragments.

All of these compositions were works conceived by Debussy beyond those in the classroom, and reveal a great deal about both his interests and his industry. But he also remained active in Guiraud's class, and produced a number of pieces associated with the Prix de Rome competition:

---

6. For further discussion of these fragments (including previously unpublished excerpts), see *L*, pp. 76–81, and James R. Briscoe, "To Invent New Forms": Debussy's *Diane au bois*," *Musical Quarterly* 74 (1990), pp. 131–169.

7. The version for piano, four-hands has survived. An orchestral setting lacks the third movement.

1882: "Salut printemps" (Probably as practice for the competition, Debussy also set the cantata, "Daniel," by Emile Cicile.)

1883: "Invocation" and *Le Gladiateur*

1884: "Le Printemps" and *L'Enfant prodigue*

Le Gladiateur was the cantata for which Debussy was awarded second prize. It is clearly a student work, with a number of clichés that confirm his study of contemporary French opera (and its fondness for diminished seventh chords at moments of dramatic intensity). But it also reveals Debussy's interest in Wagner (especially in the use of leitmotivs) and, not surprising given the songs he had composed, displays a "sensitivity to poetic values."[8]

Debussy's winning entry of 1884—*L'Enfant prodigue*—is more accomplished. The text includes roles for the Prodigal Son (Azaël), his parents (Lia and Siméon), and chorus, and is an adaptation of the biblical tale. In composing it, Debussy adhered to Guiraud's advice and wrote in a more conventional style. *L'Enfant prodigue* was created with the clear intention of offending no one and of pleasing as many as possible. For it, Debussy drew on the style of two of the most popular composers of the day, Massenet and Delibes—a selection made all the easier by the similarity between the exotic setting of *L'Enfant prodigue* and several of their operas.

It was Debussy's good fortune that the tale of the Prodigal Son enjoyed renewed popularity at the time in France, including versions by popular painters such as Puvis de Chavannes. After Debussy became better known, he decided to revise the work, and it is this version (1906–1908, apparently with assistance from André Caplet) that is heard today. When he reexamined it prior to revision, Debussy was astonished to find how inept his original scoring was, even claiming to find some double stops for the English horn.

Exoticism is an essential element of the work and a major reason for its popularity. It makes an appearance in the very first measures: the plaintive cry of the oboe is intended to be evocative of the Middle East. But equally striking is Debussy's imitation of the lyrical, operatic style characteristic of Massenet (see Example 9-4 on the following page).

For a student work, *L'Enfant prodigue* is remarkably skillful. Much of the music is enjoyable, tuneful, and memorable. Yet—despite moments of dramatic effectiveness—to those familiar with Debussy's later music, it seems like the work of someone else. It remains a tribute to his facility. He was able with comparative ease to write in the fashionable manner of his day. To the judges, it must have seemed as if he were a budding Massenet. But Debussy's subterfuge—and the artistic compromise it entailed—was not to his liking. He was never particularly pleased by the popularity of *L'Enfant prodigue*.

8. John R. Clevenger, "Debussy's First 'Masterpiece.' *Le Gladiateur*," *Cahiers Debussy* 23 (1999), p. 13.

After settling in Rome, Debussy was obliged to produce one major composition each year as an indication of his activity and development. These yearly envois were sent to Paris for evaluation. Invariably, reaction to them was not favorable. *Zuleima*, sent in 1886, has been discussed in Chapter 2. *Printemps* was hurriedly completed the following year. It was condemned for its supposed impressionistic qualities. But what was actually disliked in the work was its departure from convention—and, in that sense, the criticism was probably taken by Debussy as confirmation of his success.

Printemps is known today in a revision prepared in 1913 by Henri Büsser and authorized by Debussy (with some assistance on his part). The original has been considerably reworked: the chorus has been removed and the orchestration is far more sophisticated than would have been true of Debussy in 1887. Much of it seems intended to please, especially the work's beguiling lyricism. Yet the tonal ambiguity of its primary theme and the defiance of textbook harmony would probably have been sufficient to set the committee on edge.

They were also perplexed by its structure. "The first movement of the symphonic piece of M. Debussy is a sort of adagio prelude, of a reverie and affectation that lead to confusion," they wrote. "The second movement is a bizarre and incoherent transformation of the first."[9] To their credit, the committee recognized that the second movement was based on thematic material from the first. It might have helped Debussy's case if they had known why. As he explained in a letter to Emile Baron, "the slow and languid genesis of beings and things in nature" (Movement I) leads to "their flowering—concluding with a dazzling delight at being reborn to a new life" (Movement II)—so there was a sound poetic reason for using the same music in both movements.[10]

In 1889 Debussy had considered reworking *Printemps* for possible performance at the Société Nationale. He described it not as a choral work—for the chorus had "*no words* and is handled as if it were part of the orchestra"—but as a "*symphonic suite with chorus.*"[11] For that reason, he felt that it would be a challenge to perform, a reaction that seems to indicate that he was hesitant in entrusting it to the Société. But at the time he was creating works more indicative of new directions in his style—most notably, the Fantaisie for Piano and Orchestra and *Cinq Poèmes de Baudelaire*—and that, coupled with his invariable reluctance to revise old pieces, helps to explain why the proposed revision was delayed for nearly twenty-five years. By then, the situation had changed: his popularity was so great that any new piece he had written was eagerly awaited.

9. John R. Clevenger, "Debussy's Rome Cantatas," in *Debussy and His World*, ed. Jane Fulcher (Princeton, NJ: Princeton University Press, 2001), p. 71.

10. Letter of 9 February 1887 in *C*, p. 59.

11. Letter to Ernest Chausson of 7 March 1889 in ibid., p. 70.

Plate 1: While living with the von Mecks, Debussy regularly performed as part of a piano trio (he is on the right; the others are P. Danilchenko and Ladislas Pachulsky). One of his first compositions was written for the group in 1880.

Plate 2: Debussy at the time he was living at the Villa Medici, after winning the Prix de Rome, painted by fellow-student, Marcel Baschet. His stay there, he wrote in 1885, was "*a wasted experience* [*that*] *has merely set me back.*"

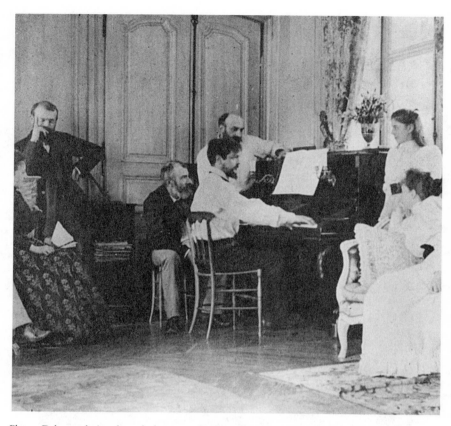

Plate 3: Debussy playing through the score of Musorgsky's *Boris Godunov* while visiting the Chaussons in 1893 at their summer residence in Luzancy. Chausson, standing alongside Debussy, became a strong supporter and advisor.

Plate 4: Debussy in 1897 relaxing in the apartment of the writer Pierre Louÿs, along with Louÿs's Algerian mistress, Zohra bent Brahim.

Plate 5: Debussy in May 1902 with his first wife, Lilly Texier. Alongside are the composer, Paul Dukas; the music critic, Pierre Lalo; and Adrien Dukas, Paul's brother.

Plate 6: The cover for Debussy's *La Damoiselle élue* by Maurice Denis (1870–1943) published by Edmond Bailly in 1892. The graceful, flowing line of her hair exemplifies the arabesque characteristic of art nouveau.

Plate 7: Debussy with his second wife, Emma Bardac. After their marriage, they lived in an elegant home in an aristocratic neighborhood near the Bois de Boulogne. But despite the popularity of his music, Debussy was constantly in debt.

Plate 8: Debussy at his work table in his study. Prominently displayed behind him is one of his favorite pieces: a wooden statue of a toad he named Arkel after the character in *Pelléas*.

Plate 9: Debussy with his daughter, Chouchou. She was the light of his life and inspired several of his compositions, including *Children's Corner* (1908).

Plate 10: Debussy at the seashore with Chouchou during a vacation to Houlgate in 1911. He was annoyed by the crowds of tourists. "I'm doing precisely nothing, not out of idleness, but because it's impossible to think amid this caravanserai."

Plate 11: A formal portrait of Debussy by Paul Nadar (1856–1939) taken in 1909. Debussy made fun of the stiff pose and joked to Nadar that the image was worthy of posterity.

Plate 12: Debussy in his garden, a constant source of inspiration to him. "On fine days, he walked along a garden path and noted down his musical ideas in a little red leather notebook which never left his pocket."

Plate 13: The cover for *La Mer* (1905). Its basis is the crest of a wave adapted from a print by the Japanese artist Hokusai (1760–1849): "The Hollow of the Wave Off Kanegawa."

Plate 14: Debussy in 1917. Cancer took a severe toll on him. "I don't take this tattered body for walks anymore," he wrote in 1916, "in case I frighten little children and tram conductors."

Plate 15: Portrait of Debussy in 1913 by Ivan Thièle (1877–1948). This is an etching from the original charcoal drawing, and was first printed in 1927 in the deluxe edition of Debussy's correspondence with his publisher.

CHAPTER TEN

Compositions, 1888–1893

In music, then, rather than in poetry, is to be found the true type or measure of perfected art. Although each art has its incommunicable element, its untranslatable order of impressions, its unique mode of reaching the "imaginative reason," yet the arts may be represented as continually struggling after the law or principle of music, to a condition which music alone completely realises.

Walter Pater, "The School of Giorgione" (1877)

Instrumental Works

Piano: *Deux Arabesques*; *Mazurka*; *Rêverie*; *Ballade slave*; *Tarentelle styrienne*; *Valse romantique*; *Suite bergamasque*; *Nocturne*; *Petite Suite*

Orchestra and Concerto: Fantaisie for Piano and Orchestra; *Marche des anciens comtes de Ross* (*Marche écossaise*)

Vocal Works

Songs: *Ariettes* [*oubliées*] (Verlaine); *Cinq Poèmes de Baudelaire*; *Fêtes galantes* (Verlaine); *Proses lyriques* (Debussy)

Opera and Cantata: *La Damoiselle élue*; *Rodrigue et Chimène*

DEBUSSY WAS ONLY THREE MONTHS SHORT OF HIS THIRTY–FIRST BIRTHDAY when he attended the unique performance in Paris of Maeterlinck's *Pelléas et Mélisande.* Although it provided him with a goal, it also brought to mind how little he seemed to have accomplished. Debussy could only have been concerned with the lack of recognition for his work thus far. But despite his growing impatience, much had been achieved. During the years immediately following his return from Rome, in working to establish a reputation he had done much to create the foundation of his musical style.

It was not as if he were uncertain about the sound he wanted to create. He described precisely what he was looking for and how it would be produced: "Sound must be drowned." "The tonal scale must be enriched by other scales." "Minor thirds and major thirds should be combined." These statements were all part of a concept expressed in conversations with Ernest Guiraud in 1889 and 1890—conversations so unusual that another student present actually took notes:

DEBUSSY: Classical signifies major and minor. In the classical style chords are resolved. The classical style implies near modulations (a closed circle). Romantic: a label that to my mind has no significance. The language of Schumann, Berlioz, and Liszt is the classical language. I hear in them all the same kind of music.

GUIRAUD: But this insipid, continuous music [the music of Wagner]. No scenes, no cuts. You can't say it is anything like Mozart!

DEBUSSY: I shouldn't say it is the opposite of Mozart. It's a later development. No square-cut phrases, nevertheless Wagner develops in the classical manner. Wagner merely abandoned the perpetual perfect cadence and the hateful six-four chord. . . .

GUIRAUD: But what about his treatment of the voices?

DEBUSSY: Yes, there we find a difference, but not a musical difference. Is it new? It may seem to resemble the spoken language; and it doesn't follow the four-bar phrase. There are no recitatives in the Italian manner and no lyrical arias. The words are subordinated to the orchestral accompaniment, but not sufficiently. It is music that sings too continuously. Singing should be reserved for certain points.

GUIRAUD: What kind of poet would you yourself have in mind?

DEBUSSY: One who only hints at what is to be said. The ideal would be two associated dreams. No place, nor time. No big scene. No compulsion on the musician, who must complete and give body to the work of the poet. Music in opera is far too predominant. Too much singing and the musical settings are too cumbersome. The blossoming of the voice into true singing should occur only when required. A painting executed in gray is the ideal. No developments merely for the sake of developments. A prolonged development does not fit, cannot fit, the words. My idea is of a short libretto with mobile scenes. . . . [The discussion then turned to concepts of rhythm and harmony.]

DEBUSSY: No faith in the supremacy of the C major scale. The tonal scale must be enriched by other scales. . . . Rhythms are stifling. Rhythms cannot be contained within bars. . . . Relative keys are nonsense too. Music is neither major nor minor. Minor thirds and major thirds should be combined, modulation thus becoming more flexible. The mode is that which one happens to choose at the moment. It is inconstant. . . .

GUIRAUD: (Debussy having played a series of intervals on the piano): What's that?

DEBUSSY: Incomplete chords, floating. *Il faut noyer le ton* [The sound must be drowned]. One can travel where one wishes and leave by any door. Greater nuances.

GUIRAUD: But when I play this it has to resolve. [Guiraud plays a Neapolitan sixth chord.]

DEBUSSY: I don't see that it should. Why? . . . There is no theory. You have merely to listen. Pleasure is the law.[1]

Debussy's comments—made at a time when he was probably working on the *Cinq Poèmes de Baudelaire*, the *Fantaisie*, and the *Petite Suite*—confirm his independence of mind, but they also reveal much about the type of music that interested him. His refusal to accept the commonplace distinction between "Classic" and "Romantic" provided a sense of direction for his own compositions. It was a perception based on his discovery that the aesthetic differences separating classicism and romanticism masked strong similarities in their musical style. His stance permitted him to assume a broad and expansive view of musical tradition and to create a deeply personal interpretation of it—with Berlioz, Schumann, and Liszt as representatives of a "classical language."

But it is also clear that Debussy's primary concern was with sound—not tradition—and certainly not with rules sanctioned or governed by tradition. Anything that did not produce the sound he wanted became irrelevant. An equally important aspect was the manner in which that sound would be created: by "nuance"—a subtle approach, and one in deliberate contrast to the dramatic and emotional climaxes characteristic of nineteenth-century music.

Debussy's sensibility—exemplified by the statement, "*Il faut noyer le ton*"—emphasized an affinity for ambiguity. Tonality continued to be present in his music, but in a new manner—more expansive, and with less distinction between major and minor. Tonality was also "enriched" by the use of scales other than major and minor, that is, different modes such as the whole tone scale. But Debussy's concern with ambiguity went beyond tonality. Articulation and texture could also be softened, in the process minimizing the difference between melody and harmony, and leading to what contemporary critics often complained was an emphasis on harmony alone.

The ideas Debussy expressed to Guiraud were not ones he had only recently articulated. Aspects of them are present in his student compositions, particularly the Verlaine songs. But beginning in the late 1880s, their presence becomes more pervasive. At the same time—while he gradually asserted his independence as a composer—Debussy's musical language and the goals he worked toward became more closely allied to a personal musical aesthetic.

1. Maurice Emmanuel (who became a critic and music historian) was a student of Guiraud and was present at about a dozen meetings between him and Debussy. He published a transcription of their conversations in 1926 in his study of *Pelléas et Mélisande*. Translation in *LK,* I, pp. 204–207.

At its heart was a dissatisfaction—in some instances, a contempt—for contemporary French music. To Debussy, most of the work performed at the Société Nationale was conventional and academic. As for French opera, it was vapid. Massenet's operas, he maintained, displayed "an extraordinary talent for satisfying all that is poetically empty and lyrically cheap in the dilettante mind! Everything in it contributes to providing mediocrity."[2] Convinced that the masses were only attracted to what was simplistic and shallow, Debussy was suspicious of any composer who (like Massenet) was popular. And he was also convinced that his own subjective and idealistic conception of music would appeal only to a select minority.

Debussy was intrigued by the elusive and evanescent qualities of music, characteristics he believed were a world apart from the sordid, callous, and ignoble standards of his day. Music, he wrote, was "a dream from which the veils have been lifted. It's not even the expression of a feeling, it's the feeling itself."[3] His connection of music with dream and feeling was not unique. Similar concepts were championed by the Symbolists. For years Debussy had been attracted to dream-like settings for his music, using texts by Banville and Mallarmé.

His association of music with feeling also resembled the view held by the Symbolists. It differed from the common nineteenth-century belief in music's ability to express specific emotions (such as grief or joy). As Debussy put it, music was "the feeling itself" (and not an intermediary). His view was allied to the concept of "états d'âme" (soul-states) current in Symbolist literature and painting (see Chapter 8). Music and, to a lesser extent, the visual arts were prized for their ability to communicate with precision what words alone could not: specific states of soul—not individual emotions, but entire, often complex, states embodying, say, happiness and elation, or despair, anger, and remorse.

One of Debussy's first steps in developing his own musical style was to reject much of what his contemporaries most valued: the traditional view of Western music of the eighteenth and nineteenth centuries. It served as the foundation at the Conservatoire, and he concluded that it was essential to get away from it "as soon as possible in order to look for and discover one's individuality."[4]

His contempt for "classical masters"—such as Beethoven (whom he "claimed to abhor")—was well known among friends and acquaintants.[5] But there were exceptions. At Rome, Paul Vidal saw Debussy enjoying performances of Beethoven's Fifth Piano Concerto and Second Symphony—so there was some posturing in his

2. Letter to André Poniatowski of February 1893 in *DL*, p. 41.

3. Ibid.

4. Claude Debussy, *Monsieur Croche et autres écrits*, ed. François Lesure (Paris: Gallimard, 1987), p. 278. Hereafter abbreviated *Écrits*.

5. Paul Vidal, "Souvenirs d'Achille Debussy," *La Revue Musicale* 7 (May, 1926), p. 14.

manner. Debussy always took pleasure in shocking the crowd, and there was no easier way for him to do it than by attacking their idols.

The classical style was confining and predictable to Debussy, and his interest in composers associated with Romanticism—Schumann, for example—was selective. What he preferred was any kind of music that differed from the academic models exhibited at the Conservatoire. The earliest recorded instance of this was his admiration for the gypsy music he heard in Moscow while with the von Mecks. It was, in the words of his first French biographer, important as "the initial instance of music without rules."[6]

Another example is his enthusiasm for the compositions of Palestrina and Orlando di Lasso that he encountered in Rome. After returning to Paris, Debussy's interest in music of the Renaissance grew. There was a revival of early music under way, and in the vanguard were the concerts created by Charles Bordes at Saint-Gervais. Debussy attended several, on at least one occasion bringing Mallarmé along. "It is incredibly beautiful," he wrote after hearing a mass by Palestrina. "Although written in a strict manner technically, its effect is one of perfect whiteness, and emotion is not expressed (as it has come to be) by shrieks and roars, but by melodic arabesques. It is the result to a certain extent of the contours, and the interlacing of the arabesques—producing something which seems to be unique: harmony created by melody!"[7] Paul Dukas recalled that at about this time he and Debussy would play pieces by Palestrina together, arranging them as piano duets.

Aspects of Palestrina's style appealed to Debussy because they provided confirmation of his own beliefs. The "perfect whiteness"—a wonderful phrase that emphasizes Debussy's visual affinity—was a result of the absence of histrionics and melodrama typical of nineteenth-century music. And he seemed pleased that although its "strict manner" embodied more than enough rules to satisfy academics, these were not the rules taught at the Conservatoire. In the end, what seemed most to impress him was the effect of Palestrina's counterpoint: "harmony created by melody"—an unusual observation, and one that could also be applied to some of Debussy's music.

Debussy was charmed by what he perceived as the essence of Palestrina's melody: melody as arabesque. Arabesque was popular at the time in the visual arts where it was represented as a free-flowing, graceful, and rippling line—both languid and dynamic. Odilon Redon, a Symbolist painter and lithographer, complained of a "preoccupation" with it.[8] And there can be little doubt that at times it must have seemed as if the arabesque

6. Louis Laloy, *Claude Debussy* (Paris: Les Bibliophiles Fantaisistes, 1909), p. 15. The incident was also mentioned in Daniel Chennevière's early study of Debussy (1913).

7. Letter to André Poniatowski of February 1893 in *C*, p. 116. The work was his *Missa brevis* for four voices.

8. Douglas Druick, ed., *Odilon Redon. Prince of Dreams, 1840–1916* (Chicago: Art Institute of Chicago, 1994), p. 236.

had invaded the arts. (A particularly fine instance is the outline of the maiden's hair in the illustration created by Maurice Denis for the cover of Debussy's *La Demoiselle élue*. Debussy gave Redon an inscribed copy of it. See Plate 6.)

Arabesque was also a pervasive component in the Japanese art admired by Debussy. And it was frequently found in art nouveau—an arts and crafts movement allied with Symbolism—where it found expression in furniture, book design, even the wrought iron entrances of the recently opened Métro in Paris. The arabesque motif was so prevalent in fin-de-siècle France that Debussy's allusion to it comes as no surprise. But to apply it as he did to Palestrina's music was striking. Arabesque as melody represented true melody to Debussy, and he discovered it in all music he admired, including that of Bach.

Debussy's interest in the music of the distant past was not limited to that of the Renaissance. He was equally fascinated with Gregorian chant, which was also performed at Saint-Gervais. Chant was being rediscovered in Paris during the 1880s and 1890s, primarily through the research of the monks at Solesmes. Debussy attended several performances, not in the romanticized style (often with keyboard accompaniment) that had become prevalent, but in a style which attempted authenticity. As with the music of Palestrina, he took pleasure in the arabesque-like quality of the melodic line.

Both chant and Palestrina's compositions were a revelation to him. One friend meeting Debussy after a performance at Saint-Gervais detected "a light in his eyes such as I had never seen before, and coming over to me, he expressed his intense emotion in these simple words: 'Now *that's* music!'" [9]

Debussy's compositions created in the half dozen years after his return from Rome confirm his eagerness to produce music as distinctive and original as the music he admired. But the varied content of his compositions also reveals the difficulties and frustration Debussy encountered. He needed to establish a reputation, but preferred not to pander to the tastes of the public. He wanted to appeal to connoisseurs, but soon realized that it was unlikely that their support would provide sufficient income. He wanted the recognition of colleagues, but seemed convinced that they would be unable to appreciate his style. In the end, he tried to appeal to all with, not surprisingly, very limited success.

His compositions during these years fall into three broad categories (with some overlapping):

1. those intended to provide income (salon works, such as the *Mazurka* and *Valse romantique*).

2. those intended to win the esteem of colleagues, usually containing elements of their style (the *Fantaisie* and *Cinq Poèmes de Baudelaire*, for example).

9. Léon Vallas, *Claude Debussy. His Life and Works* (Oxford: Oxford University Press, 1933), p. 38. (Translation corrected.)

3. those written primarily to please himself, with minimal concern with sales (such as *La Damoiselle élue*).

Debussy began by producing works of marked originality such as the *Ariettes*, and *La Damoiselle élue*. But when these did not sufficiently boost his career, his compositions became wider in their appeal. Piano pieces like the *Mazurka*, *Ballade slave*, *Tarentelle styrienne*, and *Valse romantique*—all composed in 1890— recall the salon, and were works he privately belittled.[10] They are all fairly inconsequential, often in straightforward ternary form, and with noticeable padding. The *Nocturne* (1892) also draws on the salon, but there are similarities to the manner of Fauré, and a more demanding and refined technique needed for performance.

In general these works are simple to play and easy to listen to. Melody, often vocal in style, is emphasized. And the composers who served as Debussy's models never seem to be too distant. The pieces contain some nice individual touches: clever variation of the two-measure cells of the *Ballade*, for example, or the expanded tonality of the middle section of the Chabrier-like *Tarentelle styrienne*—a composer admired by Debussy for his willingness to flout the rules.[11]

In some of his compositions Debussy was able to transform the generic salon style of his day. *Rêverie* (1890), *Suite Bergamasque* ("Prélude," "Menuet," "Clair de lune," and "Passepied"; 1890, rev. 1905), and *Deux Arabesques* (1888–1891) became extraordinarily popular. They make limited technical demands on the performer (an important element for sales), are constructed in a straightforward manner (usually in ternary form), and contain a great deal of repetition (making them both easier to learn and easier to grasp). Their simplicity is striking. But despite their popularity they represented an approach that Debussy simply did not like. In 1905 he described the *Rêverie* as "without importance...bad."[12]

In all of these works, Debussy is at his most charming. Their freshness and novelty contribute greatly to their appeal, an appeal based largely on his conception of the arabesque. The distinction between melody (often vocal in nature) and harmony (as an accompaniment to it) is deliberately obscured. In the first of the *Arabesques,* arpeggios create a melodic arabesque. The famous opening of "Clair de lune" is similar—a melding of melody and harmony, varied in cells two measures in length, and with the flow of the arabesque beginning in m. 5 (Example 10-1).

10. Both the *Ballade* and *Tarentelle* were reissued in 1903, the former simply as *Ballade* and the latter as *Danse*.

11. Chabrier's influence can also be found in the exuberant rhythms of the *Tarentelle*. And his sense of the absurd is reflected in the title. It has that exotic touch essential for sales, but no musical connection to Styria, a remote Austrian province.

12. Letter to Madame Fromont of 21 April 1905 in *C*, p. 904.

10-1 "Clair de lune"

A pair of works for piano four-hands was also composed during these years: the *Marche des anciens comtes de Ross* (commonly known as the *Marche écossaise*) and the *Petite Suite* (consisting of "En Bateau," "Cortège," "Minuet," and "Ballet"; 1888–1889). Both have become popular in orchestral versions.[13]

The *Marche* was an unusual commission given to Debussy in 1890, the story of its creation sounding too good to be true. A Scottish general approached Debussy for a march for his clan (Ross of Rosshire). The general supplied the tune. Debussy used it for the basis of a light-hearted and lively piece. The piano version is delightful, but its orchestration (with the tune now given to the trumpet) is a real crowd-pleaser. Debussy later made a point of frequently including it in programs he conducted.

The *Petite Suite* is similar in style to the *Suite bergamasque*: charming, captivating, and a stylish blend of salon and originality. But, as with all of these works, Debussy did little to promote it. The *Suite* was performed at the home of the publisher Jacques Durand in March 1889, and some weeks later (with the assistance of Paul Dukas) in Guiraud's composition class. It was a token effort, and audience response, noted Durand, "was kind, but no more than that."[14]

In contrast to the piano works, the songs composed during these years admit little compromise. The type of melody popular in the nineteenth-century—cantabile,

13. Debussy first orchestrated the *Marche* (entitling it *Marche écossaise*) c. 1893 and it was performed on 29 May 1894. It was reorchestrated in 1908. The *Petite Suite* was orchestrated by Henri Büsser in 1907.

14. *DR*, p. 30.

with symmetrical phrasing, a tune easily remembered and easily hummed—rarely makes an appearance. But although Debussy's songs are not tuneful in a conventional manner, they could hardly be more lyrical. The melodic style is one of restraint and refinement, coupled with an extraordinary sensitivity to the text. There is an intimacy to them, and the surest means of assuring a poor performance is to present them in an operatic manner.

The *Ariettes* ("C'est l'extase" [It is Ecstasy], "Il pleure dans mon coeur" [It Cries in My Heart], "L'Ombre des arbres" [The Shadow of the Trees], "Chevaux de bois" [Wooden Horses], "Green," and "Spleen"; 1885–1888), *Fêtes galantes* ("En sourdine" [Muted], "Fantoches" [Puppets], and "Clair de lune"; 1891), and *Trois Mélodies* ("La mer est plus belle" [The Sea Is More Beautiful], "Le son du cor s'afflige" [The Sound of the Horn Is Sorrowful], and "L'échelonnement des haies" [The Row of Hedges]; 1891) all use poems of Verlaine. The *Fêtes* had been previously set by Debussy in 1882. "Fantoches," the second in the group, is quite close to the earlier setting. But "En sourdine" and "Clair de lune" are new. Both now seem more sophisticated and provide greater musical contrast. But some of the spontaneity of the earlier settings has been lost. The pentatonic opening, for example, of "Clair de lune" seems recherché—but then that seems to be a trait for which Debussy is striving in many of the songs composed during these years.

"En Sourdine" works particularly well. The syncopated beginning of the opening motive in the piano (intended as a representation of the song of the nightingale referred to in the text) is hypnotic in its effect and a marvelous musical counterpart to Verlaine's poetry. In comparison, the *Trois Mélodies* seem more heavy-handed. "L'Echelonnement des haies" uses as its primary theme one very similar to the *Tarentelle styrienne* for piano. In the song it becomes ponderous and obtrusive, and a distraction to the words of the poem.

The six songs in the *Ariettes* are a fin-de-siècle counterpart to the disconsolate lover in Romantic song cycles such as Schumann's *Dichterliebe* or Schubert's *Die schöne Müllerin*. The sentimental title is deceptive. Actually these poems revel in the decadent spirit of the day, documenting a love satiated, vitiated, and filled with spleen.

All of the songs display Debussy's expanded conception of tonality. Seventh and ninth chords appear with regularity (and are usually treated as consonances). Closely related key centers are avoided. And modes unusual for the time are used ("Spleen," for example, has a pentatonic beginning). One of the most striking aspects of these songs is the manner in which Debussy's music enhances the text. The tone is set in the very first song, "C'est l'extase." A chain of pianissimo seventh and ninth chords (with the indications "lent et caressant" in the piano and "rêveusement" in the voice) complement the languid sensuality of the poem.

In "Il pleure dans mon coeur" the incessant pattern of sixteenth notes re-creates the monotony of incessant rain. And who else but Debussy could have produced the wonderfully hushed climax that follows (beginning with the words "Ce deuil est sans raison" [There is no reason for this mourning])? The utter absence of energy at the song's conclusion ("Mon coeur a tant de peine" [My heart has so much pain]) is accentuated by an extended piano/pianissimo decrescendo—lasting for eighteen beats with the vocal line dropping from C sharp to D sharp.

The poem most popular in style is "Chevaux de bois," a depiction of a Sunday visit to the merry-go-round at a fair. For it, Debussy said that he drew on his recollection of music for the fair in St. Cloud. The simplicity of the poem is complemented by the folk-like tune he wrote for it. It begins in what seems straightforward E major—but with a chromatic twist at the end of the phrase, producing tonal ambiguity (Example 10-2). At each appearance the tune is in a different tonality (E flat, G), creating tension as it rises, and returning to E as the ride winds down.

10-2 "Chevaux de bois"

Debussy's rhythmic inventiveness in these songs is subtle. In the opening of "Chevaux de bois" the incessant 3 and 2 fanfare-like pattern is abruptly syncopated to draw attention to the voice's entrance (Example 10-3).

10-3 "Chevaux de bois"

Debussy's songs were often criticized for what was regarded as their excessive chromaticism. But its use in the *Ariettes* was comparatively tame. Only after completing this set did he introduce chromaticism in an extended and deliberately provocative manner, initiating a brief phase in his musical style in which he allied himself with new trends from Germany.

The first works to display extreme chromaticism were the *Cinq Poèmes de Baudelaire* ("Le Balcon" [The Balcony], "Harmonie du soir" [Evening Harmony], "Le Jet d'eau" [The Fountain], "Recueillement" [Meditation], and "La Mort des amants" [The Death of Lovers], 1887–1889) (Example 10-4).

10-4 "Recueillement"

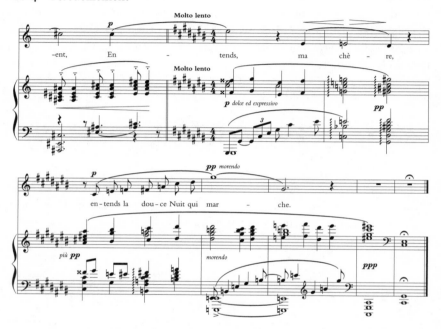

The selection of Baudelaire's poetry was a good choice—not least because of Baudelaire's well-known admiration for Wagner. When Debussy set these poems to music, Baudelaire had been dead for more than twenty years. But there was renewed interest in his work. He had been awarded a place of honor both in the *Symbolist Manifesto* of Jean Moréas and in Joris-Karl Huysmans's popular novel, *Against Nature.* For his settings, Debussy chose five of the best-known poems from Baudelaire's *Les Fleurs du mal*—each poem selected to illustrate the variety of the collection. Unlike the *Ariettes*, they are linked by no particular theme, although there are in each similar thoughts of love, melancholy, and resignation.

The inspiration for the chromaticism in them was provided by the music of Wagner. For a time it became an obsession for Debussy—a result of trips to Bayreuth in 1888 and 1889—so much so that the opening of "Recueillement" is a loosely disguised reminiscence from *Tristan.* By exploiting chromaticism (one of Wagner's most notable musical characteristics), Debussy seemed intent on drawing attention to himself—both from colleagues and from the literary circles in France infatuated with Wagner. To those who may have wondered how Wagner's musical style could be adapted to the French language, the *Cinq Poèmes* were intended to provide an answer.

The first of the set, "Le Balcon," is more like a scene from an opera than a song. It is nine pages in score, lasts nearly eight minutes in performance, and has about a dozen major changes in tempo. The piano has a dominant role, much like a Wagnerian orchestra. The increased prominence and fuller texture for all of the Baudelaire songs was clearly by design: in 1907 Debussy orchestrated "Le Jet d'eau," the third of the set.

The approach is cerebral. Vocal lines appear mannered and contrived. Even today, listening to them is not easy: there is little contrast, and slow, measured tempi are the norm. Concessions to popular taste are rare (such as the climax on the words "Nous échangerons un éclair unique" ["We will share a single bolt of lightning"] in "La Mort des amants").

For many years the sole performance of the *Cinq Poèmes* was a private one in 1890 sponsored by Ernest Chausson. But it was of great importance to Debussy and convinced many in the audience that he was a rising star. The Baudelaire settings were viewed as a response to those who felt that French music was unable or incapable of responding to Wagner's harmonic innovations. Even years later, however, critics found the songs abrasive. Writing in 1895 in *Le Guide Musicale*, Georges Servières complained of the "incorrect harmony, the incessantly loose and broken rhythms, the unsingable intervals in the melodic line," as well as the inevitable "abuse of chromaticism."[15]

Although Debussy's music had routinely drawn adverse criticism, Servières's remarks expressed the sense of outrage and indignation that was becoming common in response to much of his work. It seems inexplicable today, but the rationale for it becomes much clearer by examining the music of Debussy's French contemporaries. The songs of popular composers such as Massenet (written in a manner that would have appealed to critics like Servières) seem tame and innocuous in contrast, conceived for the salon, and with a broad market in mind. But even comparison to the songs of a musical progressive—those of Ernest Chausson—confirms how unusual Debussy's settings must have appeared.

From the start, Chausson's songs had been distinctive, in part because his earliest efforts showed little affinity to French musical tradition and reflected admiration for composers like Robert Schumann. Chausson had written more than two dozen songs prior to beginning in the summer of 1893 a setting of the five poems comprising Maeterlinck's *Serres chaudes* (Hot-House). They were dedicated to and premiered by Debussy's fiancée at the time, Thérèse Roger. Maeterlinck's unusual Symbolist imagery inspired some of Chausson's most innovative music. Yet when placed alongside Debussy's settings of Baudelaire or Verlaine, they seem to be from a bygone age. Chausson, too, was an admirer of Wagner, but his harmony always remains firmly rooted in tradition. His rhythms are static and repetitive, and melodic lines consist of

15. *LS*, p. 109.

neat four-bar phrases. It is not surprising that many critics were perplexed by Debussy's songs. There was absolutely nothing else like them at the time (Example 10-5).

10-5 Chausson: "Serre d' ennui"

The final song collection written by Debussy during this period was in many ways his most distinctive. The *Proses lyriques* (1892–1893) were composed to four of his own poems: "De rêve" (Of Dream), "De grève" (Of Shore), "De fleurs" (Of Flowers), and "De soir" (Of Evening). Their literary style is mannered and broadly Symbolist. It has become commonplace to compare them to the poems of Mallarmé, but more striking is the influence of two Belgians: Maeterlinck and Georges Rodenbach. Two of the poems—"De rêve" and "De grève"—were published (thanks to the assistance of Henri de Régnier) in *Entretiens politiques et littéraires*, a revue edited by the Franco-American poet, Francis Vielé-Griffin. That Debussy was able to write both his own poetry and music may seem a rare accomplishment, but among his contemporaries Guillaume Lekeu, Albéric Magnard, and Guy Ropartz also set their own poems to music. It was, after all, a time which prized the affinities among the arts. What set Debussy's *Proses lyriques* apart were the Symbolist qualities of his verse—and the startling music he created for it.

The *Proses lyriques* share several traits with the Baudelaire settings. Both are intensely cerebral. In the *Proses* this approach can become so marked that the songs verge on the pretentious. Yet the very artificiality of the music is one of its strengths, creating an ideal counterpart to the mannered text. As in the Baudelaire settings, the piano often takes on the role of an orchestra.[16] But unlike the expansive scena-like settings in the *Cinq Poèmes*, the *Proses* are much more fragmented, a result (best seen in "De rêve") of highlighting each musical phrase as a distinct, repetitive pattern. In "De rêve" the constant reappearance of the two-measure cell that serves as the motivic basis of the song becomes a fixation. But in "De fleurs" the repetition and static vocal line serve the text well, producing a pattern of monotony and ennui evocative of the text. The most accessible of the set is "De soir," more diatonic and clearly written to charm. In that sense, the music also reflects the poetry, which is less esoteric and more in the style of the Verlaine poems Debussy admired.

Aspects of the *Proses lyriques* anticipate later developments in Debussy's music. The whole tone scale is prominent in "De rêve." And the static vocal line and dramatic intensity of "De grève" brings to mind the sensitive, declamatory style that was to characterize his opera, *Pelléas et Mélisande* (Example 10-6).

10-6 "De grève"

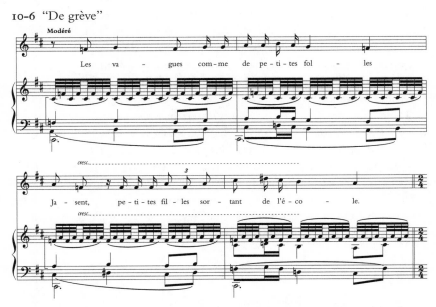

16. In the late 1890s, Debussy orchestrated part of "De grève." Early in 1901 he considered completing the settings for performance at the Société Nationale, but lost interest in the project.

Debussy's songs played an important role in making him better known, but it was in larger-scale compositions that he hoped to build his reputation. Many projects attracted his attention,. Most were scarcely started—not necessarily because Debussy quickly lost interest, but because he was a slow worker and a perfectionist. Although he may have entered into a project with élan, he never did so with the intention of finishing it quickly.

Among the projects contemplated during these years was a proposed collaboration with the poet and Poe translator, Gabriel Mourey. In 1891 he announced a collection of prose poems, *L'Embarquement pour ailleurs* (Embarking Elsewhere) with a "symphonic commentary by C. A. Debussy."[17] Debussy and Mourey shared similar interests, but there is no indication that this work went beyond the planning stages.

Of greater significance was Debussy's attraction to Villiers de l'Isle-Adam's bizarre drama, *Axël*. *Axël*—widely regarded at the time as Villiers's masterpiece—is epic (a performance lasts nearly four hours) with similarities in plot and atmosphere to *Tristan* and *Pelléas*. It was a favorite of the Symbolists. Debussy apparently set one scene of the drama to music in the late 1880s, but no additional information about the project is known. Despite its attractions, as an opera *Axël* would have required extensive cutting and skilled adaptation, and this may have discouraged Debussy from working full-time on it.

In addition to *Axël*, Debussy briefly contemplated providing incidental music for *Les Noces de Sathan* (The Marriage of Satan), a drama by Jules Blois, a friend of Mourey and secretary to Catulle Mendès. This was an occult work—but not, as the title implies, satanic in basis. At the time Debussy had a strong interest in the occult (it plays a role, too, in *Axël*), yet he found little in the play to interest him. When he discovered that the musical forces necessary to perform the work probably did not exist, he bowed out.

The composition for which Debussy entertained the highest hopes at this time was *La Damoiselle élue* (1887–1888) which he described as "a little oratorio, in a mystic, slightly pagan vein."[18] It was intended as his third envoi for the Prix de Rome. Reaction by the committee was critical but surprisingly mild. Debussy's music was described as "poetical and not devoid of charm"—although it was noted ("with regret") that some disturbing elements remained. The committee concluded, however, that these irregularities appeared "justified in a way by the nature of the subject"—that is, the "fairly obscure prose" of the text.[19]

17. *LS*, p. 123.

18. Letter to André Poniatowski of 9 September 1892 in *DL*, p. 38.

19. *LS*, p. 96.

The "fairly obscure prose" selected by Debussy was a French translation of "The Blessed Damozel," a poem by Dante Gabriel Rossetti. Rossetti (1828–1882) was one of the founders of the Pre-Raphaelite Brotherhood and an accomplished poet and painter. He was known for both his personal charm and eccentricities (his pet wombat being a favorite among his friends). Rossetti's work was popular in France and appeared in translation in books and periodicals.[20]

Part of the attraction to Rossetti was the Pre-Raphaelite style itself—broadly similar to art nouveau. Debussy was fond of it. A visitor to his apartment in 1893 was struck by the reproductions of Pre-Raphaelite art on the walls. But there was particular interest in France in Rossetti. Verlaine even wrote as a tribute the poem, "Monna Rosa d'après un tableau de Rossetti" (Monna Rosa. After a Painting by Rossetti).

Rossetti's fame was to a certain extent a result of the notoriety associated with his work. The *Times* of London in 1851 blasted his painting for its "affected simplicity, senile imitation of a cramped style, false perspective, crude colors, morbid infatuation, and the sacrifice of beauty, truth, and genuine feeling, to mere eccentricity."[21] His poems were attacked for their eroticism, and became associated with Swinburne and the "Fleshly School of Poetry." But there were strong supporters. Walter Pater praised Rossetti's work for possessing "a poetic sense which recognized no conventional standard of what poetry was called upon to be"—and it was this unconventionality which attracted Debussy.[22]

"The Blessed Damozel" was published in 1850 and became one of Rossetti's best-known poems.[23] Its subject is physical and spiritual love; its style, archaic and naive. Much about the poem—including those instances when sound seems to take priority over intelligibility—recalls Poe, and that may have provided some measure of attraction to Debussy. He arranged Rossetti's poem for female voices (solo and chorus) with orchestra, setting about half of the original text. Debussy, who did not know English, used translations of the poem by Gabriel Sarrazin.[24]

---

20. Debussy's brother, Alfred, translated an excerpt from Rossetti's "The Staff and Scrip" for the *Revue indépendent* in 1887. Alfred's literary interests during these years were strong, and this was probably the time of the closest attachment between him and his brother.

21. Arthur C. Benson, *Rossetti* (London: Macmillan, 1926), p. 44.

22. Walter Pater, "Dante Gabriel Rossetti," in *Appreciations, with an Essay on Style* (London: Macmillan, 1890). The essay was written in 1883.

23. Rossetti rarely illustrated his own poems, but the popularity of "The Blessed Damozel" led to a commission for him to create a painting on the subject, completed in 1878.

24. But Debussy's ignorance of English did not prevent him from preparing in 1908 a piano-vocal score of the work in English—with countless errors in accent.

The premiere of *La Damoiselle élue* at the Société Nationale on 8 April 1893 was an event of major importance to Debussy. Colleagues and friends were greatly impressed, but criticism was mixed. Although praised for his "subtle and rare art," Debussy was attacked for what was seen as his excessive use of chromaticism. He was blamed for having created a "very sensual, decadent" work—a remark that should have been gratifying since it indicated how successful he had been in transmitting the voluptuous elements of Rossetti's poem.[25]

Like *L'Enfant prodigue*, *La Damoiselle élue* is known today in a later revision (done in 1907–1908). A comparison of the two cantatas shows refinement of Debussy's style in the revision, both in craftsmanship and artistry. The arioso of the Damozel is subtle and more supple. And although there are occasional passages that recall contemporary French opera, they are not as prominent as in *L'Enfant prodigue*. Continuity is maintained by a variant of the Wagnerian leitmotiv. There are recurring melodic motives, the most important being the arpeggiated first inversion chord which begins the piece and serves as a structural pivot.

The orchestra is unusually prominent, and its delicate display of color provides effective contrast to the predominantly declamatory vocal setting. Perhaps the major flaw in *La Damoiselle élue* is its lack of variety, due at least in part to the use of female voices only. Debussy did not help matters by using the chorus in a consistently homophonic and static manner.

The "little oratorio" was intended for an ideal audience—an aspect emphasized by the limited edition of *La Damoiselle élue* issued by Bailly. Those were not Debussy's intentions with the two other major compositions he composed during these years: the three-movement Fantaisie for Piano and Orchestra (1889–1890) and *Rodrigue et Chimène* (1890–1893). The *Fantaisie*—conceived as his final envoi but never submitted—is a surprisingly conventional work that draws on the style of Franck and his followers. There are similarities in both structure and genre, for example, to Vincent d'Indy's *Symphonie sur un chant montagnard français,* op. 26 (Symphony on a French Mountain Air; 1886).

Debussy probably hoped that the *Fantaisie* would appeal broadly to members of the Société Nationale, in the forefront of which were students and admirers of Franck. In common with Franckist works, the *Fantaisie* uses cyclical structure, a musical device in which Debussy had previously shown little interest. Perhaps that explains why his use of it comes across as mostly academic. An association between the gamelan Debussy heard at the 1889 Universal Exposition and the pervasive ostinato rhythm of the final movement of the *Fantaisie* is a

25. *LS*, p. 134.

possibility—but arguments presented for a direct stylistic connection are less convincing.

The *Fantaisie* was withdrawn by Debussy from a scheduled performance at the Société in April 1890. He was disturbed to learn that only the first movement would be performed. While his decision may in part have been motivated by pique, there was a practical musical decision for his action: the first movement simply does not stand well on its own, especially since all three movements of the *Fantaisie* are linked motivically.

Although Debussy later mentioned thoroughly revising the work for performance, he never did so. "I've been intending for a long time to rework it almost entirely," he wrote in 1910. "Since 1889, when it was written, I've changed my views about how to combine piano and orchestra. The scoring would have to be altered too, to avoid a slightly ridiculous contest between the two characters!"[26] Debussy did find time to make some changes in the score, mostly lightening the texture. But he never began more extensive revisions. His musical style had changed considerably in the twenty years since he had composed the *Fantaisie*. There was so much in it needing revision that he may have felt overwhelmed by the idea of reworking it.

Debussy's association with Catulle Mendès and work on *Rodrigue et Chimène* has been discussed in Chapter 3. The libretto consisted of four acts, for which the last has not survived. Acts I and III exist in short score, Act II in a piano-vocal score.

None of the acts are complete. For example, choral parts are only sketched in the first act, and some pages from Act II have been lost. All three acts were frequently reworked by Debussy, and legibility of the score has suffered.

Rodrigue et Chimène is known today in a version consisting of the first three acts, edited by Richard Langham Smith and orchestrated by Edison Denisov. To those eager for any work by Debussy—even one in a fragmentary state—this edition is welcome. Despite the missing finale, the opera is comprehensible as it stands. The problem lies in its authenticity. Supplementary text had to be written to complete the three acts. And in addition to those parts for which little or no music survived, there is the orchestration for this new setting—wonderfully effective, but in the manner of Debussy's mature style, not that of the early 1890s.

Sections of *Rodrigue et Chimène*—but surprisingly few, given the conventional libretto—sound as if they could have been written decades earlier (such as the first act chorus à la Meyerbeer, "Du vin! du vin!"). Mendès's text is a world apart from the operatic ideals expressed by Debussy in his conversations with Guiraud. Much of the music, however, is more than respectable, and some (such as that of Act II,

26. Letter to Edgard Varèse of 10 August 1909 in *DL*, p. 211.

scene ii) has some of the flavor of the declamatory style of *Pelléas*. It is not surprising that when Debussy played the opera for Paul Dukas, Dukas was struck by the "dramatic breadth of particular scenes."[27] For, despite the mediocrity of the libretto, Debussy produced some fine music and in the process gained valuable experience for working on more substantial works for the stage.

27. *LS*, p. 141.

CHAPTER ELEVEN

Compositions, 1893–1899

I would rather do without potatoes than without roses. There is nothing truly beautiful except what is of no possible use. Everything useful is ugly, for it expresses a need.

Théophile Gautier, Preface to *Mademoiselle de Maupin* (1835)

Instrumental Works

Chamber: String Quartet, op. 10
Orchestra: *Prelude to the Afternoon of a Faun; Nocturnes*

Vocal Works

Songs: *Trois Chansons de Bilitis* (Louÿs)

IT IS SURPRISING THAT, ACCORDING TO HIS FRIEND ROBERT GODET, DEBUSSY DID not care for Gautier's novel, *Mademoiselle de Maupin*. Its style is distinctive, its plot is captivating, and there are statements in the Preface—in many ways an artistic manifesto—with which he certainly would have agreed. Much of it pays tribute to the concept of "art for art's sake," an idea that intrigued Debussy. The premise—that art requires no justification or validation to exist, and that it need serve no particular purpose or function—had his support. He was even willing to draw upon it in the manner of Gautier—writing, in a letter to the art critic Octave Maus, of "that forgotten truth … 'art is completely useless.'"[1]

1. Letter to Octave Maus of [mid-September 1903] in *C*, p. 184.

Art was "useless" in part because it did not fit into a utilitarian world. It definitely did not provide a dependable source of income nor should it be expected to (one of Debussy's mantras later in life). But there *was* a role for art, and meaning for music.

In his evolving program of music's qualities, Debussy began by emphasizing what music was *not* to do: it was not intended to make people "*think*."[2] He was distancing himself from much nineteenth-century music (especially German music) with its aura of profundity. Attending a concert was not supposed to be a philosophical experience with head in hand and furrowed brow. Rather Debussy wanted to "make people *listen*, in spite of themselves"—an extraordinary challenge for any composer, but surprisingly modern in its approach.[3] Once the audience had been captivated, it would be transported, as if it "had dreamt, for a moment, of a chimerical land."[4] This revelatory experience—with its emphasis on dreams and the imagination—owed much to Symbolism.

How would the audience be drawn into his music? Debussy believed that one way was to create compositions that were new and original—pieces which, as he once put it, exhibited his "latest experiments in musical chemistry."[5] But the ingredients in his experimental laboratory were not complex. "More and more I am convinced," Debussy wrote, "that music by its very nature can not be adapted to a rigorous and traditional form. It is filled with color and rhythm."[6] His focus on the general and often elusive qualities of music was in deliberate contrast to what he had been taught.

Debussy made very similar remarks concerning the performances of the gypsy violinist, Radics, whom he heard in 1910. Young musicians, he wrote, could use Radics as a source of inspiration, "not by copying his performances, but by trying to transpose their freedom, their gift for evoking color and rhythm."[7] Radics's ability to make people listen was a result of his focus on the essence of music (its color and rhythm). That essence could not be found in a classroom. Nature was its source, and close observation of it provided the key to its creation: "You learn orchestration far better by listening to the sound of leaves rustling in the wind than by consulting handbooks in which the instruments look like anatomical specimens and which, in any case, contain very incomplete information about the innumerable ways of blending the said instruments with each other."[8]

2. Letter to Paul Dukas of [11 February 1901] in *C*, p. 162.
3. Ibid.
4. Ibid.
5. Letter to Eugène Ysaÿe of 13 October 1896 in *DL*, p. 87.
6. Letter to Jacques Durand of 3 September 1907 in *C*, p. 1030.
7. Letter to Gusztáv Bárczy of 19 December 1910 in ibid., p. 1361.
8. Letter to Charles Levadé of 4 September 1903 in *DL*, p. 140.

If Nature provided the key to understanding music, tradition was typically its nemesis. Academic tradition remained the foundation of training at the Conservatoire, and Debussy waged war against it, both in the press and in his own compositions. His rationale was closely articulated in letters to the music critic, Pierre Lalo. In 1901 Debussy told him that he was "only trying—and very timidly—to free music from a heritage of burdensome traditions, falsely interpreted, which very well might crush it if care is not taken!"[9] Four years later when Lalo became a harsh critic of his music Debussy justified their parting with the following words: "The heart of the matter is that you love and defend traditions which, for me, no longer exist or, at least, exist only as representative of an epoch in which they were not all fine and valuable as people make out; the dust of the past is not always respectable."[10]

One of the most notable characteristics of that dusty tradition was its unquestioning imitation, especially of eighteenth-century classical style (and sonata form). Debussy was especially irritated by the concept of "development." "You know how little love I have for developmental padding," he wrote to one of his pupils. "It's seen long service at the hand of the masters and it's time we started to replace it by a more rigorous selection of ideas."[11] Charles Koechlin recalled that when Debussy "found himself faced with the sort of cold musical development that people call 'well-made' (what he termed 'mandarin labours') he could be heard to say: 'That's architecture, not music.'"[12]

Equally abhorrent to Debussy was the nineteenth-century preoccupation with bathos and sentiment. When coaching the singer, Jane Bathori, for a performance of the *Trois Chansons de Bilitis* he made a point of commenting at the end of "La Chevelure": "Above all, no romantic shudder."[13]

Tradition not only led musicians astray, it became a burden to them. Some were preoccupied with the past, and their music became unnecessarily complex. "One thing I'd like to see you free yourself from," he advised Chausson, "is your preoccupation with the inner parts of the texture....It would be more profitable, I feel, to go about things the other way round, that's to say, find the perfect expression for an idea and add only as much decoration as is absolutely necessary."[14] Debussy was convinced that the antidote to a preoccupation with musical tradition was in a return to natural, musical simplicity.

9. Letter to Lalo of [c. 10 November 1901] in *C*, p. 168.

10. Letter to Lalo of 25 October 1905 in *DL*, p. 163.

11. Letter to Raoul Bardac of 24/25 February 1906 in ibid., p. 166.

12. Recollection of Charles Koechlin in *DR*, p. 101.

13. Jane Bathori, "Les Musiciens que j'ai connus. II. Debussy," *Recorded Sound* (Spring 1962), p. 176.

14. Letter to Chausson of [24 October 1893] in *DL*, p. 58.

Were contemporary critics aware of his distinctive perception of music? Only one, his friend Louis Laloy, noted that Debussy in writing music "had listened to the voice of nature"—a comment that could only have come from Debussy himself.[15] To many, Debussy's compositions were seen as *un*natural and contrived.

Writing about the *Prelude to the Afternoon of a Faun* in *L'Echo de Paris*, Victorin Joncières classified Debussy as a "decadent composer who, it is said, affects a profound disdain" for all music composed before him.[16] The composer and critic Alfred Bruneau described the *Prelude* as nebulous and effeminate: "to be frank, I prefer an art that is more clear-cut, more robust, more masculine."[17] Frequently associated with this supposed effeminacy was the languor of Debussy's music, its "dream-like" qualities. Some of that can be traced to the effect of repetition, as well as the absence of abrupt contrast. But Debussy's non-functional harmony often creates a sense of drifting and inertia. Although one of Debussy's biographers came to his defense and made a point of affirming that he was "not merely a dreamer of beautiful dreams," here at least there seems to be confirmation that he had met one of his musical goals: that of moving an audience as if it "had dreamt, for a moment, of a chimerical land."[18]

To many contemporaries this effect had been primarily created by a combination of structure (or, rather, its absence) and harmony. Writing in 1907 Lawrence Gilman noted that "one is struck, first of all, in savoring his art, by its extreme fluidity, its vagueness of contour, its lack of obvious and definite outline."[19] The "fluidity" and "vagueness of contour" has some association with Debussy's melodic line (the arabesque), but the intention is to point out the absence of easily discernible, traditional, musical structure. The music itself was, according to Gilman, "a rich and shimmering texture of blended chord groups, rather than a pattern of interlaced melodic strands."[20] Harmony, then, was a significant component of Debussy's style, but arranged in an unorthodox manner. Complicating harmonic analysis, Gilman continued, was the use "almost continuously, as the structural basis of his music, [of] the medieval church modes."[21] To another contemporary critic, Louise Liebich, it was not the church modes, but Debussy's "frequent use" of the whole tone scale.[22]

15. Louis Laloy, *Claude Debussy* (Paris: Les Bibliophiles Fantaisistes, 1909), p. 73.

16. Review of 13 October 1895 quoted in *C*, p. 280.

17. Bruneau in *Le Figaro* in 1895 quoted in *LS*, p. 164. Bruneau's opinion was shared by Charles Ives for Debussy's music in general.

18. Mrs. Franz Liebich, *Claude-Achille Debussy* (London: John Lane, 1908), p. 2.

19. Lawrence Gilman, *Debussy's Pelléas et Mélisande. A Guide to the Opera* (New York: Schirmer, 1907), p. 9.

20. Ibid., p. 10.

21. Ibid., p. 15.

22. Liebich, p. 41.

It was not unusual for critics to realize that Debussy's music could not be grasped using eighteenth and nineteenth-century standards. But even those who regarded his music favorably were confused by his departure from tradition and were reduced to identifying components (such as modality) and exaggerating their role. "He introduced the Orient into music," concluded one biographer. "*With him, classicism is dead forever.*"[23] An odd pronouncement. But by substituting "tradition" for "classicism," it would have met with Debussy's approval.

The non-traditional elements in Debussy's music have always been an obstacle to its academic analysis. Since he did not follow conventional models, what served as its basis? The idea of creating a new set of rules to replace the old was far from his intention.

It is helpful from the start to think of Debussy's music simply as sonority—and to take his musical basis ("color and rhythm") as a point of departure. Simple effects, such as silence, are used to enhance the effect of sound. And timbre and texture play extraordinary roles—both serving at times to create or delineate musical sections in a manner similar to what had traditionally been assigned to tonality. Rhythm is used by Debussy to create the "fluidity" noted by contemporary critics. Associated with it is the idea of improvisation, an effect simulated by unpredictable rhythmic configurations and changes of tempo. Debussy cherished every musical performance as unique and did not want the written page to stifle interpretation.

Debussy's melodies are distinctive. Given their brevity and limited range, many can be described as motivic. But they are rarely used as a basis for traditional motivic development. Rather the idea is one of the arabesque with variation and growth from it.

Especially in his instrumental compositions, melody and harmony seem uniquely integrated. "A musical idea," Debussy wrote, "contains its own harmony (or so I believe); otherwise, the harmony is merely clumsy and parasitical."[24] Ignorance of his intentions led many contemporary critics to complain about the absence of melody in his music (a stance that infuriated Debussy). It also helps to explain why so much analysis of Debussy's music focused on harmony, often to the exclusion of other musical parameters.

The harmonic basis of much of Debussy's music rests on an expanded perception of the home key (the tonic). Full statements of the tonic are avoided. In fact, they are often only implied (by, for example, closely related keys such as the dominant or subdominant). Harmony remains tertian—with widespread use of seventh and ninth chords as consonances—but progressions are non-traditional, and, by textbook standards, unpredictable.

Debussy's harmonic approach has been described as "non-functional"—that is, harmony does not follow traditional rules and patterns. While expanding the tonic,

23. Daniel Chennevière, *Claude Debussy et son oeuvre* (Paris: Durand et fils, 1913), p. 15.

24. Letter to Mme. Gérard de Romilly of [c. 15 September 1902] in *DL*, p. 132.

he also expanded the range of acceptable harmony. Common are unorthodox chord progressions and unresolved dissonance. Chords are often altered by diatonic saturation: the addition of pitches to standard chords so that reference is made to the entire diatonic scale. Another characteristic of Debussy's music are chains of parallel chord progressions (with the parallel fifths prohibited in the textbooks he studied), a device known as planing (Example 11-1). Incidentally, these are not devices annotated by contemporary critics. Their attention rarely went beyond what they felt were the music's more "exotic" traits, such as the use of the whole tone scale or other modes.

11-1 "D'un cahier d' esquisses"

Debussy's compositional approach was determined by what pleased his ear, not by rules. How he went about it—the process of composition—remains mostly a mystery. Few sketches survive: "I destroy everything which doesn't satisfy me," he confessed.[25] But he also destroyed preliminary sketches, probably to ensure that no one would be able to pry into his manner of composition. Even though it is a late work, the best sense of his approach can be gleaned from one of the most complete surviving sets of sketches, that for *Jeux* (1912).

The initial particelle for *Jeux* consists of four staves with "practically no" indication of tempo, dynamics, or articulation—and "no more than a dozen indications

25. Quoted in Roy Howat, "A Thirteenth *Etude* of 1915: The Original Version of *Pour les arpèges composés*," *Cahiers Debussy* 1 (1977), p. 20.

of instrumentation."[26] The particelle was followed by a piano score reduction that was submitted to his publisher. About six months later Debussy began work on a draft version of the orchestration (but we know that for the *Faune* and the *Nocturnes*, the orchestration was added to the particelle itself, so it seems that a complete draft version of the orchestration was special to *Jeux*). Each of these stages of composition was an essential component in its evolution, and all witnessed modifications and alterations. The process continued even after the score had been published. Later, when he conducted his own compositions, Debussy regularly made changes in the score for revised editions.

The *Prelude to the Afternoon of a Faun* exemplifies Debussy's emerging musical style. Its genre (unlike nearly all of Debussy's orchestral works) is surprisingly direct: a tone-poem with Mallarmé's poem, *The Afternoon of a Faun*, as its basis. But its sound and structure differ greatly from the more standard tone-poems of, for example, Liszt or d'Indy. The premiere was conducted by Gustave Doret on 22 December 1894 at the Société Nationale in a program that also included works by Glazunov, Saint-Saëns, and Franck. It was a mediocre performance, despite Debussy having followed the rehearsals closely—but it won strong audience support.

Mallarmé's poem was originally conceived in 1862 as dramatic verse for recitation at the *Comédie française* (but was not accepted for production). It is a monologue by the faun, about 100 lines in length, its content ambiguous and wistful. Known at first as "Le Faune, intermède heroïque," the title was changed in the summer of 1875 to "Improvisation d'un Faune." That autumn it was published for the first time (in a limited edition) and with the title by which we know it today. Debussy became directly involved with the *Faune* in 1890 when he was asked to write incidental music for a reading of it. When that performance failed to occur, he continued the project on his own. He probably began composing the *Faune* in 1892, completing orchestration in late October 1894.

Its structure is ternary. But demarcations for each section vary with the listener. The lack of agreement is not surprising. It is a free and organic structure—and one that gives the impression of natural growth from the opening measures.

There are two primary melodic ideas: Theme A (mm. 1–4; flute), and Theme B (mm. 55–60; woodwinds) (Examples 11-2a and 11-2b on page 168). Theme A outlines the tritone, with chromatic descent and ascent. Its range and pattern embody Debussy's understanding of melody as arabesque. Tonality is vague, but "E" is implied (the tritone itself implies tonal ambiguity, but its use here is not in the often harsh manner of Schoenberg or Scriabin). Theme B is more vocal in nature. Unlike the single-measure, cell-like repetition of Theme A, it is composed of two-measure units, and is more lively, with a triplet figure (entering in m. 62) offering rhythmic variety. Its tonality is "D flat,"

26. Myriam Chimènes, "The Definition of Timbre in the Process of Composition of *Jeux*," in *Debussy Studies*, ed. Richard Langham Smith (Cambridge: Cambridge University Press, 1997), p. 5.

11-2a *Prélude à l' aprés-midi d' un faune*

11-2b *Prélude à l' aprés-midi d' un faune*

with its nebulousness emphasized by the bass outline of the diminished fifth (D flat–G). Both Themes A and B have the same dynamic level (*piano*), and similar indications of expression ("*doux et expressif* " for Theme A and "*expressif et très soutenu*" for Theme B).

The first section begins with varied statements of Theme A (three complete ones in the first thirty-one measures) with solo flute prominent, and ending with an unusual full cadence (m. 30). Mm. 31–55 are more episodic. They begin with reminiscences of Theme A for mixed orchestra, then a fresh melodic idea is introduced in m. 37 which is taken up by the violins three measures later.

The second section (mm. 55–79) provides contrast and variety. It accomplishes this with greater tunefulness and stronger tonal implications. Contrast is also provided by surprise (such as the disjointed effect of the hemiola in m. 66).

A restatement of the first section begins on m.79. But because this is a variant of Theme A—augmented, and outlining a perfect fourth—the listener does not receive the sense of resolution that would accompany a literal restatement of Theme A. There is intentional ambiguity. Is this section (which lasts until m. 94) the actual reappearance of Theme A, or is its role to set the stage for the return of Theme A?

Mm. 94–110 mark the appearance of Theme A in its original form. It is followed by a codetta and conclusion in E major. The listener, then, hears three broad sections in the *Faune*: A: mm. 1–55; B: mm. 55–79; A1; mm. 79–110. Even if mm. 79–94 are heard as a transition to the return of A (and as part of B), the effect of B still is that of an interlude.

Sections are delineated not just by contrasting thematic material and tonality. There is contrasting use of timbre and texture as well. Section A, for example, has a thinner texture with a greater use of the orchestra as a chamber ensemble. But any tripartite division of the *Faune* should not divert attention from the astonishing cohesiveness of the piece—an accomplishment enhanced by the improvisatory effect created by the score. This improvisatory character—and the unpredictability associated with it—helps to explain its continued novelty. Even after repeated hearings—and few works have been performed more frequently than the *Faune*—the listener always seems to discover something new: a subtle change in instrumentation, for example, or harmony. That is especially true with its dynamics, the *Faune* being a study in gradations of *piano* and *pianissimo*. Silence, too, is important (see, for example, the effect of m. 6—an entire measure of silence).

The orchestration is astonishingly inventive. Debussy did not approach the orchestra like his contemporaries. He avoided doubling for its own sake and never used timbre as a device simply to provide variety or contrast.

The orchestra for the *Faune* is large, but Debussy revels in the solo possibilities of each instrument. The opening theme is shared by flute, clarinets, French horn, and harp. At times it creates a chamber effect unheard of for the time, never more striking than at the conclusion, where the opening theme is taken up by the harps and French horns in turn (Example 11-3 on the next page). The strings do not have the dominant role—as they do in nineteenth-century orchestral pieces in general—nor is melody automatically allotted to the violins. Prominence is given to unexpected

11-3 *Prélude à l' aprés-midi d' un faune*

instruments, for example, the flute. Also revealing is what Debussy does *not* use: there are no trumpets or trombones in the orchestra, and the use of percussion is selective and restrained.

The *Faune* often exhibits the "dreaminess" and "languor" noted by contemporaries in Debussy's music in general. But it is an effect created by precision and clarity: with repetition, emphasis on the low end of dynamics, non-functional harmony, and timbre. Imagine, for example, if the solo flute were replaced or its part shared by an oboe. There is only a single mention of a flute in the poem (as well as "tuyaux" [pipes]). A less imaginative composer might have opted at some point for the more conventional (and rustic) sound of the oboe.

From the start, people were curious about specific connections between Debussy's music and Mallarmé's poem. Did, for example, musical sections correspond to lines from the poem? To the music critic, Willy, Debussy offered a characteristic commentary on the *Faune*: "Is it perhaps the dream left over at the bottom of the faun's flute? To be more precise it is the general impression of the poem. If the music were to follow it more closely it would run out of breath.... All the same it follows the ascending shape of the poem as well as the scenery so marvelously described in the text, together with the humanity brought to it by thirty-two violinists who have got up too early! As for the ending, it's a prolongation of the last line: Couple farewell, I go to see what you became."[27]

Given the cryptic nature of Mallarmé's poem, Debussy's "general impression" is a sensible musical response. The goal for Debussy was to produce music evocative of the text. And in this he may have been guided by the original idea of providing music to accompany a reading of the poem. For his intention seems to have been to produce music that is unobtrusive and subdued, expressive and rich in color.

The ternary structure, too, may reflect that original intention. Mallarmé's poem does not fall into three sections. But there were three sections in the title originally chosen by Debussy for his composition: *Prélude, Interlude et Paraphrase finale pour l'après-midi d'un faune*. The terminology corresponds well with the musical content. The title was promoted for the all-Debussy concert held in Brussels in March 1894, but the composition was not finished in time for performance. There are several possibilities to explain why the title was eventually simplified. Perhaps Debussy thought it was too long (or pretentious). But he may also have felt that it removed some of the mystery from his approach.

Mallarmé received a note from Debussy inviting him to attend the premiere and to hear "the arabesques...dictated by the flute of your faun."[28] "I wasn't expecting anything like that!" he told Debussy after the performance. "The music prolongs the emotion of my poem and conjures up the scenery more vividly than any color."[29]

---

27. Letter to Willy (Henri Gauthier-Villars) of 10 October 1895 in *DL*, pp. 84–85. In December 1904 he described his setting as a "very free illustration" of the poem (*C*, p. 875).

28. Quoted in *LS*, p. 157.

29. Quoted by Debussy in a letter to Georges Jean-Aubry of 25 March 1910 in *DL*, p. 218.

There could be no greater praise: Mallarmé was taken not just by the sonority of Debussy's music, but by how closely it brought to life and complemented his work.

While composing the *Faune*, Debussy was also working on his only string quartet. He wrote it during a time when he was enjoying close camaraderie with Chausson, and it shows the influence of Chausson's and Franck's music. But unlike his previous composition indebted to the Franck School—the Fantaisie for Piano—Debussy was more satisfied with the result.

It became one of his most popular works, both among audiences and musicians. Magnard, in general not an admirer of Debussy's music, wrote of its "admirable savagery."[30] And Daniel Chennevière proclaimed it as "perhaps Debussy's masterpiece"—a surprising remark, since by the time he was writing (1913) Debussy had completed far more substantial works, like *Pelléas* and *La Mer*.[31]

Throughout his career, Debussy made a point of avoiding standard musical genres. Except for a youthful piano piece, he composed no work entitled "symphony," for example, and the sonatas he wrote did not draw on the musical models that attracted his contemporaries. His only string quartet is also his *only* work with an opus number (op. 10), and it is hard to escape the feeling that its addition was intended by Debussy as a fitting ironic touch.

The String Quartet was first performed by the Ysaÿe Quartet on 29 December 1893 at a Société National concert. It has the standard four movements, with the scherzo placed second. The Quartet adopts the cyclic principle favored by Franck and his followers.[32] There are two primary themes in the first movement, the first of which is used to tie together all four movements:

11-4a String Quartet, 1st movement

30. Letter to Guy Ropartz of 16 March [1902] in Albéric Magnard, *Correspondance (1888–1914)*, ed. Claire Vlach (Paris: Publications de la Société Française de Musicologie, 1997), p. 185.

31. Chennevière, p. 30.

32. The influence of Edvard Grieg's String Quartet also appears likely. See Michael Strasser, "Grieg, the Société Nationale, and the Origins of Debussy's String Quartet," in *Berlioz and Debussy: Sources, Contexts, and Legacies. Essays in Honor of François Lesure*, ed. Barbara L. Kelly and Kerry Murphy (Burlington: Ashgate, 2007), pp. 103–117.

11-4b String Quartet, 2nd movement

11-4c String Quartet, 3rd movement

11-4d String Quartet, 4th movement

Debussy found composing the quartet to be a chore. He complained to Chausson of the difficulties: "As for the finale of the Quartet, it is not what I want it to be. And that is after three unsuccessful attempts!"[33] He wanted to dedicate it to Chausson despite his misunderstanding and apparent lack of enthusiasm for it. "I was really upset for several days ," Debussy wrote to him, "by what you said about my quartet, as I felt that it only increased your partiality for *certain things* which I would rather it encouraged you to forget. Anyway I'll write another which will be for you, in all seriousness for you, and I'll try to bring some nobility to my forms."[34]

It is uncertain where the lack of "nobility" lay. Possibly Chausson felt that Debussy did not make good enough use of the cyclic possibilities, or he may have been disturbed by the exuberant playfulness of the scherzo. What is clear is that Debussy was bothered by Chausson's reaction, especially since he had taken efforts to write in a manner respected more by Chausson than himself. The Quartet was eventually dedicated to the Ysaÿe Quartet. But Chausson actually quoted the primary theme from it near the conclusion of the first movement of his own String Quartet, op. 35 (1898; Chausson died before being able to finish it). This quotation—written at a time when he and Debussy were no longer friendly—may have been intended as a bit of nostalgia, or perhaps as a gesture toward rapprochement.

Debussy's handling of traditional form is successful in the quartet because of his assimilation of it. It does not become, as was so often the case with the Fantaisie for piano, an exercise in imitation. Much of its success can be traced to the nature of the primary theme. It is cellular and lends itself well to transformation. The contrast within it (especially the intervals of major second, minor third, and minor sixth, and the triplet figure) provides the basis for variety within the Quartet itself. Other composers tended to approach thematic transformation in the manner of Wagner

33. Letter to Chausson of [2 July 1893] in *C*, 79.
34. Letter to Chausson of [5 February 1894] in *DL*, 65.

and his use of the leitmotiv as if it were essential for the listener to identify each appearance (and at times as an opportunity for the composer to show off his skill). In contrast (and unlike the *Fantaisie* where the building-blocks are readily apparent), in Debussy's Quartet thematic material is manipulated with much resourceful-ness—but integrated seamlessly.

In addition to his friendship with Chausson, the 1890s were a time of close contact between Debussy and Pierre Louÿs. Although many projects were contem-plated, the *Trois Chansons de Bilitis* are the only substantial composition that resulted. Debussy selected three poems—"La Flûte de Pan," "La Chevelure," and "Le Tombeau de Naïades"—all taken from the first part of Louÿs's popular collection. These poems are among the most poignant in the set—and not representative of the graphic eroticism more common to it. Debussy began composition rapidly ("La Flûte de Pan" was completed in June 1897, "La Chevelure" in early July), but the remaining song was not finished until March of the following year.

Debussy's music suits the texts extremely well. Louÿs originally presented the poems not as his own, but written by Bilitis, a Greek courtesan of the sixth century B.C. To match the supposed antiquity and "oriental" flavor of the text, Debussy used great simplicity in his settings. The vocal line is mostly declamatory and chant-like, and there is greater use of modes (pentatonic for "La Flûte de Pan," Lydian for "La Chevelure"). "La Chevelure" is the most "Western" in its approach, with touches of an operatic love-scene on the text "la bouche sur la bouche" (mouth on mouth). But the settings are most effective in simpler passages, such as in "La Flûte de Pan" (11 measures from the end) where Debussy creates a startling transition by unex-pectedly shifting to G major.

For the half dozen years or so starting in 1894 Debussy wrote surprisingly little. It was a frustrating time for him, and he later blamed the lack of productivity in part on his troubled home life. Many of the aborted projects conceived during this time were related to Louÿs—an opera (or ballet or pantomime) based on his *Aphrodite* (1897), incidental music for *Oedipe à Colonne* (1895), *Daphnis et Chloë* (a ballet; 1895–1897), and an opera, *Cendrelune* (1895–1898). Debussy made some progress on a song cycle taken by Louÿs from Dante Gabriel Rossetti's collection of sonnets, *House of Life*. *La Saulaie* (*Willowwood*) was begun in 1896 and Debussy worked on it sporad-ically as late as 1900. Three pages of music (for baritone and orchestra) survive.

Much of the interest in collaboration seems to have been Louÿs's. In addition to the *Chansons de Bilitis* only one slight composition stemmed from their friendship: incidental music for the recitation of twelve poems from the *Bilitis* collection (pre-sented as part of a series of tableaux vivants). The score was for the unusual ensemble of two harps, two flutes, and celesta; the unique performance occurred on the pre-mises of *Le Journal* in February 1901. Debussy later put the music to use by arranging it for piano, four-hands, in the *Epigraphes antiques* (1914).

Debussy considered many projects besides those with Louÿs, but he actually accomplished little. In 1894 two chamber works were contemplated: a violin sonata and a second string quartet, but he wrote no music. Two years later he had the idea of producing incidental music for Verlaine's *Les Uns et les autres* (1896), but no music resulted; in the following year nothing came of the idea of writing music for a pantomime, *Le Chevalier d'Or*, to a scenario by the wife of the artist, Jean-Louis Forain. There was also a follow-up to the *Proses lyriques*: a set of five songs (with poems by Debussy), entitled, *Nuits blanches*. He worked on them in 1897–1898. Although announced in 1900, they were not published until 2000 (only two survived in manuscript). In a similar manner, he made little progress in 1898 on a projected orchestration of the *Proses lyriques* (only "De Soir" and "De Grève," partially completed).

Given the difficulty Debussy had during these years in committing himself to the completion of any project, it is gratifying that he finished the most substantial one of all: a series of three orchestral pieces eventually known as the *Nocturnes*. It has long been assumed that their origin can be traced to a series of sketches, the *Scènes au Crépuscule,* that Debussy wrote in 1892–1893. The *Scènes* were inspired by ten poems (it is not known which ones) from the *Poèmes anciens et romanesques* (1890) by Debussy's friend, Henri de Régnier. But an examination of the sketches has revealed no direct musical connection to the *Nocturnes*.[35]

The *Nocturnes* are tenuously linked to a work of the same name intended by Debussy for the violin virtuoso, Eugene Ysaÿe. It was based on an unusual concept. "I am working on three *Nocturnes*," he wrote Ysaÿe, "for violin and orchestra. The orchestra for the first consists of strings, the second of flutes, four horns, three trumpets and two harps, and the third will combine both ensembles. It is an examination of the various arrangements which produce a single color, similar to what has been done in painting: such as a study in gray."[36]

The idea was inspired by the paintings of Whistler. Using musical titles, Whistler created several works that were intended as studies in timbre, for example, the "Symphony in White, No. 2." Whistler was particularly known for his nocturne paintings, especially the "Nocturne in Blue and Silver" (c. 1872) and the more abstract "Nocturne in Blue and Gold: The Falling Rocket" (c. 1874). They did much to build his reputation, especially in France where he had a strong following. "Above all others," wrote George Moore in his study of contemporary painting, "he is surely the interpreter of the night."[37]

---

35. See Denis Herlin, "*Trois Scènes au Crepuscule* (1892–1893): Un premier projet des *Nocturnes*," *Cahiers Debussy* 21 (1997), pp. 3–24.

36. Letter to Ysaÿe of 22 September 1894 in *C*, p. 106.

37. George Moore, *Modern Painting* (New York: Charles Scribner's Sons, 1893), p. 22.

Ysaÿe was interested in what Debussy was attempting. But when Debussy showed him what he had written, for reasons unknown, in November 1896 Ysaÿe withdrew from the project. Perhaps he did not feel that Debussy's experiment in timbre was effective. Or he may have felt there was insufficient display for the violin—that the work was not enough of a concerto. But it is interesting that all went well with another elaborate work written for him at about this time: Chausson's *Poème* (full title: *Poème symphonique pour violon et orchestre,* op. 25; 1896).

Debussy continued work on the *Nocturnes*, removing references to the solo violin and arrangement in timbre. Not until December 1899 was it completed, and he complained to his publisher Georges Hartmann—who was eager to see the composition in print—that it had given him "more trouble than the five acts of *Pelléas*."[38] He told Louÿs that the slow pace was a result of challenges at home: "The three *Nocturnes* have been infected by my private life, first full of hope, then full of despair and then full of nothing! I've never been able to work at anything when my life's going through a crisis."[39]

The *Nocturnes* consist of three programmatic movements: "Nuages" (Clouds), "Fêtes" (Festivals), and "Sirènes" (Sirens). What is their genre? Symphony? A collection of tone poems? Orchestral suite (such as Chabrier's *Suite pastorale*; 1888)? The situation is complicated by the program (if not written, then authorized by Debussy) that accompanied the first performance:

> The title of nocturnes is to be interpreted in a wider sense than that usually given to it, and most especially is it understood as having a decorative meaning. Therefore the usual form of nocturne has not been considered, and the word is to be accepted as signifying in the amplest manner diversified impressions and special lights.
>
> *Nuages*: the unchanging aspect of the sky, and the slow solemn movement of the clouds dissolving in grey tints lightly touched with white.
>
> *Fêtes*: the restless dancing rhythm of the atmosphere interspersed with sudden flashes of light. There is also an incidental procession (a dazzling imaginary vision) passing through and mingling with the revelry; but the background of uninterrupted festival is persistent with its blending of music, and luminous dust participating in the universal rhythm of all things.
>
> *Sirènes*: the sea and its perpetual rhythm, and then amid waves silvered by moonbeams is heard the laughter and mysterious song of passing sirens.[40]

38. Letter to Georges Hartmann of 16 September 1898 in *DL*, p. 100.
39. Letter to Louÿs of 27 March 1898 in ibid., p. 94.
40. Liebich, pp. 42–43 (with slight change for accuracy).

In the end Debussy only increased confusion by retaining the title "nocturnes"—and its implied connection to Whistler—even though the idea of creating a related musical counterpart had been abandoned. These pieces are not musical nocturnes (or notturnos, or night-pieces, or nachtstücke) as audiences might expect. No specific reference to the night is intended. Instead Debussy supplied his own definition: "impressions and special lights." The program and the title were sufficient, incidentally, for contemporary critics to note a connection between the *Nocturnes* and Whistler.

In its initial conception the *Nocturnes* would have been a concerto (with the standard three movements), and presented as a study in timbre (with titles?). When completed, the concerto and timbre concepts were no longer present. Contemporary critics were not sure what to make of the work.

All three movements are in ternary form. But the structure for "Nuages" is ambiguous and could just as easily be seen as variations (arabesques) on two themes (mm. 1–4 in clarinet and mm. 5–8 in English horn). The key is B minor.

"Fêtes," Debussy told a friend, was inspired by "distant memories of a festival in the Bois de Boulogne" which included a procession of heavy cavalry.[41] It begins in a lively 4/4 (actually, 12/8) with the three primary sections (preceded by twenty-six measures of introduction) set off by dramatic change in theme, rhythm, and timbre. The key is A major (with section B in A flat major).

"Sirènes" adds a female chorus to the orchestra, an addition that, because of the cost, has worked against complete performances of the *Nocturnes*. There is no text; Debussy uses the chorus solely as an instrument. His goal was to produce an ethereal sound, and—for the time—his handling of the chorus is novel. The temptation is to think he might have been better served if electronic instruments such as the ondes martinet had been available. But a female chorus serves the *femme fatale* implications of the program perfectly, its unearthly effect heightened by the absence of language.

Debussy made clear that he viewed the chorus as part of the orchestra. He wanted it placed "within the orchestra and not before it, otherwise an effect diametrically opposed to what I am looking for will result. It is essential that this group of voices have no greater importance than any other section of the orchestra. It must not 'stand out,' but 'mix in.' "[42]

"Sirènes" is in B major. Its close relationship to the tonality of "Nuages" adds some credence to the "symphonic" nature of the *Nocturnes*. Early analysts such as Liebich claimed all three movements were unified by statements of the initial theme from the first movement. But that is not the case. There is a recollection of

41. Letter to Dukas of [11 February 1901] in *DL*, p. 117.
42. Letter to an unknown correspondent of 30 December 1903 in *C*, p. 812.

it in the finale, but the thematic content of each of the *Nocturnes* is as distinctive as their titles.

If the *Nocturnes* can be seen as a symphony, it is one against the grain. That is made clear in the final movement where the chorus appears, not, as in Beethoven's Ninth Symphony, to add words (with a human element) and to enhance the standard instruments of the orchestra, but rather to add timbre (and dehumanize it) to generate an unearthly effect.

Liebich concluded that the *Nocturnes* were a "category of free symphonies," a view shared by many contemporaries.[43] But Debussy's subtitle—"triptyque symphonique"—provides a more accurate interpretation. The three movements do not duplicate a triptych in the usual sense with three paintings united by subject. But they do create a picture gallery with a landscape, a genre piece, and a mythical subject (popular, incidentally, among Symbolist painters). The result is an orchestral set similar in concept to the three piano pieces Debussy assembled under the title *Estampes* (Prints) in 1903. The *Nocturnes* are nearly twice the length of the *Estampes*. But Debussy's intention seems to have been to adapt for orchestra a genre associated with the piano—in the process intentionally blurring distinctions between them.

43. Liebich, p. 43.

CHAPTER TWELVE

Pelléas et Mélisande and the Poe Operas

What strange air one breathes here!
Villiers de l'Isle-Adam,
Axël (1890)

OR A COMPOSER TO BE SUCCESSFUL IN FRANCE DURING THE NINETEENTH century it was essential to be successful as a composer of opera. The Prix de Rome provided an indication of the prevailing musical taste. Its basis was a composition, generally dramatic in content, for solo voices, ensemble, and chorus. While not an opera—that would have required too much time to compose—it resembled one. Winners of the Prix, like Debussy, were expected to build on their reputation by composing an opera not long after their return to Paris.

But Debussy was slow to follow the accepted path. If he wrote an opera, he wanted to create one unlike any other. The first requirement was a libretto that would inspire him, one, as he told Guiraud, that "only hints at what is to be said. The ideal would be two associated dreams. No place, nor time." What he was looking for was a world apart from the usual opera of the day (like *Rodrigue et Chimène*). He had tried to create something more to his taste. But his attempt to adapt dramatic scenarios from less conventional works (like those of Leconte de l'Isle or Banville) had not been successful.

Basically two predominant opera styles were current in Europe: Italian (represented by Verdi and later Puccini), and German (Wagner and his followers). French opera, though rooted in tradition, was more of a hybrid. The most popular, that of Massenet, combined elements of grand opera (established by Giacomo Meyerbeer in Paris in the 1830s) with aspects of lyric opera (Gounod and Thomas). None of those approaches appealed to Debussy.

No one was more aware of literary trends than Debussy, and he knew of the attention being directed toward the unusual dramas of the future Nobel laureate, Maurice Maeterlinck. They were in the Symbolist manner of works Debussy admired (like *Axël*), but were more concise and broader in their appeal. Performances in Paris of Maeterlinck's "The Intruder" and "The Blind" in 1891 had been very successful. His "Pelléas et Mélisande" was eagerly awaited, but because of financial complications, it was presented in only a single matinee performance on 17 May 1893. Debussy was present, as were distinguished representatives of all the arts, including Mallarmé, Whistler, Régnier, and Louÿs.[1]

Debussy had read "Pelléas et Mélisande" before the performance and probably had been struck by its potential as a libretto.[2] But seeing the play had a powerful impact on him. The performance was by all accounts striking, clothed in the distinctive dramaturgy associated with Symbolist works for the stage.

Despite its qualities as a drama, "Pelléas et Mélisande" was an odd choice for an opera. Based on the operatic standards of the day, it was totally unsuitable. There is little action. There are no aria-like sections, or ensembles, or distinction between contemplative scenes. In fact much of it seems deliberately anti-operatic and in opposition to nineteenth-century operatic convention.[3]

As set by Debussy, the opera opens with Golaud, lost in a forest, coming upon a mysterious, young woman (Mélisande) weeping beside a fountain. In spite of her fear, he manages to persuade her to leave with him. Six months later in a letter to his half-brother, Pelléas, Golaud announces his marriage to Mélisande and return to his ancestral home: the castle of his grandfather, King Arkel. Mélisande soon feels oppressed by the castle and the gloom of the surrounding forest. Life with Golaud is strained, a tension that is exacerbated when she carelessly loses her wedding ring. At the same time she gradually grows closer to Pelléas. Golaud becomes aware of their relationship and suspicious, using his young son from an earlier marriage, (Yniold), in an attempt to spy on them. Eventually he tells Pelléas to avoid Mélisande, using as a basis her "delicate condition" (Mélisande is pregnant). But he continues to keep the pair under observation, and at the very moment when they first declare their love, he rushes upon them and kills Pelléas. The opera concludes with

1. For additional study of *Pelléas*, see David Grayson, *The Genesis of Debussy's Pelléas et Mélisande* (Ann Arbor: UMI Research Press, 1986), and Roger Nichols and Richard Langham Smith, *Claude Debussy. Pelléas et Mélisande* (Cambridge: Cambridge University Press, 1989). For detailed information on all of Debussy's works for the stage (including ballets and abortive projects), see Robert Orledge, *Debussy and the Theatre* (Cambridge: Cambridge University Press, 1982).

2. He had previously been interested in Maeterlinck's "Princess Maleine," but rights had already been granted to d'Indy.

3. That would not have been by design. Maeterlinck was not musical, and he conceived "Pelléas et Mélisande" solely as a play, not as a statement on opera.

Mélisande's death, not long after having given birth prematurely. For much of the time Golaud is by her side, overwhelmed by remorse, but obsessed by her betrayal.

The basis of the plot—the love between a wife and her husband's brother—is far from original. But its presentation is. Mélisande, Golaud, and Pelléas inhabit their own dream-like world. Their grasp of reality is limited. Their speech and behavior are child-like. Words are spoken without concern for their impact. Attempts at concealment of thought or action are clumsy and simplistic. Communication often seems indirect, as if the characters were addressing themselves first and anyone who might be present as an afterthought. The dream-like—or, if you prefer, nightmarish—qualities of this somber drama are enhanced by the strongly realistic basis of the plot, but a plot presented by essentially abnormal personalities. Golaud, for example, seems delusional, and on the verge of madness.

Conspicuous by their absence are the high-flown phrases and sentiments of nineteenth-century romanticism. But the general absence of emotional display only lightly covers the profound transformation taking place within Pelléas, Golaud, and Mélisande. That change—and the soul-states which trace it—is the focus of the play.

Traditionally if a composer had been interested in "Pelléas et Mélisande" as an opera, Maeterlinck's text would have served as a point of departure. A writer would have been commissioned to prepare an adaptation. That was not Debussy's intention. For his musical setting, he assembled the libretto himself, making frequent, but minimal cuts (generally of repetitious text, a hallmark of Maeterlinck's style). Four scenes (with no bearing on the primary action) were omitted in their entirety. But for the most part, Debussy set to music the text as Maeterlinck had written it.

The staging of the play—in many ways remarkable—was a major source of inspiration for Debussy's musical approach. Pelléas, for example, had been played by a woman. But most memorable had been the visual impact of the sets and the style of acting.

Few stage properties had been used. Instead there had been an emphasis on painted paper and "abstract foliage."[4] Lighting was dim; makeup was a pale gray. The acting was typical of Symbolist plays: "hieractic gesture, stylized posing, and monotone declamation."[5] The tone was similar to that used for the recitation of poetry:

> I believe it was there [at the Théâtre d'Art] that for the first time poems were said as they should be said. Thus the *syllabic music* achieved through *natural accentuation* of *long syllables* and *short syllables* based on the premise that the poet did not choose short or long syllables without an intention, and that in order to give a poetic line its meaning, we need only

4. Contemporary review quoted in Frantisek Deak, *Symbolist Theater. The Formation of an Avant-Garde* (Baltimore, MD: Johns Hopkins University Press, 1993), p. 166.
5. Ibid., p. 54.

stress where the syllable is deep with sound, and glide over the mute and the "weak" syllables, without arbitrary effect left to an actor's caprice.[6]

The goal was to rely on simplicity to create an aura of mystery and detachment from reality. Contemporary reviews noted that the speech patterns of the actors provided glimpses into their souls, and comparisons were made to their words as "chant."[7] Although one reviewer complained that the actors spoke "in a tone of recitative with an irritating monotony," the general response was favorable.[8]

Debussy was excited by the possibility of "Pelléas et Mélisande" as an opera. Unlike nearly all of his other operatic projects, he took on this one without regrets and without hesitation, receiving permission to use the text from Maeterlinck in August 1893. Debussy may have begun composition earlier but did not work in earnest until late in August. Two years later, on 17 August 1895, composition (short score, excluding orchestration) was basically completed.

During that time he was absorbed with other pieces (like the *Marche écossaise,* the String Quartet, and the *Faune*), but *Pelléas* remained the focus, even if Debussy's approach seemed scattered. He began by setting the most extraordinary (and atypical) scene from the drama: Act IV, scene iv, the scene where Pelléas and Mélisande confess their love and are surprised by Golaud. Its intensity proved a challenge, and he had to rework it twice: in September–October 1893 (Debussy claimed the previous version sounded too much like Wagner), and in May 1895.

From that scene, Debussy jumped to the beginning of the drama, and from December 1893 through February 1894 set Act I to music. Act III (which shows Golaud's growing paranoia) and the remainder of Act IV (using the scenes with Yniold as a pivot) followed:

Act III, scene i	May–June (July?) 1894
Act III, scene ii	July–August 1894
Act III, scene iii	August 1894
Act IV, scene iii	August 1894
Act III, scene iv	August–September 1894
Act IV, scenes i, ii	January–February? 1895

Debussy composed Act V in April–June 1895 before turning to Act II to complete the opera (June–August 1895).

6. Charles Morice quoted in ibid., p. 172.
7. Ibid., p. 189.
8. Ibid., p. 167.

Debussy's compositional process for *Pelléas* consisted of making an initial draft (done in haste), followed by a short score with revisions. Many of the changes focused on the text, often subtle ones intended to enhance clarity and meaning. The vocal score was probably not fully completed until April 1900 (at the insistence of Debussy's publisher, and in preparation for rehearsals), and was revised in the summer of 1901. Orchestration went smoothly over a three- to four-week period early in 1902 (with additional revisions later, based on performance).

One of the greatest challenges facing Debussy was inherent in the plot of *Pelléas*. Its climax occurs in Act IV with Golaud's discovery of Pelléas and Mélisande. How could Debussy retain audience interest for an additional act? How could he reduce its sentimentality and maintain a semblance of reality in Mélisande's lengthy deathbed scene? He responded with understatement, by quickening the pace, and by treating Act V almost as an epilogue.

While composing *Pelléas* Debussy immersed himself in the text. Portions were played for friends. Letters documented his absorption. The scene in the vault was "full of deceitful terror, and mysterious enough to give vertigo to the most hardened souls. . . . Now I am at work on the scene between father and son. . . . There is a 'petit père' there that gives me nightmares."[9]

Once the opera had been accepted and a date set for its performance, he became actively engaged in how it would be presented on stage. Rehearsals began on 13 January 1902 and lasted until the premiere on 30 April. Debussy was present for sixty-nine days of them, an extraordinary amount. But he was convinced that *Pelléas* needed unusual guidance to ensure adequate presentation.

Fortunately he was seconded in his work by the conductor, André Messager. Messager, a popular composer of operetta, seemed an unlikely supporter, but he grasped the significance of *Pelléas* and early on convinced the management at the Opéra-Comique of its importance—and of the possibility that it might attract a following.

Debussy was equally fortunate to have for the roles of Pelléas and Mélisande two singers who were gifted musicians and able to respond to the new style the opera represented. Jean Périer excelled as Pelléas, and, as Mélisande, Mary Garden drew exceptional praise (despite criticism of her French pronunciation; she was born in Scotland and had lived in the United States).

Two factors contributed to Périer's and Garden's success in *Pelléas et Mélisande*: their acting skill, and their ability to sidestep operatic tradition. Their performance has led to the myth that they were extraordinary finds by Debussy. But both were part of the standard troupe at the Opéra-Comique and were also successful in more conventional operas. Garden had made her debut two years earlier in Charpentier's *Louise*, a role she loved—and one that could not have been more different from Mélisande. After

9. Letter of [28 August 1894] to Henry Lerolle in *C*, p. 220.

Pelléas et Mélisande she appeared as Violetta in Verdi's *La Traviata*. That was followed by starring roles in the standard repertory (she became a favorite in Massenet's *Thaïs*).

There has never been an opera quite like *Pelléas et Mélisande*, and that has worked to its advantage. Many who do not like opera in general, find it to be an exception. Others, more tradition-bound, find it to be a refreshing change. From the start, reaction to it was unpredictable. Audiences generally enjoyed it (a small, energized minority developed into a cult following). There was strong appeal to the younger generation, especially composers.

Criticism in the press ran the gamut. To traditionalists, Debussy was nothing less than the "head of the anarchists in music."[10] Debussy's former collaborator, Catulle Mendès, expressed disappointment. Debussy had missed the "poetic essence," he claimed, and the result was similar to what some had criticized in the performance of the play: "systematic exaggeration of monotony."[11] But there was also approval in unexpected quarters. Massenet, who heard it in rehearsal, described it as "so new, so unexpected."[12]

A common complaint was that the music had too complementary a role, and that the emphasis was on the text (producing the type of "monotony" Mendès mentioned). Richard Strauss went even further. *Pelléas et Mélisande*, he concluded, was "not music."[13] But it continued to attract audiences, and reached its hundredth performance at the Opéra-Comique in January 1913. Figures for the first half of the twentieth century are impressive: 343 performances, ranking fifteenth overall (first on the list, with 1,808 performances, was Bizet's *Carmen*).

The authors of early studies of Debussy were enthralled with *Pelléas et Mélisande*. Louise Liebich wrote that *Pelléas* constituted nothing less than "an epoch in the history of operatic music.... [It was] entirely without precedent, bearing no resemblance to any other opera."[14] Lawrence Gilman was equally effusive. It was "not simply a new manner of writing opera, but a new kind of music...this dim and wavering and elusive music, with its infinitely subtle gradations, its gossamer fineness of texture, its delicate sonorities, its strange and echoing dissonances, its singular richness of mood, its shadowy beauty, its exquisite and elaborate art."[15]

10. Arthur Pougin quoted in Jann Pasler, "*Pelléas* and Power: Forces behind the Reception of Debussy's Opera," *19th-Century Music* 10 (1987), p. 262.

11. Ibid., p. 250.

12. Demar Irvine, *Massenet: A Chronicle of His Life and Times* (Portland, OR: Amadeus Press, 1997), p. 243.

13. *LS*, p. 285.

14. Mrs. Franz Liebich, *Claude-Achille Debussy* (London: John Lane, 1908), p. 79.

15. Lawrence Gilman, *Debussy's Pelléas et Mélisande. A Guide to the Opera* (New York: Schirmer, 1907), pp. 3, 4–5.

Singled out for discussion was the manner in which Debussy had set the text to music: it not only avoided traditional distinctions between recitative, arioso, and aria, but the Wagnerian concept of "endless melody," as well. Gilman described it as "virtually a chant; an opera in which there is no vocal melody whatsoever, and comparatively little symphonic development of themes in the orchestra."[16] Liebich reacted similarly, writing of the opera's "intensified speech occasionally resembling plain or Gregorian chant."[17] Actual resemblance between Debussy's setting and plainchant is slight. And the reference to "no vocal melody whatsoever" is wide of the mark. What those statements emphasize is how unusual Debussy's music must have sounded at the time, and how difficult it was to try to explain what made it so.

We know that Debussy worked hard to create a unique, declamatory style. One objective during the course of his revision was to produce the effect of more natural speech patterns (and at the same to undo the occasional bad habit, such as predictable phrasing). As in his songs, Debussy was acutely sensitive to words, meaning, and drama. When in the final act Golaud asks for Mélisande's forgiveness, in order to heighten its effect there is suddenly no orchestral accompaniment.

Debussy's effort to create music to enhance, yet not overwhelm, the text, led him back to the essence of the spoken word. Sung text, he advised Manuel de Falla in 1911, should not last longer than speech. The style and dramatic pace of Maeterlinck's text lent itself singularly well to that type of musical approach.

Operatic, vocal lyricism is absent from Debussy's score. On the one hand there are no lengthy speeches or soliloquies in Maeterlinck's setting that could function as an aria. But even when an opportunity arises—as in Mélisande's song in Act III—Debussy turned his back on operatic tradition and created instead a folk-like setting.

Since much of Debussy's vocal line is nuanced, relying on repetition of notes and stepwise motion, any departure from it can become strikingly lyrical, as in the following instance from Act IV. Here the effect is further enhanced by slowing the pace from eighth to quarter notes (Example 12-1 on the next page).

The style Debussy created for *Pelléas* has tended to complicate performance, where an emphasis has sometimes been placed on acting over musicality. In moments of great intensity—Act IV, for example—there has been a tendency for singers to turn to spoken word or to offer only an approximation of the pitch notated in the score—as if, for some reason, music were no longer suitable. But Debussy went to great pains to be precise in his notation, and it always works. When he did not want notated pitch, he indicated it (as in Golaud's poignant "ahs" in the final act; in an earlier version Debussy had actually set them to music).

16. Ibid., pp. 49–50.
17. Liebich, p. 68.

Even today Debussy's handling of the text seems a marvel, a synthesis of word and music that appears completely natural. But what makes it particularly effective is the role of the orchestra. Voice and orchestra are not independent. But in a reversal of traditional roles, the orchestra is often more "melodic." There is variety of tone and timbre, and greater lyricism. But it is complementary, and subdued (Debussy's dynamic indications, often *piano*, are a key).

At times the orchestra provides commentary on the text. The sudden appearance of the harps, for example, in the grotto scene in Act III, scene iii, has the effect of a bolt of light. Equally effective are the orchestral interludes, most of which originally were no more than several dozen measures in length. Debussy was asked to expand them for

12-1 *Pelléas et Mélisande*

continued

12-1 Continued

performance to allow time to change scenery on stage. But beyond that practical need, they often provide a moment of catharsis, helping to dissipate some of the stress and emotion of the previous scene while providing a transition to the new one.

Much of the drama in *Pelléas* occurs not in exterior action but as character development—as a response to what has become an increasingly untenable situation. That inward tension and its progression is a characteristic of Symbolist drama, and one that draws heavily on the concept of soul-states. Debussy's concern with it helped fashion his music, and provides further insight into his intentions. "On hearing opera," he wrote, "the spectator is accustomed to experiencing two distinct sorts of emotion: on

the one hand the *musical emotion*, and on the other the emotion of the characters—
usually he experiences them in succession. I tried to ensure that the two were perfectly merged and simultaneous. Melody, if I dare say so, is antilyrical. It cannot express
the varying states of the soul, and of life. Essentially, it is suited only to the song that
expresses a simple feeling."[18] Being "antilyrical" was one way to express in music the
complexity of a soul-state. Yet another device Debussy employed was to adapt in his
own manner the concept of the leitmotiv developed by Richard Wagner.

Debussy had mixed feelings about Wagner's music. It was, he felt, inimitable, with
glorious elements, but the summation of an age. *Parsifal* ("of the utmost beauty")
was the work of Wagner that Debussy most admired.[19] But he was critical of
Wagner's use of leitmotivs in his music dramas, comparing them to "calling cards"
which tended to disrupt rather than enhance the dramatic flow.[20]

In *Pelléas et Mélisande* Debussy associated readily identifiable musical motives with
the primary characters. Each is clearly recognizable, by both pitch and rhythm (for
example, the triplet and dotted rhythm for Golaud, as well as the repeated major
second: Example 12-2). They reappear subtly and unobtrusively. Often their function
is more as a musical representation of a soul-state than of a person or a situation (as in
Wagner)—and their change and transformation is a musical response to the complexity of the emotions, feelings, and thoughts embodied by the soul-state.

12-2 *Pelléas et Mélisande*

Debussy's use of leitmotivs was noted by audiences and critics. Too much was
made of them. Maurice Emmanuel, for example, identified thirteen major ones,
and analyzed the entire opera with them as the basis.[21] Although the leitmotivs are

18. Interview in *Le Figaro* of 16 May 1902 in *DM*, p. 80.

19. Review of 6 April 1903 in *DM*, p. 167.

20. For a full discussion of Debussy's understanding of Wagner, see Robin Holloway, *Debussy and Wagner* (London: Eulenburg Books, 1979).

21. Maurice Emmanuel, *Pelléas et Mélisande de Debussy* (Paris: Mellottée, [1924]).

one of the most obvious musical characteristics of the opera, focusing on them tends to detract from the other musical elements of the score.

Many of the expected features of Debussy's music are found in *Pelléas*: modality, non-functional harmony, varied repetition of cells as a means of musical development. More debatable is the claim of tonality as means of musical symbolism. It was, we know, a device favored by composers such as Vincent d'Indy. His letters confirm that, like Debussy, he thought of leitmotivs as symbolic of musical soul-states. But on a larger dimension d'Indy created tonal architecture designed to enhance an opera's symbolism. In *Fervaal* (1895) D major represented light and triumph; A flat minor was associated with suffering. Some have seen similar symbolism in *Pelléas et Mélisande* with, for example, F sharp major as the equivalent of "light, revelation, vision."[22] The case of proof, however, is not as strong—both because Debussy's tonality is less clear-cut than d'Indy's, and because Debussy never referred to its use.

D'Indy was Debussy's greatest rival at the time of *Pelléas*. His opera, *Fervaal*, was intended as a regeneration of the genre in France. D'Indy wrote the text himself and worked on the score for six years. First performed at the Opéra-Comique in 1898, its basis was legend; its setting, the Saracen invasion of the Cévennes in the eighth century. D'Indy was an admirer of Wagner, and Wagner's style permeates all elements of *Fervaal*. In that sense *Fervaal* was typical of many fin-de-siècle operas. It is difficult today to grasp the astonishing effect Wagner's music had on French composers of the time. "Yesterday," Emmanuel Chabrier wrote to his wife, "I heard *Parsifal* for the first time. I have never in all my life had an artistic experience at all comparable to this; it is overwhelming: one comes out after each act (I do, at least) absolutely overcome with admiration, bewildered, distraught with tears running down one's cheeks."[23] In trying to create a new style of opera, French composers fell under Wagner's spell (Chabrier's unfinished *Briséis* [1894], and Chausson's *Le Roi Arthus* [1895], are good examples). Debussy's independent stance was unique.[24]

Except to increase the vogue of Maeterlinck, the success of *Pelléas* did not alter operatic taste in France. The Massenet style continued to be popular, whether by him or in the hands of other composers, such as Xavier Leroux and Henry Février.[25]

22. Arthur B. Wenk, *Claude Debussy and Twentieth-Century Music* (Boston: Twayne, 1983), p. 48.

23. Letter to his wife of 22 July 1889 in Rollo Myers, *Emmanuel Chabrier and His Circle* (London: J. M. Dent, 1969), p. 85.

24. The search for possible influences on *Pelléas* led beyond Wagner and the use of leitmotivs to Debussy's supposed indebtedness to Musorgsky's *Boris Godunov* (1874). But although he had access to the score, rather than specific musical traits what they share is a departure from operatic convention. In style and content (*Boris* is, after all, basically a historical drama), *Pelléas et Mélisande* and *Boris Godunov* are a world apart.

25. Even if, as in the case of Février's *Monna Vanna* (1909), the source was a play by Maeterlinck.

D'Indy followed *Fervaal* with *L'Etranger* (1903). The influence of Wagner was diminished. But even though the text (again his own work) could not be more Symbolist, the music owes little to *Pelléas* (excepting perhaps its preference for greater musical simplicity).

The exception was Dukas's *Ariane et Barbe-bleue* (1907), a sparkling work based on Maeterlinck's play of the same name. Dukas adapted Debussy's approach in *Pelléas*, but with less circumspection for the text (and Debussy's declamatory style). Debussy was not impressed. He complained to Dukas that "throughout, at every turning, the music dominates the words."[26] Privately he described *Ariane et Barbe-bleue* as "a masterpiece, but not a masterpiece of French music"—a dubious pronouncement that says more about Debussy's growing nationalism than his critical judgment.[27]

The popularity of *Pelléas et Mélisande* led to the expectation that Debussy would soon favor the public with another opera. But he was fearful of repeating himself and cautious in selecting another subject. In 1895 he had briefly considered a tale by Balzac, "La Grande Bretêche." It is in the frenetic style of Pétrus Borel with overtones of Poe: a husband revenges himself on his wife by entombing her lover alive. Nothing came of the idea, but it gives some indication of Debussy's interests. Of the many plans for opera after *Pelléas*, two seemed to hold his attention: an adaptation of Shakespeare's *As You Like It* (1902–1904), and an opera based on the legend of Orpheus (1907–1909). But no music was composed for either one.

Debussy eventually settled on a little-known short story by Poe: "The Devil in the Belfry" (1839). Poe was extraordinarily popular in France where he had had the benefit of two translators of genius: Charles Baudelaire and Stéphane Mallarmé. For years he had been one of Debussy's favorite writers.

The tale selected by Debussy is not in the gothic genre generally associated with Poe but is a humorous piece intended for the local press. Poe wrote several stories like it, with an affinity for the "tall tales" popular at the time in the United States. The plot is basic: the devil disrupts life in a dull and conventional Dutch village (with the name of Vondervotteimittiss) by having the town clock strike thirteen.

Unlike Poe's tales that focus on the macabre, the intent in "The Devil in the Belfry" is to entertain with humor and hyperbole. The following extract (where Poe explains how Vondervotteimittiss received its name) is typical of its style:

> Among a multitude of opinions upon this delicate point—some acute, some learned, some sufficiently the reverse—I am able to select nothing which ought to be considered satisfactory. Perhaps the idea of Grogswigg—nearly coincident with that of Kroutaplenttey—is

---

26. Letter of 8 May 1907 in *DL*, p. 178.
27. Letter to Vittorio Gui of 25 February 1912 in *C*, p. 1494.

to be cautiously preferred:—It runs:—"*Vondervotteimittis*—*Vonder, lege Donder*—*Votteimittis, quasi und Bleitziz*—*Bleitziz obsol: pro Blitzen.*" This derivative, to say the truth, is still countenanced by some traces of the electric fluid evident on the summit of the steeple of the House of the Town-Council. I do not choose, however, to commit myself on a theme of such importance, and must refer the reader desirous of information, to the "*Oratiunculæ de Rebus Præter-Veteris,*" of Dundergutz. See, also, Blunderbuzzard "*De Derivationibus,*" pp. 27 to 5010, Folio, Gothic edit., Red and Black character, Catch-word and No Cypher; wherein consult, also, marginal notes in the autograph of Stuffundpuff, with the Sub-Commentaries of Gruntundguzzell.[28]

What attracted Debussy to Poe's short story (it is only about a half dozen pages in length)? The humor can be heavy-handed, but absurdity, exposure of human folly, satire on conventionality—all were aspects with appeal to Debussy. He also felt that the type of devil Poe created ("ironical and cruel") was much more effective than the traditional one.[29] And then there is the important role of sound: the tolling of the clock's bell in the belfry, and the devil himself, a virtuoso bass fiddler and dancer extraordinaire.

But there were real difficulties in adapting the story as an opera (or, for that matter, as a drama). It is a fable (Poe originally subtitled it, "An Extravaganza"), so much so that depicting its fantastic occurrences on stage would be a challenge. Then there is the narration itself. Much of it is descriptive with commentary on past occurrences intended to set the scene. All would need to be summarized and transferred to the stage to explain the devil's presence.

Debussy began work on *The Devil in the Belfry* in the summer of 1902. In October 1903 he signed a contract with Durand stipulating that the work would be in two acts, and would be completed by May 1905. But although he worked sporadically on the project until 1912, he made little progress. In the end there are only six pages of notes (with a summary of the text) and three pages of music, all bearing the date 25 August 1903. While at work on the score, Debussy wrote to Durand of a distinctive manner he had developed in writing for voices. But there is no way of knowing what he intended based on what has survived. About a dozen measures of the music were used by Debussy in the brief piano piece, "Morçeau de concours," published in *Musica* in 1905.

Because of Debussy's lack of progress, he was given an extension to April 1907. In the following year he signed an additional contract for its production with the

---

28. *The Works of Edgar Allan Poe,* ed. John H. Ingram. 4 vols. (London: A. & C. Black, 1899), II, p. 300. Incidentally, Baudelaire retained "Vondervotteimittiss" in his translation, but Debussy did not use it.

29. Letter to André Messager of [9 June 1902] in *C*, p. 668.

Metropolitan Opera in New York City, but with an important addition. *The Devil in the Belfry* was intended to be part of a double-bill along with another opera based on Poe: "The Fall of the House of Usher" (1839).[30]

Debussy's interest in adapting "The Fall of the House of Usher" was nearly two decades old. Around 1890 he contemplated an orchestral piece based on it. He probably started creating a libretto in 1908 and began composing music the following year. As with *The Devil in the Belfry*, his work was irregular, but it continued as late as 1916. What have survived are two versions of the text (a twenty-seven-page sketch and a final version of seventeen pages) and twenty-one pages of music for voice and piano (with some orchestral indications).

"The Fall of the House of Usher" is one of Poe's best-known works, a tale of unremitting gloom and depression, chronicling the hypersensitivity, incipient madness, and death of Roderick Usher. Usher is an aesthete and a musician known for his "wild improvisations" on the guitar.[31] The story is set as the first-person narrative of a friend of Usher and is almost entirely descriptive. Only Usher speaks. In creating his libretto, Debussy increased the role of a very minor character (a physician), in the process presenting dramatic possibilities but minimizing the effect of the gradual, but inexorable dissolution of Usher.

Not enough material has survived to assemble an edition of *The Fall of the House of Usher* that can accurately reflect what Debussy ultimately wanted the work to be. One attempt at completing Debussy's unfinished work was made in 1979 by Juan Allende-Blin and has been published and recorded.[32] There are interesting moments in it (Debussy seems to have captured some of the eerie, ominous atmosphere well), but at best it can only provide glimpses of what may have been intended. Debussy completed no music for substantial portions of the text, and none of the orchestration.

Why after more than fifteen years was Debussy unable to complete either of his Poe operas? Involvement with other musical projects was undoubtedly an impediment. But he was also concerned about comparisons with *Pelléas et Mélisande*. Debussy was determined that his next opera would be completely different, and not another version of *Pelléas*. That required a different type of text and a different approach—and, although he may not have recognized it, there are strong similarities in style, plot, and mood between *Pelléas* and *Usher*. There also must have been at least some anxiety that whatever he wrote might not match the success of *Pelléas*, both financially and critically.

30. Also part of the contract was a Tristan opera. Debussy was candid with the Met management on the implausibility of completing all the works.

31. *Works*, I, p. 186.

32. Another version by Carolyn Abbate and Robert Kyr was performed in 1977.

Yet an additional obstacle was psychological. Debussy never appeared resolved to compose music for *The Devil in the Belfry*. As had been the case with so many operatic projects, he seemed to lose interest in it, even though he occasionally made an effort to return to it.

But that was not the case with *The Fall of the House of Usher*. Debussy became obsessed with it. Letters to friends record his fascination. "I am living," he wrote to Durand, "in "The House of Usher" . . . it bears no resemblance to a rest home, and at times I leave it with my nerves stretched as tautly as those of a violin."[33] Poe, he confessed, "holds nearly an agonizing tyranny over me."[34]

The "insufferable gloom" and "utter depression of soul" that permeates "The Fall of the House of Usher" is skillfully manipulated by Poe and can produce an uncanny effect on a sensitive reader.[35] For Debussy, that was not the type of immersion in the subject that had proved so beneficial in composing *Pelléas et Mélisande*. It was as if it had become a struggle to maintain the sense of detachment necessary to compose, as if composing itself had become an ordeal. The result—a composer so captivated by his subject that he is unable to finish his work—is not as far-fetched as it may appear, and worthy in itself of a tale by Poe.

But Debussy may also have felt stymied by his attempt to adapt the story as an opera. His libretto seems several steps removed from Poe and lacks the brooding atmosphere that is such a crucial component of the tale. In the end, it is hard to believe that Debussy was completely satisfied with the text he had produced, yet another factor that may have contributed to *The Fall of the House of Usher* remaining little more than a fragment.

33. Letter of 15 July 1910 in *C*, p. 1302.

34. Letter to André Caplet of 21 September 1909 in ibid., p. 1214.

35. *Works*, I, p. 179.

CHAPTER THIRTEEN

Compositions 1900–1912

In fact the best pupil from my point of view will be the "bad" pupil, the one
who takes nothing on trust!

Pierre Boulez, "The Teacher's Task" (1961)

Instrumental Works

Solo Piano: *Images oubliées* (1894); *Pour le piano*, *Images* (Books I and II);

Estampes; *L'Isle joyeuse*; *Masques*; *D'un cahier d'esquisses*; *Pièce pour piano* (*Morçeau de concours*);
   Children's Corner; "The Little Nigar"; *Hommage à Haydn*; *Préludes* (Books I and II); *La
   plus que lente* (also for orchestra)

Two Pianos: *Lindaraja*

Chamber: Rhapsody for Clarinet (with piano; also for orchestra)
          Petite pièce for Clarinet (with piano)

Orchestral and Concerto: *La Mer*; Rhapsody for Saxophone and Orchestra (completed
   after Debussy's death by Roger-Ducasse); *Deux Danses* (for harp and orchestra); *Images
   pour orchestre*

Ballet: *Khamma*

Vocal Works

Songs: *Fêtes galantes* (2nd series) (Verlaine); *Trois Chansons de France* (Charles d'Orléans,
   Tristan L'Hermite); *Trois Chansons de Charles d'Orléans*; *Trois Ballades de François Villon*;
   Le Promenoir des deux amants (Tristan L'Hermite)

Works for the Stage:
   Incidental music for *King Lear*; *Le Martyre de St. Sébastien*

W HILE STILL A STUDENT DEBUSSY DECIDED THAT IT WAS ESSENTIAL TO DISCARD much of what he was being taught. Blindly adopting rules and traditions produced music that was bland and predictable. There was the added risk that it might become fashionable. So it could only have been a shock for Debussy to discover after the success of *Pelléas* that his own music was becoming popular. What he wrote was in vogue, and widely imitated. Although he may have been amused at first by references in the press to a "School of Debussy" or to "Debussy and His Followers," in time the idea only horrified him.

There were in Debussy's eyes three major drawbacks to fame. The loss of privacy annoyed him. Then there were the simplistic labels—like Impressionism—that were applied to his music. Finally, there seemed to be a widespread belief that somehow his music fit into a mold, that what he composed would be predictable and a continuation of what he had previously produced.

He was determined to remain distinctive, and to write music free from formulas. But it was not a simple task. "For every bar [I write] that has some freedom about it," wrote Debussy while at work on his Poe operas, "there are twenty that are stifled by the weight of one particular tradition; try as I may, I'm forced to recognize its hypocritical and destructive influence. The fact that this tradition belongs to me by right is hardly relevant."[1]

★ ★ ★ ★ ★

No work serves as a stronger point of demarcation between Debussy and his contemporaries than *La Mer*. It revealed an entirely new compositional approach, and one so distinctive that it alienated and perplexed many who had been eager supporters of his music.[2]

Composing *La Mer* was a grueling project. Debussy dedicated more than a year and a half to it—from August 1903 to March 1905. Its source of inspiration testified to the depths of his recollections and sensibility, for *La Mer* was begun far from the sea, deep in the heartland of France during a visit to his in-laws in Burgundy. By the time it was completed, Debussy had left Lily and established a new life with Emma Bardac.

Given the extraordinary changes in his personal life (and the slow pace adopted by Debussy in general on a new work), *La Mer* was completed rapidly. Unlike the major orchestral work that preceded it—the *Nocturnes*—he did not complain about writing or finishing *La Mer*. Yet it is a far more complex work than the *Nocturnes* and provided much more of a challenge.

Its complexity is not readily apparent. *La Mer* is an instrumental composition with a program inspired by nature, the type of program with broad appeal not just in the open-

1. Letter to André Caplet of [22 December 1911] in *DL*, p. 252.

2. For additional study of *La Mer*, see Simon Trezise, *Debussy: La Mer* (Cambridge: Cambridge University Press, 1994).

ing decade of the twentieth century but for much of the nineteenth century as well. Bodies of water, whether lakes, streams, or the sea, were a popular musical subject.

Paul Gilson's *La Mer* provides an interesting comparison. Gilson, a Belgian composer, was three years younger than Debussy. *La Mer* (1892) was his first major composition, and it became one of his most successful.

Gilson's *La Mer* is an orchestral composition with a poem as its basis, but vague in genre (it is identified neither as a tone poem nor a symphony). The subtitle is "symphonic sketches," and there are four, each with a title: "Lever de soleil" (Sunrise), "Chants et danses de matelots" (Sailors' Songs and Dances), "Crépuscule" (Twilight), and "La Tempête" (The Tempest). The program offers a bit of everything, from sailors at leisure to the changing faces of nature. Gilson's musical approach could not be simpler. As a unifying device, a single, easily recognizable theme appears in all the movements.

On the surface Debussy's *La Mer* shows similarity to Gilson's. "I am working," he wrote at the beginning of the project, "on three symphonic sketches entitled: 1. 'Mer belle aux iles sanguinaires'; 2. 'jeu de vagues'; 3. 'le vent fait danser la mer'; the whole to be called *La Mer*."[3] As the project progressed over the next eighteen months, three basic components remained unchanged: that *La Mer* consisted of symphonic sketches, that there were three of them, and that each had a title.

The titles were eventually altered, and the ones selected by Debussy—"De l'aube à midi sur la mer" (From Dawn to Noon at Sea), "Jeux de vagues" (Play of the Waves), and "Dialogue du vent et de la mer" (Dialogue of the Wind and the Sea)— were an improvement. They are less restrictive than the original titles, more poetic, more evocative, and, in the case of the final movement, they avoid the association with dance (and the ballet).

Unlike Gilson's, Debussy's *La Mer* focused solely on the sea. People may be implied as observers, but the commonplace associations of Gilson's titles have been deliberately avoided. And while the temptation might be strong to associate Debussy's titles to paintings or prints with similar names, there is no indication that was his intention. Unlike the *Nocturnes* that drew directly on the visual arts, *La Mer* draws solely on nature. There is no intermediary.

One curious link between Debussy and Gilson is the description of their work as "symphonic sketches." Each could just as easily have been called a symphony. Gilson's format is identical to a typical four-movement symphony (with the second movement as a scherzo). Debussy only uses three movements (Fast-Slow-Fast). But for a symphony to have three movements was not unusual in France.

---

3. Letter to André Messager of 12 September 1903 in *DL*, p. 141. The Iles sanguinaires are part of an archipelago near Ajaccio, Corsica. There has been speculation that the odd, original title of the first movement may have been derived from a short story by Camille Mauclair, or from a newspaper's daily meteorological update ("la mer est toujours belle aux Iles Sanguinaires"). *LS*, p. 246.

Debussy avoided the title "Symphony," both because he questioned the vitality of its tradition and because he wanted to avoid easy categorization. But beyond that—and this may have been the reason the concept of "sketches" appealed to Gilson as well—the subtitle helped to provide specificity. Unlike sketches as images, these were musical sketches from nature. To Debussy there was yet another reason for the subtitle's appeal. "Sketches" gives the impression of a work still evolving, dashed off, improvisatory—all elements that Debussy tried to capture in his music.

By writing music inspired by the sea, Debussy could draw on a potentially broad base of interest. There was a fascination among the arts with the sea, an appeal that surpassed genre and artistic credos to include Impressionist seascapes, Symbolist painting (such as Alphonse Osbert's *Hymne à la mer* [1893]), as well as poetry (Francis Vielé-Griffin and Jean Richepin, for example). But Debussy's attraction to the sea went beyond current interest. As a child he had been captivated by his first view of the Mediterranean at Cannes and later expressed interest in becoming a sailor. As an adult, he found that a vacation by the seashore (curiously, Debussy was unable to swim) provided both relaxation and regeneration for work. He was an acute observer of the sea. The idea, then, of composing a piece of music inspired by the sea was in many ways a fulfillment for him of deeply held convictions.

Debussy was also concerned about the appearance of *La Mer* in print. For the cover, rather than a generic illustration (or, more likely, none at all), a detail was adapted (the crest of a wave) from a print by the Japanese artist, Hokusai: "The Hollow of the Wave Off Kanegawa" (one of his *Thirty-Six Views of Mount Fuji*, 1820–1829). It was a striking choice—exotic, distinctive, yet wonderfully conceptualized. There was the advantage that Hokusai had a growing circle of admirers in France, including Gauguin.[4]

Since *Pelléas*, each new work by Debussy found an eager audience. But those who had expected something in his previous manner were disappointed by *La Mer*. Critics were confused. They noted the general resemblance to a symphony but found that using the symphonic repertory as a point of comparison led to confusion. A symphony—whether one in name or disguised under another, like Gilson's *La Mer*—organized its musical material in a traditional manner and presented it in easily comprehensible structures. Debussy did neither.

How, then, did *La Mer* actually compare with contemporary symphonies in France? Some composers continued the standard nineteenth-century approach established in Germany: four movements, in contrasting tempi (Fast-Slow-Moderate-Fast). D'Indy and Magnard followed that practice but adapted the cyclic principle as a unifying device. D'Indy's Second Symphony (1903) is in four movements and is based on a pair of theme groups, both of which reappear as a grandiose conclusion in the finale. Magnard's Fourth Symphony (1913) adopts a similar approach.

4. A print of Hokusai's "Wave" hung prominently in Debussy's study.

But there was no rule restricting the number of movements to four. The symphonies of Franck (1888), Chausson (1890), and Dukas (1896) all contained three (Fast-Slow-Fast). Using their work as a basis, Debussy's *La Mer* certainly looked like a symphony—but one with titles (and a program of sorts).

Whether three or four movements, symphonies used contrast, typically melodic and tonal, to delineate structure. For a listener, identifying tonal centers requires perfect pitch. But many in the audience listened for and identified melodies, and used their reappearance to determine compositional process and the evolving musical structure.[5] When traditional structures were adopted, audiences could locate their position within a piece (the recapitulation in sonata form, for example), and would then be able to anticipate—if only in a general sense—the next likely musical event. Over time (and, in the case of long-familiar structures like sonata form, over generations) the listening experience became predictable and comforting (much like a journey, the direction set with minimal variation, the path well trodden, accompanied by recognizable but changing scenery). It was the coupling of the new with the predictable that provided both the charm and firm grounding for the listener.

But both seem to be missing from *La Mer*. There is some tunefulness, and a good deal of contrast. Listeners can hear when a melody enters or when bold change happens. They can recognize when structural transformation has occurred. But because traditional forms are not being indicated by these shifts, listeners are left adrift. To recognize that a structural change has occurred but not to know what role it plays appears pointless. What is its relationship to what has come before? And where is it going? Those seem to be unanswered questions in *La Mer*.

The most ingenious attempt to solve the riddle of its musical structure uses golden section as its key. The concept of golden section has been used in the visual arts since antiquity and is said to be based on a proportion ubiquitous in nature. It is represented by the following theorem: the ratio of the shorter to the longer length is equal to the ratio of the longer to the whole (b/a = a/a+b; the ratio equals approximately .618). In the visual arts, that position may indicate the focal point of an image (for example, placement of a halo). Golden section was in vogue in fin de siècle Europe, and was used by painters like Seurat and Segantini. Debussy likely came into contact with the concept early, perhaps through his association with Edmond Bailly.

Transferring the golden section to music is not easy. The proportion would be indicated by an important structural change, perhaps the entry of new thematic material, or the significant return of a theme heard previously. But what should be used as the basis of measurement? Beats? Bars? The performance time of the composition? In the visual arts, the eye can see the structural point of reference. But how can the ear hear it?

---

5. See Eric F. Jensen, "Sound as Symbol: Fin de Siècle Perceptions of the Orchestra," *Music Review* 57 (1996), pp. 227–240.

One Debussy scholar, Roy Howat, used bars as a basis and justified its selection by pointing to what he felt was a clue in a letter by Debussy. Looking through the proofs of *Estampes*, Debussy complained to his publisher that a measure—"necessary from the point of view of number; the divine number, as Plato and Mlle Liane de Pougy would say, though each for a different reason, admittedly"—was missing.[6] The tone of the letter is bantering, and the meaning unclear. But using Debussy's comment as a point of departure, Howat examined several of Debussy's compositions, including *La Mer*, to see if golden section were present.

Golden section in music is not as far-fetched a concept as it might appear. Béla Bartók, for one, used it. And it seems likely that the idea of reproducing in his music a proportion present throughout nature would have had appeal to Debussy. But the examples presented by Howat are not convincing. There do not seem to be enough significant structural points in Debussy's compositions to coincide with golden section—at least not without some proportional adjustment.

But even if the idea of replicating nature in his music did appeal to Debussy, how would he have reacted to the idea of creating it through such a tedious and mechanical manner? Conventional musical development (as in sonata form) he dismissed as "mandarin labors." "That's architecture," he once told Charles Koechlin, "not music."[7] Would he have felt the same about golden section? And there may be another reason the practice might not have appealed to him. Although it had the advantage (in Debussy's eyes) of being a compositional concept not taught in music conservatories, golden section remained associated with the Western tradition from which Debussy was increasingly distancing himself.

Much of the novelty of structure in *La Mer* can be traced to Debussy's approach in earlier orchestral compositions like the *Faune* and the *Nocturnes*. The basis is the same: repetition and variation of two- and four-bar phrases. In *La Mer* that repetition takes on added meaning: musical repetition becomes a counterpart to the repetitive motion of water.

Like the ocean's waves, Debussy's musical phrases are never identical. In earlier compositions the final measure of a phrase often served as a bridge to a new musical idea or a variant. But there is a difference in its application in *La Mer*. Previously the principle was applied in the context of broad, structural outlines—generally an ABA form—and the repetition and variation was contained within, while helping to differentiate musical sections. In *La Mer* there is no set form, like ABA or sonata. The structure itself is unique and is generated in a continuous and unpredictable manner by a succession of musical ideas—not by their position within a traditional, recognizable structure.

6. Letter to Jacques Durand of [18 September 1903] in *DL*, p. 137. The piece in question is "Jardins sous la pluie." Liane de Pougy was a well-known courtesan of the time.

7. *DR*, p. 101.

Debussy's approach is cellular and brings to mind Bach's. Bach's motivic cells relied more on imitation and less on predictable phrase length (and often more than one were presented simultaneously). But Debussy achieves the same generative effect in his music, one of natural growth and expansion. The most significant change is that phrases are no longer conceived as a component of a section or subdivision, a concept that encouraged listeners in the eighteenth and nineteenth centuries to keep track of what had happened musically in order to determine what point they had reached in their musical journey (and where they were going).

In *La Mer* the focus is on the present. There are no structural formulas, no padding—every bar is essential and serves in the growth of the composition. That explains the root of the problem contemporary critics had with *La Mer*, even though they were unable to explain it. Based on its appearance, *La Mer* was a symphony. They listened and looked for traditional symphonic structures—and were soon lost. There were no comprehensible points of reference. This was not the familiar path.

The novel approach Debussy adopted for *La Mer* assures that it always appears fresh and inventive. The structure is astonishingly subtle and flexible, and it varies not just from listener to listener, but from hearing to hearing. What is heard, and how it is interpreted, depends on what the listener chooses to emphasize.

To begin to follow the compositional process in *La Mer*, focus on what is being heard at the moment. Listening remains an evolving presentation, but Debussy's practice becomes clearer by concentrating on patterns (the two- and four-measure repetitive phrases of *La Mer*). The last movement, "Dialogue du vent et de la mer," is a good place to start. Here the compositional procedure is followed with an almost rigorous logic. Listen to the opening phrase, its varied repetition, and transition to new material. Hear how phrases exist independently but flow easily into one another, how the music itself is generated in a natural process (but with no direct relationship to the traditional tonal or thematic centers that used to serve as structural markers). It is an exciting experience—lively, unpredictable, and a world apart from the music people in Europe had been listening to for hundreds of years.

Despite its apparent freedom, there are parameters in place for the innovative structural process Debussy developed for *La Mer*. Associated with it are musical concepts more conventional in basis that help to remove some of its novelty and provide cohesion. The sound of *La Mer* is based on concepts long associated with Debussy's music: melody as arabesque; nonfunctional harmony; exoticism (as in the use of whole tone and pentatonic scales in the first movement). Debussy also adapted a method associated with Franck and his school: a primary theme, varied and appearing in all three movements as a unifying device. There are several readily identifiable elements in it, rhythmic (the triplet) and melodic (ascending minor third; descending major and minor seconds—Example 13-1 on the next page).

In the first movement this theme reappears near the end of the movement as the climax (the appearance of the sun at midday). In the second movement it appears

with less emphasis (based mostly on the triplet figure). For the final movement, the second half of the theme receives prominence (Example 13-2).

13-2 *La Mer*: "Dialogue du vent et de la mer"

Debussy's thematic transformation is by design far less obtrusive than Franck's. But he seems to emphasize a connection with the Franckian School by using in the last movement a theme that alternates between flat sixth and natural sixth (implying major and minor mode), a notable characteristic of Franck's melodic style. At the most exciting moment in the movement, Debussy presents simultaneously this Franck-like theme in the woodwinds alongside the primary theme in the brass (Example 13-3).

13-3 Continued

Debussy's use of rhythm in *La Mer* is extraordinarily supple. The major seconds that begin "De l'aube à midi sur la Mer," when echoed by the harps, give the impression of wave-like, repetitive patterns. On another level, intricate rhythmic patterns—each associated with a particular timbre—yield a dense, multi-layered approach that Debussy developed with uncanny effect in later works, like the *Images pour orchestra*.

Among audiences and critics there was no real understanding of what he had accomplished in *La Mer*. Even the best-intentioned of admirers were confused by it (Daniel Chennevière in his early biography of Debussy, for example). But probably the most disappointing response was that of Pierre Lalo. Lalo's previous criticism seemed to indicate a kindred spirit. Now he attacked more than the music. He criticized Debussy's sensibility and musicianship, and focused on what he described as the artificiality of *La Mer*. It was, he wrote, "a reproduction of nature; a wonderfully refined, ingenious, and carefully composed reproduction....I do not hear, I do not see, I do not smell the sea."[8]

Debussy felt compelled to respond to Lalo. He began with an air of detachment: "There's no problem in your not liking *La Mer* and I've no intention of complaining about it. I shall perhaps suffer regret that you haven't understood me and astonishment at finding you (though one such occasion doesn't establish a habit) in agreement with your fellow music critics." But anger mounted as he continued to write: "You say—keeping your unkindest cut for the last—'that you do not see or smell the sea throughout these three sketches'! That's a large claim and I don't know who is going to evaluate it for us....I love the sea and I've listened to it with the passionate respect it deserves. If I've been inaccurate in taking down what it dictated to me, that is no concern of yours or mine. You must admit not all ears hear the same way. The heart of the matter is that you love and defend traditions which, for me, no longer exist or, at least, exist only as representative of an epoch in which they were not all as fine and valuable as people make out; the dust of the past is not always respectable."[9]

★ ★ ★ ★ ★

In addition to *La Mer* Debussy composed more than two dozen works during the first twelve years of the twentieth century. They represent a wide variety of styles. Not all made a point of avoiding "the dust of the past." Much depended on their intended market (and Debussy's often pressing need for additional income).

The first compositions of the new century—*Lindaraja*, and the Rhapsody for Saxophone (both written in 1901)—adopt a simpler musical style, a reaction perhaps to the less than rousing response given to the *Nocturnes*. But it was also a time

8. Review of 16 October 1905 in *Le Temps* quoted in *DL*, p. 164.
9. Letter of 25 October 1905 in ibid., pp. 163–164.

when Debussy needed to focus his attention on the forthcoming premiere of *Pelléas* and had little time or energy for other projects.

Lindaraja is a light, entertaining piece for two pianos, four-hands. The title was taken from the name of one of the courtyards of the Alhambra in Grenada. The engaging and distinctive style of *Lindaraja* (such as the habanera rhythm) anticipates other Spanish-inspired pieces by Debussy ("La Soirée dans Granade" in *Estampes* and "Ibéria" in the orchestral *Images*). *Lindaraja* is in ternary form with arabesque-like elaboration of its two primary themes. But Debussy did not show much interest in it. He made no attempt to publish it, and there is no mention of it in his correspondence. It did not appear in print until 1926.

The Rhapsody for Saxophone was commissioned by Elise Hall using the oboist of the Boston Symphony Orchestra, Georges Longy, as intermediary. Mrs. Hall, a skilled saxophonist and a wealthy patron of the arts, was the primary supporter of the Orchestral Club of Boston, an organization conducted by Longy that focused on contemporary music. About this time she also commissioned works for saxophone from d'Indy and Charles Loeffler. Debussy worked on the Rhapsody intermittently from 1901 to 1911, but never finished it. Years after the commission had been spent, he admitted Mrs. Hall was still asking about it.

His lack of enthusiasm for the project was a result of ambivalence. "The saxophone," Debussy wrote, "is a reedy animal with whose habits I'm largely unfamiliar. Is it suited to the romantic sweetness of the clarinets or the rather vulgar irony of the sarrusophone (or the contra-bassoon)? In the end I've got it murmuring melancholy phrases against rolls on the side-drum....The whole thing's called 'Rapsodie arabe.'"[10] Although the title *Rapsodie arabe* was dropped, the work retained a Spanish/Moorish flavor. It is a short, single-movement concerto about ten minutes in length with three primary themes, all recognizably "Spanish" sounding. But Debussy's lack of interest in the saxophone did not work in the piece's favor. The writing is so removed from the distinctive sound of the sax that the score could just as easily be adapted for clarinet—or even viola.

At about the same time—and as a sign of his growing fame—Debussy was asked to write a short piano piece for the journal, *Musica*. Published in January 1905, it was part of a contest in which readers were asked to identify six unattributed pieces by well-known and very different composers (the others were Cécile Chaminade, Saint-Saëns, Massenet, Gaston Serpette [an operetta composer], and Rodolphe Berger [known for his popular dances for piano]). Debussy's composition (*Morçeau de concours*) is a slight piece, only about a minute in length, and is based on a sketch from his projected opera, *The Devil in the Belfry*.

10. Letter to Pierre Louÿs of [beginning of August 1903] in *DL*, p. 136. Other titles considered: *Rapsodie orientale* and *Rapsodie mauresque*.

Similar in style and approach was a short work for piano commissioned by the Société Internationale de Musique to honor the centenary of the death of Franz Joseph Haydn. Published in the *Revue Musicale* in January 1910, versions by other notable French composers were part of the presentation, including Dukas, Reynaldo Hahn, d'Indy, Ravel, and Charles Widor. All used the same theme, an anagram (with substitution when necessary) approximating the musical spelling of H (B natural in German nomenclature)-A-Y (d)-D-N (g). Haydn had never been a favorite with Debussy, and the piece he wrote is of little interest.

Also dating from this time are two pieces for clarinet written for performance and evaluation at the juries of the Conservatoire: the *Petite pièce* (for clarinet and piano; composed in July 1910) and the *Première rapsodie* (clarinet and piano, January 1910; orchestrated in 1911). The *Pièce* is less than two minutes in length, monothematic, and bland (it was intended as a sight-reading piece). The *Rapsodie* is more challenging. Debussy described it as one of his "most amiable," and it is pleasant and unpretentious.[11] The clarinet shows to advantage (it is on display throughout most of the movement's nearly nine minutes), with two strongly contrasting themes and the opportunity for much lyricism. The orchestral version is also effective, even though there is a reliance on the strings (unusual for Debussy, but hardly surprising given the intended audience).

Works commissioned from Debussy, whether the source was an individual or an institution, are generally a disappointment. They provided little inspiration, and Debussy seemed eager to pocket the fee and move on. The exception was a commission in 1904 from the Brussels Conservatory. The idea behind it was to promote a new instrument: the chromatic harp. It was cross-strung and marketed by the firm of Pleyel as an improvement over the pedal harp advocated by their rival Erard. The advantage was supposed to be its simplicity, but the harp never caught on. Performances today use the pedal version.

Debussy's *Deux Danses pour harpe* (for solo harp with string accompaniment) consist of a "Danse sacrée" and a "Danse profane." They are charming, elegant, and serene—but they met with a surprisingly mixed reception at their premiere on 6 November 1904 as part of the Colonne concert series. Gabriel Fauré, writing for *Le Figaro*, was dismissive:"Over and over one encounters the same harmonic singularities. Sometimes they seem curious and seductive—and at other times simply unpleasant."[12]

Both recall the antiquity of Debussy's *Bilitis* settings. The theme for the "Danse sacrée" is not by Debussy but by Francisco de Lacerda, a Portuguese composer based in Paris. Debussy discovered it in the *Revue Musicale* published under the title, "Danse du voile." Although not indicated in the score, Debussy freely acknowledged the source of the melody and later became a generous supporter of Lacerda, a student of d'Indy.

11. Letter to Jacques Durand of 8 December 1911 in *C*, p. 1468.

12. Review of 7 November 1904. *LS*, p. 267.

One source of the success of Debussy's *Danses* is the vivid contrast between them. Debussy alluded to it when he referred to the "'gravity' of the first, and the 'grace' of the second."[13] The "gravity" of the opening dance is indebted to its stately tempo and singular modality. The "grace" of the second owes much to the arabesque-like unfolding of the melodic line. But perhaps the most beguiling aspect of the *Danses* is their orchestration. A major challenge for Debussy was to provide contrast in timbre (using only strings), yet not to overshadow the harp. He achieved his goal with characteristic subtlety and delicacy—an approach that demands sensitivity from the conductor in interpreting Debussy's use of silence and reliance on a full spectrum of subdued dynamics.

The Songs

Debussy's commissions were a result of his growing fame but incidental to his direction as a composer. As in the past, song and solo piano were major outlets for his music, both as a primary source of income and as a way to enhance his reputation. He published five sets of songs in the early 1900s. The first was a return to Verlaine; the others were indicative of a new interest.

The *Fêtes galantes I* consist of three texts by Verlaine, poems Debussy had previously set as a student and returned to in 1892. They were not published, however, until 1903. *Fêtes galantes II* followed one year later (with three poems by Verlaine: "Les ingénus," "Le Faune," and "Colloque sentimental"). As with the first set, simplicity is their essence, but with more variety and playfulness. There is a wonderful sense of irony, as in the understated commentary on the text at the end of "Les ingénus" ("That our soul since that time trembles and is astonished"; heightened by Debussy with change in tempo and register in the piano, and, harmonically, with the tonal ambiguity of an augmented triad).

The remaining four sets of songs—*Trois Chansons de France* (1904), *Trois Chansons de Charles d'Orléans* (1898, 1908), *Le Promenoir des deux amants* (1910), and *Trois Ballades de François Villon* (1910)—share a common link: Debussy's increasing nationalism. As in his music criticism, Debussy turned to the music and literature of France—often to the distant past—as a source of inspiration.

The Charles d'Orléans songs are for a cappella four-part mixed chorus. The first ("Dieu! qu'il la fait bon regarder!" [God, how good it is to look on her!]) and third ("Yver, vous n'estes qu'un vilain" [Winter, you are nothing but a knave]) were composed in April 1896 for the Fontaines' choral group that Debussy directed. The second ("Quand j'ay ouy le tabourin" [When I heard the drum], for solo tenor or baritone and chorus) was completed in 1908. All three are a surprising departure from Debussy's usual style. They are madrigalesque, lyrical with little dissonance, and, in the final piece of the set, there is even some imitation in *stile antico*.

13. Letter to Manuel de Falla of 13 January 1907 in *DL*, p. 176.

Debussy continued to use the poetry of Charles d'Orléans in the *Trois Chansons de France*: the first "Rondel. Le temps a laissé son manteau" (Time has left its mantle), and third, "Rondel. Pour ce que Plaisance est morte" (Since pleasure is dead). The second song from the set ("La Grotte") is by Tristan L'Hermite. Republished two years later alongside two other poems by L'Hermite ("Crois mon conseil, chère Climène" [Trust my advice, dear Climène] and "Je tremble en voyant ton visage" [I tremble at seeing your face]), this new set was published under the title, *Le Promenoir des deux amants*. Debussy's tribute to the poetic heritage of France concluded with the *Trois Ballades* of Villon: "Ballade de Villon à s'amye" [Ballad of Villon to his friend], "Ballade que Villon fait à la requeste de sa mère pour prier Nostre-Dame" [Ballad written by Villon at the request of his mother as a prayer to Our Lady], and "Ballade des femmes de Paris" [Ballad of the women of Paris].

All of these songs share limited audience appeal. There is, first of all, the poetic language. Charles d'Orléans (1394–1465), François Villon (1431–c.1463), and Tristan L'Hermite (1601–1655) used a vocabulary and style far removed from modern practice. While working on the *Trois Chansons de Charles d'Orléans*, Debussy actually turned to the scholarly Louis Laloy for assistance in understanding them.

That remains a problem for audiences today. At the same time Debussy's music is extraordinarily distinctive. It is, as always, intimately crafted to the text. That is especially the case with the Villon settings where there is a fluidity and flexibility that seem to defy notation. Much of the music is extremely simple, and driven by one or two rudimentary motives. There are deliberate "archaisms"—such as modality and parallel, open fourths and fifths. But that "sound" had become a natural part of Debussy's musical language by 1910. Perhaps most striking is the subdued and reflective temper of most of these songs, aspects that do not work to their advantage in a concert hall setting.

Music for Piano

Unlike the songs, the music for piano that Debussy composed during these years has broad appeal and has made itself at home among both amateurs and professionals. It contains some of his best-known work, including *Pour le piano*, *Estampes*, the two sets of *Images*, *Children's Corner*, and the *Préludes*.

Pour le piano (1901) has become one of Debussy's most popular pieces. The title itself appears vague and perfunctory—very much against the grain of the florid, programmatic titles popular in nineteenth-century piano music. The three pieces in the set have titles associated with Baroque keyboard music: "Prélude," "Sarabande," and "Toccata." Each is distinctive (but not at all Baroque-sounding). The "Prélude" and its extensive cadenza emphasize the improvisatory. The "Toccata" is the showpiece of the set. In between is the more lyrical "Sarabande." All three pieces are in the style of Debussy's piano pieces of the 1890s.

The "Sarabande" is actually a reworking of a composition with the same title composed seven years earlier. That earlier "Sarabande" was published alone in February 1896 in the magazine, *Le Grand Journal*. But it was intended as part of a set, one that was not published until 1977 with the title, *Images oubliées* (not be confused with the other sets of piano *Images* composed by Debussy in 1901–1905 and 1907). Debussy wrote this first set for Yvonne Lerolle, daughter of his friend Henry Lerolle. They were completed in the winter of 1894 and dedicated to her.

The dedication to Mademoiselle Lerolle provides insight, both into Debussy's perception of their relationship and his musical intentions. He alluded to the personal nature of the pieces, describing them as "'conversations' between the Piano and Oneself."[14] As in *Pour le piano*, there are three pieces in the set with the "Sarabande" second in order. But these 1894 *Images* are far from polished. The opening piece ("Mélancolique et doux") is strongly improvisatory but not related thematically to the "Toccata" in *Pour le Piano*. The whimsical finale is entitled "Quelques aspects de 'Nous n'irons plus au bois,'" a reference to the quotation in it of a French nursery tune much loved by Debussy.[15] The "Sarabande" is captivating, and its melodic charm is probably what convinced Debussy to put it to use, even if only published separately.

After the success of *Pelleas* Debussy turned in his piano work to a style less indebted to his earlier music. The change first became apparent in *Estampes* (1903), and in what was likely intended as a set comprising *Masques, D'un cahier d'esquisses,* and *L'isle joyeuse* (1903–1904, for the group). These are the first piano works, too, that readily bring to mind the typical Debussy "sound," one that owes a great deal to the way he played the piano.

Debussy performed in public infrequently and never enjoyed fame as a pianist. The most insightful accounts of his performances are from those who heard him in private. In his home in the Bois de Boulogne Debussy had three pianos. There was a Pleyel in his office (supplied by the firm without charge). He owned two others: a Bluthner (known for its warm tone) and a Bechstein upright. The Bluthner contained an unusual feature: an extra set of strings in the upper register. They were not struck by the piano's hammers but vibrated when those alongside were played.

There was general agreement about what set Debussy apart from other pianists. His tone, described as "the most elusive and ethereal," was accompanied by a "soft, deep touch which evoked full, rich, many-shaded sonorities."[16] "Personally I have never heard more supple, elegant or velvety playing," wrote Emile Vuillermoz. "He obtained sonorities from the piano which softened the angles and asperities generated

14. *C*, p. 227. Debussy mentioned an additional piece, a waltz, but it has not been found.

15. "Nous n'irons plus au bois" also appears in the song, "La belle au bois dormant" (1890), *Estampes,* and in *Rondes de printemps* of the orchestral *Images*.

16. Maurice Dumesnil in *DR*, p. 159; Louise Liebich in ibid., p. 202.

by his forward-looking inspiration."[17] The composer Alfredo Casella was convinced that Debussy's pianism was impossible to duplicate: "Not that he had actual virtuosity, but his sensitivity of touch was incomparable; he made the impression of playing directly on the strings of the instrument with no intermediate mechanism; the effect was a miracle of poetry. Moreover he used the pedals in a way all his own. He played, in a word, like no other living composer or pianist."[18] The printed scores only give an indication of this fluidity, for, as Debussy himself put it, "pedaling can not be written down. It varies from one room, or one hall, to another."[19] Characteristics of Debussy's piano playing—"elusive," "supple," "elegant"—can also be applied to elements of his piano music during the next decade.

Estampes

Estampes (Prints), like the *Nocturnes*, consists of three pieces with titles intended to invoke images associated with the visual arts: "Pagodes," "La Soirée dans Grenade," and "Jardin sous la pluie." The concept for *Estampes* drew on the popularity of print-making in France at the time. There was an extraordinary variety available—Japanese prints were especially popular—and in his titles Debussy brought together a bit of everything, from the glamor of the Orient to a landscape evocative of an Impressionist painting. Debussy was particularly concerned about the set's appearance in print, discussing with Durand the typeface and color of the cover (blue and pale gold). "Thank you," he wrote to him, "for humoring my cover mania."[20] Over the years Debussy became increasingly involved in the visual presentation of his music.

All of the *Estampes* adopt a broad ternary structure, but their contrasting musical styles set each piece apart. The exoticism of "Pagodes" is stimulated both by its pentatonicism and by a percussive, tam-tam-like effect recalling the gamelan. Its peculiarity struck listeners at the time, one admirer confessing that it "strikes the ear as almost ugly. Then the ear gets caught with a certain bizarre charm and the final effect is one of odd stimulation."[21]

In "La Soirée dans Grenade" the habanera is used with effect (see mm. 38–66). "Jardin sous la pluie" was, according to Jacques-Emile Blanche, inspired by a June rainstorm at his home during which everyone sought refuge inside except Debussy. For reasons unknown, two nursery tunes are quoted in it: "Do, do, l'enfant do," and "Nous n'irons plus au bois." Both are adapted to produce the type of lively finale Debussy preferred for sets of this type.

17. Ibid., p. 156.

18. Charles Timbrell, "Debussy in Performance," in *The Cambridge Companion to Debussy*, ed. Simon Trezise (Cambridge: Cambridge University Press, 2003), p. 261.

19. Dumesnil in *DR*, p. 163.

20. Letter of [27 August 1903] in *DL*, p. 138.

21. William H. Daly, *Debussy: A Study in Modern Music* (Edinburgh: Methuen Simpson, 1908), p. 41.

Images

Estampes was followed by two works similar in intent, the *Images* (set 1: 1901–1905, "Reflets dans l'eau," "Hommage à Rameau," "Mouvement"; set 2: 1907, "Cloches à travers les feuilles" [Bells through the Leaves], "Et la lune descend sur le temple qui fut" [And the Moon Descends on the Temple Which Was], "Poissons d'or" [Golden Fish]). Debussy took unusual pride in the first set: "Without false vanity," he wrote, "I believe these three pieces work together well, and will take their place in piano literature."[22]

Four of the *Images* have strongly visual titles, two with specificity. "Cloches à travers les feuilles" derives from a narrative by Laloy of a rural scene on All Saint's Day with the tolling of bells from Vespers. "Poissons d'or" was inspired by a black and gold, lacquered, Japanese panel owned by Debussy showing two carp swimming beneath a weeping willow.

There are two exceptions to titles with a visual emphasis: "Hommage à Rameau," and "Mouvement." The pair are in a broadly ternary structure reminiscent of the *Estampes*. The homage is (appropriately) a Debussyan sarabande. "Mouvement" serves as a lively finale to the first set of *Images*. Its tonality is tantalizingly ambiguous. At the conclusion C seems to be the key, but extensive diatonic saturation (especially the B flats) provides an unexpected element of shock.

It is an instance, too, of what Debussy meant when he made reference to his "most recent discoveries of harmonic chemistry" (words he used to describe "Reflets dans l'eau").[23] Some of this "harmonic chemistry" was rooted in modality (such as the pentatonicism of "Reflets," "Poissons," and "Et la lune"). But there is also an increasingly layered approach, one that often leads to the use of three staves—not because it would have been impossible to notate the music on two, but because the use of an additional staff provides greater clarity. It removes the appearance of textural density, and emphasizes the many musical events occurring simultaneously. In "Cloches," for example, Debussy creates a marvelously hypnotic effect (recalling what Bartók would develop in works like his *Out-of-Doors*, 1926) with repetitive clusters of pitches in close proximity (especially major and minor seconds). Notated on two staves, it would have appeared cluttered. The additional staff provides independence to the musical idea, while at the same time integrating it into what is happening elsewhere.

As in much of his earlier work for piano, the *Images* are founded on the structural principle created by two contrasting themes. Listeners can follow their movement, and track an ABA form. But—and this is especially true in the second set of *Images*—the increasing reliance on varied repetition (which on the printed page, the eye still perceives as sectionalism) creates a sense of extraordinary fluidity to the ear. At the

---

22. Letter to Jacques Durand of 11 September 1905 in *C*, p. 919.
23. Letter to Jacques Durand of [18] August 1905 in *DL*, p. 155.

same time, it becomes much more of a challenge to distinguish the thematic contrast which is the basis of the structure. Here, then, seems to be a step toward the compositional approach Debussy used in *La Mer*.

The Second *Suite bergamasque*

For both *Estampes* and the *Images*, Debussy drew on the visual arts to complement his music. The linkage for the other piano set from this period—*Masques*, *D'un cahier d'esquisses*, and *L'isle joyeuse*—was more musical. They were intended as a suite to be called, *Suite bergamasque*. But Debussy's earlier work of the same title was being republished by Hartmann's heirs. That seemed to eliminate his interest both in the title and in the idea of issuing the three pieces together. The first and third eventually appeared separately. We know that Debussy intended to complete the set with a "Deuxième Sarabande." But no such piece was published, and it appears likely that *D'un cahier d'esquisses* was the work in question.[24]

D'un cahier d'esquisses is a curiosity. There is no manuscript for it (and no mention of it in Debussy's published correspondence). It was first published (under the title *Esquisse*) in February 1904 in the magazine, *Paris illustré* (which commissioned it). Later that year it was issued by Schott in Brussels. Both incidents are odd. Debussy had had no previous contact with either the magazine or Schott. Adding to the oddity is the music itself. While it makes no great demands on the technique of the performer, it is not the type of salon music a magazine would usually be interested in publishing. It is in D flat major, improvisatory, and with distinctly indeterminate structure. Although it does not follow the compositional approach used by Debussy for *La Mer*, its arrangement and use of registers can appear orchestral—so it may have been conceived as a study for *La Mer*.

The other components of Debussy's suite are less experimental. *L'Isle joyeuse* and *Masques* are complementary. For *L'Isle joyeuse*, there was a biographical association: the 'joyous isle' is a reference to the Isle of Jersey where Debussy lived that summer with his new love, Emma Bardac. Debussy compared it to Watteau's idyllic painting, *L'Embarquement pour Cythère* (1717), though the music was, he wrote, 'less melancholy.'[25] Both *L'Isle* and *Masques* were revised in the summer of 1904, and both are in the broad ternary form characteristic of Debussy's larger scale works for piano prior to *La Mer*. In style *Masques* is toccata-like and percussive, *L'Isle joyeuse* more lyrical (and in Debussy words, "difficult to play…[because] it joins together force with grace").[26]

24. See Roy Howat, "En Route for *L'Isle Joyeuse*: The Restoration of a Triptych," *Cahiers Debussy* 19 (1995), pp. 37–52.

25. Letter to Désiré Walter of 13 July 1914 in *C*, p. 1835.

26. Letter to Jacques Durand of [12 October? 1904] in ibid., p. 869.

Children's Corner

The market for pieces like *L'Isle joyeuse*—and for Debussy's piano work in general—was mixed. Who was the intended audience? Amateur? Professional? Both? And what was the milieu: concert, or performance at home? By requiring increasingly greater technique (both physical and interpretative), Debussy seemed to be ruling out typical amateur performances for many of his most recent compositions. That was not the case, however, with his next piano set, *Children's Corner*, which was intended for a specific niche in the home market.

The set came about as the result of a request for a piece from a piano teacher, Octavie Carrier-Belleuse. She was assembling an introductory piano course. Debussy responded in March 1906 with a short piece, "Sérénade à la poupée," and then decided to build a collection around it. Five additional pieces were added, and the work was completed in July 1908.

The project was of special interest to Debussy. He drew the illustration for the cover himself (including a character from the set: Golliwogg) and was particular about the coloring for publication (incidentally, the original background was gray, not, as in current editions, yellow). *Children's Corner* was in print by 30 September (Chouchou's birthday) with the dedication: "For my dear little Chouchou, with her Father's tender apologies for what is about to follow."

Works of this type fall into two categories: pieces written for children to study and perform (with the goal of developing their musicianship), or pieces written for adults (with the intention of evoking recollections of childhood). *Children's Corner* is a unique blend of the two, but with an emphasis on the latter. Their closest parallel is Robert Schumann's *Scenes from Childhood* (1839). But Debussy's pieces are not drawn from Schumann's idyllic, idealistic world. They are more personalized—and more whimsical.

Many of the pieces are directly connected to Chouchou. Several use as a basis the concept of her toys coming to life, and singing or dancing: Jimbo, for example (actually a mispronunciation of its English name, Jumbo; Chouchou had an English governess, hence also the English title for the set). Popular at the time were ornate, mechanical toys, such as those produced by Fernand Martin. His "La Danseuse de cakewalk" and "Bamboula" may have provided inspiration for one of the most popular pieces in *Children's Corner*: "Golliwogg's Cakewalk."

The cakewalk was an African American plantation dance, taken up by minstrel shows in the latter nineteenth century. It was characterized by high-stepping and prancing. Music for it was in the style of ragtime: a heavily syncopated tune with a repetitive, steady, and rhythmically predictable accompaniment. Debussy loved ragtime's playfulness and simplicity.

In addition to "Golliwogg," he wrote another cakewalk for piano ("The Little Nigar"), published in 1909 in Théodore Lack's *Methode élémentaire de piano*. Perhaps it was originally conceived as a sketch for "Golliwogg." Both are meant as fun. Their harmony is erratic (and at times mismatched with the tune) and parody both rag-time and classical music.[27]

Humor is an important element not just of "Golliwogg's Cakewalk" but of many of the pieces in *Children's Corner*. It is a distinctive kind of humor—playful, capricious, at times slightly mocking. It can have a curious effect on the listener, creating a sense of ironic detachment—as if it were intended by Debussy as a defense against the world of enchantment he has conjured.

All of the pieces in *Children's Corner* are unpretentious. But their brevity and simplicity are deceptive. The first piece in the set, "Doctor Gradus ad Parnassum," begins with monotonous repetition of a scale in the style of a typical, beginner's etude. Debussy's performance indication ("without dryness") does little to moderate the bleakness. But as the piece moves along, it becomes more demanding techni-cally—and more tuneful. There is no reason, Debussy seems to be saying, why exer-cises should be tedious.

"Jimbo's Melody" is a wonderful example of the great care Debussy took in creating these pieces—and of the unexpected discoveries within them. There are

13-4 "Jimbo's Melody"

27. Wagner's *Tristan und Isolde* is recalled in mm. 61–80 of "Golliwogg," marked "with great emotion."

two strongly contrasting themes in the piece. Theme A (pentatonic) has been constructed with fluidity and transcends notions of a bar line. Theme B is more conventional and more repetitive. When Theme A appears for the final time, it is transformed by what seems to be a new accompaniment. But actually what Debussy has done is adapt Theme B as the accompaniment. For the listener it is a moment of extraordinary poignancy, at least in part because of the unexpected linkage of what had been two entirely disparate musical ideas (Example 13-4).

The *Préludes*

Debussy's *Préludes* are, like *Children's Corner*, short, programmatic pieces (though for the *Préludes* the titles appear at the end of each piece and in parentheses—all part of Debussy's attempt at assuring that the music take precedence over the program). There are two sets and twelve pieces in each, but they are not intended to cover all major and minor keys, as had become traditional. Neither is there any performance indication. Whether they should be performed as a set or individually is left to the pianist's taste. Technical requirements vary from the moderate to the very challenging, indicating Debussy's interest in attracting as broad a market as possible.[28]

The first book of *Préludes* was composed quickly, from 7 December 1909 to 4 February 1910. Sketches survive for three of them (numbers 2, 8, and 10) in a sketchbook from 1907–1908, so the idea for creating them was not immediate. The second book was composed at a more leisurely pace during 1911 and 1912. Each set is distinct in both content and style.

Debussy did not want the titles to take precedence, but in many instances they are helpful aids in interpretation.[29] In the first book, "Danseuses de Delphes" (Delphic Dancers) refers to a Greek sculpture (in the Louvre) that represents three women in a ritualistic dance. "Voiles" is ambiguous and can be translated as either "sails" or "veils," the latter possibly a reference to the veil dancing made famous by Loïe Fuller. The title for "Le Vent dans la plaine" (The Wind on the Plain) is taken from Charles-Simon Favart's drama, *Ninette à la cour* (1753) which in turn was quoted as an epigraph in Verlaine's "C'est l'extase langoureuse" (set by Debussy in 1887). A similar poetic connection exists for two other titles: "Les sons et les parfums tournent dans l'air du soir" (Sounds and Perfumes Swirl in the Evening Air) and "La Fille aux cheveux de lin" (The Girl with the Flaxen Hair). The former is from Baudelaire's "Harmonie du soir" (set to music by Debussy in 1889); the latter is the fourth of Leconte de Lisle's "Chansons écossaises" (set by Debussy in 1881).

28. "Ce qu'a vu le vent d'Ouest" (from the first set) could not be more virtuosic and at times brings to mind "Mazeppa" from Liszt's *Transcendental Etudes*.

29. Most of the interpretation and sources—some of it speculative—for Debussy's titles is a result of research, not of information supplied by Debussy.

Literary associations are likely for three additional preludes in the first book. "La Cathédrale engloutie" (The Sunken Cathedral) is indebted to a Breton legend that tells of a sunken city whose cathedral spire periodically appears above the water's surface, accompanied by the chanting of monks.[30] "Ce qu'a vu le vent d'Ouest" (What the West Wind Saw) may have been inspired by Hans Christian Andersen's tale, "The Garden of Paradise." And there are two possibilities for "La Danse de Puck": Kipling's Puck stories and Shakespeare's *A Midsummer Night's Dream*.

Tracking sources for the titles for the second set of *Préludes* is more challenging. "Feuilles mortes" (Dead Leaves) may come from the title of a poem by Debussy's friend, Gabriel Mourey; the poetic phrase, "La terrasse des audiences du clair de lune" (The Terrace for Moonlight Audiences) may have been taken from a very matter-of-fact newspaper article on the coronation of George V. "Canope" was an ancient Egyptian city whose name was adapted for small ritual, funeral urns (canopic jars). Debussy owned a pair and kept them on his work table. Like *Lindaraja*, "La puerta del vino" is associated with the Alhambra, in this instance the name of a Moorish gate.

As in the first set, several of the Book II *Preludes* have a literary connection. "Hommage a S. Pickwick Esq. P.P.M.P.C." is a reference to the droll hero of Dickens's *Pickwick Papers* (P.P.M.P.C. = Perpetual President and Member of the Pickwick Club). The title, "Les fées sont d'exquises danseuses" (The Fairies Are Exquisite Dancers) is taken from an illustration by Arthur Rackham for J. M. Barrie's *Peter Pan in Kensington Gardens* (1907). In a similar manner, "Ondine" may have been inspired by a Rackham illustration for La Motte-Fouqué's novella, *Undine*. Both were likely encountered as reading for Chouchou.

With "Feux d'artifice" (Fireworks) we are on surer ground. It refers to the firework celebrations associated with Bastille Day in France (and the " Marseillaise" is quoted in it to provide a French flavor—just as "God Save the King" adds an English touch to the Pickwick homage). "General Lavine excentric" is another of Debussy's cakewalks, in this case the inspiration being the American clown, Edward Lavine.[31]

The music for the first book of *Préludes* is rich in variety but owes much stylistically to Debussy's previous piano music. "La Fille aux cheveux de lin" is an elegant example of melody as arabesque. And there is no better instance of Debussy's mingling of modality and pandiatonicism than "La Cathédrale engloutie" (a curious point is the conventional crescendo climax, a device all the more effective because so rarely encountered in Debussy's music).

"Minstrels" is yet another of Debussy's ragtime pieces, probably inspired by a minstrel show he had seen in Eastbourne in 1905. It is, like all of his "rags," a playful

---

30. A similar legend served as the basis for Edouard Lalo's opera, *Le Roi d'Ys* (1888).

31. Lavine performed in Paris in 1910 and 1912. It was said he played the piano with his toes.

pastiche. "La Sérénade interrompue" evokes Spain (and alludes to Debussy's *Ibéria*, discussed later in this chapter).

In the second book of *Préludes* tonality is expanded, and there is greater use of dissonance ("Bruyères" [Moors] and "Feuilles mortes" are good examples). But even more striking is how idiomatic the pieces are. Debussy takes full advantage of the extensive and varied sounds only the piano can produce. "Les fées sont d'exquises danseuses" showcases trills. In "Ondine" rapid runs and arpeggios obscure pitch and tonality. In "Feux d'artifice" glissandos produce the same effect. These are all, of course, devices not original to Debussy. But the manner in which he uses them—often simultaneously—is individual and emphasizes how involved he was with the concept of sound as distinct from pitch. At the same time Debussy's use of three staves in the second set of *Préludes* (although not always necessary) emphasizes once again his concern with clarity; the additional staff helps the performer track Debussy's musical thoughts through what often becomes a veritable maze of pitches. For "Feux" Debussy even devised four note heads of different size to differentiate musical material.

Music for Orchestra

Debussy's concern with timbre—coupled with the expansive range of sound he increasingly exploited for the piano—found a direct outlet in the music he wrote for orchestra. One orchestral project was conceived as a companion to the *Images* for solo piano and derived from Debussy's intent in writing a series of musical images for two pianos. The two pianos concept evolved into the *Images pour orchestre*, Debussy's largest instrumental work. It contains five movements: *Gigues* (1912), *Ibéria* (1906–1909) (itself consisting of three movements: "Par les rues et les chemins" [In the Streets and Byways], "Les parfums de la nuit" [The Fragrances of the Night], and "Le matin d'un jour de fête" [The Morning of the Day of a Festival]), and *Rondes de printemps* (1905–1909).

Like *La Mer*, the *Images pour orchestre* are difficult to categorize. Their title and conception brings to mind the piano *Images*. But the imagery for the orchestral *Images* is quite different. The titles are more poetic than visual. At their center is what might best be described as a genre piece, *Ibéria*. But at either end are dances (even though imagery of some type might be associated with them). Debussy's approach for this orchestral set is distinctive—different not just from the direct linkage to the visual arts characteristic of the piano *Images*, but distinct, too, from the picture gallery concept of the *Nocturnes*.

Debussy gave the subtitle "triptych for orchestra" to the *Nocturnes*. Some have applied a similar approach to the *Images pour orchestre*, dividing the work into a triptych (*Gigues-Ibéria-Rondes de printemps*), occasionally with subdivision of *Ibéria* as a separate triptych. But does the approach add to our understanding of the work? For the *Nocturnes* the idea of a triptych helped to link movements disparate in content, creating for the listener a linear track—a musical counterpart to what might be the effect of viewing paintings (images) alongside one another. But there is no indication that Debussy intended a similar approach for the *Images pour orchestre*.

Instead the *Images* rely on musical parameters for their linkage. Of the five movements in the *Images*, the first and last, and second and fourth, are comparable in size and effect. At the center is the most intense and concentrated movement of the set: *Les parfums de la nuit*. The result can be seen as an arch: A–B–C–B–A.

The musical style of the *Images* is indebted to *La Mer*. There is the same reliance on the musical moment to generate structure, but it is created with greater reliance on variation (complemented by the introduction of new musical material), and less on repetition. To the listener, it produces a greater sense of discontinuity, an effect that Debussy deliberately cultivated by juxtaposing strongly contrasting, even incongruous, musical elements.

The opening of *Gigues* evokes the essence of music: a single pitch gradually varied by timbre. The initial theme that serves as the movement's basis is folk-like (and rustic sounding). But because it appears fragmented—with permutations well into *Gigues*—listeners with a traditional approach in mind are deceived, convinced for much of the piece that they are listening to an elaborate introduction and waiting in vain for a full statement of the theme. As in *La Mer*, the structure relies on expansion of the moment.

Rondes de printemps is similar. The primary theme is motivic and presented as fragments with variants. But here the effect is far more disruptive. Much of the musical material is strongly contrasting and presented not in the generative manner of *La Mer* but in sections of widely varying and unpredictable length. About halfway into the movement, the tune, "Nous n'irons plus au bois," becomes recognizable. But deconstruction of the tune continues, and there is no full statement of it until nearly the end, a moment of extraordinary resolution for the listener.[32]

Ibéria is the longest of the *Images*. It would be impossible to imagine a more vivid musical evocation of Spain—a country, incidentally, that Debussy never visited. The initial piano sketches for it were produced in 1906–1908. An orchestral draft followed that autumn, and he produced the final version in the spring of 1909. The Spanish flavor is pronounced, most notably with rhythm (sevillana, seguidilla, habanera), and timbre (even including castanets).[33] The primary theme from the very beginning of the first movement appears in all three movements.

---

32. In a broad sense, there is structural resemblance to d'Indy's tone poem, *Istar* (1896), a theme and variation in reverse order.

33. For a full discussion of *Ibéria*, see Matthew Brown, *Debussy's Ibéria* (Oxford: Oxford University Press, 2003).

One of the most striking elements of *Ibéria* is Debussy's manipulation of time and movement. In "Par les rues et les chemins," phrases are frequently elided, giving the effect (depending on the musical material at hand) not of progressive, forward movement, but of hesitancy or delay. At times, too, varied repetition becomes circuitous, a retracing of direction. These effects obscure the listener's perception of the music's motion, adding a level of complexity that can lend unusual drama to the simplest devices—such as the return of the primary theme near the end of the first movement. Debussy's use of the orchestra enhances the effect, as in the following example from "Les parfums de la nuit" (Example 13-5 on the next page) where the layers of sound produce an extraordinarily intricate texture—but one so tightly knit and cohesive it is as if movement were suspended. There is independence of line and great variety of timbre: nine different types of sound predominantly in the upper register (with divided strings—but no basses—performing with tremolos, harmonics, mutes, and on the fingerboard).

Despite the splendor of *Ibéria* (and of the orchestral *Images* as a unit), the work, many would agree, is less successful than *La Mer*. The most likely explanations are the sense of musical discontinuity experienced by the listener and the order of the movements as a whole. To listen to the *Images* as Debussy intended them to be heard—ending with *Rondes de printemps*—seems a disappointment. It appears to end weakly, with inadequate emphasis. That has led to experimentation with the order of the *Images* in performance, placing *Ibéria* at the end. But while the close of "Le matin d'un jour de fête" is more vigorous, the ending still seems inconclusive.

Debussy knew precisely what effect he was creating by ending the *Images* with *Rondes de printemps*. The music, he explained, was "immaterial and as a result one can not manage it like a robust symphony."[34] By placing *Rondes* at the end, Debussy seems to be demonstrating that the *Images* were neither robust nor a symphony. Instead he has relied on the broader effect of all five movements (and the arch they created). A more rousing conclusion might have made the *Images* more of a crowd pleaser. But listening to the five movements in the order Debussy planned makes sense—and highlights (in a manner recalling the symmetry in Bach's cantatas) his well-developed sense of architecture.

One other orchestral work dates from these years: *La plus que lente* (The Even Slower Waltz) (subtitled in the original piano version: *Valse pour piano*). Published in 1912 (the piano setting was written two years earlier), it emulates the type of music performed at a bistro or brasserie.[35] *La plus que lente* demonstrates how convincingly Debussy was able to push a popular idiom to its limits. Its audacious and unexpected harmonies are engaging, the excessive syncopation is amusing—all produce a charming yet slightly demented version of the pop music of the day.

---

34. Letter to Jacques Durand of 3 September 1907 in *C*, p. 1030.

35. There has been speculation that it was intended as a take-off on Massenet's popular "Valse très lente."

13-5 *Iberia*: "Les parfums de la nuit"

The Martyrdom of St. Sebastian, Khamma, and Projects for the Stage

During these years Debussy was involved in a substantial number of collaborative projects. Most were abandoned. In 1902 he discussed using Shakespeare's *As You Like It* as the basis for an opera with Paul-Jean Toulet. But although the play was a favorite with Debussy and a libretto was finished, he wrote no music (Debussy continued to refer to the project as late as 1917).[36]

In tune with previous interests was a projected scenario for the Ballets Russes: "Masques et bergamasques" (1909). Set in eighteenth-century Venice, Louis Laloy was selected to provide the text. But it was Debussy who went ahead and sketched the scenario (but no music). Another project, "Crimen amoris," was similar in theme. It was to be based on Verlaine's "Fêtes galantes," with Charles Morice supplying the text. A contract was signed in May 1912 (updated in January 1913 with the addition of Laloy). Announced as part of the 1912–1913 season at the Opéra, Debussy did not progress beyond some sketches for the work.

The most intriguing collaborations during these years were operatic works inspired by the legends of Tristan, Siddhartha, and Orpheus. Gabriel Mourey developed the text for Tristan. Debussy discussed the project (anti-Wagnerian in basis) in 1907–1908. The press picked up on it, and mention was made of it as late as 1914. But despite Debussy's enthusiasm ("Frankly the whole project is so attractive, I'm almost frightened of getting the libretto"), he wrote no music.[37]

Victor Segalen provided the momentum for the Siddhartha and Orpheus projects. At first Debussy was enthusiastic about the possibilities of Siddhartha (1906–1907; based on the life of Buddha), but backed out, claiming he was incapable of writing suitable music. That became a major reason, as well, for the lack of progress with Orpheus: "As for the music to accompany the drama, I hear it less and less. And then, one does not make Orpheus sing, because he is song itself."[38] In 1907–1908 Debussy received the text in stages from Segalen and was pleased by much of it. Published in 1921, Segalen's *Orphée* is a reverie, very much in the style of the Symbolists. Debussy suggested some cutting for the sake of simplicity and complained of "too much lyricism" in the fourth act.[39] But despite being a project with appeal to both men, no music was composed. Segalen was persistent and wrote to Debussy about their project in 1916, years after substantive work on it had halted.

One bright spot among these projects was Debussy's involvement with André Antoine's production of *King Lear.* Some music for it was completed. The idea was to provide incidental music, and Debussy planned a prelude and three interludes, in

36. The Shakespeare project led to another based on a play: in June 1904 he expressed interest in writing music for the drama *Dionys*, by Joachim Gasquet.

37. Letter to Jacques Durand of [6–8 August 1907] in *DL*, p. 182.

38. Letter to Victor Segalen of 5 June 1916 in *C*, p. 1999.

39. Conversation of 6 May 1908 in *DR*, p. 146.

addition to background music for two scenes: "Le sommeil de Lear," and "Le Roi Lear dans la lande." He worked at it in the fall of 1905—mention of it being made as late as the following summer—but only two pieces were finished: a short fanfare and "Le Sommeil de Lear." Neither was used in the production, but both (the dream-like scena that would not have been out of place in *Pelléas*, and the mellow fanfare) are effective.

Of the proposed and contemplated collaborations during these years, Debussy completed only two in their entirety: *The Martyrdom of St. Sebastian,* and *Khamma*. It can be no coincidence that they were the only collaborations that promised to pay well.

The *Martyrdom* consists of five acts (called "mansions" by Debussy's collaborator, Gabriele d'Annunzio): "La Cour de lys" (The Court of Lilies), "La Chambre magique" (The Magic Room), "Le Concile des faux dieux" (The Council of False Gods), "Le Laurier blessé" (The Wounded Laurel), and "Le Paradis" (Paradise). Debussy's endorsement of the text—"the poem is of great beauty, and it contains real treasures in the field of imaginative lyricism"—was more in the vein of publicity for the forthcoming performance.[40] Despite d'Annunzio's bombastic setting, Debussy continued to hope for the best. Perhaps he felt that d'Annunzio's text resembled that for Rameau's opera *Hippolyte et Aricie* (at the time being rediscovered), a libretto he described as "poetically quite abominable, but having the makings of a varied and entertaining spectacle."[41]

Debussy received d'Annunzio's text piecemeal during January and February 1911, with all of the text in hand in early March. The music was scheduled to be completed by 15 May, and that left little time for Debussy to compose it. André Caplet was contacted to help (primarily with the orchestration). Debussy closely supervised his work. The orchestration of the second, third, and fourth Mansions was mostly done by Caplet. Debussy orchestrated all of the fifth Mansion, most of the first, as well as scene ii in the second, scenes ii and vii in the third, and scene ii in the fourth.

The music for the *Martyrdom* (choral settings, instrumental preludes, and interludes) comprises about an hour in a work nearly five hours in length. It would be difficult for the music not to be overwhelmed by the sheer amount of spoken text. Even so, the music is a disappointment. Much of it is clichéd and predictable—in its way a suitable counterpart to d'Annunzio's drama. The most successful pieces are the chamber-like choral settings; perhaps the weakest is the conclusion (an alleluia).

When it became clear that the *Martyrdom* was not the success that Debussy had hoped for, Caplet worked to arrange portions as an orchestral suite ("fragments symphoniques"), and it is in these excerpts that the work is best known today. In 1922 Ida Rubinstein revived the drama (with Debussy's music), hoping that an abridged version might be more successful. But it, too, failed to please.

Unlike the *Martyrdom*, Debussy came to hold no illusions about the possibility of success for *Khamma*. Collaboration with Maud Allan could not have been more

40. Interview of 18 January 1911 in *DM*, p. 244.
41. Review in *Le Figaro* of 8 May 1908 in ibid., p. 228.

tortuous. The scenario, set in ancient Egypt at the Temple of Amon-Re, was created as a showpiece for her. The god is implored by his grand priest to rescue the city, which is under attack. With a series of three dances, Khamma persuades the god to intercede, but sacrifices her life in the process.

The piano version is the only music for the work solely by Debussy. He lost interest in the project (not least because of Allan's demands) and eventually asked Charles Koechlin to do the bulk of the orchestration. Koechlin was an admirer of Debussy's music, especially *Pelléas*. He was also an experienced and gifted orchestrator, of his own music and others'.[42]

Debussy orchestrated the beginning of *Khamma*. Koechlin's goal became (in his words) "to remain within the orchestral 'color'" of what Debussy had done.[43] He and Debussy met once a week from 14 December 1912 to 31 January 1913. "We didn't chat," Koechlin recalled. "We concentrated on my orchestration, which he was happy with, although he warned me that it might be rather hard to perform."[44] *Khamma* was not performed until 1924 (in a concert version). Koechlin's role remained a secret and only became widely known after World War II.

Khamma is rarely heard today, surprisingly so for a work that was written during a time when Debussy was in his prime. But its absence from the repertoire is not as great a loss as it might seem. In its orchestral setting *Khamma* simply does not sound like Debussy. That is not a disparagement of Koechlin, who was a fine orchestrator and a gifted composer. But he was not Debussy, and what he produced, while faithful to the notes, could never capture Debussy's unique orchestral sound. *Khamma* makes clear that orchestration was an essential component in Debussy's compositional process, one that provided more than a measure of vitality. The piano version—conceived by Debussy not as a piece for solo piano but more as an orchestral reduction—merits greater attention. It is there that the listener can best experience what Debussy described as "the trumpet calls which evoke the riot and conflagration—and which send chills up your spine."[45]

Khamma is sectional and episodic (about twenty minutes in length), and not in the generative style of *La Mer*. Three musical motives serve as its basis (the predominant one, emphasizing the intervals of a major and minor second, appears in scene 1, mm. 14–17). The ending is a bit of an anti-climax (both plot and music seem to drag after *Khamma*'s death)—and that in itself might work against *Khamma* gaining an audience, either by means of orchestra or piano. Still, *Khamma* contains sections of extraordinary beauty, especially in the first dance. One can only speculate how much better known it might be today had Debussy been fully committed to the project.

---

42. He had orchestrated Fauré's *Pelléas et Mélisande* (1898) and Saint-Saën's *Lola* (1901).

43. Robert Orledge, "Debussy's Orchestral Collaborations, 1911–13. 2. *Khamma*," in *Musical Times* 116 (1975), p. 31.

44. *DR*, p. 102.

45. Letter to Jacques Durand of [1 February 1912] in *C*, p. 1491.

CHAPTER FOURTEEN

Compositions, 1912–1918

We came to seriously believe that it was absolutely essential for an artist to be "original," to provide the public with a work that was completely different from anything that had ever appealed to them in the past.

Téodor de Wyzéwa, *Nos Maîtres* (1895)

Instrumental Works

Solo Piano: *La Boïte à joujoux* (orchestral version by André Caplet); *Berceuse héroïque* (also for orchestra); *Douze Etudes*; *Page d'album*; *Elégie*; *Les soirs illuminés*

Two Pianos: *Six Epigraphes antiques* (originally piano, four-hands); *En Blanc et noir*

Chamber: *Syrinx* (for solo flute); Sonata for Cello; Sonata for Flute, Viola, and Harp; Sonata for Violin

Ballet: *Jeux*

Vocal Works

Songs: *Trois Poèmes de Mallarmé*; "Noël des enfants" (Debussy)

Choral: *Ode à la France* (unfinished)

"THE GENERAL EFFECT [OF DEBUSSY'S MUSIC]," STATED *BAKER'S BIOGRAPHICAL Dictionary of Musicians* in 1919, "is that of monotony.... After *Pelléas et Mélisande* there is no advance, not one feature which is not familiar from the earlier works; rather a decline, for the music seems to become even more intangible."[1] In his study of contemporary music Cecil Gray agreed, but placed the start of the decline after *La Mer*, attributing it to "premature exhaustion and sterility. By the time Debussy had reached his fullest maturity he had no longer anything left to say."[2] Such pronouncements—especially from usually discerning critics, like Gray—illustrate widespread misunderstanding of Debussy's music. There were those who (like Pierre Lalo) were devoted to his earlier compositions, detected a difference in his later works, and were disconcerted and perplexed by it. Then there were those who felt that there had been no change at all, and that Debussy was simply repeating himself.

By design there had been consistent development and change in Debussy's music over the years, but much of it had either passed unnoticed or been misunderstood. Complicating the situation was the work of a new generation of composers. By 1912 the non-traditional approach adopted by Debussy was being put into practice by others—especially Stravinsky. It placed Debussy in a difficult position. Unlike those who were offended by the novelty of new musical styles, his fear was of being out-paced.

★ ★ ★ ★ ★

Although completed nearly six years before his death, the ballet, *Jeux*, was Debussy's last orchestral composition. It has long attracted a devoted following, but it remains one of his lesser-known works—and a bit of an enigma.[3]

The motivation for its composition was financial. Debussy was eager to share in the success of the Ballets Russes. Diaghilev had discussed with him in 1909 the idea of a collaboration, for which Louis Laloy was to write the scenario and Debussy the music. In the end Debussy sketched the scenario, but no music (for what received the tentative title of "Masques et Bergamasques"). The Ballets Russes production of the *Faune* (with what was regarded as at least one sexually explicit moment) followed in May 1912 with choreography by Nijinsky.

That production only emphasized that France's best-known composer had yet to compose any original music for the Ballets Russes. An agreement was reached in June 1912 between Debussy and Diaghilev. Debussy was to receive 10,000 francs, with the piano score due at the end of August and the orchestral score at the end of March 1913. It was, by Debussy's standards, to be quick work.

1. *Baker's Biographical Dictionary of Musicians*, 3rd ed., revised and enlarged by Alfred Remy (New York: Schirmer, 1919). The text was written prior to Debussy's death.

2. Cecil Gray, *A Survey of Contemporary Music* (Oxford: Oxford University Press, 1924), p. 107.

3. Herbert Eimert's essay on *Jeux* in *Die Reihe* in 1957 helped to establish interest in it among the avant-garde.

Nijinsky supplied the scenario, one that was vague and general enough to provide freedom to the composer, but hardly inspired:

In a park, at dusk, a tennis ball is lost; a young man and two girls are eagerly looking for it. The artificial light from large electric lamps spreads a fantastic glow all around them and gives them the idea of playing childish games: aimlessly they hunt each other, hide, give chase, quarrel and sulk; the night is warm, the sky clear and gentle, they kiss. But the innocent charm is broken by a tennis ball, thrown by some malicious hand. Surprised and frightened, the young people disappear into the deep shadows of the park.[4]

Jeux consists of five musical sections, each closely allied to the plot of the scenario:

Section 1   Introduces the characters.
            Until section mark 17; about 3 minutes in length
            Half of this section sets the scene before the curtain rises, and consists of two
            distinct motives: 1) three rising semitones, and 2) a descending outline of an
            augmented triad.
Section 2   The girls dance (the young man is not present).
            This section lasts until section mark 27 (about 2 minutes in length), and is set
            off from the previous section by lively syncopation.
Section 3   The youth returns and dances with the first girl.
            Until section mark 35 plus 6 measures; about 2 ½ minutes in length
            Set off by abrupt change in timbre and texture.
Section 4   He dances with the second girl.
            Until section mark 51 (about 4 ½ minutes in length)
            Set off by pizzicati.
Section 5   All three dance
            Until section mark 80, with the remainder as a coda (which draws on the
            introduction); about 5 1/2 minutes, with about 1 minute for the coda.

The two themes from the introduction (Example 14-1, on following page) serve as the basis for subsequent musical material in the ballet. See, for example, how the first theme (now in contrary motion) is used as a bridge to Section 3. The thematic transformation used by Debussy is subtle, so much so that it is possible to listen to *Jeux* many times without noticing it.

4. See Claude Debussy, *Oeuvres complètes*, ed. Pierre Boulez and Myriam Chimènes, Vol. VIII, *Jeux*. (Paris: Durand-Costallat, 1988), p. ii. Nijinsky later wrote that the idea for the scenario came from Diaghilev, a case of erotic wishful-thinking, with himself as the youth and two boys replacing the women.

The compositional process in *Jeux* resembles the generative approach used in *La Mer* and the *Images pour Orchestre*. But it has been adapted to the plot of the scenario. Each section has distinctive musical material, suitable for the mood and action of the scenario. And even though much can in some measure be traced to music heard earlier, its transformation is so complete that the musical effect of *Jeux* is one of astonishing variety. The construction is seamless, with each section providing impetus toward the climactic dance in Section 5. Debussy's harmonic approach (part of his "musical chemistry") is more adventurous than usual.[5] The works of Stravinsky he had examined provided some impetus.

There is a more expansive view of tonality in *Jeux* (the emphasis on the augmented triad opening the work helps to prepare the listener for it), and dissonance is more biting and acerbic. Coupled with it is a noticeable increase in volume, along with repetitive, driving rhythms. But these are not the pounding rhythms of Stravinsky. They are still characterized by great suppleness and fluidity, and give, as does much of *Jeux*, the effect of inspired improvisation.

Perhaps the greatest marvel of *Jeux* is its orchestration. While working on the piano score, Debussy wrote: "I am thinking of that orchestral color which seems to be illuminated from behind, and for which there are such marvelous displays in *Parsifal*."[6] The idea, then, was to produce timbre without glare, subdued (its source almost concealed), but to do so with clarity and precision. How Debussy achieved that effect requires a look at the standard perception of the role of orchestration at the time.

Orchestration became an increasingly important part of the compositional process during the nineteenth century, a time when the size of the orchestra (and its audience) increased significantly. Berlioz's treatise on orchestration (1844) was the first to systematically approach the subject. Many others (all dependent on his work) followed. The goal was to reveal the mysteries of orchestration by focusing on its craft. What pitches could instruments play? What did they sound like in various registers? What instruments sounded well together? These and other fundamental questions were answered concisely, often using excerpts from nineteenth-century compositions as examples.

For most composers orchestration was the final stage in the process of composition. The music already existed in a version for piano. Now it was simply a matter of dressing it up, of rearranging the sound using well-practiced techniques as the basis.

Orchestration was the final step for Debussy as well, but for him it was a crucial, and in many ways the most important, component in the process. How important

---

5. Letter to Jacques Durand of 9 August 1912 in *C*, p. 1536. Also included in the chemistry was the octatonic scale. See Sylvia Kahan, *In Search of New Scales. Prince Edward de Polignac, Octatonic Explorer* (Rochester: Boydell & Brewer, 2009).

6. Letter to André Caplet of 25 August 1912 in *C*, p. 1540.

it was—and how gifted he was as an orchestrator—becomes clearer after listening to works intended for orchestra, but orchestrated by someone else (as was *Khamma*), or by listening to a version of his piano pieces orchestrated by another hand (*Children's Corner*). Rather than focusing on fidelity to pitches, Debussy was concerned with their implications. He tried to envision what was missing from the page. And he was fascinated by new combinations of instruments, never forgetting the basic premise that the same pitches sound completely different (and with completely different effect) when performed on different instruments. Orchestration was never an automatic process for Debussy. And it was disingenuous for him to present as original works pieces, such as *Khamma*, that had been orchestrated by someone else.

It should come as no surprise that Debussy was not an admirer of books on orchestration. He felt they relied on formulas. Debussy countered with Nature as a teacher and once recommended learning how to orchestrate by listening to the "sound of leaves rustling in the wind."[7] As for his own approach, he rarely put into words his concept of the orchestra. But on one occasion he offered some general advice to a friend: "As for the disposition of the orchestra, the strings should make, not a barrier, but a circle around the others. Split up the woodwind. Mix the bassoons up with the cellos, the clarinets and oboes with the violins; so that their entries don't sound like somebody dropping a parcel."[8]

In the short score for *Jeux* (with four staves) Debussy provided "no more than a dozen indications of instrumentation."[9] But he took the unusual step of producing a draft orchestral score in March and April 1913 as preparation for the final version. He used the ensemble as a unit with full effect but never lost sight of the individual capabilities of each instrument, or of the advantages of a chamber-like effect. There are novelties, such as the surprising appearance of the tambourine in the next to last measure. And there is the increasing use of groups as soloists, especially in the strings. But most noticeable is the manner in which thematic material is shared among instruments, an approach that could appear choppy or contrived but in Debussy's hands seems natural and effortless. He used orchestration to create focal points and to direct the ear to specific locations in the score—not to sections (the usual manner of composers), but to strands. In Example 14-2 (pages 232–233) there is spontaneous movement from strings to French horns to bassoons to clarinets to flutes (with harps).

---

7. Letter to Charles Levadé of 4 September 1903 in *DL*, p. 140.

8. Conversation with Victor Segalen of 17 December 1908 in *DR*, p. 149.

9. Myriam Chimènes, "The Definition of Timbre in the Process of Composition of *Jeux*," in *Debussy Studies*, ed. Richard Langham Smith (Cambridge: Cambridge University Press, 1997), p. 5.

14-2 Continued

After completing *Jeux* Debussy had high hopes for it. But he did not take into account Nijinsky's choreography, nor the work that was scheduled to be performed next on the Ballets Russes schedule: the premiere of Stravinsky's *Rite of Spring*. Not only did the scandal created by Stravinsky's ballet tend to efface recollection of *Jeux*, but the Stravinsky work was given a large number of rehearsals, limiting the time available to prepare *Jeux*.

Debussy's private reaction to Nijinsky's choreography was candid. "It is horrible!" he wrote.[10] For the *Faune,* Nijinsky had emphasized stiffness. Choreography for *Jeux* was less extreme, but it remained in complete contrast to the fluidity and suppleness of Debussy's score. In its emphasis on the ungainly, Nijinsky's choreography was ahead of its time—just as it was ahead of its time in presenting choreography that did not complement the music, but was in conflict with it. But it was a disservice to Debussy's intentions.

From the completion of *Jeux* until the summer of 1915 Debussy composed little. He was frustrated by his lack of productivity and complained about it. There were many likely contributing factors. His personal life was a disappointment. Marriage remained a challenge, and there was a continual need for money to maintain the lifestyle associated with it. But his artistic life was also in disarray. Audiences seemed to prefer his earlier compositions. Adding to his concern was the fear that the music he was composing had become too dependent on the styles he had created.

The outbreak of the First World War made even day-to-day life a challenge. But the artistic implications of the war were particularly alarming to Debussy. The growing success of the German army placed in jeopardy the French culture that had become an increasingly important component of his artistic stance.

At times it must have seemed like a hopeless situation. In 1913, in addition to *Jeux*, he completed only three small works: *Trois Poèmes de Mallarmé, La Boîte à joujoux*, and *Syrinx*. The Mallarme settings—"Soupir" (Sigh), "Placet futile" (Futile Petition), and "Eventail" (Fan)—were finished that summer. The piano version of the *Boîte* was composed from July to October (for the orchestral version, Debussy orchestrated several dozen measures at the beginning; the remainder was done by André Caplet after Debussy's death).

The Mallarmé songs are short pieces, averaging only about two and a half minutes for each. Debussy's satisfaction with them was offset by Ravel's setting to music at the same time two of the same texts (although in a chamber setting for nine instruments). Like much of Debussy's late music, they are performed infrequently—and deserve to be much better known.

10. Letter to Robert Godet of 9 June 1913 in *C*, p. 1619.

Simplicity and restraint are primary characteristics of them. There is tonal ambiguity, extreme fluidity, and, for listeners even today, a sense of suspense, a result of the unpredictability of the music. The frequent changes in tempo sound improvisatory. Much of the vocal line resembles heightened speech, but one in which even rudimentary movement becomes lyrical. The lulling effect of the broadly tertian harmony produces a dream-like and hypnotic atmosphere that is an ideal counterpart to Mallarmé's poetry.

La Boîte à joujoux is a ballet for children (originally conceived for puppets) based on a scenario by the children's book illustrator, André Hellé. Like *Children's Corner* it was associated in Debussy's mind with Chouchou (and her toys). It is light and entertaining, consisting of a prelude, an epilogue, and four scenes. The plot tells of toys coming to life and of the complications of a toy soldier's love for a doll (the soldier is represented by the main theme from "The Little Nigar"). Unlike *Khamma* where the piano version was conceived from the start as an orchestral reduction, the piano score for the *Boîte* is charming—and in many ways more engaging than Caplet's orchestral score.

Syrinx, a short piece for unaccompanied flute, was written in November 1913. Although the project dated to 1909, it is the only piece that Debussy completed as incidental music for Gabriel Mourey's verse play, *Psyché* (first performed in December 1913). It is about three minutes in length, and although Debussy's ultimate intentions for it are unclear (the title is the publisher's), it has become a standard part of the flautist's repertoire. *Syrinx* gives the impression of an extraordinary improvisation, its lyricism rooted in Debussy's concept of the arabesque.

Over the next eighteen months Debussy continued to write little. Even the number of projects he attempted fell off considerably. There is only one of substance. On 21 November 1913 Debussy signed a contract to provide a one-act ballet (with scenario by Georges de Feure) for performance in London. It was known as "La Palais du silence," (later, "No-Ja-Li"). The subject was to be Chinese (with a gamelan orchestra), and Debussy was expected to provide a piano score by April 1914. He only completed some sketches, and when the ballet was created as part of a medley at the Alhambra Theater on 4 May, Büsser's orchestration of *Printemps* was substituted.[11]

The most substantial composition of 1914–1915 was, strictly speaking, not even new. The *Six Epigraphes antiques* (for piano, four-hands; later arranged for two-hands) are an adaptation—at first thought of as a suite—of some of the music Debussy had composed in 1901 for the readings of excerpts from Louÿs's *Chansons de Bilitis*. He had composed twelve pieces for that performance at the offices of *Le Journal*. Now

---

11. There was also a project with Charles Morice for a "lyric tale" for the Opéra entitled *Crimen amoris* (1912–1915). Its basis was the poetry of Verlaine. Later Louis Laloy became part of the abortive project with the title changed to *Fêtes galantes*.

he drew on half of them for the *Epigraphes* (in order of adaptation: original numbers 1, 7, 2, 10, 8, and 12). The music is very much in the style of Debussy's *Bilitis* songs.

Other than the *Epigraphes*, his compositions during these years were limited to pieces related to the First World War. The art of propaganda was in its infancy but developed quickly. The first *cause célèbre* of the war was Germany's violation of Belgium's neutrality in its invasion of France. The Rape of Belgium was used effectively to paint a portrait of Hun barbarism, its foil being the heroic, but helpless, defense of Belgium by its small army.

Debussy was involved in one of the earliest projects associated with the fall of Belgium. In November 1914 his *Berceuse héroïque* (there is both a piano and an orchestral version) was published in *King Albert's Book. A Tribute to the Belgian King and People from Representative Men and Women throughout the World*. Proceeds from the sale of the book were donated to the *Daily Telegraph* Belgium Fund.

The popular English novelist Hall Caine was listed as "general organizer" for *King Albert's Book*. There were more than 200 contributors, from all branches of the arts. The emphasis was on those from Great Britain, but there was an international and populist flavor to the publication. Elgar, Jack London, Edith Wharton, Walter Crane, André Messager, Maeterlinck, and Anatole France were among the contributors.

The *Berceuse* is a simple, well-crafted, and somber piece, about four minutes in length. It quotes the Belgian national anthem. Debussy described his contribution as "melancholy and discreet...with no pretensions other than to offer a homage to so much patient suffering."[12] A "berceuse" is a lullaby, hardly an apt title for the mood of Debussy's music. Its selection was intended to be ironic, and a way to bring to mind the suffering of the children in Belgium as a result of the war.

The *Berceuse* was followed by two extremely short, minor piano pieces: *Page d'album* and *Elégie*. *Page d'album* was composed in June 1915 for a concert series sponsored by a philanthropic group devoted to supplying clothing to the wounded. Emma was involved with the project, and that helps to explain Debussy's participation.[13] The *Elégie*, a simple and solemn work, was published six months later in facsimile in *Pages inédites sur la femme et la guerre*. Profits from sale of the book were intended for war orphans.

That same month Debussy completed his final work inspired by the war effort: "Noël des enfants qui n'ont plus des maisons" (Christmas of Homeless Children). The focus was again on children as an illustration of the horror and atrocities of war. Debussy composed both the words and music for this straightforward, strophic setting. Its recurrent refrain—"Revenge the children of France!"—gives an indication of its mood and intent.[14] But Debussy's approach was subtle. Rather than have

12. Letter to Emile Vuillermoz of 25 January 1916 in *DL*, p. 313.

13. It was not published until 1933.

14. During 1916–1917 Debussy also completed a few sketches for a patriotic choral work, *Ode à la France*. Completed and arranged by Marius-François Gaillard, it was premiered in 1928.

the music document the horrors described in the text, it enhances the naiveté of the children and their reaction to a frightful situation.

Between the composition of the *Berceuse* and the *Elégie* lay one of Debussy's most productive periods. After years of creative frustration, Debussy discovered in the summer of 1915 inspiration in the rural seclusion of "Mon Coin." Its beauty and serenity led to the creation of his five final compositions.

En Blanc et Noir (for two pianos) was composed from 4 June to 20 July 1915. Writing an original piece of music for two pianos was unusual for Debussy, but he wanted timbre of a particular type. The title gives some indication of its starkness. Debussy felt that the pieces "draw their color, their emotion, simply from the piano, like the 'grays' of Velázquez."[15] The work was originally called *Caprices en blanc et noir*, and another source of inspiration for them was Goya's *Los Caprichos* (1799). Goya's etchings focus on human folly and share with some of Debussy's music for *En Blanc et Noir* an emphasis on the grotesque. "I must confess," Debussy wrote to Durand, "that I have slightly changed the color of the second *Caprice*...it was becoming too black, and nearly as tragic as a *Caprice* of Goya."[16] In the end, "caprice" was dropped from the title because of Debussy's realization that the pieces would then be confused with the standard musical caprice.

In this, the first of his works from "Mon Coin," Debussy was unable to leave the war behind. Each piece is prefaced with an excerpt from a French poem (for the second, it is Villon's "Ballade contre les ennemis de la France"). The first piece in the set (all three are untitled) is the most accessible. It is primarily monothematic, sectional, and of the three, the lightest in mood.

The second piece is the odd one of the group. Luther's "A Mighty Fortress Is Our God"—as a symbol of the Germans—is quoted and distorted nearly beyond recognition. Representing the French are echoes of the "Marseillaise," and bugle calls. It is a dramatic piece, stark, disjunct, and one of Debussy's most dissonant. In some ways it is a curious throwback to earlier "battle" pieces of music, Biber's *La Battalia* (1673), for example. The concluding piece in the set is, like the first, monothematic. Near the conclusion, it restates the main theme from the second piece.

En Blanc et Noir was followed by a set of twelve Etudes for piano (23 July to 29 September). There can be a dry and forbidding connotation to the word, etude, but Debussy was unusually enthusiastic about these. He told Durand that "they will occupy a special place."[17] And he put a great deal of care and effort into them, entirely recasting "Pour les arpèges composés."[18]

---

15. Letter to Robert Godet of 4 February 1916 in *DL*, p. 314. Velázquez relied heavily on grays and blacks in his paintings.

16. Letter to Jacques Durand of 14 July 1915 in *C*, p. 1909.

17. Letter to Jacques Durand of 27 September 1915 in ibid., p. 1939.

18. See Roy Howat, "A Thirteenth *Etude* of 1915: The Original Version of *Pour les arpèges composés*," in *Cahiers Debussy* 1 (1977), pp. 25–36.

Rather than the student etude (such as the one Debussy made fun of in *Children's Corner*), these etudes draw on the nineteenth-century concept of the *etude de concert*, the type of etude written by piano virtuosi like Alkan, Henselt, and Chopin. Debussy's ideal is made clear by his dedication: "To the Memory of Frédéric Chopin." (François Couperin was also considered as a possible dedicatee.)

They are presented in two sets of six, but not arranged by key centers. Each set mixes etudes focusing on technique with those more concerned with the exploration of piano sonority. Debussy aims at encouraging self-reliance: no fingering is supplied. Humor, too, is an essential component. "A little charm," Debussy explained to Durand, "never did any harm."[19] "Pour les agréments," the eighth in the set, Debussy compared to a "Barcarolle on the sea, a bit Italian," possibly an allusion to Chopin's *Barcarolle,* op. 60.[20]

The Etudes are extraordinarily difficult pieces to perform. The physical demands are many (such as the sixth which focuses on scales but asks that they be performed contrary to habit—without using the thumbs). The challenge to Debussy was to create entire pieces based on the repetition of a particular pattern (like scales or thirds), and yet retain the listener's interest. Debussy's sense of humor—such as the consistent "wrong" notes in the first etude—helps.

Several of the Etudes are strikingly dissonant. What makes the dissonance so effective (in "Pour les quartes" and "Pour les sonorités opposés," for example) is both its abrasiveness and the contrast produced. It is a concept Debussy uses more consistently in the Etudes than in any other of his piano pieces.

Much has been made of the "modernistic" tendencies of these Etudes, and the more prominent use of dissonance is one indication of it. But compared to the younger generation making a name for itself (Stravinsky, for example), Debussy was more restrained. In the last etude ("Pour les accords") the emphasis is on driving, rhythmic patterns, but Debussy still manages to convince the listener that the piano is more a melodic than a percussive instrument.[21]

Debussy's last compositions were a set of sonatas. He explained to Durand that he would compose six of them and among the group would be solo sonatas for popular instruments like the violin, as well as unusual combinations. Debussy lived to complete three: the Cello Sonata (July and August 1915), the Sonata for Flute, Viola, and Harp (September and October 1915), and the Violin Sonata (October 1916 to April 1917). They were signed, "Claude Debussy, musicien français"—an

19. Letter to Jacques Durand of 28 August 1915 in *C*, p. 1925.

20. Letter to Jacques Durand of 12 August 1915 in ibid., p. 1920.

21. Debussy composed one final piece for piano in February–March 1917: *Les soirs illuminés*. Intended as payment for his coal merchant (when heat was at a premium, and at his request), it is a sketch inspired by Baudelaire's "Le Balcon." It was published in 2003.

indication not just of Debussy's nationalism during a time of war, but of the heritage he drew upon for writing them.[22]

The sonata as a genre was alive and well in France during the final decades of the nineteenth century and opening decades of the twentieth. The model was the four-movement variety that had been developed, primarily in German-speaking lands during the 1800s. Sonatas for violin provide a good example. There were three outstanding ones composed by Debussy's contemporaries: Guillaume Lekeu (1890), Albéric Magnard (1901), and Vincent d'Indy (op. 59; 1904). Each is more than twice the length of Debussy's sonata for violin. And all draw on the grandiloquent tradition of nineteenth-century virtuosity. Franck is their model, and the sonata structures and cyclic principle which he advocated are adapted by them.

Not surprisingly, Debussy's sonatas are quite different. They are shorter than the standard sonata, call for unusual instruments, do not use sonata form, and avoid virtuosity in the grand style. Why, then, did he call them "sonatas"? What Debussy actually had in mind in writing his sonatas was French chamber music of the eighteenth century. It was more intimate in nature, more indebted to dance, and, compared to later sonata structures, far more unpredictable. That Debussy would turn to these lesser known accomplishments of a distinguished French legacy—and use them as a point of departure—was very much in character.

The Cello Sonata is the most extroverted of the sonatas completed. It contains three movements (with the titles "Prologue," "Sérénade," and "Finale," the last two movements to be played without pause). Debussy wrote that he "loved its proportion and form, nearly classical in the good sense of the word."[23] In the first movement the cello is lyrical and self-reliant, so much so that at times it seems as if the piano accompaniment is merely an afterthought. The structure is heard as ABA since there is an easily recognizable return of the opening theme. But there is actually no B—that is, no new thematic material to serve as contrast. Rather Debussy relies on the type of generative compositional approach of *La Mer*. The entire length of this first movement, incidentally, would approximate the size of an exposition section in the sonatas of his contemporaries.

The finale is similar in conception, though with cyclic overtones since the presentation of the wonderfully soaring melody that Debussy created for it is interrupted by rubato recollections from the second movement. As had been the case with *En blanc et noir*, that movement is an oddity: grotesque (with unexpected dance-like segments), brittle, dissonant, and filled with humor. Debussy may have had characters from the commedia dell'arte in mind. But it also recalls Poe's devil in "The Devil in the Belfry," and perhaps that served as a source of inspiration.

22. The fourth sonata was planned for oboe, French horn, and harpsichord; the fifth for trumpet, clarinet, bassoon, and piano; and the sixth for the previous instruments with addition of string bass.

23. Letter to Jacques Durand of 5 August 1915 in *C*, p. 1916.

14-3 Violin Sonata

The Sonata for Flute, Viola, and Harp (originally conceived with oboe instead of viola) is Debussy's version of a trio sonata but with equality for each of the instruments. Like the Cello Sonata, there are three movements ("Pastorale," "Interlude," "Allegro moderato ma risoluto"), but the dramatic change in texture and tonality within the Interlude can give the impression to the listener of several movements instead of a single one. The opening theme of the "Pastorale" (with its emphasis on the intervals of minor and major third, and perfect fourth) serves as the basis for much of the thematic material in the sonata. An excerpt from the "Pastorale" is restated at the end of the finale, providing unity as well as a sense of finality.

Debussy drew on the timbre of the instruments with extraordinary effect. Distinctive qualities (such as the rich, mellow sound of the viola) are highlighted, as well as unusual combinations (viola harmonics with harp), all emphasizing Debussy's inventiveness. The sonata overall creates a sense of extraordinary serenity, all the more remarkable given the trauma Debussy had experienced as a result of the war.

The Violin Sonata was Debussy's last work. Completing it was difficult, both because the pace of war in 1916 and 1917 produced additional hardship (it was the time of Verdun and failure on the Somme) and because Debussy's illness and treatment often left him exhausted. Creating a finale that satisfied him (like the other sonatas, there are three movements) was a challenge.[24]

Unlike the two previous sonatas, the Violin Sonata relies less on the generative concept Debussy had adopted for much of his later work and more on thematic contrast. There is one primary theme in the first movement (heard at the very beginning in the violin, and outlining a major seventh), and a contrasting motive. They appear simultaneously near the conclusion of the movement (Example 14-3 on page 240).

The biting dissonance and humor of the second movement ("Intermède") is a counterpart to the Cello Sonata's "Sérénade." The finale begins with a surprising, literal restatement of the theme from the first movement. Like the "Intermède" there are dance-like elements in the finale, though in this instance Debussy seems to have contemporary, popular dance in mind (see the section marked "le double plus lent"). With extended trills in the violin and a tolling, bell-like ostinato in the piano, Debussy concludes the sonata with a dramatic burst of excitement and exhilaration.

Permeating all three movements is Debussy's vision of the gypsy violinist Radics, a performer whom he admired for his extraordinary musicality. There are aspects that sound "gypsy-like"—the provocative glissandos, for example. But Debussy's concern was less with specific elements than with encouraging performances in the spirit of Radics, performances that embodied music's essence: its "color and rhythm."

24. See Denis-François Rauss, "'Ce terrible finale': les sources manuscrites de la sonate pour violon et piano de Claude Debussy et la genèse du troisième mouvement," in *Cahiers Debussy* 2 (1978), pp. 30–62.

CHAPTER FIFTEEN

Debussy as Critic

Critics are people who trade on the authority and name of newspapers to talk about something of which they know nothing.

Debussy, conversation with Sylvain Bonmariage

Debussy's involvement with music—as conductor, performer, composer, teacher, and critic—could not have been more active. But only composing provided real satisfaction to him. Performing, teaching, and conducting were nuisances, necessary for income and publicity. As for music criticism, it paid poorly, provided meager recognition, and ate up valuable time that could be better spent composing—all good reasons why Debussy managed to avoid writing any music criticism until he was nearly forty.

By the time Debussy began his career as a critic in 1901, it had become common in France for composers—even those with negligible literary skills—to supplement their income by writing for the press. Had he wanted to, Debussy could have become a critic years earlier. He was enormously interested in all the arts, wrote well, and was close to writers who could have recommended him to the leading papers of the day.

But Debussy had several concerns. First, becoming a critic might imply a lack of success as a composer (as one early study reported: "[Debussy] has even resorted— one wonders how desperately—to the writing of music criticism for various journals and reviews")[1]. He was also a slow worker. Writing did not come easily to him. Would he be able to write to order? Would he be able to meet deadlines?[2]

---

1. Lawrence Gilman, *Debussy's Pelléas et Mélisande. A Guide to the Opera* (New York: Schirmer, 1907), p. 8.

2. His anxiety helps partially to explain why at times he resorted to rewriting old material for different papers.

Despite Debussy's reservations, there were definite advantages to bringing his name before a broader public. At the start of the twentieth century his reputation was beginning to grow, and interest in him and his work was increasing. Although untested as a writer, he was well-read and intimate with the literary, artistic, and musical scene. He was known to be an original. It remained to be seen whether he could write in a way to attract readers and sell papers.

Debussy began writing music criticism in April 1901 and worked sporadically at it for about a dozen years. He started with one of the most prestigious papers of the day, *La Revue blanche*, but stayed for only eight months, giving overwork—he was preparing *Pelléas* for its premiere—as one of his reasons for leaving.

More than two years passed before he again wrote any music criticism, this time for *Gil Blas* (January–June 1903). *Gil Blas* was more lively and entertaining than *La Revue blanche*, and for it Debussy's reviews were paired with those of the popular writer, Colette. Her current bestsellers were novels written in the guise of a naive, provincial schoolgirl: Claudine. And it was Claudine's unsophisticated reviews that were published alongside Debussy's, providing an additional level of humor now that Debussy was the famous composer of *Pelléas*.

In the years following his work with *Gil Blas*, Debussy wrote for the press infrequently. He returned on occasion—concerned by the rise of "pretentious mediocrity"—and chose topics meaningful to him for journals such as *Musica*, and papers like *Le Figaro* and *Le Matin*.[3] His final criticism was for a more scholarly journal: *Société Internationale de Musique* (*SIM* ; 1912–1914). His intent was to try to "put things back where they belong: in an attempt to recover the values falsified by arbitrary judgements and capricious interpretations."[4] His friends Emile Vuillermoz and Louis Laloy were associated with *SIM*—and that overcame Debussy's suspicion of academics sufficiently for him to contribute nearly a dozen articles.

★ ★ ★ ★ ★

Debussy's start in musical journalism was auspicious. *La Revue blanche* was one of the finest artistic journals of the day. Founded in 1889, it was published twice per month and was an intriguing blend of intellectual and entertaining content. Contemporary French literature was a major focus, including the avant-garde (Alfred Jarry was a frequent contributor). Many of Debussy's friends had been published in *La Revue blanche*, including Mallarmé, Régnier, Louÿs, and Toulet. But it was truly cosmopolitan, and writers outside France, such as Tolstoy and Hamsun, also received attention.

In addition to literature, a great deal of space was devoted to the visual arts, a reflection of the tastes of the publisher, Thadée Natanson, who was an avid art

---

3. Letter of 10 March 1906 to Louis Laloy in *DL*, p. 167.
4. Letter to Robert Godet of 18 January 1913 in ibid., p. 269.

collector. Natanson's preferences were seen as well in his choice of editor. Félix Fénéon, a well-known art critic and supporter of Seurat, served in that capacity from 1895 to 1903. That helps to explain the wide range of artists who were contributors to La Revue blanche (Edouard Vuillard, Pierre Bonnard, and Toulouse-Lautrec). In addition, Félix Valloton regularly supplied portraits of notables of the day.

Coverage of literature and the visual arts was exceptional. That for music was mediocre. The first music critic for La Revue blanche was Willy (Henri Gauthier-Villars, husband of Colette). Although he was one of the most popular critics of the day (in such demand that he hired others to write under his name), his knowledge and background in music were negligible. To supplement Willy, Alfred Ernst, a Wagnerian, wrote occasional music columns.

Debussy's immediate predecessor—and at the time the most regular music contributor to La Revue blanche—was Alfred Corneau, music critic from 1898 to 1901.[5] But there continued to be additional contributors, such as Edouard Dujardin (novelist, poet, and Wagnerian), who supplied a study of Beethoven's late works.

The uneven and often superficial music criticism in La Revue blanche prior to Debussy's arrival is surprising. Nantanson's wife Misia took an active role in the publication—and she was an accomplished musician. A talented pianist and student of Fauré, she was also a good friend of Mallarmé (for whom she regularly played). She might have had a part in hiring Debussy, but he had many friends associated with the journal, any one of whom could have been influential in his employment.[6] No matter who might have been responsible for bringing Debussy on board, it can be no coincidence that his initial work for La Revue blanche corresponded with a time of increased debt for him. Music criticism was one of the few ways he could hope to increase his income.

Debussy's first article appeared on 1 April 1901, the last, eight months later. During that time Debussy contributed eight pieces, more frequently at the beginning of his association. He began his declaration of war against the critical standards of his day with disarming bluntness:

> What you will be finding here are my own sincere impressions, exactly as I felt them—more than criticism, which is all too often no more than a brilliant set of variations on the theme of "you didn't do it as I would, that's your mistake," or even "you have talent, I have none, and that certainly cannot go on." I shall try to see the works in perspective, to discover the various seeds from which they spring, and what they contain of inner life.[7]

5. He was also music critic for the paper, Le Matin.

6. Both she and her husband were aware of his reputation: he had privately performed portions of Pelléas for them.

7. Review of 1 April 1901 in DM, p. 13.

There was little revolutionary about Debussy's agenda. It was *how* Debussy expressed himself—as much as what he had to say—that captured readers' attention. His style was light, yet assured; almost conversational, yet always bearing the conviction of his musical expertise. His reviews were amusing, flippant, caustic, outspoken, shocking, and invariably entertaining. What ensured their freshness was their wit and unpredictability:

> We heard Monsieur Léopold Auer, violin soloist to his Majesty the Emperor of Russia. He showed enormous talent playing a concerto by Brahms and a melancholy serenade by Tchaikovsky. These two works competed with each other in boredom.[8]

> The attraction that binds the virtuoso to his public seems much the same as that which draws the crowds to the circus: we always hope that something dangerous is going to happen. Monsieur Ysaÿe is going to play the violin with [the conductor] on his shoulders. Or [the piano virtuoso] will finish by seizing the piano with his teeth.[9]

> Monsieur Chagnon [father of a child prodigy] complains that his son hasn't a good enough piano, and that he can go to the Conservatoire only once a week....These two problems are easily remedied: let his son not go to the Conservatoire at all, and let him spend the money thus saved on a better piano.[10]

Debussy lost little time in introducing a fictional character into his reviews—one who made few appearances but who came to represent much of Debussy's critical stance: Monsieur Croche. Debussy offered only a vague, general description of Croche: "short and wizened...[he] spoke very softly and never laughed."[11] The choice of name was clever. "Croche" means eighth-note, so a musical connection was established. But the word also brings to mind "crochet" (hook, spiked), implying that he might not be the most amiable of characters.

Croche battled mediocrity and championed the unconventional. Often he became a spokesman for some of Debussy's most controversial opinions and in that sense seemed useful in distancing Debussy from possible retaliation.

Croche was blunt, and a master at confrontation, but much more than a skillful antagonist. Debussy made him a philosopher of profundity, and one who, like himself, was often perplexed by the dullness and unthinking acts of those around him: "Just remember," he observed, "something which is truly beautiful commands only silence. Every day we witness the magical beauty of the sunset. Does one think of applauding that?"[12]

8. Review of 16 March 1903 in ibid., p. 146.

9. Review of 1 May 1901 in ibid., p. 26.

10. Review of 30 March 1903 in ibid., p. 158.

11. Review of 1 July 1901 in ibid., p. 45.

12. Ibid., p. 46.

Croche appeared (or was mentioned) in fewer than a half dozen of Debussy's reviews (he briefly reappeared in 1903 in *Gil Blas*), but he enjoyed a broad measure of popularity, one that led to charges if not of plagiarism, then of something close to it. Paul Valéry detected a strong similarity between his own creation, Monsieur Teste, and Debussy's Monsieur Croche—an impression that many shared. Teste had first appeared in Valéry's "Soirée of Monsieur Teste" in *Le Centaure* in 1896. Debussy knew of Teste (he and Valéry were friends).

Although Messieurs Teste and Croche share some personal features and idiosyncracies, there are far more differences between them. Croche is less cryptic in his pronouncements, for example, and far more intelligible. He is also much more of an iconoclast. Teste could have served as inspiration to Debussy. But the actual source may have been closer at hand: in many ways Croche bears an uncanny resemblance to Debussy's good friend, Erik Satie.[13]

Debussy's light and engaging style tended to obscure his seriousness of purpose. He was on a mission to expose what he felt was lacking in contemporary music life and to offer suggestions to remedy the situation. Over the years his focus remained the same. But because of friends and colleagues who might have taken his criticism too personally, he made a point of tempering his views. On its own, then, Debussy's published music criticism presents only what he wanted the public to see. A complete view needs to draw on his private opinions as well, and those are scattered throughout his correspondence.

★ ★ ★ ★ ★

One of the foundations of Debussy's music criticism was his unusual perception of the role of nature in music. Music, he wrote, approaches "the mysterious correspondences between Nature and the Imagination."[14] He discovered practical examples of it in musical compositions. In looking for something good to say about Beethoven's "Pastoral" Symphony he made a point of attributing to the music the "sentimental transposition of what is 'invisible' in nature."[15] Bach and his use of the melodic arabesque was another instance, one where "music was subject to laws of beauty inscribed in the movement of nature itself."[16]

Debussy's somewhat mystical convictions might seem out of place with the modernist stance of some of his compositions and writings—but they are very much in

13. Robert Orledge, "Debussy and Satie," in *Debussy Studies*, Richard Langham Smith, ed. (Cambridge: Cambridge University Press, 1997), p. 163.

14. "Why I Wrote *Pelléas*," April 1902 in *DM*, p. 61.

15. Review of 16 February 1903 in *Ecrits*, p. 96.

16. Review of October 1902, in *DM*, p. 84.

accord with his view of the essence of music, for which he is indebted to the Symbolists. It also brings to mind his seeing Nature as a teacher (of orchestration, for example), and ultimately as an inspiration for simplifying the process of learning. "Let us purify our music," he wrote in one of his last articles. "Let us work to relieve its congestion."[17]

The "congestion" was, Debussy felt, layers of encumbrances added by tradition. In his criticism he did all he could to fight against its unthinking acceptance. "Beethoven's real lesson to us," he wrote, "was not that we should preserve age-old forms, nor even that we should plant our footsteps where he first trod. We should look out through open windows into clear skies."[18] Too much attention, he believed, was paid to "the 'authorities.' It seems to me they stifle a more individual voice within."[19] He was eager for people to think for themselves, to study and evaluate music on their own. And he was irritated by complacency. "I admire Beethoven and Wagner," he wrote, "but I refuse to admire them because they have been deemed to be masters. Never!"[20]

Uncritical attachment to "The Masters" led to the creation of a repertory that was moribund. That was one reason Debussy showed interest in the music of lesser known composers. Writing of the music of Alessandro Scarlatti (1660–1725; the little-known father of Domenico), he dryly noted that "we are perhaps wrong in playing the same old things time and time again."[21]

Music education became a major target for his criticism. Institutions like the Conservatoire were responsible for perpetuating much of the tradition that Debussy found so stifling. In one review he singled out a composer's youth as his salvation. There was still, he explained, "time to get rid of his present respect for what he has been taught and exchange it for a mind of his own, free of any arbitrary formulae."[22] And he was infuriated by the basis for determining excellence at the Conservatoire— competitions that only led to "creating more and more idiots."[23] "Among the institutions on which France prides itself," concluded Monsieur Croche, "do you know of any more ridiculous than the Prix de Rome?"[24]

17. Review of 1 November 1913 in *Ecrits*, p. 247.

18. Review of 1 April 1901 in *DM*, p. 15.

19. Ibid., p.16.

20. Interview of 18 January 1911 in *Ecrits*, p. 318.

21. Review of 13 April 1903 in *DM*, p. 174.

22. Review of 15 March 1913 in ibid., p. 285.

23. Review of 14 February 1909 in ibid., p. 238.

24. Review of 15 November 1901 in ibid., p. 52.

Competitions, Debussy maintained, tended to reward upper-level mediocrity (or at least the readily comprehensible), and led both to a deterioration of artistic standards and misconceptions concerning art's function and stature. Winners of the Prix needed to "be told that Art must be loved through all its visions, all its miseries, and should never be relied upon to supply a 'job.'"[25] Debussy felt that the teaching of Art and an emphasis on its craft had led to some curious misconceptions: "When will someone come along and put an end to this dreadful notion, so popular at the moment, that it is as easy to be an artist as a dentist?"[26]

Think for yourself—Question tradition—Be suspicious of what you are taught. These were not concerns of the typical music critic. Such statements have led to Debussy's music criticism being described as the "first major outpouring of anarchist ideas in music."[27] But while it may make sense to associate him with a form of intellectual anarchism—directed in particular to a younger generation—it is misleading to couple him with anarchism as a political movement, a branch of which was prominent in France in the 1890s and early 1900s.

Although there were sympathizers in the arts for anarchism (including Mallarmé), many who supported its philosophy were at the same time horrified by its violence. Anarchist bombings, murders, and assassinations—terrorist acts characterized at the time as "anarchism in practice"—became increasingly common in France during the 1890s. But there is no indication that Debussy supported anarchism. And his view of art—which was always critical of the taste of the masses—differed from the broadly egalitarian standards adopted by the anarchists. True—he placed "value…on independence" and "derided…institutionalism," both traits of anarchism.[28] But the principles of Debussy that most resembled those of anarchism—opposition to convention, suspicion of tradition, an emphasis on self-reliance—were ideals held in common with many artists (and hardly the hallmarks of anarchism).

As a music critic, Debussy continued to question the "authorities." His stance determined his view of music history and made him wary of a great deal of nineteenth-century music that served as the basis of the repertory. He admired Chopin for example, but liked only some of the early piano music of Schumann. Schumann's settings of Heine's poems—which were often singled out for their sensitivity—he criticized for their ignorance of Heine's "fine spirit of irony."[29] Debussy was convinced that many

25. Review of May 1903 in *Ecrits*, p. 179.

26. Review of November 1912 in *DM*, p. 265.

27. Ibid., p. 9.

28. Déirdre Donnellon, "The Anarchist Movement in France and Its Impact on Debussy," *Cahiers Debussy* 33 (1999), pp. 53, 54.

29. Review of March 1911 in *DM*, p. 250.

well-known genres had served their purpose. He wrote of the "uselessness of the symphony since Beethoven" and described the Opéra as "a place where monumental luxury is unable to conceal the poverty of what is performed."[30]

The type of change essential for the growth of French musical life was, Debussy felt, opposed by most French composers of his day, especially the most illustrious. Debussy was openly critical of prominent figures like Fauré ("the Master of Charms").[31] Whatever good he discovered in the music of his contemporaries was consistently overshadowed by its drawbacks. These were discussed openly in letters to friends. For publication, his reservations were often concealed by hyperbole. For one review he described Paul Dukas's Piano Sonata as "somewhat special," and concluded that "by its grandeur of conception it takes its place immediately after the sonatas of Beethoven" (hardly intended as a compliment coming from Debussy).[32]

The music of Vincent d'Indy was a special case. Debussy admired d'Indy's artistic convictions, if not his musical style. Above all, he wanted to avoid the controversy fueled by those in the d'Indy and Debussy camps. In print he made a point of being praiseworthy, sometimes excessively. For d'Indy's opera, *L'Etranger*, "the music appeared to be very beautiful, but as if enclosed; it stupefied with such mastery that one scarcely dared to be moved—that would not have been respectable."[33] In private, he was more blunt, criticizing d'Indy's dogmatic approach.

Debussy was far warmer in his praise of Russian music—in part because of its distance from Western conventions. He described Rimsky-Korsakov's *Antar* as a "pure masterpiece of renewal in which [he] sends the traditional forms of the symphony packing."[34] Musorgsky's music, he concluded, is "unique....There is no question of any such thing as 'form,' or, at least, any forms there are have such complexity that they are impossible to relate to the accepted forms—the 'official' ones."[35]

Debussy's knowledge of contemporary music from countries other than France was surprisingly sketchy. He knew little of Mahler (though Mahler had conducted all of Debussy's major orchestral works).[36] He was more familiar with Richard Strauss. They had met at a lunch arranged by his publisher, Jacques Durand. Strauss

---

30. Reviews of 1 April 1901 in ibid., p. 15, and of 9 March 1903 in *Ecrits*, p. 116.

31. Review of 9 March 1903 in *DM*, p. 138.

32. Reviews of 15 April 1901 and May 1903 in *Ecrits*, pp. 31, 178.

33. Review of 12 January 1903 in ibid., p. 70.

34. Review of 16 March 1903 in *DM*, p. 147.

35. Review of 15 April 1901 in ibid., pp. 20–21.

36. Incidentally, the often cited incident of Debussy, Pierné, and Dukas walking out in protest at a performance of Mahler's Symphony No. 2 (17 April 1910) has no basis in fact. It is unlikely that Debussy would have found much to admire in Mahler's music, but the episode is entirely out of character (and would have made little sense). The source for it is Alma Mahler's unreliable memoirs.

used the occasion to talk about the intricacy of copyright laws, a disappointment to Debussy who had hoped for a less worldly discussion. According to Durand, Debussy "generally dealt with embarrassing situations by thinking of something else and losing himself in his dream world. Lunch therefore passed in active conversation on the part of Strauss and obstinate silence on that of Debussy."[37]

Debussy knew most of Strauss's best-known pieces. Privately, he described *Salomé* as "an absolute masterpiece," but he was more critical of the tone poems (*Till Eulenspiegel*, for example).[38] In general Debussy discovered in Strauss's music "curious similarities" to the Symbolist paintings of Arnold Böcklin.[39] Precisely what Debussy had in mind he never revealed. But it is the type of comparison to the visual arts that appealed to him. He found it interesting, too, that in *Ein Heldenleben* Strauss "no longer uses the rigorous architectural methods of a Bach or a Beethoven. Instead he develops with rhythmic colors."[40] But privately Debussy had previously concluded that *Ein Heldenleben* was no more than "a good solid piece," and one that required a "strong stomach to swallow."[41]

Arnold Schoenberg's music he found to be indigestible, even though his firsthand knowledge of it was slight. Apparently he never heard any performances of it. Varèse said that he showed Debussy Schoenberg's *Three Piano Pieces,* op. 11, and *Five Pieces for Orchestra,* op. 16. What particularly bothered Debussy about it was its foreignness. He was concerned that it might become popular enough to serve as a model in France.

For, despite Debussy's contempt for tradition, there was one tradition he came increasingly to champion: that of French music. That tradition, he wrote, was characterized by "clarity of expression, concise and compact in form, qualities particular and significant to French genius."[42] It was, he concluded, a tradition that was in danger of vanishing, the culprits being "influences from the North and from Byzantium."[43] French composers had been too eager to emulate foreign music. Wagner—"a beautiful sunset that has been mistaken for a sunrise"—was the most recent example.[44] He had devised "a number of formulas to accommodate music for the theatre. One day we shall recognize their complete uselessness."[45]

37. Recollection of Jacques Durand in *DR*, p. 120.

38. Letter to Gabriel Astruc of 23 May 1907 in *DL*, p. 179.

39. Review of December 1912 in *DM*, p. 270.

40. Review of 30 March 1903 in ibid., p. 160.

41. Letter of 4 March 1900 to Georges Hartmann in *DL*, p. 111.

42. Review of 2 February 1903 in *Ecrits*, p. 91.

43. Letter to d'Annunzio of 12 June 1913 in *DL*, p. 273.

44. Review of January 1903 in *DM*, p. 83.

45. Review of 15 May 1901 in *Ecrits*, p. 41.

Debussy was convinced that the bane of foreign influence on musical life in France had existed long before Wagner. Earlier in the century Rossini and Meyerbeer had corrupted French taste. And in the 1700s, there had been Gluck. Debussy maintained that he was the composer who had first set French music astray.

Since his student days Debussy had been critical of Gluck, a composer who had long been idolized in France for the dramatic effectiveness of his operas. But there was nothing Debussy could find in his favor. He criticized the "very poor" prosody of Gluck's settings, and Gluck's "habit of impolitely interrupting the action," destroying dramatic coherence.[46] The collaboration between Debussy and Victor Segalen on an Orpheus opera had been intended, he said, to right the wrongs of Gluck's *Orfeo* (1762)—a setting Debussy felt was banal and sentimental.

By imitating Gluck (and following advocates of his style such as Spontini), composers had allowed the French tradition Debussy cherished to be forgotten. Its last true representative—Jean-Philippe Rameau—had been dead for nearly a century and a half. In both his correspondence and music criticism Debussy extolled the "perfect taste and strict elegance" of Rameau's music.[47] And he paid tribute to him in his own music (the "Hommage à Rameau," for example, in the first set of the *Images* for piano). The relationship was symbolized to perfection in a concert given by Debussy's amanuensis, André Caplet, in 1912: it was devoted solely to the music of Debussy and Rameau.

Rameau at the time was little known. Debussy's praise began in 1903 (inspired by a performance he saw of the first two acts of *Castor et Pollux* [1737]). He never wavered in his support and became convinced that the "purely French tradition" that Rameau exemplified provided not only a true and distinctive path for contemporary music but an antidote to the corruption of foreign influence.[48]

Debussy's enthusiasm for Rameau came at what he believed was a crucial time for the development of music in France. But his glorification of French music—combined with a willingness to emphasize weaknesses at the expense of strengths in other composers—led at times to negativism and unmerited fault-finding. At its worst it became narrow-minded provincialism, as when he claimed Dukas's *Ariane et Barbe-bleue* was "not a masterpiece of French music."[49] Even prior to the rampant nationalism fostered by the Great War, Debussy was using fidelity to his perception of French musical tradition as a measure of excellence.

Debussy's relationship with Igor Stravinsky was affected by it, even though they were on friendly terms. Here it was not a question—at least in public—of Stravinsky not writing French music. In the years preceding the First World War Stravinsky became

---

46. Reviews of 23 February 1903 and 2 February 1903 in ibid., pp. 101, 91.

47. Letter to Louis Laloy of 10 September 1906 in *DL*, p. 172.

48. Review of 2 February 1903 in *DM*, p. 112.

49. Letter of 25 February 1912 to Vittorio Gui in *DL*, p. 256.

a phenomenon, and Debussy was fascinated by his music. Privately, he described *Firebird* as "not perfect [but] an excellent piece of work."[50] After hearing *Petrushka* he wrote to Stravinsky: "You will go beyond *Petrushka*—that's certain—but you can already be proud of what this work represents."[51] As for the *Rite of Spring*, he confessed it "haunts me like a beautiful nightmare."[52]

Debussy's fulsome compliments are an indication both of his recognition of Stravinsky's accomplishment and astonishment by it.[53] But privately, he was far more critical: "[Stravinsky] says: my *Firebird*, my *Sacre*, like a child saying : my top, my hoop. And that's exactly what he is—a spoilt child....He's also a young savage who wears noisy ties and kisses the ladies' hands while treading on their toes. When he's old, he'll be intolerable. That's to say, he won't be able to tolerate any music; but, for the moment, he's amazing."[54]

Debussy's music criticism generally tried to give the impression of being above the fray. But he never regarded or treated any composer as an equal. His own music, he felt, was unique; his only real competitor was himself. That helps to explain why he felt intimidated by Stravinsky's originality, why, given his preoccupation with French elegance, he dismissed him as barbaric—and why he never took the time to write a review on Stravinsky's behalf.

Debussy reserved wholehearted praise for those who were no longer alive, Musorgsky, for example. Bach became a special instance of it: "a benevolent God to whom musicians should offer a prayer before setting to work in order to protect themselves from mediocrity."[55]

Debussy was enthralled by what he described as Bach's use of melody as arabesque, a characteristic of his own music as well. In a Bach violin concerto, he discovered "nearly intact that 'musical arabesque.'...Bach, in reworking the arabesque, made it more supple, more fluid, and despite the severe discipline that the great master imposed on beauty, it is imbued with a constantly renewed, free fantasy that astonishes us even today. In Bach's music it is not the character of the melody that affects us but its curve. Even more often it is the parallel movement of several lines whose meeting—whether fortuitous or by agreement—stirs our emotions."[56] At times Debussy felt transported

---

50. Letter of 8 July 1910 to Jacques Durand in ibid., p. 221.

51. Letter of 13 April 1912 in *C*, p. 1503.

52. Letter of [7 November 1912] to Stravinsky in *DL*, p. 265.

53. The complex relationship between Debussy and Stravinsky is documented in Mark McFarland, "Debussy and Stravinsky: Another Look into Their Musical Relationship," *Cahiers Debussy* 24 (2000), pp. 79–112.

54. Letter to Robert Godet of 4 January 1916 in *DL*, p. 312.

55. Review of 15 February 1913 in *Ecrits*, p. 228.

56. Review of 1 May 1901 in ibid., p. 34.

by Bach's music: "It haunts us long after it is ended, so that on coming out into the street one cannot but be astonished that the sky is not more blue, and that the Parthenon does not rise out of the ground before one's very eyes."[57]

What generally served as the basis for Debussy's admiration was Bach's unconventionality—the "freedom and fantasy in both composition and form," the fact that Bach "scorned harmonic formulae."[58] "I acknowledge," he concluded, "one great master....This is Bach; but I will not say the same of Beethoven, as I consider him a man of his epoch, and with a few exceptions his works should have been allowed to rest."[59]

There were times—always when an audience was not present—that he felt less compelled to place Bach on a pedestal. In 1917 when preparing an edition of Bach's violin sonatas he complained that if "the old Saxon cantor hasn't any ideas he starts out from any old thing and is truly pitiless. In fact he's only bearable when he's admirable. Which, you'll say, is still something! At the same time, if he'd had a friend—a publisher perhaps—who could have told him to take a day off every week, perhaps, then we'd have been spared several hundreds of pages in which you have to walk between rows of mercilessly regulated and joyless bars, each one with its rascally little 'subject' and 'countersubject.' "[60]

At the encouragement of Godet and Laloy—and to provide an additional source of income—in 1913 Debussy collected some of his music reviews for publication as a book. The idea of preparing a book about music—in contrast to writing criticism for the press—appealed to Debussy and had long been at the back of his mind. It provided more permanence and put on display the breadth of his writing. He selected barely half of what he had written, edited it sparingly, and in March 1914 was at work checking the proofs. But because of the war, publication of *Monsieur Croche, Antidilettante* (in an edition of only 500 copies) was delayed until 1921— three years after Debussy's death. Even incomplete, it served its purpose and drew attention both to his skill as a writer and to his artistic beliefs.

Although a century has passed since it was written, Debussy's music criticism remains a model of its kind. Much of its vigor can be traced to its uncompromising idealism and to its willingness—even eagerness—to go against the grain. Debussy wanted to animate and provoke discussion not just about individual pieces of music, but about the role and function of Art itself. He accomplished his goals without giving the impression of preaching, and with a refreshing freedom from cant. And even though a good portion of the music he examined was ephemeral, the incessant questioning of convention that served as the basis for his criticism has assured its freshness and vitality.

57. Review of 15 January 1913 in *DM*, p. 276.
58. Reviews of 1 November 1913 and October 1902 in ibid., pp. 297, 84.
59. Interview of 6 August 1908 in ibid., p. 233.
60. Letter to Jacques Durand of 15 April 1917 in *DL*, p. 323.

Calendar

Year	Age	Life	Contemporary musicians and events
1862		Birth on 22 August of Achille–Claude to Manuel–Achille and Victorine Debussy at Saint-Germain-en-Laye.	Delius born;
			Les Miserables
1864	1	Baptized on 31 July.	Meyerbeer dies; Toulouse-Lautrec born; Richard Strauss born.
1866	4		Busoni born; Satie born; Austro-Prussian War.
1868	6	Family settles in Paris.	Rossini dies.
1870	8	In Cannes. First music lessons.	Lekeu born; Franco-Prussian War.
1871	9	Begins piano lessons in Paris with Mme Mauté.	Auber dies.
1872	10	22 October: admitted to Conservatoire.	Scriabin born; Vaughan Williams born.

Year	Age	Life	Contemporary musicians and events
			Whistler's *Nocturne*
			in Blue and Silver
1873	11	Manuel Debussy is released after serving two years in prison, a result of his participation in the Commune.	John Stuart Mill dies.
1876	13	16 January: first public performance.	Goetz dies;
			Jack London born.
1879	17	Summer: at Chenonceaux.	Zulu War.
		Removed from piano program at	
		Conservatoire.	
		First compositions.	
1880	18	Summer: travel with the von Mecks.	Offenbach dies;
		Accompanist in Moreau-Sainti's singing class.	Medtner born.
		December: enters Guiraud's	
		composition class.	
1881	19	Summer: in Russia and Italy with the von Mecks.	Musorgsky dies;
			Bartók born.
			Bruckner's Fourth
			Symphony
1882	20	Start of affair with Marie Vasnier (or 1883). Writes first Verlaine songs.	Rossetti dies;
		July: first attempt at Prix de Rome.	Stravinsky born.
		Final stay with the von Mecks.	*Parsifal*
			From the Cradle
			to the Grave
			Redon's *A Edgar Poe*

Year	Age	Life	Contemporary musicians and events
1883	21	June: awarded 2nd place in the Prix de Rome.	Wagner dies;
			Webern born.
1884	21	June: wins the Prix de Rome with *L'Enfant prodigue*.	Siege of Khartoum
			Huckleberry Finn
			Manon
1885	23	January: arrives in Rome.	Hugo dies;
		Complains about his life there.	Berg born.
			Brahms's Fourth Symphony
1887	25	March: returns to Paris.	Borodin dies.
1888	26	First trip to Bayreuth.	Alkan dies.
		La Damoiselle élue	*Mörike-Lieder*
1889	27	Summer: attends Universal Exhibition.	Villiers dies;
		Second trip to Bayreuth.	Khnopff's *Memories*
		Petite Suite	
		Cinq Poèmes de Baudelaire	
1890	28	Spring: meets Gaby Dupont.	Franck dies.
		Autumn: begins to attend Mallarmé's mardis.	
1892	30	Beginning of friendship with Pierre Louÿs.	Milhaud born.
			Bruges-la-Morte
1893	31	May: attends performance of *Pelléas et Mélisande*.	Gounod dies; Chaikovsky dies.
		Friendship with Chausson.	
		August: begins composition of *Pelléas*.	
		December: premiere of String Quartet.	
1894	32	February: brief engagement to Thérèse Roger.	Chabrier dies;
		December: premiere of *Prélude à*	Lekeu dies;
			Warlock born;

Year	Age	Life	Contemporary musicians and events
		l'après-midi d'un faune.	Mahler's Second Symphony
			Monet's *Rouen Cathedral*
			Delville's *Angel of Splendor*
1895	33	Completes vocal score of *Pelléas.*	Godard dies;
			Morisot dies;
			Hindemith born.
			Moreau's *Jupiter and Semele*
1897	35	February: Gaby attempts suicide.	Brahms dies.
1899	37	19 October: marriage to Lilly Texier.	Chausson dies;
			Poulenc born.
			Boxer Rebellion
1900	38	February: publication of the *Nocturnes.*	Nietzsche dies;
			Mahler's Fourth Symphony
1901	39	April: becomes music critic for *La Revue blanche.*	Verdi dies.
1902	40	30 April: premiere of *Pelléas.*	*The Hound of the Baskervilles*
1903	41	Signs contract for *The Devil in the Belfry.*	Wolf dies;
		Estampes	Whistler dies;
			First airplane flight.
			D'Indy's Second Symphony
1904	42	August: leaves Lilly and settles with Emma Bardac in Pourville.	Dvorak dies; Russo-Japanese War
		October: Lilly attempts suicide.	
1905	43	Signs exclusive publishing contract with Jacques Durand.	Strauss's *Salomé*
		30 October: birth of Chouchou.	
		La Mer	

Year	Age	Life	Contemporary musicians and events
1907	45	Works on the orchestral *Images*.	Grieg dies.
		Images (2nd Series)	
1908	46	12 January: makes debut as a conductor with *La Mer*.	MacDowell dies. *Gaspard de la nuit*
		30 January: marries Emma Bardac.	
		Begins work on *The Fall of the House of Usher*.	
		Children's Corner	
		Ibéria	
1910	48	September: signs contract for *Khamma*.	*Der Rosenkavalier*
		28 October: death of Manuel Debussy.	*Prometheus*
		November–December: conducts in Vienna and Budapest.	*The Firebird*
		Préludes, Book I	
1911	49	22 May: premiere of *The Martyrdom of St. Sebastian*.	Mahler dies.
			Petroushka
		June: conducts in Turin.	
1912	50	29 May: performance of the *Faune* at the Ballets Russes.	Massenet dies; Sinking of Titanic
		Continued financial difficulties.	*Pierrot lunaire*
		Préludes, Book II	
1913	51	January: premiere of the orchestral *Images*.	*Rite of Spring*
		15 May: premiere of *Jeux*.	
		December: conducts in Moscow and St. Petersburg.	
		Trois Poèmes de Mallarmé	
1914	52	February: conducts in Rome and Amsterdam.	Magnard dies;

Year	Age	Life	Contemporary musicians and events
		April: conducts in Holland.	
		September: temporary move to Angers because of the German invasion.	First World War.
1915	53	July–October: settles at "Mon Coin."	Scriabin dies;
		Diagnosis of cancer.	Gourmont dies.
		Etudes; *En Blanc et Noir*;	
		Cello Sonata;	
		Sonata for Flute, Viola, and Harp	
1916	54	Condition gradually worsens.	Battle of the Somme;
			Battle for Verdun.
			Nielsen's Fourth
			Symphony
1917	55	May: premiere of the Violin Sonata.	Degas dies.
			October Revolution
1918	56	25 March: death of Debussy	
1919		16 July: death of Chouchou	

List of Works

	Date of Composition	Date of Publication
Instrumental		
Piano		
Solo		
Danse bohémienne	Summer 1880	1932
Deux Arabesques	1890–1891	1891
Mazurka	1890–1891	1903
Rêverie	1890	1891
Tarentelle styrienne	1890	1891
		1903 (as *Danse*)
Ballade slave	1890	1891
		1903 (as *Ballade*)
Valse romantique	1890	1891
Nocturne	1892	1892
Images oubliées	Winter 1894	1977
1. Lent		
2. Sarabande (first published: 1896)		
3. Quelques aspects de "Nous n'irons plus au bois"		

	Date of Composition	Date of Publication
Pour le piano	1894–1901	1901
1. Prélude		
2. Sarabande		
3. Toccata		
Images (1st Series)	1901–1905	1905
1. Reflets dans l'eau		
2. Hommage à Rameau		
3. Mouvement		
Estampes	July 1903	1903
1. Pagodes		
2. La Soirée dans Grenade		
3. Jardins sous la pluie		
L'Isle joyeuse	1903–August 1904	1904
Masques	1903–July 1904	1904
D'un cahier d'esquisses	January 1904	1904
Pièce pour piano	End 1904	1905
(*Morçeau de concours*)		
Children's Corner	1906–July 1908	1908
1. Docteur Gradus ad Parnassum		
2. Jimbo's Lullaby		
3. Serenade for the Doll		
4. The Snow Is Dancing		
5. The Little Shepherd		
6. Golliwogg's Cake Walk		
(set was orchestrated by Caplet in 1908)		
Images (2nd Series)	October 1907	1908
1. Cloches à travers les feuilles		
2. Et la lune descend sur le temple qui fut		
3. Poissons d'or		
The Little Nigar (Cake-Walk)	1909	1909
Hommage à Haydn	1909	1910

	Date of Composition	Date of Publication
Préludes (Book I)	December 1909– February 1910	1910
1. Danseuses de Delphes		
2. Voiles		
3. Le Vent dans la plaine		
4. "Les sons et les parfums tournent dans l'air du soir" (Baudelaire)		
5. Les collines d'Anacapri		
6. Des pas sur la neige		
7. Ce qu'a vu le vent d'Ouest		
8. La Fille aux cheveux de lin		
9. La Sérénade interrompue		
10. La Cathédrale engloutie		
11. La Danse de Puck		
12. Minstrels		
La plus que lente (see also Orchestral)	1910	1910
Préludes (Book II)	1911–1912	1913
1. Brouillards		
2. Feuilles mortes		
3. La Puerta del Vino		
4. Les Fées sont d'exquises danseuses		
5. Bruyères		
6. "Général Lavine" eccentric		
7. La Terrasse des audiences du clair de lune		
8. Ondine		
9. Hommage à S. Pickwick Esq. P.P.M.P.C.		
10. Canope		
11. Les Tierces alternées		
12. Feux d'artifice		

	Date of Composition	Date of Publication
Bérceuse héroïque	November 1914	1915
(see also Orchestral)		
Page d'album	June 1915	1933
Douze Etudes	July–September 1915	1916
Book I:		
1. Pour les "cinq doigts" d'après M. Czerny		
2. Pour les tierces		
3. Pour les quartes		
4. Pour les sixtes		
5. Pour les octaves		
6. Pour les huit doigts		
Book II:		
7. Pour les degrés chromatiques		
8. Pour les agréments		
9. Pour les notes répétées		
10. Pour les sonorités opposées		
11. Pour les arpèges composés		
12. Pour les accords		
Elégie	December 1915	1997
Les Soirs illuminés	February–March 1917	2003
Four-hands		
Symphony in B minor	1880–1881	1933
Andante cantabile	Early 1881	2002
Diane, Overture	1881	2002
Le Triomphe de Bacchus	Early 1882	2002
Divertissement	Summer 1884	2002
Petite Suite	1888–1889	1889
1. En bateau		
2. Cortège		
3. Menuet		
4. Ballet		

	Date of Composition	Date of Publication
Suite bergamasque	1890–1905	1905
1. Prélude		
2. Menuet		
3. Clair de lune		
4. Passepied		
Marche écossaise sur un thème populaire (*Marche des anciens comtes de Ross*) (see also Orchestral)	1890	1891
Six Epigraphes antiques (uses musical material from *Musique de scène pour les Chansons de Bilitis*; see Chamber)	July 1914–1915	1915
Two Pianos, four-hands		
Lindaraja	April 1901	1926
En Blanc et Noir	June–July 1915	1915
Chamber		
Piano Trio in G Major	September—October 1880	1986
Intermezzo (for cello and piano)	1882	1944
Nocturne et scherzo (for cello and piano)	June 1882	Unpublished
String Quartet, op. 10	1892–1893	1894
Musique de scène (for *Chansons de Bilitis*) (for 2 flutes, 2 harps, and celesta; the celesta part is absent from the surviving MS)	1900–1901	1971
First Rhapsody for Clarinet (with piano accompaniment) (see also Concerto)	December 1909–January 1910	1910
Petite Pièce (for clarinet and piano)	July 1910	1910

	Date of Composition	Date of Publication
Syrinx	1913	1927
(for solo flute)		
Sonata for Cello and Piano	July–August 1915	1915
Sonata for Flute, Viola, and Harp	September–October 1915	1916
Sonata for Violin and Piano	October 1916–April 1917	1917
Concertos		
Fantaisie for piano and orchestra	1889–1890	1920
Rhapsody for saxophone and orchestra	1901–1911	1919
(completed by Roger-Ducasse)		
Two Dances (for harp and strings)	April–May 1904	1904
1. Danse sacrée		
2. Danse profane		
First Rhapsody for Clarinet	December 1909–1911	1911
Orchestral		
Intermezzo	June 1882	2002 (4-hands)
Première Suite d'orchestre	January 1883	Unpublished
1. Fête		
2. Ballet		
3. Rêve		
4. Bacchanale (Cortège et Bacchanale)		
Zuleima (G. Boyer after Heine)	1885	Lost
Printemps	February 1887	1904 (4-hands)
(originally for piano, chorus, and orchestra;		
Büsser orchestration: 1913)		
Marche écossaise sur un thème populaire	1893–c.1908	1911

	Date of Composition	Date of Publication
(*Marche des anciens comtes de Ross*)		
Prélude à l'après-midi d'un faune	1891–September 1894	1895
Nocturnes	1897–December 1899	1900
1. Nuages		
2. Fêtes		
3. Sirènes (with female chorus)		
La Mer	August 1903–March 1905	1905
1. De l'aube à midi sur la mer		
2. Jeux de vagues		
3. Dialogue du vent et de la mer		
La plus que lente	1910	1912
Images for Orchestra		
1. *Gigues*	1912	1913
2. *Ibéria*	1906–1909	1910
a. Par les rues et les chemins		
b. Les parfums de la nuit		
c. Le matin d'un jour de fête		
3. *Rondes de printemps*	1905–1909	1910
Berceuse héroïque	December 1914	1915
Ballets		
Khamma (orchestrated by Koechlin)	1911–1912	1912
Jeux	August 1912–April 1913	1913
La Boîte à joujoux (orchestrated by Caplet)	July–October 1913	1913
Vocal		
Solo Songs		
Madrid (Musset)	End 1879	Unpublished

	Date of Composition	Date of Publication
Nuit d'étoiles (Banville)	1880	1882
Rêverie (Banville)	1880	1984
Caprice (Banville)	1880	1966
Aimons-nous et dormons (Banville)	End 1880	1933
Les Baisers (Banville)	Early 1881	Unpublished
Rondel chinois (?)	Early 1881	Unpublished
Mélodie (Léon Valade after Heine)	Early 1881	Unpublished
Jane (Leconte de l'Isle)	Early 1881	1982
La fille aux cheveux de lin (Leconte de l'Isle)	Early 1881	Unpublished
Fleur des blés (Girod)	Early 1881	1891
Rondeau (Musset)	Summer 1881	1932
Souhait (Banville)	October–November 1881	1984
Triolet à Philis (Zéphir)	November 1881	1932
Les Papillons (Gautier)	End 1881	2004
L'Archet (Cros)	End 1881	Unpublished
[Les Baisers d'amour] (Bouchor)	End 1881	Unpublished
[Chanson triste] (Bouchor)	End 1881	Unpublished
Les elfes (Leconte de l'Isle)	End 1881	Unpublished
Fantoches (1st version) (Verlaine)	Jan. 1881	Unpublished
Les Roses (Banville)	Early 1882	1984
Sérénade (Banville)	Early 1882	1984
Pierrot (Banville)	Early 1882	1969
Fête galante (Banville)	Early 1882	1984
Il dort encore (*Hymnis*; Banville)	Early 1882	1984
Le lilas (Banville)	April 1882	1984
Flots, palmes, sables (A. Renaud)	June 1882	Unpublished
En sourdine (1st version) (Verlaine)	September 1882	1944

	Date of Composition	Date of Publication
Mandoline (Verlaine)	November 1882	1890
Séguidille (Gautier)	End 1882	Unpublished
Clair de lune (1st version) (Verlaine)	End 1882	1969
Pantomime (Verlaine)	Early 1883	1969
Coquetterie posthume (Gautier)	March 1883	1983
Romance (Bourget)	September 1883	1983
Musique (Bourget)	September 1883	1983
Paysage sentimental (Bourget)	November 1883	1891
Romance (Bourget)	January 1884	1903
Apparition (Mallarmé)	February 1884	1969
La Romance d'Ariel (Bourget)	February 1884	1983
Regret (Bourget)	February 1884	1983
Ariettes oubliées (Verlaine)		1903
1. C'est l'extase langoureuse	March 1887	
2. Il pleure dans mon cœur	March 1887	
3. L'ombre des arbres	January 1885	
4. Tournez, tournez	January 1885	
5. Voici des fruits	January 1886	
6. Les roses étaient toutes rouges	January 1886	

(The set was entitled *Ariettes* when first published in 1888. The title became *Ariettes oubliées* when issued by Fromont in 1903.)

Romance (Bourget)	1885	1891
Les Cloches (Bourget)	1885	1891
Barcarolle (Guinand)	c.1885	Unpublished
Cinq Poèmes de Baudelaire		1890
1. Le Balcon	January 1888	
2. Harmonie du soir	January 1889	
3. Le Jet d'eau	March 1889	
4. Recueillement	1889	
5. La Mort des amants	December 1887	

	Date of Composition	Date of Publication
La Belle au bois dormant (Hypsa)	July 1890	1903
Beau soir (Bourget)	1890 or 1891	1891
Trois Mélodies (Verlaine)	1891	1901
1. La mer est plus belle que les cathédrales		
2. Le son du cor s'afflige vers les bois		
3. L'échelonnement des haies moutonne à l'infini		
Fêtes galantes (1st set) (Verlaine)	1891–1892	1903
1. En sourdine (2nd version)		
2. Fantoches (2nd version)		
3. Clair de lune (2nd version)		
Les Angélus (G. Le Roy)	February 1892	1893
Proses lyriques (Debussy)	1892–July1893	1895
1. De Rêve		
2. De Grève		
3. De Fleurs		
4. De Soir		
Chansons de Bilitis (Louÿs)	June 1897– August 1898	
1. La flûte de Pan		1899
2. La Chevelure		1897
3. Le Tombeau des naïades		1899
Berceuse (for solo voice)	April 1899	Unpublished
from *La Tragédie de la mort* (René Peter)		
Nuits blanches (Debussy)	May–September 1898	2000
1. Nuits sans fin		
2. Lorsqu'elle est entrée		
Dans le jardin (Gravollet)	May 1903	1905
Fêtes galantes (2nd set) (Verlaine)	1904	1904
1. Les Ingénus		

	Date of Composition	Date of Publication
2. Le Faune		
3. Colloque sentimental		
Trois Chansons de France (Charles d'Orleans,	1904	1904
Tristan L'Hermite)		
1. Rondel ("Le temps a laissé")		
2. La Grotte		
3. Rondel ("Pour ce que Plaisance")		
Trois Ballades de François Villon	May 1910	1910
1. Ballade de Villon à s'amye		
2. Ballade que Villon fait à la requeste de sa mère pour prier Nostre-Dame		
3. Ballade des femmes de Paris		
Le Promenoir des deux amants (Tristan L'Hermite)		1910
1. La Grotte (see *Trois Chansons de France*)	1904	
2. Crois mon conseil, chère Climène	1910	
3. Je tremble en voyant ton visage	1910	
Trois Poèmes de Stéphane Mallarmé	Summer 1913	1913
1. Soupir		
2. Placet futile		
3. Éventail		
Noël des enfants qui n'ont plus de maison (Debussy)	November 1915	1915
Duets		
Eglogue (Leconte de l'Isle) (S, T)	January 1882	Unpublished
Ode bachique (*Hymnis*; Banville) (S, T, with piano)	Summer 1882	Unpublished

	Date of Composition	Date of Publication
Chanson espagnole (Musset) (for two voices in the same range)	Early 1883	1983
Choral		
Chanson des brises (Bouilhet) (for soprano and three female voices)	Early 1882	Unpublished
Le Printemps (de Segur) (for female voices and orchestra)	May 1882	1928; 1956 (orch.)
Invocation (Lamartine) (for male voices and orchestra)	May 1883	1928; 1957 (orch.)
Le Printemps (Barbier) (for chorus and orchestra)	May 1884	Unpublished
Trois Chansons de Charles d'Orléans		1908
1. Dieu! qu'il la fait bon regarder!	April 1898	
2. Quand j'ay ouy le tabourin	1908	
3. Yver, vous n'estes qu'un villain	April 1898	
Opera, Cantata, and Works for the Stage		
Hélène (Leconte de l'Isle) Incomplete.	Early 1881	Unpublished
Daniel (Emile Cicile) (Cantata for three soloists and orchestra)	Early 1882	Unpublished
Diane au bois (Banville) Incomplete.	1883–1885	Unpublished
Le Gladiateur (E. Moreau)	June 1883	Unpublished
L'Enfant prodigue (Guinand) (extensively revised in 1907)	May 1882	1907
La Damoiselle elue (Rossetti; tr. Sarrazin)	1887–1888	1903 (revised)
Axël (Villiers de l'Isle-Adam) Incomplete.	c. 1890	Unpublished
Rodrigue et Chimène (Mendès) Incomplete.	1890–1893	2003
Pelléas et Mélisande (Maeterlinck)	1893–1902	1904

	Date of Composition	Date of Publication
The Devil in the Belfry (Poe) (*Le Diable dans le beffroi*) Incomplete.	1902–1911	2006

Incidental Music for *King Lear*
   1. Fanfare
   2. *Le Sommeil de Lear*
 Incomplete.
	1904	2006

The Fall of the House of Usher (Poe) (*La Chute de la Maison Usher*) Incomplete.	1908–1917	2006
The Martyrdom of St. Sebastian (mostly orchestrated by Caplet)	February–May 1911	1911

Personalia

Allan, Maud (1873–1956). Dancer. Raised in San Francisco, Allan was self-taught. She became famous for free-spirited interpretations of well-known pieces like Mendelssohn's "Spring Song." But her reputation was established by the sexuality of *The Vision of Salomé* (with music by Marcel Rémy). In 1910 she approached Debussy with a commission for *Khamma*, an exotic ballet set in ancient Egypt. Debussy committed himself to the project but completed only the piano score.

d'Annunzio, Gabriele (1863–1938). Novelist, poet, and dramatist. Although d'Annunzio was the most prominent Italian writer of his generation, the widespread success of his poetry, novels, short stories, and plays was unable to support his extravagant lifestyle. In 1910 he left Italy to escape debts. His collaboration with Debussy on *The Martyrdom of St. Sebastian* was part of a campaign to establish a new life for himself in France. After the First World War, d'Annunzio became an ardent nationalist and supporter of Mussolini.

Bailly, Edmond (1850–1918). Bookseller, publisher, writer, and amateur composer. Debussy was a regular visitor to his shop. There he met some of the most famous writers and artists of the time, many of whom were part of Bailly's circle. Bailly published in luxurious format Debussy's *Blessed Damozel* and *Five Poems of Baudelaire*.

Banville, Théodore (1823–1891). Poet. Banville's first works were published in the 1840s and were much indebted to the poetry of Victor Hugo. In the 1870s he was associated with the Parnassians, a school of poetry that focused on craft and objectivity, and was opposed to the sentimentality of Romanticism. While a student, Debussy was strongly attracted to Banville's poetry and left unfinished an adaptation of his drama, *Diane au bois* (1863).

Baudelaire, Charles (1821–1867). Poet, critic, translator, and Wagnerian. Baudelaire's collection of poems, *The Flowers of Evil* (1857), included taboo sexual content for which the author was successfully prosecuted for obscenity. His work grew in popularity after his death and was championed by the Symbolists. Debussy's settings of Baudelaire's poems (1887–1889) are among his most chromatic and helped to establish his reputation as a rising star.

Büsser, Henri (1872–1973). Prolific composer and conductor. Büsser was a student of Gounod and Franck, and winner of the Prix de Rome in 1893. He was associated with Debussy both as conductor (he succeeded André Messager during the first run of *Pelléas et Melisande*) and arranger (he orchestrated Debussy's *Printemps* and *Petite Suite*). In the 1930s and 1940s Büsser was a professor of composition at the Conservatoire. He was elected to the French Academy of Fine Arts in 1938.

Caplet, André (1878–1925). Conductor and composer. Winner of the Prix de Rome in 1901, Caplet often served as Debussy's amanuensis. As a conductor (he led the Boston Opera from 1910 to 1914), he was in a position to make Debussy's music better known. His ability as a composer was particularly valuable to Debussy, both in helping to complete large-scale works like *The Martyrdom of St. Sebastian* and in preparing orchestral versions of others (including *La Boîte à joujoux*). He shared with Debussy an interest in Poe and in 1923 wrote an instrumental chamber piece inspired by Poe's "Masque of the Red Death": *Conte fantastique d'après Poe*.

Chabrier, Emmanuel (1841–1894). Composer. Obliged until 1880 to earn his living as a bureaucrat in the Ministry of the Interior, Chabrier is best known today for lively and spirited pieces like *España* and the *Pièces pittoresques*. Debussy admired the unconventionality of his music. But there was also a more "serious" side to Chabrier, best seen in the opera, *Briséïs*. This work was left unfinished at his death; Debussy was approached, but declined to complete it.

Charpentier, Gustave (1860–1956). Composer. Charpentier was a student of Massenet and winner of the Prix de Rome in 1887. Unlike Debussy, he soon made a name for himself as a composer. His opera, *Louise* (1900), is an early example of naturalism (it depicts lower middle-class life in Paris), and was an immediate success. Debussy disliked both the content and musical style and was disturbed that a work so different from *Pelléas et Melisande* seemed to set the tone for the age.

Chausson, Ernest (1855–1899). Composer. Chausson became an important supporter of Debussy not long after Debussy's return from Rome. Independently wealthy, he recognized the young composer's extraordinary ability and was eager to help. Their relationship ended abruptly after the fiasco of Debussy's engagement to Therèse Roger, who was a friend of Chausson. Chausson died in a freak bicycle accident.

Claudel, Camille (1864–1943). Sculptor. Sister of the writer, Paul Claudel. Around the age of twenty, she became associated with Auguste Rodin (1840–1917) as student, lover, and inspiration. Extraordinarily gifted, she soon established a reputation for her work on its own merit but began to exhibit bizarre and unpredictable behavior. She was committed to an asylum for the mentally ill in 1913, and, despite support from the staff for her release, spent the remainder of her life in confinement.

Dalcroze, Emile (1865–1950). Swiss music educator. Dalcroze's method (of which eurhythmics was a part) associated movement with specific musical concepts. Vaslav Nijinsky adapted Dalcroze's models for the choreography he created for Debussy's *Jeux*, an approach that Debussy privately attacked. Dalcroze's concepts continue to be taught in seminars and workshops around the world.

Diaghilev, Serge (1872–1929). Impresario. After being associated with theatrical productions in St. Petersburg, Diaghilev conquered Paris with performances of Russian music in 1907 and 1908. He created the Ballets Russes and over the years commissioned music from Stravinsky, Poulenc, Satie, and Ravel, among others. His sole commission from Debussy was *Jeux*, one of the composer's most inventive works.

Dukas, Paul (1865–1935). Composer. Best known today for his tone poem, *The Sorcerer's Apprentice* (1897), Dukas was a perfectionist who composed comparatively little. He and Debussy knew one another for decades and got along well, but they never became close. His *Ariane et Barbe-bleu* (1907) is, along with Debussy's *Pelléas*, one of the most original French operas of the time. Dukas became a professor of composition at the Conservatoire in 1928.

Fénéon, Félix (1861–1944). Art critic. Fénéon, a champion of Seurat and neo-Impressionism, was editor at the *Revue blanche* where Debussy began his career as a music critic. His involvement with the anarchist movement led to one of the most celebrated trials of the time. Fénéon was acquitted of having planted and detonated a bomb at a restaurant in Paris (as a result of which the Symbolist poet, Laurent Tailhade, had lost the use of an eye).

Flaubert, Gustave (1821–1880). Novelist. An impeccable stylist, Flaubert wrote in opposition to Romantic sentiment. *Madame Bovary* (1857) is a realistic account of a woman's attempt to counter the banality of her life (because of the novel, Flaubert was unsuccessfully tried for obscenity). Flaubert was admired by Marguerite Pelouze and was a regular guest at her residence, Chenonceaux, where Debussy spent the summer of 1879.

Franck, César (1822–1890). Belgian composer. A child prodigy, Franck settled in Paris in the 1830s where he became a student at the Conservatoire. For much of his life he made his living as an organist and was associated with Sainte-Clotilde Basilica from 1858 until his death. He became professor of organ at the Conservatoire in 1872 where his skill in improvisation and growing reputation as composer attracted young composers like Debussy. He also taught composition privately. Among his pupils were Vincent d'Indy, Guillaume Lekeu, and Ernest Chausson.

Gourmont, Rémy de (1858–1915). Novelist, poet, and critic. Gourmont was the leading critic for Symbolism and a founder of the *Mercure de France*. Disfigured by lupus, he led an increasingly private life. His novel, *Sixtine* (1890), was both provocative and highly cerebral, and exemplified many of the tenets of Symbolism.

Ghil, René (1862–1925). Poet. At first a disciple of Mallarmé, he soon set out on his own, becoming one of the most distinctive poets of his day. Ghil was fascinated by the interrelationships among the arts. He developed in his poetry the concept of "verbal instrumentation" in which timbre and color were associated with particular vowels.

Huysmans, Joris-Karl (1848–1907). Novelist and critic. Huysmans began as a writer of fiction associated with the Naturalist school of Zola. But he changed course dramatically with *Against the Grain* (1884), a novel that documents the bizarre tastes of its jaded hero. It became one of the best-known works associated with the decadent side of Symbolism. It was followed by *Down There* (1891) which focusesd on contemporary practice of satanism. Huysmans's later novels explored mysticism and complemented his move toward acceptance of Catholicism.

d'Indy, Vincent (1851–1931). Composer, educator. No musician was more influential in French musical life of his day than d'Indy. He was a prolific composer, active worldwide as a conductor, and a founder of the Schola Cantorum which, after the Conservatoire, was the most significant establishment for training musicians in France. Despite the differences in style and aesthetic in their music, d'Indy and Debussy were publicly respectful of one another, and d'Indy was a sincere admirer of some of Debussy's compositions.

Lekeu, Guillaume (1870–1894). Belgian composer. In the late 1880s Lekeu and his family settled in Paris where he became a student of Franck (whom he idolized). After Franck's death he studied for a time with d'Indy. Eugène Ysaÿe became a strong supporter, and it was for him that Lekeu wrote his two most mature works, a violin sonata and a piano quartet. Like all students of Franck, Lekeu shows influences of Franck's style, mostly structural, in his music; at the same time his work displayed extraordinary mastery for one so young. Lekeu died of typhus, leaving his piano quartet unfinished.

Maeterlinck, Maurice (1862–1949). Belgian poet, essayist, and dramatist. Maeterlinck was one of the most influential writers associated with Symbolism. His idealistic essays (such as those collected in *The Treasure of the Humble*, 1896) and enigmatic plays (like *Pelléas*) attracted wide criticial and popular notice, leading to the Nobel Prize for Literature in 1911. Musicians were fascinated by Maeterlinck's dramas, and a large number of composers wrote music inspired by his work (including, in addition to Debussy, Schoenberg, Fauré, Loeffler, Vaughan Williams, and Sibelius).

Magnard, Albéric (1865–1914). Composer. Magnard was independently wealthy and published privately many of his compositions, a lifestyle that unfortunately misled some contemporaries into thinking of him as a gentlemanly, amateur composer. Foremost among Magnard's instrumental works are four symphonies that cover the gamut of his career and are among the most ambitious orchestral compositions of the day. Magnard died in the opening weeks of the First World War in a suicidal attempt to defend his home from German troops.

Mallarmé, Stéphane (1842–1898). Poet. Mallarmé was the leading poet of Symbolism, famous for his weekly salons (Debussy was an irregular visitor) where many of the most famous writers and artists of the day met to discuss their art. Debussy came into contact with Mallarmé's arcane work early in his career and was profoundly affected by it.

Mendès, Catulle (1841–1909). Poet, critic, novelist, and dramatist. Mendès wrote in a variety of styles for a variety of markets. He started in the 1860s as a poet associated with the Parnassians. But his passion for the music of Wagner seemed to provide him with a new sense of direction. The novels that Mendès came to be known for were often psychological in mood with a focus on sexuality (*Zo'Har*, 1886; *Méphistophéla*, 1890). Debussy's proposed collaboration with Mendès on the opera, *Rodrigue et Chimène*, was a disappointment to them both.

Messager, André (1853–1929). Composer and conductor. As a conductor Messager was equally at home in Covent Garden and Paris. Much the same was true of the operettas he composed. They invariably charmed whether in French or English productions. But despite several attempts, his "serious" operas never gained an audience. His association with Debussy was crucial to his success. Messager was among the first to recognize *Pelléas* as a masterpiece, and he worked on its behalf at the Opéra-Comique (where he conducted the first performances).

Monet, Claude (1840–1926). Artist. Known for his landscapes (including scenes from his garden) and seascapes, Monet became the best-known artist associated with Impressionism. Debussy was an admirer of his work and was privately flattered by comparison to him (not based on similarity of style, Debussy felt, but similarity of artistic stance and intention).

Moreau, Gustave (1826–1898). Artist. Moreau was the eldest and most prominent painter associated with Symbolism. His first success was in 1864 with the enigmatic *Oedipus* *and the Sphinx.* Moreau's painting became increasingly hermetic, culminating in works like *Jupiter and Semele* (1895), a jewel-like canvas teeming with symbols. Moreau bequeathed his art and studio to the state, which continues to administer it as a museum in Paris.

Nijinsky, Vaslav (1890–1950). Dancer. Nijinsky was the most gifted male dancer in the Ballets Russes. He was also the lover of its director, Serge Diaghilev, who did much to promote Nijinsky's career until Nijinsky's marriage in 1913. Nijinsky created the choreography for the Ballets Russes productions of Debussy's *Faune* and *Jeux*, productions that Debussy felt ill-suited his music.

Pierné, Gabriel (1863–1937). Conductor, composer. Pierné was a fellow student of Debussy at the Conservatoire and went on to win acclaim in France. His involvement as conductor with the Concerts Colonne began in 1903 and continued for more than thirty years. He composed in a wide variety of genres, including orchestral, chamber, and opera. Pierné was elected to the French Academy of Fine Arts in 1924.

Poe, Edgar (1809–1849). Writer. Poe's reputation in the United States has never been as enthusiastic as the one he has in France. There the full spectrum of his poetry and tales has been admired, not least because of the wonderful translations of it by Charles Baudelaire and Stéphane Mallarmé. Debussy was enthralled by Poe's writing and spent many years working on operatic adaptations of two short stories ("The Fall of the House of Usher" and "The Devil in the Belfry"), but left both unfinished at his death.

Rameau, Jean-Philippe (1683–1764). Composer, music theorist. Rameau came from a musical family, and until the early 1720s he made his living primarily as an organist. Theoretical publications (1722, 1726), both learned and practical, helped to broaden his reputation. But his fame came to rest on a series of operas and ballets (including *Hippolyte et Aricie* and *Castor et Pollux*) composed during the 1730s and received to acclaim. Rameau remained little more than a relic of the past until a revival of interest in his work during the 1890s, with Vincent d'Indy as one of its leaders. At that time several of Rameau's operas were performed, and a complete edition of his compositions was initiated. Debussy became one of Rameau's most outspoken champions, hailing him as an ideal of French genius.

Ravel, Maurice (1875–1937). Composer. Like Debussy, Ravel was a student who found the academicism at the Conservatoire to be stifling. His repeated failure to win the Prix de Rome became scandalous. Ravel's international reputation took off after the end of the First World War. That was particularly the case in the United States and the United Kingdom, where his music found an enthusiastic public, and where composers as diverse as Gershwin and Vaughan Williams were admirers of it. Ravel's music has often been coupled with Debussy's, but while there is superficial similarity in sound, their style and structure differ considerably.

Redon, Odilon (1840–1916). Artist. Redon's reputation was made with imaginative series of lithographs, one of which was inspired by Poe, and all of which focused on the bizarre. During the 1890s Redon turned to oils and pastels, producing a series of still lifes, portraits, and mythological subjects of astonishingly vibrant color. Redon was also a gifted amateur musician and admirer of Debussy's music.

Régnier, Henri de (1864–1936). Poet, novelist. A patrician and influential disciple of Mallarmé, Régnier made his debut as a poet in 1889. He later (primarily in the first decade of the twentieth century) published short stories and novels. Régnier's work, while distinctive, is indebted to a classical tradition and owes little stylistically to Mallarmé. He was a good friend of Debussy in the 1890s, and helped him gain permission to set Maeterlinck's *Pelléas et Mélisande* to music. Régnier was elected to the French Academy in 1911.

Satie, Erik (1866–1925). Composer. Satie was one of the most unconventional and inventive composers of his generation. His dry and lively wit plays an important part in his music, whether in the form of "incorrect" harmonic progressions or unexpected text published in the score to complement the music. Satie and Debussy were extraordinarily close, a friendship that survived all trials over nearly three decades.

Verlaine, Paul (1844–1896). Poet. Verlaine's first poetry appeared in the 1860s and showed many of the stylistic characteristics of the Parnassians. His later works (such as *Jadis et naguère* [1884]) were championed by the Symbolists. Debussy was the first composer to recognize Verlaine's unique poetic sensibility and create comparable music for it.

Vidal, Paul (1863–1931). Composer, teacher. Vidal was a fellow student of Debussy at the Conservatoire and winner of the Prix de Rome in 1883. In addition to writing music, he worked as a conductor at the Opéra and Opéra-Comique in the 1890s and early 1900s. He eventually became a professor of composition at the Conservatoire.

Villiers de l'Isle-Adam, Auguste de (1838–1889). Writer. Villiers was a brilliant but eccentric writer who developed a strong following among the Symbolists. His focus was the bizarre and unusual (*Contes cruels*, 1883). Villiers worked off and on for the final two decades of his life on *Axël*, an occult drama with Wagnerian overtones that Debussy considered setting to msic.

Select Bibliography

Correspondence and Writings

Avec Stravinsky. Monaco: Editions du Rocher, 1958.

Debussy, Claude. *Correspondance (1872–1918)*. Edited by François Lesure and Denis Herlin. Annotated by François Lesure, Denis Herlin, and Georges Liébert. Paris: Gallimard, 2005.

Debussy, Claude. *Debussy Letters*. Edited by François Lesure and Roger Nichols. Cambridge, MA: Harvard University Press, 1987.

Debussy, Claude. *Lettres de Claude Debussy à sa femme, Emma*. Edited by Pasteur Vallery-Radot. Paris: Flammarion, 1957.

Debussy, Claude. *Debussy on Music*. Edited by Richard Langham Smith. Ithaca, NY: Cornell University Press, 1988.

Debussy, Claude. *Monsieur Croche et autres écrits*. Edited by François Lesure. Paris: Gallimard, 1987.

Joly-Segalen, Annie and André Schaeffner, eds. *Segalen et Debussy*. Monaco: Editions du Rocher, 1961.

Prunières, Henri. "A la Villa Médicis." *La Revue Musicale* 7 (May 1926), pp. 23–42.

Timbrell, Charles. "Claude Debussy and Walter Rummel: Chronicle of a Friendship, with New Correspondance." *Music & Letters* 73 (1992), pp. 399–406.

Tosi, Guy, ed. *Claude Debussy et Gabriele d'Annunzio. Correspondance inédite*. Paris: Denoël, 1948.

Toulet, P.-J. *Correspondance de Claude Debussy et P.-J. Toulet*. Paris: Le Divan, 1929.

Reminiscences

Bathori, Jane. "Les Musiciens que j'ai connus. II Debussy." *Recorded Sound* (Spring 1962), pp. 174–180.

Bonheur, Raymond. "Souvenirs et impressions d'un compagnon de jeunesse." *La Revue Musicale* 7 (May 1926), pp. 3–5.

Koechlin, Charles. "Souvenirs sur Debussy." *Cahiers Debussy* 7 (1983), pp. 3–6.

Koechlin, Charles. "Souvenirs sur Debussy, la Schola et la S.M.I." *Revue Musicale* 15 (1934), pp. 241–251.

Mourey, Gabriel. "Souvenirs sur Debussy." *Cahiers Debussy* 15 (1991), pp. 55–58.

Nichols, Roger, ed. *Debussy Remembered*. Portland, OR: Amadeus Press, 1992.

Peter, René. *Claude Debussy*. Paris: Gallimard, 1931.

Pierné, Gabriel. "Souvenirs d'Achille Debussy." *La Revue Musicale* 7 (May, 1926), pp. 10–11.

Régnier, Henri de. "Souvenirs sur Debussy." *La Revue Musicale* 7 (May, 1926), pp. 89–91.

Romilly, Mme Gérard de. "Debussy professeur, par une de ses élèves (1898–1908)." *Cahiers Debussy* 2 (1978), pp. 3–10.

Vasnier, Marguerite. "Debussy à dix-huit ans." *La Revue Musicale* 7 (May 1926), pp. 17–22.
Vidal, Paul. "Souvenirs d'Achille Debussy." *La Revue Musicale* 7 (May 1926), pp. 12–16.

Books: Debussy, Debussy's Music

Abravanel, Claude. *Claude Debussy, a Bibliography*. Detroit: Information Coordinators, 1974.
Almendra, Julia d'. *Les Modes grégoriens dans l'oeuvre de Claude Debussy*. Paris: G. Enault, 1948.
Barraqué, Jean. *Debussy*. Paris: Editions du Seuil, 1994.
Boulez, Pierre. *Orientations. Collected Writings*. Cambridge, MA: Harvard University Press, 1986.
Boulez, Pierre. *Relevés d'apprenti*. Paris: Editions du Deuil, 1966.
Briscoe, James R. *Claude Debussy: A Guide to Research*. New York: Garland, 1990.
Briscoe, James R., ed. *Debussy in Performance*. New Haven, CT: Yale University Press, 1999.
Brown, Matthew. *Debussy's Ibéria*. Oxford: Oxford University Press, 2003.
Chennevière, Daniel. *Claude Debussy et son oeuvre*. Paris: Durand et fils, 1913.
Cogeval, Guy and François Lesure, eds. *Debussy e il simbolismo*. Rome: Fratelli Palombi, 1984.
Daly, William H. *Debussy. A Study in Modern Music*. Edinburgh: Methuen Simpson, 1908.
Dietschy, Marcel. *A Portrait of Claude Debussy*. Oxford: Clarendon Press, 1994.
Emmanuel, Maurice. *Pelléas et Mélisande de Debussy*. Paris: Mellottée, 1950.
Fulcher, Jane, ed. *Debussy and His World*. Princeton, NJ: Princeton University Press, 2001.
Gilman, Lawrence. *Debussy's Pelléas et Mélisande. A Guide to the Opera*. New York: Schirmer, 1907.
Grayson, David A. *The Genesis of Debussy's Pelléas et Mélisande*. Ann Arbor: UMI Research Press, 1986.
Holloway, Robin. *Debussy and Wagner*. London: Eulenburg Books, 1979.
Howat, Roy. *Debussy in Proportion*. Cambridge: Cambridge University Press, 1983.
Ingelbrecht, Germaine and D. E. *Claude Debussy*. Paris: Costard, 1953.
Jankelevitch, Vladimir. *Debussy et le mystère de l'instant*. Paris: Plon, 1976.
Jarocinski, Stefan. *Debussy. Impressionisme et symbolisme*. Paris: Editions du Seuil, 1970.
Laloy, Louis. *Claude Debussy*. Paris: Les Bibliophiles Fantaisistes, 1909.
Lesure, François. *Catalogue de l'oeuvre de Claude Debussy*. Paris: Fayard, 2003. See also the online list provided by the Centre du Documentation Claude Debussy: http://www.debussy.fr/cdfr/centre/centre.php.
Lesure, François. *Claude Debussy*. Paris: Klincksieck, 1994. (Republished by Fayard in 2003 with a revised list of works.)
Lesure, François. *Claude Debussy avant Pelléas, ou les années symbolistes*. Paris: Klincksieck, 1992.
Lesure, François. *Debussy (Iconographie musicale)*. Geneva: Minkoff, 1980.
Liebich, Mrs. Franz. *Claude-Achille Debussy*. London: John Lane, 1908.
Lockspeiser, Edward, ed. *Debussy et Edgar Poe. Documents inédits*. Monaco: Editions du Rocher, 1961.
Lockspeiser, Edward. *Debussy: His Life and Mind*. 2 vols. London: Cassell, 1962, 1965.
Nichols, Roger. *Debussy*. Oxford: Oxford University Press, 1973.
Nichols, Roger. *The Life of Debussy*. Cambridge: Cambridge University Press, 1998.
Nichols, Roger and Richard Langham Smith. *Claude Debussy. Pelléas et Mélisande*. Cambridge: Cambridge University Press, 1989.

Orledge, Robert. *Debussy and the Theatre*. Cambridge: Cambridge University Press, 1982.

Parks, Richard S. *The Music of Claude Debussy*. New Haven, CT: Yale University Press, 1989.

Roberts, Paul. *Images: The Piano Music of Claude Debussy*. Portland, Oregon: Amadeus Press, 1996.

Smith, Richard Langham, ed. *Debussy Studies*. Cambridge: Cambridge University Press, 1997.

Thompson, Oscar. *Debussy: Man and Artist*. New York: Dodd, Mead, 1937.

Trezise, Simon. *Debussy. La Mer*. Cambridge: Cambridge University Press, 1994.

Trezise, Simon, ed. *The Cambridge Companion to Debussy*. Cambridge: Cambridge University Press, 2003.

Trillig, Johannes. *Untersuchungen zur Rezeption Claude Debussys in der zeitgenössichen Musikkritik*. Tutzing: Hans Schneider, 1983.

Vallas, Léon. *Achille-Claude Debussy*. Paris: PUF, 1949.

Vallas, Léon. *Claude Debussy et son temps*. Paris: Albin Michel, 1958.

Vallas, Léon. *Claude Debussy. His Life and Works*. Oxford: Oxford University Press, 1933.

Vallas, Léon. *The Theories of Claude Debussy*. Oxford: Oxford University Press, 1929.

Weber, Edith, ed. *Debussy et l'évolution de la musique au XXe siècle*. Paris: Editions du Centre National de la Recherche Scientifique, 1965.

Wenk, Arthur B. *Claude Debussy and the Poets*. Berkeley: University of California Press, 1976.

Wenk, Arthur B. *Claude Debussy and Twentieth-Century Music*. Boston: Twayne, 1983.

Zenck-Maurer, Claudia. *Versuch über die wahre Art, Debussy zu analysieren*. Munich: Emil Katzbichler, 1974.

Books Related to Debussy

Literature, the Visual Arts, Cultural History

Aranjo, Daniel. *Paul-Jean Toulet (1867–1920). La vie—l'oeuvre*. 2 vols. Pau: Marrimpouey Jeune, 1980.

Becker, Jean-Jacques. *The Great War and the French People*. Providence, RI: Berg, 1993.

Bernier, Georges. *La Revue blanche*. Paris: Editions Hazan, 1991.

Bertrand, Adrien. *Catulle Mendès*. Paris: Sansot, 1908.

Billy, André. *L'Epoque 1900*. Paris: Tallandier, 1900.

Bulteau, Michel. *Présence de Paul-Jean Toulet*. Paris: La Table Ronde, 1985.

Chaix, Marie-Antoinette. *La Correspondance des arts dans la poésie contemporaine*. Paris: Alcan, 1919.

Chastenet, Jacques. *Histoire de la Troisième République. Jours inquiéts et jours sanglants (1906–1918)*. Paris: Hachette, 1955.

Chastenet, Jacques. *Histoire de la Troisième République. La République des Républicains (1879–1893)*. Paris: Hachette, 1954.

Chastenet, Jacques. *Histoire de la Troisième République. La République triomphante (1893–1906)*. Paris: Hachette, 1955.

Clive, H. P. *Pierre Louÿs (1870–1925): A Biography*. Oxford: Clarendon Press, 1978.

Cornell, Kenneth. *The Symbolist Movement*. New Haven, CT: Yale University Press, 1951.

D'Anthonay, Thibaut. *Jean Lorrain*. Paris: Plon, 1991.

Dantzig, Charles. *Rémy du Gourmont*. Paris: Editions du Rocher, 1990.

Da Silva, Jean. *Le Salon de la Rose+Croix (1892–1897)*. Paris: Syros Alternatives, 1991.

Daudet, Léon. *Souvenirs littéraires*. Paris: Grasset, 1968.

Deak, Frantisek. *Symbolist Theater. The Formation of an Avant-Garde*. Baltimore, MD: Johns Hopkins University Press, 1993.

Delevoye, Robert. *Symbolists and Symbolism*. Geneva: Skira, 1982.

Druick, Douglas, ed. *Odilon Redon. Prince of Dreams, 1840–1916*. Chicago: Art Institute of Chicago, 1994.

Dumas, Véronique. *Le Peintre Symboliste: Alphonse Osbert (1857–1939)*. Paris: CNRS Editions, 2005.

Fauser, Annegret. *Musical Encounters at the 1889 Paris World's Fair*. Rochester, NY: University of Rochester Press, 2005.

Gaubert, Ernest. *Rachilde*. Paris: E. Sansot, 1907.

Ghil, René. *De la poésie scientifique*. Paris: Messein, 1909.

Goldwater, Robert. *Symbolism*. New York: Harper & Row, 1979.

Goujon, Jean-Paul. *Pierre Louÿs, une vie secrète (1870–1925)*. Paris: Seghers, 1988.

Gourmont, Rémy de. *The Book of Masks*. Translated by Jack Lewis. Boston: John W. Luce, 1921.

Gourmont, Rémy de. *Sixtine. Roman de la vie cérébrale*. Paris: Mercure, 1926.

Halperin, Joan. *Félix Fénéon. Aesthete and Anarchist in Fin de Siècle Paris*. New Haven, CT: Yale University Press, 1988.

Huysmans, Joris-Karl. *L'Art moderne*. Paris: Plon, [1883].

Huysmans, Joris-Karl. *Certains*. Paris: Plon, 1908.

Jullian, Philippe. *D'Annunzio*. New York: Viking Press, 1972.

Jumeau-Lafond, Jean-David. *Carlos Schwabe. Symboliste et visionnaire*. Paris: ACR Edition, 1994.

Kuhn, Reinhard. *The Return to Reality: A Study of Francis Vielé-Griffin*. Paris: Droz-Minard, 1962.

Lacambre, Genevieve. *Gustave Moreau. Between Epic and Dream*. Chicago: Art Institute of Chicago, 1999.

Lefebvre, Louis. *Charles Morice*. Paris: Perrin, 1926.

Legrand, Francine-Claire. *Le Symbolisme en Belgique*. Brussels: Laconti, 1971.

Lehmann, A. G. *The Symbolist Aesthetic in France. 1885–1895*. Oxford: Basil Blackwell, 1950.

Lowell, Amy. *Six French Poets. Studies in Contemporary Literature*. New York: Macmillan, 1916.

Maitron, Jean. *Le Mouvement anarchiste en France. Des origines à 1914*. Paris: Gallimard, 1975.

Manceron, Gilles. *Segalen*. Paris: J. C. Lattès, 1991.

Masini, Lara-Vinca. *Art Nouveau*. New York: Arch Cape Press, 1987.

Mathieu, Pierre-Louis. *Gustave Moreau*. Boston: New York Graphic Society, 1976.

McIntosh, Christopher. *The Rosicrucians*. London: Crucible, 1987.

Morice, Charles. *La Littérature de tout à l'heure*. Paris: Perrin, 1889.

Michaud, Guy. *Message poétique du symbolisme*. Paris: Nizet, 1951.

Millan, Gordon. *The Life of Stéphane Mallarmé*. New York: Farrar, Straus and Giroux, 1994.

Moore, George. *Modern Painting*. New York: Charles Scribner's Sons, 1893.

Nectoux, Jean-Michel. *Harmonie en bleu et or. Debussy, la musique et les arts*. Paris: Fayard, 2005.

Nectoux, Jean-Michel. *Mallarmé. Un clair regard dans les ténèbres. Peinture, Musique, Poésie*. Paris: Adam Biro, 1998.

Pierrot, Jean. *The Decadent Imagination, 1880–1900*. Chicago: University of Chicago Press, 1981.

Raitt, A. W. *The Life of Villiers de l'Isle-Adam*. Oxford: Oxford University Press, 1981.
Redon, Odilon. *A Soi-Même. Journal (1867–1915)*. Paris: Floury, 1922.
Retté, Adolph. *Le Symbolisme*. Paris: Vanier, 1903.
Richard, Noël. *A l'aube du symbolisme*. Paris: Nizet, 1961.
Richard, Noël. *Le mouvement décadent*. Paris: Nizet, 1968.
Richard, Noël. *Profils symbolistes*. Paris: Nizet, 1978.
Thomson, Belinda. *Impressionism: Origins, Practice, Reception*. London: Thames & Hudson, 2000.
Valéry, Paul. *Masters and Friends*. Translated by Martin Turnell. Princeton, NJ: Princeton University Press, 1968.
Vinchon, Emile. *Maurice Rollinat*. Paris: Jouve, 1921.
Walzer, Pierre Olivier. *Paul-Jean Toulet*. Paris: Segners, 1963.
Woodhouse, John. *Gabriele D'Annunzio. Defiant Archangel*. Oxford: Clarendon Press, 1998.

Music and Ballet

Bailly, Edmond. *Le Son dans la nature*. Paris: Librairie de l'art indépendant, 1900.
Borgex, Louis. *Vincent d'Indy*. Paris: Durand et fils, 1913.
Chausson, Ernest. *Ecrits inédits*. Edited by Jean Gallois. Paris: Editions du Rocher, 1999.
Cherniavsky, Felix. *The Salome Dancer. The Life and Times of Maud Allan*. Toronto: McClelland & Stewart, 1991.
Cooper, Martin. *French Music from the Death of Berlioz to the Death of Fauré*. Oxford: Oxford University Press, 1951.
Depaulis, Jacques. *Ida Rubinstein. Une inconnue jadis célèbre*. Paris: Champion, 1995.
Gallois, Jean. *Ernest Chausson*. Paris: Editions aujourd'hui, 1981.
Garafola, Lynn. *Diaghilev's Ballets Russes*. New York: Oxford University Press, 1989.
Garafola, Lynn and Nancy Van Norman Baer, eds. *The Ballet Russes and Its World*. New Haven, CT: Yale University Press, 1999.
Garden, Mary and Louis Biancolli. *Mary Garden's Story*. New York: Simon and Schuster, 1951.
Huebner, Steven. *French Opera at the Fin de Siècle: Wagnerism, Nationalism, and Style*. New York: Oxford University Press, 1999.
d'Indy, Vincent. *César Franck*. Translated by Rosa Newmarch. London: John Lane, 1929.
Irvine, Demar. *Massenet. A Chronicle of His Life and Times*. Portland, OR: Amadeus Press, 1994.
Sylvia Kahan, *In Search of New Scales. Prince Edward de Polignac, Octatonic Explorer*. Rochester: Boydell & Brewer, 2009.
Kufferath, Maurice. *Parsifal de Richard Wagner*. Paris: Fischbacher, 1890.
Leblanc, Georgette. *Souvenirs*. New York: Dutton, 1932.
Lekeu, Guillaume. *Correspondance*. Edited by Luc Verdebout. Liège: Mardaga, 1993.
Lorrain, Jean. *Pelléastres*. Paris: Albert Mericant, [1910].
Lourié, Arthur. *Sergei Koussevitzky and His Epoch*. New York: Knopf, 1931.
Magnard, Albéric. *Correspondance. (1888–1914)*. Edited by Claire Vlach. Paris: Publications de la Société Française de Musicologie, 1997.
Mason, Daniel Gregory. *Contemporary Composers*. New York: Macmillan, 1918.
Mauclair, Camille. *La Religion de la musique*. Paris: Fischbacher, 1924.
Myers, Rollo. *Emmanuel Chabrier and His Circle*. London: Dent, 1969.

Nectoux, Jean-Michel. *Fauré*. Paris: Editions du Seuil, 1995.

Northcote, Sydney. *The Songs of Henri Duparc*. London: Dennis Dobson, 1949.

Noske, Frits. *French Song From Berlioz to Duparc*. New York: Dover, 1970.

Orledge, Robert. *Charles Koechlin (1867–1950). His Life and Works*. Chur, Switzerland: Harwood Academic Publishers, 1989.

Palmer, Christopher. *Impressionism in Music*. London: Hutchinson, 1973.

Rolland, Romain. *Musicians of To-Day*. New York: Henry Holt, 1914.

Séré, Octave. *Musiciens français d'aujourd'hui*. Paris: Mercure, 1921.

Smith, Moses. *Koussevitzky*. New York: Allen, Towne, & Heath, 1947.

Studd, Stephen. *Saint-Saëns. A Critical Biography*. London: Cygnus Arts, 1999.

Tiénot, Yvonne. *Chabrier*. Paris: Henri Lemoine, 1965.

Turnbull, Michael T. R. B. *Mary Garden*. Portland, OR: Amadeus Press, 1997.

Vallas, Léon. *Vincent d'Indy*. 2 vols. Paris: Albin Michel, 1946, 1950.

Vander Linden, Albert. *Octave Maus et la vie musicale belge (1875–1914)*. Brussels: Palais des Académies, 1950.

Varèse, Louise. *Varèse. A Looking-Glass Diary*. New York: Norton, 1972.

Wagstaff, John. *André Messager. A Bio-Bibliography*. Westport, CT: Greenwood Press, 1991.

Articles

"Correspondance inédite entre Saint-Saëns et Maurine Emmanuel à propos de Claude Debussy." *Revue Musicale* 69 (1988), pp. 44–48.

"Debussy de 1883 à 1885 d'après la correspondance de Paul Vidal à Henriette Fuchs." *Revue de Musicologie* 48 (1962), pp. 98–101.

Abbate, Carolyn. "*Tristan* in the Composition of *Pelléas*." *19th-Century Music* 5 (1981), pp. 117–141.

Barras, Marie-Cécile. "La Présence de Chopin dans la musique de piano de Debussy." *Cahiers Debussy* 20 (1996), pp. 41–60.

Berman, Laurence D. "*Prelude to the Afternoon of a Faun* and *Jeux*: Debussy's Summer Rites." *19th-Century Music* 3 (1980), pp. 225–238.

Bertrand, Anne. "Debussy et Jacques-Emile Blanche." *Cahiers Debussy* 17/18 (1993–1994), pp. 73–93.

Bleau, Alexandre. "Chemins de Mallarmé. Un état de la question." *Cahiers Debussy* 32 (2008), pp. 27–49.

Branger, Jean-Christophe. "Une oeuvre de jeunesse inédite de Debussy: la *Première Suite d'orchestre*." *Cahiers Debussy* 32 (2008), pp. 5–26.

Briscoe, James R. "Debussy *d'après* Debussy: The Further Resonance of Two Early Mélodies." *19th-Century Music* 5 (Fall 1981), pp. 110–116.

Briscoe, James R. "Debussy, Franck, and the 'Ideas of Sacrifice.'" *Revue Belge de Musicologie* 45 (1991), pp. 27–39.

Briscoe, James R. "To Invent New Forms: Debussy's *Diane au bois*." *Musical Quarterly* 74 (1990), pp. 131–169.

Brody, Elaine. "La Famille Mendès. A Literary Link between Wagner and Debussy." *Music Review* 33 (1972), pp. 177–189.

Brussel, Robert. "Claude Debussy et Paul Dukas." *La Revue Musicale* 7 (May 1926), pp. 92–109.

Charle, Christophe. "Debussy in Fin-de-Siècle Paris." In *Debussy and His World*, edited by Jane Fulcher. Princeton, NJ: Princeton University Press, 2001, pp. 271–295.

Chimènes, Myriam. "La Chimie musicale de *Khamma*." *Cahiers Debussy* 12/13 (1988–1989), pp. 123–140.

Chimènes, Myriam. "Les Vicissitudes de *Khamma*." *Cahiers Debussy* 2 (1978), pp. 11–29.

Chimènes, Myriam. "The Definition of Timbre in the Process of Composition of *Jeux*." In *Debussy Studies*, edited by Richard Langham Smith. Cambridge: Cambridge University Press, 1997, pp. 1–25.

Christoforidis, Michael. "De la composition d'un opéra: conseils de Claude Debussy à Manuel de Falla." *Cahiers Debussy* 19 (1995), pp. 69–76.

Clevenger, John R. "Achille at the Conservatoire (1872–1884)." *Cahiers Debussy* 19 (1995), pp. 3–35.

Clevenger, John R. "Debussy's First 'Masterpiece.' *Le Gladiateur.*" *Cahiers Debussy* 23 (1999), pp. 3–34.

Clevenger, John R. "Debussy's Paris Conservatoire Training." In *Debussy and His World*, edited by Jane Fulcher. Princeton, NJ: Princeton University Press, 2001, pp. 299–361.

Clevenger, John R. "Debussy's Rome Cantatas." In *Debussy and His World*, edited by Jane Fulcher. Princeton, NJ: Princeton University Press, 2001, pp. 9–98.

Cobb, Margaret G. "Au Temps de *La Demoiselle élue*." *Cahiers Debussy* 12/13 (1988–1989), pp. 48–53.

Cobb, Margaret G. "Debussy and *Le Roman de Rosette*." *Cahiers Debussy* 22 (1998), pp. 75–87.

Cobb, Margaret G. "The Several Versions of "Trois Mélodies de Claude Debussy." *Cahiers Debussy* 10 (1986), pp. 24–27.

Dal Molin, Paolo and Jean-Louis Leleu. "Comment composait Debussy: les leçons d'un carnet de travail (à propos de *Soupir* et d'*Eventail*)." *Cahiers Debussy* 35 (2011), pp. 9–82.

Davidian, Teresa. "Debussy, d'Indy, and the Société Nationale." *Journal of Musicological Research* 11 (1991), pp. 285–301.

Davidian, Teresa. "Debussy's *Fantaisie*: Issues, Proofs and Revisions." *Cahiers Debussy* 17/18 (1993–1994), pp. 15–25.

Delage, Roger. "Debussy et Chabrier." *Cahiers Debussy* 17/18 (1993–1994), pp. 57–64.

DeVoto, Mark, "The Debussy Sound: Color, Texture, Gesture." In *The Cambridge Companion to Debussy*, edited by Simon Trezise. Cambridge: Cambridge University Press, 2003, pp. 179–196.

Devriès, Anik. "Les Musiques d'Extreme-Orient à l'Exposition universelle de 1889." *Cahiers Debussy* 1 (1977), pp. 25–36.

Dickinson, A. E. F. "The Neo-Modal Style." *Music Review* 33 (1972), pp. 108–121.

Donnellon, Déirdre, "Debussy as Musician and Critic." In *The Cambridge Companion to Debussy*, edited by Simon Trezise. Cambridge: Cambridge University Press, 2003, pp. 43–61.

Donnellon, Déirdre. "The Anarchist Movement in France and Its Impact on Debussy." *Cahiers Debussy* 33 (1999), pp. 45–63.

Douche, Sylvie. "Résonances du *Diable dans le Beffroi* d'Edgar Poe chez Debussy, Bruneau et Inghelbrecht." *Cahiers Debussy* 29 (2005), pp. 27–70.

Duchesneau, Michel. "La musique française pendant la Guerre 1914–1918. Autour de la tentative de fusion de la Société Nationale de Musique et de la Société Musicale Indépendante." *Revue de Musicologie* 82 (1996), pp. 123–153.

Eigeldinger, Jean-Jacques. "Debussy et l'idée de l'arabesque musicale." *Cahiers Debussy* 12/13 (1988–1989), pp. 5–14.

Gelleny, Sharon. "Cyclic Form and Debussy's *Nocturnes*." *Cahiers Debussy* 20 (1996), pp. 25–39.

Goldman, David Paul. "Esotericism as a Determinant of Debussy's Harmonic Language." *Musical Quarterly* 75 (1991), pp. 130–147.

Grayson, David. "Bilitis and Tanagra: Afternoons with Nude Women." In *Debussy and His World*, edited by Jane Fulcher. Princeton, NJ: Princeton University Press, 2001, pp. 117–139.

Grayson, David. "Claude Debussy Addresses the English-Speaking World: Two Interviews, an Article, and *The Blessed Damozel*." *Cahiers Debussy* 16 (1992), pp. 23–47.

Grayson, David. "Debussy on Stage." In *The Cambridge Companion to Debussy*, edited by Simon Trezise. Cambridge: Cambridge University Press, 2003, pp. 61–84.

Grayson, David. "The Interludes of *Pelléas et Mélisande*." *Cahiers Debussy* 12/13 (1988–1989), pp. 100–122.

Grayson, David. "The Libretto of Debussy's *Pelléas et Melisande*." *Music & Letters* 66 (1985), pp. 34–50.

Gubisch, Nina. "Le Journal inédit de Ricardo Viñes." *Revue Internationale de Musique Française* 1 (1980), pp. 154–248.

Guillot, Pierre. "Claude Debussy et Déodac de Séverac." *Cahiers Debussy* 10 (1986), pp. 3–16.

Herlin, Denis. "Le Dédale des corrections dans 'Sirènes.'" *Cahiers Debussy* 12/13 (1988–1989), pp. 82–99.

Herlin, Denis. "Les Esquisses du *Quatuor*." *Cahiers Debussy* 14 (1990), pp. 23–55.

Herlin, Denis. "Une Oeuvre inachevée: *La Saulaie*." *Cahiers Debussy* 20 (1996), pp. 3–15.

Herlin, Denis. "Sirens in the Labyrinth: Amendments in Debussy's *Nocturnes*." In *Debussy Studies*, edited by Richard Langham Smith. Cambridge: Cambridge University Press, 1997, pp. 51–77.

Herlin, Denis. "*Trois Scènes au Crepuscule* (1892–1893): Un premier projet des *Nocturnes*." *Cahiers Debussy* 21 (1997), pp. 3–24.

Hepokoski, James. "Formulaic Openings in Debussy." *19th-Century Music* 8 (1984), pp. 44–59.

Hirsbrunner, Theo. "Claude Debussy und Pierre Louÿs. Zu den 'Six Epigraphes antiques' von Debussy." *Die Musikforschung* 31 (1978), pp. 426–442.

Hirsbrunner, Theo. "Debussy—Maeterlinck—Chausson. Literary and Musical Connections." *Miscellanea Musicologica* 13 (1984), pp. 57–65.

Hirsbrunner, Theo. "Debussys Ballett, *Khamma*." *Archiv für Musikwissenschaft* 36 (1979), pp. 105–121.

Hirsbrunner, Theo. "Zu Debussys und Ravels Mallarmé-Vertonungen." *Archiv für Musikwissenschaft* 35 (1978), pp. 81–103.

Howat, Roy. "Debussy et les musiques de l'Inde." *Cahiers Debussy* 12/13 (1988–1989). pp. 141–152.

Howat, Roy. "Debussy's Piano Music: Sources and Performance." In *Debussy Studies*, edited by Richard Langham Smith. Cambridge: Cambridge University Press, 1997, pp. 78–107.

Howat, Roy. "En Route for *L'Isle Joyeuse*: The Restoration of a Triptych." *Cahiers Debussy* 19 (1995), pp. 37–52.

Howat, Roy. "A Thirteenth *Etude* of 1915: The Original Version of *Pour les arpèges composes*." *Cahiers Debussy* 1 (1977), pp. 25–36.

Jean-Aubry, G. "L'Oeuvre critique de Claude Debussy." *Revue Musicale* 1 (1 December 1920), pp. 191–202.

Jensen, Eric F. "Adventures of a French Wagnerian: The Work of Villiers de l'Isle-Adam." *Music Review* 46 (1985), pp. 186–198.

Jensen, Eric F. "Towards a Symbolist Aesthetic in Music: The Work of Guillaume Lekeu." *Music Review* 50 (1989), pp. 134–142.

Jensen, Eric F. "Satie and the *Gymnopédie*." *Music & Letters* 75 (1994), pp. 236–240.

Jensen, Eric F. "Sound as Symbol: Fin de Siècle Perceptions of the Orchestra." *Music Review* 57 (1996), pp. 227–240.

Jordan, Stephanie. "Debussy, the Dance, and the *Faune*." In *Debussy in Performance*, edited by James R. Briscoe. New Haven, CT: Yale University Press, 1999, pp. 119–134.

Kasaba, Eiko. "*Le Martyre de Saint Sébastien*. Etude sur sa genèse." *Cahiers Debussy* 4/5 (1980–1981), pp. 19–37.

Kasaba, Eiko. "Retour sur le *Martyre de Saint Sébastien*." *Cahiers Debussy* 24 (2000), pp. 57–78.

Koechlin, Charles. "*Pelléas et Mélisande*, étude inédite présentée et établie par Aude Chaillet." *Cahiers Debussy* 27/28 (2003–04), pp. 29–123.

Lado-Bordowsky, Yves A. "*L'Archet*. Un Croquis musical de Debussy." *Cahiers Debussy* 16 (1992), pp. 3–23.

Lado-Bordowsky, Yves A. "La Chronologie des oeuvres de jeunesse de Claude Debussy (1879–1884)." *Cahiers Debussy* 14 (1990), pp. 3–22.

Laloy, Louis. "Claude Debussy et le Debussyisme." *Société Internationale de Musique* 6 (1910), pp. 507–519.

Lang-Becker, Elke. "Aspekte der Debussy-Rezeption in Deutschland zu Lebzeiten des Komponisten." *Cahiers Debussy* 8 (1984), pp. 18–41.

Lesure, François. "Achille à la Villa (1885–1887)." *Cahiers Debussy* 12/13 (1988–1989). pp. 15–28.

Lesure, François. "*Crime d'amour ou Fêtes galantes*. Un Projet verlainien de Debussy." *Cahiers Debussy* 10 (1986), pp. 17–23.

Lesure, François. "Debussy et le Chat Noir." *Cahiers Debussy* 23 (1999), pp. 35–43.

Lesure, François. "Debussy et le syndrome de Grenade." *Revue de Musicologie* 68 (1982), pp. 101–109.

Lesure, François. "Debussy, le Symbolisme, et les arts plastiques." *Cahiers Debussy* 8 (1984), pp. 3–12.

Lesure, François. "La Longue Attente de *Pelléas* (1895–1898)." *Cahiers Debussy* 15 (1991), pp. 3–12.

Lesure, François. "Raymond Bonheur: Un ermite, ami de Debussy." *Cahiers Debussy* 17/18 (1993–1994), pp. 65–72.

Lesure, François. "Une Interview romaine de Debussy (février 1914)." *Cahiers Debussy* 11 (1987), pp. 3–8.

Malvano, Andrea Stefano. "Claude Debussy à l'Exposition internationale de Turin en 1911." *Cahiers Debussy* 36 (2012), pp. 25–46.

Martins, José Eduardo. "Les trois dernières lettres connues de Chouchou Debussy." *Cahiers Debussy* 31 (2007), pp. 77–81.

McFarland, Mark. "Debussy and Stravinsky: Another Look into Their Musical Relationship." *Cahiers Debussy* 24 (2000), pp. 79–112.

McGinness, John. "From Movement to Moment: Issues of Expression, Form, and Reception in Debussy's *Jeux*." *Cahiers Debussy* 22 (1998), pp. 51–74.

McKay, James R. "The Bréval Manuscript: New Interpretations." *Cahiers Debussy* 1 (1977), pp. 5–15.

Monelle, Raymond. "A Semantic Approach to Debussy's Songs." *Music Review* 51 (1990), pp. 193–207.

Mouton, Henri. "Les Rapports d'Indy—Debussy," *Schweizerische Musikzeitung* 113 (1973), pp. 209–211.

Mueller, Richard. "Javanese Influence on Debussy's *Fantaisie* and Beyond." *19th-Century Music* 10 (1986), pp. 157–186.

Nadeau, Roland. "Brouillards: A Tonal Music." *Cahiers Debussy* 4/5 (1980–1981), pp. 38–50.

Nectoux, Jean-Michel. "Debussy et Fauré." *Cahiers Debussy* 3 (1979), pp. 13–30.

Nectoux, Jean-Michel. "Debussy et Mallarmé." *Cahiers Debussy* 12/13 (1988–1989), pp. 54–66.

Nichols, Roger. "Debussy's Two Settings of 'Clair de lune.'" *Music & Letters* 48 (1967), pp. 229–235.

Nichols, Roger. "The Reception of Debussy's Music in Britain Up to 1914." In *Debussy Studies*, edited by Richard Langham Smith. Cambridge: Cambridge University Press, 1997, pp. 139–153.

Orledge, Robert. "Another Look Inside Debussy's 'Toybox.'" *Musical Times* 117 (1976), pp. 987–989.

Orledge, Robert. "Debussy and Satie." In *Debussy Studies*, edited by Richard Langham Smith. Cambridge: Cambridge University Press, 1997, pp. 154–178.

Orledge, Robert. "Debussy the Man." In *The Cambridge Companion to Debussy*, edited by Simon Trezise. Cambridge: Cambridge University Press, 2003, pp. 9–25.

Orledge, Robert. "Debussy's Musical Gifts to Emma Bardac." *Musical Quarterly* 60 (1974), pp. 544–556.

Orledge, Robert. "Debussy's Orchestral Collaborations, 1911–13. 2. *Khamma*," *Musical Times* 116 (1975), pp. 30–35.

Orledge, Robert. "Debussy's Orchestral Collaborations, 1911–13. 1. *Le Martyre de Saint Sébastien*." *Musical Times* 115 (1974), pp. 1030–1035.

Orledge, Robert. "Debussy's Piano Music." *Musical Times* 122 (1981), pp. 21–27.

Pasler, Jann. "Debussy's *Jeux*: Playing with Time and Form." *19th-Century Music* 6 (1982), pp. 60–75.

Pasler, Jann. "*Pelléas* and Power: Forces behind the Reception of Debussy's Opera." *19th-Century Music* 10 (1987), pp. 243–264.

Rauss, Denis-François. "'Ce terrible finale': les sources manuscrites de la sonate pour violon et piano de Claude Debussy et la genèse du troisième mouvement." *Cahiers Debussy* 2 (1978), pp. 30–62.

Rolf, Marie. "Debussy, Gautier, and 'Les Papillons.'" In *Debussy and His World*, edited by Jane Fulcher. Princeton, NJ: Princeton University Press, 2001, pp. 99–115.

Rolf, Marie. "Des *Ariettes* (1888) aux *Ariettes oubliées* (1903)." *Cahiers Debussy* 12/13 (1988–1989), pp. 29–47.

Rolf, Marie. "Mauclair and Debussy: The Decade from "Mer belle aix îles sanguinaires" to *La Mer*." *Cahiers Debussy* 11 (1987), pp. 9–23.

Rolf, Marie. "Orchestral Manuscripts of Claude Debussy: 1892–1905." *Musical Quarterly* 70 (1984), pp. 538–566.

Rosen, Charles. "Where Ravel Ends and Debussy Begins." *Cahiers Debussy* 3 (1979), pp. 31–38.

Rumph, Steven. "Debussy's *Trois Chansons de Bilitis*: Song, Opera, and the Death of the Subject." *Journal of Musicology* 12 (1994), pp. 464–490.

Smith, Richard Langham. "Debussy and the Pre-Raphaelites." *19th-Century Music* 5 (1982), pp. 95–109.

Smith, Richard Langham. "La Genèse de *La Damoiselle élue*." *Cahiers Debussy* 4/5 (1980–1981), pp. 3–18.

Smith, Richard Langham. "'La Jeunesse du Cid': A Mislaid Act in *Rodrigue et Chimène*." In *Debussy Studies*, edited by Richard Langham Smith. Cambridge: Cambridge University Press, 1997, pp. 201–228.

Smith, Richard Langham. "*Rodrigue et Chimène*. Genèse, histoire, problèmes d'édition." *Cahiers Debussy* 12/13 (1988–1989), pp. 67–81.

Spencer, Williametha. "The Relationship between André Caplet and Claude Debussy." *Musical Quarterly* 66 (1980), pp. 112–131.

Strasser, Michael. "Grieg, the Société Nationale, and the Origins of Debussy's String Quartet." In *Berlioz and Debussy: Sources, Contexts, and Legacies. Essays in Honor of François Lesure*, edited by Barbara L. Kelly and Kerry Murphy. Burlington: Ashgate, 2007, pp. 103–117.

Timbrell, Charles. "Debussy in Performance." In *The Cambridge Companion to Debussy*, edited by Simon Trezise. Cambridge: Cambridge University Press, 2003, pp. 259–278.

Timbrell, Charles. "Debussy's 'Prince of Virtuosos.'" *Cahiers Debussy* 11 (1987), pp. 24–33.

Vis, Jurjen. "Debussy and the War. Debussy, Luther, and Janequin." *Cahiers Debussy* 15 (1991), pp. 31–50.

Warburton, Thomas. "Bitonal Miniatures by Debussy from 1913." *Cahiers Debussy* 6 (1982), pp. 5–15.

Youens, Susan. "From the Fifteenth Century to the Twentieth: Considerations of Musical Prosody in Debussy's *Trois Ballades* de François Villon." *Journal of Musicology* 2 (1983), pp. 418–433.

Youens, Susan. "Music, Verse, and 'Prose Poetry': Debussy's *Trois Chansons de Bilitis*." *Journal of Musicological Research* 7 (1986), pp. 69–94.

Index